A TIME
FOR
CRITIQUE

NEW DIRECTIONS IN CRITICAL THEORY

NEW DIRECTIONS IN CRITICAL THEORY

Amy Allen, General Editor

New Directions in Critical Theory presents outstanding classic and contemporary texts in the tradition of critical social theory, broadly construed. The series aims to renew and advance the program of critical social theory, with a particular focus on theorizing contemporary struggles around gender, race, sexuality, class, and globalization and their complex interconnections.

For a complete list of titles, see page 309

A TIME
FOR
CRITIQUE

EDITED BY
DIDIER FASSIN AND
BERNARD E. HARCOURT

Columbia University Press
New York

Columbia University Press
Publishers Since 1893
New York   Chichester, West Sussex
cup.columbia.edu

A complete CIP record is available from the Library of Congress.
ISBN 978-0-231-19126-5 (cloth)
ISBN 978-0-231-19127-2 (paper)
ISBN 978-0-231-54931-8 (ebook)

Columbia University Press books are printed
on permanent and durable acid-free paper.
Printed in the United States of America

Cover design: Noah Arlow

CONTENTS

ACKNOWLEDGMENTS

The present volume has been prepared during the year 2017 through a series of seminars followed by a two-day workshop in the School of Social Science at the Institute for Advanced Study. We express our gratitude to Laura McCune for the congenial organization of these events and to Munirah Bishop for the thorough copyediting of the manuscript. We are also thankful to Wendy Lochner and Lowell Frye at Columbia University Press for their unwavering support of our project.

A TIME

FOR

CRITIQUE

INTRODUCTION

DIDIER FASSIN AND BERNARD E. HARCOURT

T he first decades of the twenty-first century have been marked by an accumulation of deeply troubling political events occurring in the wake of a global war on terror and the consolidation of neoliberal policies worldwide. The unexpected vote on Brexit, the unforeseen election of Donald Trump as president of the United States, the coming to power of authoritarian leaders in Italy and Austria, the illiberal turn of presumably democratic countries, such as Hungary and Poland, and the spectacular rise of nationalist and xenophobic parties in France, Germany, Denmark, Sweden, and the Netherlands have shaken the Western world order. But this preoccupying polymorphic drift of politics has not spared the rest of the planet, from Egypt to Israel, from Turkey to India, from Venezuela to Brazil, from Thailand to the Philippines.

The global instability has generated a flow of somewhat baseless and sometimes contradictory interpretations by media commentators and public intellectuals always quick to recycle ready-made theories or offer skin-deep concepts, like posttruth. Meanwhile, this political evolution has left many social scientists in disarray. They were all the more distraught that they had not seen this wave coming and did not have adequate tools to analyze it. Moreover, they were confronted with the multiplication of so-called fake news and conspiracy theories, which mimicked critical thinking, and with the expansion of social media, which tended to displace traditional channels used by critics in the public sphere.

In these times of crisis, the predicament of critique coincided with contestation over its relevance and even the foretelling of its death, often by the very representatives of its self-proclaimed avant-garde in the social sciences and literary studies. Had not criticism gone too far, they asked? Was it not in part because of its excesses that people had lost their discernment in their questioning of knowledge and power, thereby rendering us all receptive to alternative facts and threatening ideologies? Was there not, then, a moral obligation, as well as an epistemological necessity, to reconsider critique's pertinence, and to move on, in order to address more pressing issues?

This reactionary stand was contemporaneous with a series of attacks launched in the academic world against critical theory as well as feminist studies, postmodern theory as well as postcolonial studies. Interestingly, the offensive also came at a time when positivism appeared to be at its peak in the social and cognitive sciences, with the ascendency of big data, the development of experimental techniques, the hegemony of the rational actor paradigm, and the supremacy of evidence-based research. This trend was itself supported by governments as part of the growing field of expertise and encouraged by the corporate world in the name of efficacy. Critical thinking carried little weight by contrast to this powerful alliance of science, politics, and economy.

The present undertaking stems from this dual series of challenges presented by both critical events and critical interpellations. Concerned by the increasingly disconcerting situation, a group of scholars from various disciplines of the social sciences and humanities decided to meet on a regular basis over the course of a year to discuss these challenges. What sort of critical thinking is needed in a time when its very existence seems threatened? How can one maintain sufficient distance from the ubiquitous and eventful present without doing it an injustice? How can we address contemporary issues without repudiating the intellectual legacies of the past? To what extent could critique still be a project for the future? These are some of the questions that we tackled based on our experiences of theoretical and empirical research in political science, philosophy, law, history, literature, sociology, and anthropology.

However, while it is important to evoke this context, which did incentivize our project, it is also crucial to emphasize that the book is neither a direct response to the current state of the world from a critical perspective, nor a systematic defense against the multifaceted rebuke to critical thinking. Indeed, whereas we take these challenges seriously, we want to distance ourselves from their immediacy and avoid the all-too-common reactive attitude to events and interpellations. With the sense of urgency often come hasty analyses, which are later refuted. For us, on the contrary, critique must allow time for consideration. We firmly believe that the challenges critique faces today call for a reappraisal of its practice, and simultaneously a deepening and a displacement of our own reflection. Reappraisal requires a reexamination of the meaning, significance, and complications of the critical gesture, and its reinscription in its political genealogy, historical temporality, and cultural diversity. Displacement entails the systematic questioning of the self-evidences of critical interventions and the recognition of their obscured issues, ignored debates, and neglected alternative traditions. In sum, far from deploring the challenges that critique faces today, we consider that they offer a unique opportunity for its thorough reassessment and a potential for novel openings. To be faithful to its core principle, critique must involve its self-critique. That is the only way, in these critical times, to move forward.

* * *

The volume comprises two sections that explore the relationship between critique and practice from two symmetrical viewpoints. Introduced by an analysis of the changing landscape of critical discourses during the past half century, the first part, "Critique as Practice," provides a reflection on the practice of critique from various theoretical perspectives. It therefore calls into question the idea of a unity of critical thinking. Concluded by a discussion of recent expressions of critical praxis, the second part, "Critique in Practice," offers case studies analyzing critique as it is actually practiced by social agents from diverse backgrounds in concrete situations. It thus shows the multiplicity of potential critical interventions.

In a famous lecture, Michel Foucault asked: What is critique? It is a complementary question that Didier Fassin addresses in the opening of the first section: How is critique? Rather than a philosophical inquiry, his chapter proposes a sort of clinical diagnosis. More specifically it examines the contrast between the 1960s–70s and the 2000s–10s in France and the United States in terms of the historical, institutional, and disciplinary environment within which critique developed in each period. The general argument is that critical thinking cannot be apprehended as an isolated intellectual phenomenon. In order to grasp it, one has to consider the state of the world and of the global public sphere in which it is inscribed, as well as the changing structures of the academy, where it originates, and their relations with the political domain and the media. This broader context determines in part the conditions of possibility— or impossibility—of critique and its particular manifestations. Certain critical discourses and practices that were common half a century ago are difficult to imagine today, whereas new ones appear, which were not then conceivable. In this respect, what does the evolution of critique over the past decades reveal? A general observation is that it is affected by a relative loss of leverage and decline in legitimacy both in the public sphere and in the academic realm. However, this analysis does not validate the reckless pronouncements on the death of critique. It signals instead the increasingly difficult circumstances of its production. Critique faces hard times. Its space has shrunk. Yet, it is alive and well, not only within scholarly circles, but also in novel forms within social movements.

It is precisely to resist its increasing confinement to the academy and to professional thinkers that Linda M. G. Zerilli proposes to rethink critique as a political practice of freedom, that is, as a mode of acting and interacting with various publics about matters of shared concern. Rather than elaborate on the ontological or ethical roots of critique—both of which she recognizes to be important—she invites us to locate critique in the public sphere, so as to question the arts of governing as well as the resistance to them. In doing so, she offers an alternative reading of Michel Foucault's conception of critique to those put forward by John Rajchman and Judith Butler, the former insisting on the "ontology of ourselves" while the latter focuses on "self-transformation." Whereas most Foucauldian interpretations have emphasized the individual dimension of the processes of desubjugation and subjectivation, she is interested instead in their collective aspect, as manifested in their extreme forms during the French Revolution. Here, Arendt's analysis of publicity is crucial as it takes critics out of their cave to encounter publics. Far from the Platonic tradition, which protects the philosopher within the academy, away from the polis and at a distance from public affairs, critique must address political issues and be exercised in the public sphere. In Zerilli's view, critique reveals itself as a mode of being politically in common. It reflects the Arendtian emphasis on the need for dialogue among citizens in public, as a way forward to test and critically evaluate our truths. These then become the public conditions of true critical thought. Only outside the university can we hope to reinvigorate critique, she writes—in the public sphere, in the political realm, where it properly belongs.

Indeed, critique has traditionally been associated with hope since it implied the expectation of an emancipation of human beings in the Kantian tradition or of a revolutionary transformation of society in Marxist theory. But as suggested by Ayşe Parla, the declining faith in utopian projects has disconnected critique and hope, or has at least rendered their connection more problematic. Is contemporary critique so disillusioned about the possibility of political improvement that there is no more space for hope, she inquires, or, conversely, is hope itself an obstacle to the advent of critique and therefore of political change in today's world? Rather than providing a simple response to this question, Parla reformulates it by asking why hope should be a necessary condition to progressive politics. Using the example of the campaign in 2017 for the referendum to decide whether Turkey would move from a parliamentary to a presidential regime, which meant a de facto legitimation of Recep Tayyip Erdogan's authoritarianism, she exposes the ambiguity of many opponents to the reform who viewed hope as a bulwark against apathy and denounced pessimism as leading to inaction. Against this moralizing dichotomy, she mobilizes the resources of Afro-pessimism to show that the politics of hope is unevenly distributed and that it may sometimes be, in the hands of the privileged, a comfortable instrument to neutralize the legitimate resentment of the dominated, elude their potentially radical questioning, hinder effective counterpowers, and, in the end, block critique.

But are we so sure that critique is even useful? wonders Peter Redfield. And if it is, in what way? To answer these questions, he analyzes two case studies that complicate our understanding of how critique works. The first case concerns global health, an international strategy relying on evidence-based knowledge and cost-effective programs at the expense of the understanding of more complex cultural and structural issues. Due to the moral force of the claim to make the world a better place and to the political power of the positivist assumption that science gives access to truth, critique has little space and even little legitimacy to express itself unless it appears to be constructive and renounces its challenge to the very premises of global health. The second case regards humanitarian design, an international trend in development practices that is based on the creation of simple and original devices potentially offering major beneficial consequences for the poor. Instead of proposing reforms or revolutions, its promoters provide modest but effective and inexpensive tools aimed at solving practical problems, from helmets for motorcycle drivers to so-called single-use toilets consisting of a biodegradable plastic bag eventually serving as fertilizer. Since objecting to these minimal yet helpful improvements is delicate, critique seems to be reduced to a marginal and uncertain role as it faces the hope raised, in the first case, by the grandiose mission of saving the lives of human beings and, in the second one, by the humble project of small betterments in the world. However, in front of this triumphant utilitarian politics, it can still ask: Such politics may be useful, but to what end?

The question is particularly relevant and sensitive when critique concerns morally invested and broadly consensual politics. This is the case of human rights, which Karen Engle argues are often seen as being in need of protection from critique. While critical approaches to human rights have become more common, in particular by critics from the left who express reservations with respect to the underlying liberal preconception, she shows that they have been accompanied by a certain discomfort. Critical human rights scholarship is often received as valid and important, she observes, but rejected in practice—brushed aside as unhelpful or unseemly, as going against the best interests of the emancipatory project. The result is that critical scholars themselves are often hesitant to fully embrace their positions, she writes, and draw on a repertoire of discursive devices to either soften or render their critiques more palatable. As an illustration of these rhetorical strategies, she offers a phenomenological account of the ways in which critics deal with this reticence, analyzing her own experiences and those of other critics such as David Kennedy, Samuel Moyn, or Gayatri Chakravorty Spivak. Based on this review, Engle marshals four of the main rhetorical measures that critics deploy to negotiate the discomfort, namely, affirming one's own commitment to human rights, emphasizing that rights are the kind of things that one cannot not want, separating theory from practice and advocacy, and internalizing and responding to criticism. But whereas contemporary left political discourses tend to distance themselves from human rights in favor of alternative approaches to economic inequality or climate change, she notes that the emergence of an unashamed right-wing populism promoting misogynistic, xenophobic, and white-supremacist politics—which often, paradoxically, deploys the language of human rights—brings to the fore a new demand for the defense of human rights. Will human rights provide sufficient leverage to combat these trends? she asks. Perhaps not, but if emancipatory projects flourish elsewhere, critique will need to follow—or, rather, lead—into the future.

As it does, Massimiliano Tomba suggests, critique will continue to instantiate a unique temporality. The dominant interpretation of history as universal is typically Eurocentric, he argues, and in order to apprehend the globalization of the contemporary world, a pluralization of historical temporalities is necessary. In other words, we need to provincialize our conception of time, which has served not only to normalize but also to colonize the rest of the planet. Such different temporal trajectories are, for Tomba, tied to other forms of self-government and to communal notions of property. Weaving together these alternative notions of time and of the commons, he proposes the geological metaphor of subduction, that is, the movement of the edges of the Earth's plates, as a way to think about history as overlapping historical-temporal layers. On this basis, he explores Ernst Bloch's idea of historical multiverse as well as Walter Benjamin's differential of time as potential paths to account for the richness of political attempts in democratic experiments ranging from the revolt of German peasants in 1525 led by the preacher Thomas Müntzer to the Paris Commune of 1871 and the Spartacist uprising of 1919. His is a radical call to emancipate ourselves from our linear conception of time and rediscover earlier experiences of transformations of society, not to fetishize these legacies of the past but to retrieve the sense of a possibility of a different life. This endeavor to reinvent or stimulate or activate our sense of criticality is meant to be collective and political.

A vexing problem remains however little addressed, Vanja Hamzić asserts: it is that of the limits of knowledge or of what he calls the unknowable—the tangible spaces that we believe cannot be properly understood. For him, this is a particular challenge to critique, which has always been guided by the quest to know better and to offer better interpretations. The central thrust of the Kantian idea of critique has been understood as the search for the limits of knowledge as a way to place what we can know on more firm ground; and the ambition of critical theory, from the Frankfurt School on, has always been to unveil illusions and generate alternative analysis to understand our times and our crises. What then of what is left behind? he wonders. How should critique engage those unknown and perhaps unknowable territories? To answer these questions, he examines three contemporary trends in three disciplines. In social anthropology, the ontological turn, conceptualized by Martin Holbraad and Morten Axel Pedersen, among others, encourages the ethnographer to suspend familiarity with ordinary understandings and explore the unfamiliar life of things. In continental philosophy, the speculative turn, especially in the ontological structuralism proposed by Slavoj Žižek, represents an effort to limit our ability to observe reality and the human. In political theory, notably in the writings of Susan Buck-Morss, who asserts that the ontological cannot be political, there is a renewed quest to open a space for experimentation in order to explore whether our world can be otherwise. The inquiry into these sophisticated and somewhat contradictory approaches suggests that the unknowable is not limited to the posthuman but also concerns the human—which is, after all, ethically comforting.

But critique is neither an exclusive scholarly preserve nor a solely theoretical practice. It is also the affair of laypersons and a practical exercise of rights, as demonstrated by Lori Allen, whose contribution initiates the second section. Local elites, in historical contexts of domination, can be regarded as subaltern critics in their own right, Allen argues, taking the Palestinian situation as a case in point. Whereas the common Western discourse asserts that Arabs lacked proper narratives to defend their cause and were therefore unable to justify their independence and later rhetorically oppose the Zionist project, she insists that the problem was not the absence of proper narrators, but the fact that they were not listened to by the international community. Although she acknowledges that he does not fit the typical profile of the subaltern, she views as eloquent the example of Fayez Sayegh, a Palestinian intellectual trained at Georgetown University and a leading figure of the Palestine Liberation Organization, who later became the Special Rapporteur of the United Nations to the International Convention on the Elimination of All Forms of Racial Discrimination. The critique that he was able to convey within the global public sphere entailed both a deconstructionist moment, which contested the prevailing interpretations of the history of Palestine, and a constructive intervention, which called for the just settlement of the Palestinian problem. As shown by the diplomatic battle that opposed the assimilation of Zionism to a form of racism and the denunciation of this position as anti-Semitic, and contrary to the usual distinction established between critique and politics, the two dimensions proved to be in fact inseparable.

Such is also the case for the reactions to the Syrian revolution within the left, particularly in the Arab world, as Fadi A. Bardawil demonstrates. Because they did not correspond to the traditional leftist political alignments, especially with regard to anti-imperialism and secularism, the men and women who rebelled against the Assad regime could not make their cause heard in the global public sphere. The quandary of the left in front of this uprising against an oppressive state apparatus thus signaled a broader difficulty to apprehend unanticipated events that do not conform to ready-made categories and emancipatory movements that do not have capitalism and the West for their primary targets. To remedy this misrecognition of events and movements, an inventive labor of critique must be undertaken. The examples of Aimé Césaire leaving the French Communist Party because it did not acknowledge the singularity of anticolonial struggles, of Franz Fanon imagining novel forms of national liberation beyond reified revolutionary theories in the wake of the Algerian War of Independence, or of Hannah Arendt vindicating the force of events against the materialist mantra of social forces in the context of the Hungarian Revolution are powerful precedents, which can help us reconsider how to address new realities that emerge, especially when they do so out of our comfort zone of interpretation. As Edward Said convincingly showed through his own work and attitude, what is at stake in the critical ethos is not simply the better account of what is going on in the world but also the capacity to energize and mobilize publics through ideas and wordings that thus contribute to generate combativeness.

An illustration of this combativeness can be found in the campaign against police abuse orchestrated by Sri Lankan activists belonging to an organization named People Against Torture, whose practices are analyzed by Nick Cheesman as pragmatic critique. By this expression, he means an empirical inquiry aiming at unveiling the conditions of existence of institutionalized practices beyond their traditional or official justifications in order to engage a political action to change it or abolish it. In the case under study, extreme forms of abuse by police forces in the southern part of the country were documented on the basis of numerous detailed testimonies by survivors and relatives of deceased persons. This implied what Eyal Weizman calls critical proximity with the victims of torture, their families, and, more broadly, local communities. However, beyond this meticulous recording, the activists strove to uncover the logics at work by showing, first, that torture was not the exception but the rule in law enforcement; second, that it targeted almost exclusively the poor and powerless; third, that it was tolerated by public authorities who did not investigate the cases and did not prosecute the authors; and fourth, that it did not have the usual excuse of the context of war since the region was at that time not part of the conflict zone. Significantly, the fact that they conducted this inquiry with local communities generated among the inhabitants a sentiment of hope and a sense of their own worthiness.

Subaltern critique is certainly not new, however. The problem is its absence from the historical archives, where little remains of the voices of the dominated.

Through a close reading of the legal case that opposes an enslaved black man named Adam and his master called John Saffin in Boston at the end of the seventeenth century, David Kazanjian tries to fill the blanks of the missing voice of the slave who never represents himself in the legal documents but is represented by others, starting with his master. Contrary to the Lockean interpretation of possession and the Marxist theory of dispossession, he argues, Adam is not claiming that he was dispossessed of something that he earlier possessed. Rather his critique is directed against both possession and dispossession. To establish his thesis, Kazanjian resorts to a form of speculative historiography, which does not infer its analysis from evidence-based facts but from unverifiable hypotheses, which are grounded, in the present case, in what the other agents say about Adam. His deviance, as it is narrated in the court records, appears to be a performance that contests the moral as much as the social order. What seems unbearable does not have to do with the labor he carries out but with the conduct he exhibits. His critique resides in the sense of freedom he manifests.

A renewed and radical critique is what Andrew Dilts calls for under the rubric of abolitionist politics. The political crises we find ourselves in today, he argues, reflect in truth a deeper crisis within the left, characterized by the many liberal and center-left political critics who accuse critical theory of identitarianism and call for more responsible incrementalism. Rather than succumb to these centrist demands to be realistic, Dilts draws on a strand of critical thought that links together the emancipatory moment of abolition with the constructive moment of building new institutions and practices. Called "Abolition Democracy" by W. E. B. Du Bois, later embraced by Angela Davis and others such as Cedric Robinson and Robin D. G. Kelley, the critical impulse here is to conjoin the dismantling of oppressive institutions with the simultaneous creation of new social, economic, and political ones for true emancipation. This approach is put into practice through the writing and advocacy of Critical Resistance, especially in the way in which this abolitionist organization collaborated with INCITE! Women of Color Against Violence, a national organization dedicated to ending violence against women of color, to address their mutual aspirations and institutional efforts at building a new political body. Through these and other examples of abolitionist politics, Dilts demonstrates that the critical tools necessary to overcome the current crisis within the left and to counter the recurring critique of critique are available.

In a similar vein, dismayed at the marginal place of critical legal scholarship within the legal academy in the United States, Allegra M. McLeod turns our attention to other legal spaces where critique is thriving today—often unexpected sites and in unanticipated ways. In particular, she shines a light on spaces dubbed the undercommons by Fred Moten and Stefano Harney, more specifically inside the prison system and within the protest movements challenging excessive police violence, where she identifies new and promising forms of critique of law. In the carceral world, the Short Corridor Collective is a self-initiated reading group formed by inmates imprisoned in solitary confinement over decades in the California Pelican Bay State Prison Security Housing Unit—all men identified by the state as belonging to different racially identified prison gangs. Drawing on their underground discussions of a variety of critical texts on themes ranging from the Irish prison hunger strikes and the Black Panthers to Michel Foucault's works, these men began writing, developing a critique of their conditions of confinement and of the logics of the punitive system. The critical exercise inspired a hunger strike of their own, which called for solidarity across prisons and forged a collective voice from within Pelican Bay—ultimately resulting in the release of hundreds of prisoners from decades-long solitary confinement and the development of a New Abolitionist movement across the country. With respect to police violence, the Movement for Black Lives engaged in a critical examination of communities' own governance mechanisms and invented experiments in self-governance, leading to innovative efforts to reduce community dependence on the police in order to actualize the abolitionist ambition. Several organizations, including the Black Youth Project 100, internalized their critique of criminal justice by developing mechanisms to address internal grievances within the organization, and enacted transformative justice projects. In the end, such alternative spaces radically question and expand our understanding of critical interventions as they open new forms of critique in action.

It is precisely on this theme of the new and emerging forms of critical practice that Bernard E. Harcourt concludes the book. We stand today at a pivotal moment for praxis, he argues. After decades-long contestation and challenges to the older orthodox modes of political action associated with a more Marxist-oriented critical theory tradition, and in light of newer experiments with forms of assembly and occupation, the terrain of critical praxis is now open to a range of new modalities of uprising—from temporary autonomous zones to hashtag social movements to political disobedience. To answer a pressing question—What is to be done?—Harcourt traces a genealogy of contemporary critical praxis and surveys eight broad categories of political action that now exist in this space of contemporary critical thought and social movements. He sets forth different visions to rejuvenate political practice and challenges us to address what is perhaps the most important task in these critical times: to develop a new critical praxis for the twenty-first century.

PART I

CRITIQUE AS PRACTICE

CHAPTER 1

HOW IS CRITIQUE?

DIDIER FASSIN

There is something in critique which is akin to virtue.

—Michel Foucault

O n May 27, 1978, Michel Foucault[1] delivered before the Société française de philosophie a lecture on critique for which he somewhat affectedly announced that it was without title, nevertheless adding that he had in fact found one but considered it to be "indecent." In the last words of his conclusion, he revealed that what he had imagined and not dared articulate was "What is the *Aufklärung*?" Yet, six years later, this is how he actually titled a text that he wrote on the occasion of the two hundredth anniversary of the publication of Kant's eponymous essay and in which he expanded his earlier analysis. It is not certain, however, that the substitute wording that he ended up adopting for the title of his original lecture—"What is critique?"—was less ambitious or emphatic. To this bold question his answer was famously a series of variations on the theme: the art of not being governed in this way. Beyond this catchy but ultimately not so transparent definition, what Foucault proposed was to apprehend critique as a method combining archeological, genealogical, and strategic analysis to identify how the historical responses to social problems such as madness, illness, crime, or desire have come to be what they are, how they could have been different, and how they could still differ in the future. This is what he called "eventualization," the advent of realities via interactions between knowledge and power that make the contingent outcomes of these interactions appear to be not only acceptable but even necessary: the asylum, the hospital, the prison, or sexuality, respectively. Such outcomes are regarded as truths, that is, facts deemed true and no more disputed. Critique is therefore "the movement by which the subject gives himself the right to question truth on its effects on power, and question power on its discourses of truth." The "critical attitude" consists in challenging the self-evidence of the world as it is.

It is a different, although similarly reckless, interrogation that I want to raise. Rather than "what is critique?" it can be formulated as "how is critique?" Here, "how" means an inquiry into the condition of critique, in the same way as one would ask someone: How are you? In this sense, it is a sort of clinical investigation into the health of critique in the contemporary moment. This medical bulletin is obviously to be taken with a grain of salt since, to be seriously established, such a diagnosis would necessitate a long-term research program in its own right. More modestly, I will offer the outline of a reflection on some of the issues faced by critical thinking. In order to do so, I consider that it is indispensable to contextualize critique both temporally and spatially. Indeed, as a practice, it always exists within a given time and space, and we must account for both dimensions. To that effect, I will mostly concentrate my analysis on two periods—roughly the 1960s–70s and the 2000s–10s—and two countries—France and the United States—not excluding, nevertheless, occasional incursions into other periods and countries. Through this tentative exploration, I want to analyze the transformation of critique in light, on the one hand, of the historical contexts in which it is situated, as emphasized by John Dewey,[2] for whom "the most pervasive fallacy of philosophical thinking goes back to neglect of context," and, on the other hand, of the social fields within which it is inserted, the most obvious being "the intellectual field as a system which is governed by its own laws," as Pierre Bourdieu[3] writes. Both elements are crucial, albeit overlooked, as critique is often discussed only from an internal perspective, that is, within a philosophical or more broadly theoretical framework. While such reading is necessary, it does not exempt from historical and sociological approaches, which account for the conditions of possibility of critique as it is, in a specific time and place. Critique is always, at least in part, a response to a certain state of the world being developed within a certain configuration of power and knowledge in the academic and public spheres.

At this point, four caveats may be necessary. First, this essay must be read as a provisional cartography of a complex landscape; even when its conclusions might sometimes seem assertive, they should be read as hypotheses for future research. Second, the emphasis is mostly on critique as it emerges from the intellectual world and the academic field in connection with the political and economic domains; however, there are other significant forms of critique, coming from society more broadly, through action in particular, which deserve attention. Third, the focus is limited to the two countries I am more familiar with but can be construed as epitomizing in distinct ways some of the challenges facing critique; this is obviously a bias, which I have tried to partially correct by inserting these cases in their global background and occasionally comparing them with other parts of the world. Fourth, revisiting the past is at risk of appearing to be nostalgic of a golden age, which I do not think ever existed; indeed, any temptation to idealize better times for critique and to heroicize earlier critics runs the risk of ignoring new forms and new actors.

These cautionary words being formulated, the general argument developed here is that the public presence of critical thinking has been considerably transformed during the past half century. In particular, it has lost much of its radical edge and academic legitimacy, while being increasingly confined to marginal circles. However, this is neither a linear nor an unequivocal process, and there exist important differences across time and place, but also significant emergences of novel expressions of critique. I will show how this process has operated by examining first historical contexts, second social fields, third disciplinary variations. I will conclude by showing that the reconfiguration has not led to the disappearance of critique and has even rendered possible interesting emerging forms. Critique may have lost some of its momentum, but even in the present unfavorable environment (and perhaps because of it) there are multiple signs of its being alive and well, provided that we be able to recognize them.

Contexts

France, 1961. Jean-Paul Sartre,[4] who is undoubtedly the most prominent French philosopher of his time, and for that matter one of the world's most famous public intellectuals, writes the preface to *The Wretched of the Earth*. Reflecting on the uprisings in the colonies analyzed and defended by Frantz Fanon in his book, he comments: "This irrepressible violence is neither sound and fury, nor the resurrection of savage instincts, nor even the effect of resentment: it is man re-creating himself. . . . The native cures himself of colonial neurosis by thrusting out the settler through force of arms. . . . In the first days of the revolt you must kill. To shoot down a European is to kill two birds with one stone, to destroy an oppressor and the man he oppresses at the same time. There remain a dead man and a free man." Violence is not only a means for political liberation but also a means for ethical subjectivation—the self-realization of the individual as a free man. He is, indeed, so free that he is even liberated from the fear of dying: "This new man begins his life as a man at the end of it; he considers himself as a potential corpse. He will be killed; not only does he accept this risk, he is sure of it. . . . He prefers victory to survival; others, not he, will have the fruits of victory. . . . We find our humanity on this side of death and despair; he finds it beyond torture and death." To realize how powerful this analysis of violence is, let us imagine substituting today "Palestinian" for "native" and "Israeli" for "European" in a similar text accounting for the attacks of the former against the latter as a response to the occupation of his land and the oppression of his people: it is easy to fancy the uproar. In the contemporary world, Sartre would be accused of anti-Semitism, notwithstanding his "reflections on the Jewish question," and prosecuted for "expressing support for terrorism," under French legislation recently voted. Half a century ago, he was awarded the Nobel Prize—only three years after the publication of his preface to Fanon's book.

United States, 1964. As the Civil Rights movement is at its height and the anti-Vietnam War movement is just starting, a student protest, which has come to be known as the free speech movement, erupts at the University of California, Berkeley, in response to the repression of various initiatives taken on campus to generate debate about political issues and support for antiracist causes. During the ensuing civil disobedience campaign, Mario Savio[5] delivers a famous speech in which he criticizes the president of the university for having compared the institution to a firm: "There's a time when the operation of the machine becomes so odious, makes you so sick at heart, that you can't take part. . . . And you've got to put your bodies upon the gears and upon the wheels, upon the levers, upon the apparatus, and you've got to make it stop." After months of demonstrations and confrontations with the police, the students finally obtain significant achievements in terms of freedom of speech in universities, opening the way to years of leftist activism. Five decades later, in September 2017, it is on the historic site of these protests, Sproul Plaza, which has since then become the symbol of the defense of the First Amendment in academia, that alt-right and white supremacist speakers, such as the former senior editor of *Breitbart News* Milo Yiannopoulos, are invited. The ironically named Free Speech Week gives rise to mostly peaceful but occasionally violent student demonstrations, leading the bankrupt university to spend more than $100,000 to ensure the security of the events through a massive presence of the police on campus. As conservative and far-right pundits multiply their public interventions in higher-education institutions all over the country, some of the latter decide and implement new policies aiming at punishing protests against such speakers, in reference to the First Amendment of the Constitution and in the name of civility.

For critique, contexts thus matter. And contexts change. The 1960s and 1970s were a time of radical transformations and radical thinking worldwide. From the 1980s on, a reaction occurs, increasingly marginalizing leftist positions and mobilizations, and leaving a growing public space to not only neoliberal discourse but also, in the 2000s, right-wing radicalism. To understand this remarkable shift, which is certainly not unprecedented if one thinks, for instance, of Germany and France in the 1920s and 1930s, we need to apprehend the larger historical picture.

In the aftermath of the Second World War, most African and Asian countries conquered their independence, often after violent conflicts with the colonizers, mostly British and French, while Communist regimes were installed in the Soviet Union, Eastern Europe, most of Asia, and part of Africa and Cuba, with the Cold War as background. In that regard, the debacle of the French army at Dien Bien Phu in 1954 can be viewed as an omen for the retreat of the US army from Saigon two decades later, both troops being defeated by the same Viet Cong backed by China. In parallel, the Bandung Conference in 1955 paved the way soon afterward for the Non-Aligned Movement, which involved two-thirds of the United Nations' members and was fundamentally an anti-imperialist coalition attempting to free itself from the so-called great powers and their bloc politics. A new world order was being built, raising new tensions. Latin America, Southeast Asia, sub-Saharan Africa, and the Middle East became sites of direct or indirect confrontation between the United States and the Soviet Union, and more generally between the West and the East. In other words, the ideological lines were clearly traced between right and left, between liberal democracies and socialist regimes. In academia, progressive ideas were dominant, anti-imperialism succeeded anticolonialism. In France, the intellectual realm was dominated by the struggle between Stalinists, Trotskyists, and Maoists. In the United States, the New Left was increasingly present on campuses. Each country had its specific historical configuration: France with the painful metropolitan developments of the undeclared Algerian War as an enduring conclusion of the decolonization process, the United States with the Civil Rights movement attempting to put an end to more than two centuries of oppression of the African American population. And each country had its specific political response: May 1968 students' demonstrations and workers' strikes on one side of the Atlantic, anti–Vietnam War protests on the other side.

But the subversive mood did not only affect international and domestic politics. It also concerned culture, largely understood as both bourgeois for its moral narrowness and capitalist for its commodity fetishism. Such critique was already present in the 1950s in the writings of the Frankfurt School, most notably Theodor Adorno and later Herbert Marcuse, who connected Marx and Freud in a radical questioning of the values, practices, and spirit that characterized the societies of their times. Importantly, what was coined critical theory was not limited to everyday culture; it also encompassed scientific culture, including that of the social sciences, which can be traced back to Walter Benjamin; in particular, positivism was criticized by Max Horkheimer for its unadmitted embedding in the economic structures that it served and strengthened. Thus, capitalism was seen as underpinning both ordinary behavior, with its unbridled consumption, and intellectual work, with its false claim to neutral knowledge. Notably, however, this radical critique translated little into action as most of these German authors, having learned from the experience of Nazism, were somewhat pessimistic about the possibilities of change. In parallel, and with some time lag, what later came to be known as French theory, but was then often referred to as poststructuralism, began to delve deeper into the very structures of language, representation, meaning, and thought, with Jacques Derrida, Gilles Deleuze, Roland Barthes, and Jacques Lacan, among others. From their perspective, deconstruction was an infinite methodological process unendingly putting to the test any pretense to truth. The archeology of the human sciences developed by Michel Foucault even led to the affirmation that man was a recent invention, hardly more than a few centuries, and that he could well disappear in the near future, as a new episteme would emerge. Significantly, for these French scholars, critique was more than an intellectual exercise. It also involved participation in social and political movements, from students' protests to workers' strikes, from institutional psychotherapy at La Borde clinic to denunciation of the carceral condition by the Group of Information on Prisons, from the struggle against apartheid in South Africa to the assistance to boat people in Vietnam. Beyond their impact on their national public, in Germany and France, both Frankfurt School and French Theory had a considerable influence on academia elsewhere, notably in the United States, as the former fostered neo-Marxist contestation of capitalism in the 1960s, while the latter contributed to the birth of feminist and postcolonial studies in the 1970s and beyond.

In short, these decades were a period of turmoil on the international scene, of contestation of the social, moral, and political order in many countries, and of effervescence of radical thinking in the intellectual realm, which spared few of the certainties inherited from the Enlightenment. Revolution was in the street as well as in the academy.

The backlash, which began in the second half of the 1970s and developed in the 1980s, took multiple forms. In Latin America, often described as the backyard of the United States, right-wing dictatorships spread over the continent; in Brazil, Argentina, Chile, and Paraguay, among others, the brutal repression of the left with the help of the CIA as part of Operation Condor was accompanied by the development of experiments in neoliberal economics promoted by the Chicago Boys. In Western Europe, the reaction to the mobilizations of the 1960s, which increasingly turned to riotous confrontations in the following decade, led to the access to, or the consolidation in, the power of conservative majorities in parliaments and governments, most significantly in Britain with Margaret Thatcher; in various countries, leftist exasperation reached a paroxysm, notably with the Red Army Faction in Germany and the Red Brigades in Italy, thus serving as a justification for authoritarian measures in return.

In the United States, the popular response to the protests on Californian campuses was Ronald Reagan's election as governor, which opened the way to a presidential term marked not only by the combination of market deregulation, government trimming, and tax reduction, but also by the beginning of mass incarceration, as a result of the so-called war on drugs, which had replaced the war on poverty of the previous decade. A sign of the stability of the new ideology, the coming to power of Bill Clinton only reinforced the neoliberal and repressive turn initiated by his predecessors. In the meantime, in France, the brief parenthesis of the left in government after the election of François Mitterrand paradoxically comforted the trend. On the one hand, the shift, after only two years of Socialists in power, toward austerity measures and privatization policies spelled the end of the idea of a possible alternative to strictly market-driven economies. On the other hand, the rise of the National Front, by weakening the traditional conservative parties, transformed the political agenda as it put at its center immigration and security issues that were subsequently adopted by the right and later the left. Thus, both in the United States and in France, the ideological line was blurred between Republicans and Democrats, and between conservatives and socialists, respectively, the very idea of a progressive left in government seeming an antiquated fantasy or more flatly a doomed project.

At the international level, the culmination of this process came in 1989 with the fall of the Berlin Wall, the dislocation of the Soviet Union, and the end of communist regimes in Eastern Europe. An orphan of its socialist imaginary, the left became "spiritually homeless" with "haunting pasts without utopias," as Enzo Traverso[6] formulated it. Even if they did not signify the end of history proclaimed by some, these events marked the failure of most major experiments in socialism of the twentieth century, leaving the field open to conservative and neoliberal parties. As an indication of this trend,[7] in terms of who governed in the twenty-eight countries of the European Union at the end of 2017, only one, Greece, was classified as left, although an alliance was formed there with the nationalist right; ten were center-left, four of them being in coalition with right-wing parties; for the rest, four were center-right, four right, and two far-right. In France, the Communist Party, which was the greatest political force at the end of the Second World War, remained for three decades the first component of the left, and structured the political life of the working class, only won 2.7 percent of the vote in the 2017 legislative elections, condemning it to the margins of political life. The trajectory of the historian François Furet,[8] who was the president of the École des hautes études en sciences sociales from 1977 to 1985, epitomizes this rightward evolution: born into a wealthy family, he studied in the most exclusive school of Paris; in 1949, he joined the Communist Party, which he left ten years later; in 1968, he became advisor for the center-right minister of education, Edgar Faure; in 1982, he created a neoliberal think tank, the Foundation Saint-Simon; in 1995, he published a book analyzing the fall of the idea of communism, which he described as the passing of an illusion. Such retreat from progressive thinking and turn to reactionary positions were far from rare in France and beyond.

In fact, it is often noted that the shift to the right of the entire ideological spectrum is such that what used to be considered to be center-left or even center-right ideas a few decades ago, for instance, in matters of distributive and retributive justice or respect for the rule of law and human rights, is now often regarded—or even denounced—as leftist, while the center has itself definitely moved rightward. Thus, during the 2017 presidential campaign, Emmanuel Macron, rejecting the traditional ideological divisions, described his program as centrist. Triumphantly elected, his agenda actually turned out to be a conventional mix of neoliberalism, with tax reduction on capital, contraction of public expenses, and revision of the labor code, and of authoritarianism, with the incorporation of state of emergency measures into normal legislation, the hardening of border control, and the construction of new prisons. Ironically, the book he had published one year earlier to present his ideas was titled *Révolution*.[9] Whereas hardly any critical thinker dared to use such a watchword anymore, it was hijacked by a politician coming from the financial world who implemented this combination of minimal government for the economy and maximal government for repression.[10] But such travesty of radicalism in the language of political communication is indeed not new.

In this new context, the place of critique, its adequacy with the present state of the world, and its relevance to the public's expectations for intellectuals seem growingly problematic.

Fields

Contexts—international and national, political and cultural—are therefore indispensable to take into account when trying to interpret the evolution of critique, to understand why certain discourses, such as Sartre's, applauded in a given moment, become unacceptable some years later, and to make sense of why certain means, the call for free speech at Berkeley, for example, can serve opposite ends at two different moments. But the conditions of possibility of critique are not only to be grasped in light of these macrohistorical backgrounds. They must also be apprehended in relation with meso-social elements. What I have more specifically in mind is the structuring and interconnecting of social spaces, in particular the academic world, the public sphere, the political arena, and the economic realm. These four fields obey in principle different logics. The academic world is about research and education. The public sphere is about communication and debate. The political arena is about decision and governance. The economic realm is about market and profit. Of course, none of these fields can be reduced to these explicit logics: thus, life in the academic world has also much to do with debate, with decision, and even with profit. Besides, within each of the four fields, it is power relations that define both the rules of the game and the position of the players: for instance, the dominance of economists in the social sciences has led to a reorientation of political science and sociology. Finally, these fields interact with one another: thus, the way in which research programs and scholars are currently promoted, funded, and assessed in institutions of higher education is a recent importation from the corporate world that has substantial effects on the production of knowledge. Not only can critique not ignore the structuring and interconnecting of these social spaces, but it is entirely embedded and shaped by them, even when it criticizes them.

The United States is probably the most studied and most extreme case in terms of the corollary transformations of, and increasing interactions between, these various fields. It reveals some of the major trends that can be observed on a minor scale elsewhere in the world as a result of both the influential position occupied by the country with regard to these four fields and the common mechanisms at work in various parts of the globe.

Over the past decades, academia has come more and more under dual pressures, one external, the other internal, which proceed, at least in part, from a shared ideology and, in the end, contribute to their mutual strengthening. The external pressure is that of neoliberalism, and manifests itself through market-oriented logics that infuse the whole higher education system, leading to what Wendy Brown[11] calls a "stealth revolution." Universities ferociously compete for the supposedly best professors and best students, the criterion of quality being in both cases not independent from financial consideration: the fame of the professors tends to overrate their intrinsic scientific value; the profile of the students includes their potential addition to lucrative sports and their expected contributions as future alumni. Liberal arts with their comprehensive approach to knowledge remain the privilege of the elites' children, while the general tendency in the college system is to favor vocational training that is supposed to secure employment and income as well as correspond to the needs of the economic world. Students are viewed as human capital in which society invests, beginning with their parents as soon as their offspring is born, but in which these young people themselves must become self-investors, through the loans that they must take out to pay their tuition and will reimburse over several decades. The closing of departments in the humanities, the repeated targeting of the social sciences by representatives for their alleged lack of benefit for national economic interest, and the announcement of substantial budget cuts for public research, in particular when it might undermine industrial companies by revealing their impact on health or climate, are signs of this evolution. In parallel, the internal pressure is that of positivism, understood simply here as the belief in the existence of undisputable facts that scientists merely have to collect and of underlying laws that govern social life, a belief that seems to have an "uncanny persistence," in George Steinmetz's[12] words. There is indeed a long tradition of this conception of both science and the social, and it has had heydays in the 1930s and 1960s, often occurring at the confluence of new methods, technologies, or sometimes theories within the disciplines, and of forceful social, political, and economic influences. The contemporary moment does not escape these logics. Exemplary of such trends, the import of big data relies on the combination of rapidly increasing processing power and the ubiquitous implementation of data mining as a way to discover invisible patterns as well as strategic implications for both the computing industry and hedge funds. Science and economy tend to go hand in hand. In fact, many top mathematicians and physicists leave the academic world for the world of finance where their competence is more highly valued in terms of remuneration.

To summarize, the convergence of these external and internal pressures has reoriented the higher-education system toward a corporate model described by Philip Mirowski[13] as the "new knowledge economy," in which the space for critique has been significantly restricted, critical thinking being regarded as useless for markets, irrelevant for science, and, on the whole, potentially negative for the nation. This analysis leads to reconsider the thesis developed by Luc Boltanski and Ève Chiapello,[14] according to whom "the principal operator of creation and transformation of the spirit of capitalism is critique" and even, "in certain conditions, critique can itself be one of the factors of a change in capitalism" as such. For them, reflexive managers and indignant critics jointly contribute to modifying the ideas and, in some cases, the practices of capitalism. But while such possibility certainly attests to the remarkable adaptability of the latter, it only operates within the range of the expected benefits, including symbolic. Capitalism's most common response to critique is not appropriation but marginalization. Again, the United States offers the most extreme illustration of this trend. In quantitative as well as qualitative terms, it is not unreasonable to affirm that this country's universities concentrate the highest proportion of radical thinkers worldwide. Yet, these critics are mostly confined in the higher-education system and even, within it, in a few departments and centers, themselves situated at the margin of the system, such as those in literary, feminist, postcolonial, or African American studies, while the dominant disciplines, namely, political science, economics, and law, remain generally impervious and even hostile to such thinking. This process—let us call it *reductio ad scholam*—is probably the most effective way of containing without censoring critique, which is left to develop freely inasmuch as it does not overflow into society or contaminate positive science. Thus, it might not be exaggerated to affirm that, in this context, the more radical critique is, the more circumscribed it remains—and in the end, the more inoffensive.

In this respect, it is crucial to consider the characteristics of, and interactions between, the various fields involved in the production, circulation, and consumption of critique. Of particular interest is the reconfiguration of the public sphere over the past decades. Two major series of transformations have occurred, one technological, the other economic, the second being in large part a condition of possibility for the development of the first. Thus, since the 1960s, television has considerably affected the place and profile of authors and books in society: rather than the capacity to reflect, it is the aptitude to perform that is expected from an author; more than depth or creativity, simple messages and if possible polemical stances are required for the success of books; in fact, today's public intellectuals do not even have to be authors and write books as long as they are able to make good performances in the media. But this evolution is not mainly due to the introduction of the new technology; it is the economic model underlying it that plays the determining role. Indeed, public channels such as Arte, the BBC, or PBS continue to offer space for intellectual programs, whereas private ones, which dominate the media, do not. Infamously but lucidly, the CEO[15] of the main French broadcast company, TF1, declared that his programs "had for vocation" to "entertain and relax" the viewer's brain "so as to prepare it between two commercials," adding that "what we sell to Coca-Cola is time of available human brain." In these circumstances, it is clear that critics do not have a place in the media unless they accept its rules of the game, for instance, in talk shows, which imply short interventions, overt simplifications, frequent interruptions, fierce attacks by columnists, an anchor's dubious humor, and the loud reactions from the audience. Announced and denounced by Guy Debord,[16] the "society of the spectacle" is certainly not critique-friendly. Furthermore, in the United States in particular, the progressive disappearance of bookstores eliminated by the competition of online ordering of books, combined with the whittling down of social sciences and humanities volumes from the shelves of the surviving chains, is another sign of the reduction of the potential space to disseminate critical thought, even if some local booksellers endeavor to develop alternative models in defense of literary and scholarly quality. As a result of these various processes of commodification and spectacularization, the public presence of critical intellectuals seems limited to a small number of individuals, who get to write regular columns in newspapers, and a small number of media outlets, which may operate via individual or syndicated blogs, therefore constituting a vibrant but marginal critical public sphere with little echo within society at large. Such marginalization contrasts with the increasing role of social media, which have begun to vie with television but which are not necessarily more sympathetic to critique.

No less significant in that regard is the relationship between the intellectual world and the political arena. Traditionally, critical thinkers have played an important role in right-wing parties, under the Nazi and Fascist regimes in particular, and even more in left-wing ones, especially communist ones, either in power as in the Soviet Union or in the opposition as in France. Such affinity sometimes led to symbiosis, as was the case for Antonio Gramsci, who was the leader of the Italian Communist Party and became one of the most influential figures of Western Marxism. From the 1960s on, the evolution of the political world has been largely dependent on the already evoked transformations of the public sphere, in particular the commodification of the media and the spectacularization of society. Although it is now part of ordinary politics, with the highly dramatized public debates between presidential candidates and the increasing presence of politicians in popular talk shows, extreme manifestations of this trend have been the election of celebrities to the highest office in the United States, with the B-movie actor Ronald Reagan and the reality television host Donald Trump, but the list of comedians, singers, anchors, and even porn stars who have had a second life in politics across the planet is long. These migrations from show business to the political domain have signaled as well as contributed to a shift from substance to performance and, consequently, to the rise of populism, which has in turn reinforced with its hostile slogans the discredit of intellectual life.

In fact, even when some room is left to scholars in the circles of power, those chosen are the most apt to assist with governing, namely, the experts who are appreciated for both their specific competence and their mainstream accommodating approach. Moreover, in the case of economic advisors to governments, they often have close ties with investment banks, hedge funds, insurance companies, and more broadly the financial world. One can easily imagine that such a combination of positive science and problematic liaisons is hardly favorable to critical thinking. In fact, the rare encounters between politicians and intellectuals generally take place in worldly circumstances. For instance, French heads of state are in the habit of having occasional lunches or dinners with scholars, philosophers, or writers, a practice that is reminiscent of those of the ancient régime court system. Obviously, neither expert committees nor social events are particularly favorable environments for the flourishing of critical thinking.

In the end, when considering how the features of and relations between the academic world, the public sphere, the political arena, and the economic realm have evolved over the past decades, it appears that the intellectual domain has been largely reconfigured and that the space for critique has been seriously constrained. This is at least the case in Western societies, most dramatically in the

United States and significantly less in France. Indeed, the observer who travels to other regions of the world, visiting Latin American or African countries, draws a somewhat different picture. There, more porosity often exists between fields, permitting an easier circulation of people and ideas, including critical ones, from the academy to the polis and the media, and vice versa. One might even have a sense that society is more politicized and debates more open. In some aspects, a campus in Bogotá or Johannesburg in the 2010s presents some resemblance with a campus in Berkeley or Paris in the 1970s. However, the combined trend toward more autonomy, more specialization, and more claim to science, as well as the increasing dominance of the neoliberal model within academia, including in the methods of evaluation of scholarly activity, tends with time to attenuate these differences.

Disciplines

If historical contexts and the configurations of social fields are crucial to apprehend the recent evolution of critique, we should not underestimate its internal logics. Certainly, these logics are not independent from contexts and configurations. The fall of communism has contributed to the retreat of revolutionary ideas and the empire of neoliberalism in higher education has participated in the turn to positivism. However, the disciplines themselves have inner mechanisms of transformation. New theories and new methods develop, responding in part to criticisms of previous approaches, in part to institutional calls for innovations. It would be arduous, if not impossible, to try to delineate a single coherent tendency, but a more reasonable task might be to limit the analysis to one significant discipline.

Sociology is often considered to be the most critical of the social sciences, both in an epistemological sense, as it questions the self-evidence of social worlds as they appear to be, and in a political sense, since it addresses issues to which societies are confronted. The combination of the two elements typically leads to a more specific criticism: that of symbolic power and social violence. "Whose side are we on?" Howard Becker[17] famously asked in a presidential address to the Society for the Study of Social Problems. His answer was unambiguous. For interactionist sociologists like him, since a "hierarchy of credibility" makes the superordinate groups more legitimate "to define the way things are," and therefore their version of any event more authoritative than any account by the subordinate groups, the mere fact of giving as much credence to the latter's statements as to the former's assertions signifies the refusal of "an established status order, in which knowledge of truth and the right to be heard are not equally distributed." One can therefore not avoid taking sides, and sociologists are necessarily seen as adopting the perspective of the dominated against that of the dominant. Taking sides may, however, have a different meaning if one thinks in terms of social structures rather than social interactions, as critique analyzes broader and deeper phenomena. This is what Marxist and neo-Marxist sociologists do when they unveil the deleterious effects of the relations of production on those who are exploited and reveal the pernicious mechanisms of the ideology by which domination is obscured to those it affects. Such critical approach is epitomized by C. Wright Mills's *The Sociological Imagination*,[18] which was in the 1960s the manifesto of the radical segment of the discipline in the United States.

In each period of its short life, sociology has been traversed by various theoretical currents and empirical practices. It is therefore impossible to describe it at any time as a unified discipline. Certain trends can nevertheless be identified. In his study of half a century of the professional association's flagship journal, the *American Sociological Review*, Ben Agger[19] shows that although "the discipline of U.S. sociology was positivist from the beginning" in its intention, "only quite recently, in response to sociology's loss of institutional prestige, has *ASR* come to resemble a science journal." According to his analysis, the most consequential transformation that occurred during that time was the passage from "substance-driven" to "methods-driven" research, the professionalization of the discipline being accompanied by its "mathematization" and more generally by the project of making it "bench-science." This positivist turn, which was an attempt to relegitimize a discipline in crisis as a result of a dual process of internal fragmentation and external contestation in the 1980s, partially took its inspiration in the orientation taken by what had then become the most authoritative social science—economics. Today, the most prominent sociological journals in the United States are dominated by empirical studies, often using quantitative techniques, readily relying on digital archives, leaving little space to narratives, and demonstrating moderate interest in critical thinking.

Yet, interestingly, what has perhaps been the major debate within the discipline in recent years was not about its positivist turn: it was about its social utility, as Michael Burawoy[20] proposed to recenter the discussion around two questions: "for whom and for what do we pursue sociology?" Distancing himself from what he designated as professional sociology, policy sociology, and critical sociology, the then president of the American Sociological Association called instead for a "public sociology," which he decomposed into "traditional" interventions into the public sphere and "organic" collaborations with local publics. Although Burawoy was much criticized for these somewhat artificial and exclusive distinctions, he had the merit to draw attention to the increasing enclosure of the discipline in its academic ivory tower, especially with regard to its critical expressions that have little echo beyond university campuses, and to the importance of alternative forms of intellectual life exterior to the scholarly realm, thus recognizing the often-ignored significance of social critique outside the social sciences.

The positivist evolution of the discipline, as a corollary of the consolidation of its institutional position, also occurred in France. In that regard, Boltanski[21] recounts how the creation by Bourdieu of the *Actes de la recherche en sciences sociales* in 1974 was a response to the difficulty their group of critical sociologists had publishing their research in "official academic journals," as "colleagues, not necessarily worthy of esteem, guardians of norms coming out of nowhere but regarded as sacred, who, in the name of science and of what they called epistemology, conceived of on the model of a repressive morality," blocked them with constraining demands. By contrast, the new journal allowed for the publication, without having to wait "months for the verdict of a committee," of lengthy texts avoiding "predefined formats" in which it was possible "to both describe and criticize, in sum, to do sociology." One of the first articles published was a seventy-page essay cosigned by Boltanski and Bourdieu and titled "The Production of Dominant Ideology,"[22] of which Boltanski writes that every time he opens it he remains "struck—or better astounded—by the critical force of the text: how could we dare?" Not only did they "denounce the injustice, lies and transgressions by the powerful of the time," but they also "questioned the very moral order by describing it as a political order entirely directed towards the perpetuation" of inequalities. "In those times, what would have been unthinkable ten years earlier, what will ten years later become not only incongruous but also unacceptable, was sheerly obvious." Indeed, three decades later, even in this journal, one does not find any more such outliers in terms of form and content: it has become part of normal science, and even its critical edge has become normalized.

In hindsight, it is therefore ironic that the fiercest battle that took place in French sociology during the past decades would have opposed the very authors of this essay: the professor and his former assistant, both engaged in the same radical intellectual endeavor a few years before.[23] Indeed, whereas from the early 1960s until the end of the 1980s Bourdieu had imposed his critical sociology as the most creative and influential approach to social worlds, his interpretive framework became in the 1990s an object of criticism by Boltanski, who distanced himself from it and developed a different paradigm, which he named sociology of critique. Beyond the personal dispute and the rebellion of the disciple against his master, it is crucial to understand that two opposed visions of critique were involved. For critical sociologists, heirs of Marxism, what we consider self-evident, whether it is the idea that the education system is solely based on merit, that science is a disinterested activity, or that aesthetic taste is intrinsic, is in fact produced by social forces. Such self-evidences are deceptive not only in relation to truth but also in relation to power. Symbolic violence precisely consists in imposing as natural or obvious what is determined by social relations, and more specifically by social relations of domination. The role of the sociologist is therefore to uncover the mechanisms and logics that obfuscate reality, to show how free will is largely determined by habitus, and to lift the veil on the way social fields function. For sociologists of critique, inspired by pragmatism, and particularly Dewey's version of it, social actors are neither duping nor duped. They engage in disputes in which they develop arguments based on principles and in tests by means of which agreements are ultimately found. The task of the sociologist is therefore not to unmask the dominant and enlighten the dominated, but to provide a formal grammar of social action by describing the disputes, the arguments exchanged, the principles invoked, and the tests implemented. While Bourdieu's theory has been questioned for emphasizing too much social determination and leaving little place to individual agency, for overestimating domination and discouraging emancipation, Boltanski's approach has been challenged for focusing almost exclusively on discourses and ignoring social practices in their contexts, and for dehistoricizing and depoliticizing social research.

What is most interesting in this debate is the question of the location of critique and of the social role of social scientists. It is in some ways the epitome of Plato's cave allegory discussed by Michael Walzer[24] with regard to intellectuals, who can either "find their peers only outside the cave, in the blaze of Truth," or "find peers or even comrades inside, in the shadow of contingent and uncertain truths." One can easily rank Bourdieu among the former and Boltanski among the latter. The point is whether social scientists can legitimately have a critical perspective on the world that may escape agents (with the possibility of ignoring the latter's sense of critique) or whether their task primarily consists in recording and analyzing the agents' critical approach to the world (with the risk of renouncing their own role as critics). In fact, one can argue that by being on the threshold of the cave, it is possible to acknowledge the social intelligence of agents as well as recognize the need for an intellectual autonomy of social scientists, and therefore to reconcile the two positions.[25] One does not have to choose between critical sociology and the sociology of critique. Yet, there was a time when, in France, sociologists had to make this choice as the two sides clashed. By an apparent and ironic paradox, from the 1990s on, critical sociology, which was attacked for hindering emancipation, turned out to be immensely popular in the public sphere, with Bourdieu becoming the main figure of the intellectual à la Sartre, whereas the sociology of critique, which was attentive to people's claims, gained a dominant position within the academy, with Boltanski becoming the leader of the pragmatic school of thought in higher education and scientific research institutions.

Thus, both in the United States and in France, a major trend of the past decades has been the relative marginalization of the most radical forms of critical thinking within sociology. In the first case, positivist approaches have prevailed; in the second one, pragmatic theories have succeeded. In fact, even critical sociology receded, becoming more moderate in its tone and more cautious in its analysis. This is not to say that our understanding of contemporary societies has lost out in this evolution. On the contrary, research has allowed us to get a finer and sometimes more extensive knowledge of numerous phenomena via methods-driven studies as well as a better comprehension of social action by paying more attention to the agents' justifications. Similarly, there has been some merit to critics' prudence as it acknowledges the failures of grand theories and past revolutions, and opens avenues to the recognition of people's worldviews even in their less pleasant aspects. But undoubtedly there has been a significant change in what is simply conceivable to think, discuss, or investigate within the discipline.

What has just been described about sociology would certainly find, if not similar, at least roughly comparable tendencies in other social sciences. Economics is certainly a case in point, as the overwhelming domination of rational-choice theory and its methods, with admittedly refinements and variations, goes hand in hand with the extreme marginalization of alternative models, in particular when they propose to rethink the very foundations of the present economic system and of our understanding of economic practices: of all disciplines, it is undoubtedly the one whose single paradigm is not only the least contested but also the most pervasive within the rest of the social sciences.[26] History has definitely turned the page of its critical moment, whether it was inspired by materialist or poststructuralist theories: objective facts, quantifiable data, scholarly apparatus, and implicit moral stances tend to be valued more than subjectivation processes, qualitative information, literary material, and critical theory.[27] Anthropology may have a somewhat different evolution, at least if one considers its cultural variety in the United States and its more or less social equivalent in France, as it is probably the social science that has resisted positivism with the most passion, remained the closest to the humanities, and demonstrated the most constant zeal for diversification of its paradigms; such general comments, however, should not minimize the attraction exercised by biological and evolutionary models or the decline in the centrality of cultural and social critique within the discipline.[28] In sum, a pattern emerges from this limited review of some of the social sciences: that of a blunting of their critical edge, due to external logics, such as professional and institutional expectations, as well as to internal rationales, in particular the dominant representations of what science is.

* * *

How is critique? Fifty years after the 1968 protests,[29] which marked in a way the encounter of critique within academia and critique within society at large (symbolized by the presence of students and workers together in the street) as well as a rejection of a certain order of things and state of the world (racial discrimination in the United States and cultural breakdown in France), the question seems opportune. At the end of this outline of the transformation of the political, social, and scientific environment in which critique is produced, the answer is decidedly "Not so well" (it was precisely a strong incentive for the present volume). In past decades, critique seems to have lost much of its leverage in the public sphere and legitimacy in the academic realm. And where it is expressed, it often appears to be normalized or marginalized. The meaning of this clinical diagnosis must be specified. Since what I have studied here is the environment of the production of critique—what I have called contexts, fields, and disciplines—it is a diagnosis on the external, so to speak, conditions of possibility of critique, in other words, on how the social, cultural, economic, political, institutional, and professional environment influences or transforms the emergence or development of critical thinking. It is not—or only marginally—a diagnosis on the internal, to keep the same spatial metaphor, life or liveliness of critique as such. Consequently, it is very different from the various pronouncements on the death of critique,[30] whose reception and influence powerfully confirm my thesis on the increasingly difficult conditions of production of critique, even within academia.

Should this realistic diagnosis render us pessimistic? I do not think so for the following two reasons. First, the analysis proposed here is certainly shared by many critical thinkers today. That the space available for their work has been reduced and restrained is not only something they know and experience but also something that has made them react in various ways, by developing alliances, creating networks, organizing conferences, editing volumes, launching journals, and rethinking their mode of intervention. Constraints and pressures, it is a well-known fact observed for instance in former communist countries, can stimulate rather than silence critique, and there are signs that this is what is occurring today. Second, the less favorable environment of critical thinking within academia has led critics to identify and acknowledge emergent forms of critique outside its traditional avenues in the intellectual realm. From the Me Too campaign to the Standing Rock protest in the United States, from the Notre-Dame-des-Landes "Zone to Defend" to the 470 organizations gathered in the "Estates-General of Migration" in France, sites of critical intervention have multiplied, offering new possibilities of critique, more directly connected with concrete issues and practical responses. The question to be posed and the lessons to be drawn, in line with the analysis presented here, regard the conditions of possibility of such mobilizations. For instance, in the case of the Black Lives Matter movement,[31] it is important to understand better what made the issue of the violent and discriminatory practices of the police invisible, and what rendered public criticisms against it suddenly possible, and in the case of the Yellow Vests uprising,[32] it is essential to examine how a protest against an increase in the price of gasoline has been extended into a mobilization for more equality and more democracy, and how it has maintained for months a high level of sympathy in the population despite the government's attempts to discredit it.

Times are definitely difficult for critique, and they are much more so in certain places in the world and certain moments in history: think of what it means to be a critical thinker or participate in a critically oriented movement in Saudi Arabia, Egypt, Syria, Iran, Turkey, Israel, Russia, Azerbaijan, China, Nicaragua, or Venezuela, to name a few. But the convergence of the two factors—the exacerbated resistance of critics under harsh conditions and the recognition of emergent forms of criticisms within society at large—provides promising circumstances to which we should be attentive in the near future.

Notes

1. Conspicuously, this text is not included in the three thousand pages of the *Dits et écrits*. The English version is reconstituted through a recorded version. Michel Foucault, "What Is Critique?," in *The Politics of Truth*, ed. Sylvère Lotringer, 41–81 (Los Angeles: Semiotext[e], 1997), 43, 45, 67.

2. For Dewey, thought cannot be understood outside of its cultural context, a notion that can be extended to that of historical context. John Dewey, "Context and Thought," in *The Essential Dewey*, vol. 1, *Pragmatism, Education, Democracy*, ed. Larry Hickman and Thomas Alexander, 206–16 (Bloomington: Indiana University Press, 1998), 206–7.

3. For Bourdieu, intellectual activity cannot be comprehended outside the social field in which the agents interact with other agents along a system of lines of force that serve not only to give them access to positions but also to define the stakes of the field. Pierre Bourdieu, "La production de l'idéologie dominante," *Actes de la recherche en sciences sociales* 2, nos. 2–3 (1976): 3–73, 89–90.

4. In this text, Sartre shows how Fanon's book obliges us to "confront an unexpected sight: the striptease of our humanism—not a pretty sight in its nakedness." Jean-Paul Sartre, "Preface," in *The Wretched of the Earth*, by Franz Fanon, trans. Richard Philcox, xliii–lxii (New York: Grove, 2004), lv–lvii.

5. *The Essential Mario Savio* gathers the most important oral and written contributions of the activist who was the major figure of the Free Speech movement. Mario Savio, *The Essential Mario Savio: Speeches and Writings That Changed America*, ed. Robert Cohen (Berkeley: University of California Press, 2014), 188.

6. According to Traverso, the fall of the Berlin Wall and East European regimes "seemed to have exhausted the historical trajectory of socialism itself" as "the entire history of communism was reduced to its totalitarian dimension" and "the so-called velvet revolutions frustrated any previous dream and paralyzed cultural production." Enzo Traverso, *Left-Wing Melancholia: Marxism, History, and Memory* (New York: Columbia University Press, 2016), 1–3.

7. This distribution is presented by Toute l'Europe, www.touteurope.eu/actualite/les-regimes-politiques-europeens.html.

8. In a later article in *Le Monde*, dated August 20, 2008, the literary critic Jean Birnbaum writes that with Furet, the radical left "believed it had found its Francis Fukuyama: an ideologue at the service of the powerful who announced the end of revolutionary hope." Indeed, the last sentences of the book are "The idea of another society has

become almost impossible to conceive of. . . . Here we are, condemned to live in the world as it is." François Furet, *The Passing of an Illusion: The Idea of Communism in the Twentieth Century* (Chicago: University of Chicago Press, 1999), 502.

9.   An online paper by Robert Zaretsky in *Foreign Policy*, dated August 14, 2017, less than three months after the election, was titled "Macron's Revolution Is Over Before It Started."

10. A combination that Bernard Harcourt traces back to the eighteenth century to account for the way in which the United States simultaneously developed deregulation of markets and mass incarceration at the end of the twentieth century. Bernard Harcourt, *The Illusion of Free Markets: Punishment and the Myth of Natural Order* (Cambridge, MA: Harvard University Press, 2011).

11. Affirming that "broadly accessible and affordable higher education is one of the great casualties of neoliberalism's ascendance," Brown adds that "this casualty in turn threatens democracy itself" as it reduces "the desire for democracy." Wendy Brown, *Undoing the Demos: Neoliberalism's Stealth Revolution* (New York: Zone, 2015), 175, 200.

12. In his work, Steinmetz relates the success of positivism in the social sciences in the aftermath of the Second World War with the logics of Fordism. George Steinmetz, "Positivism and Its Others in the Social Sciences," in *The Politics of Method in the Human Sciences*, 1–56 (Durham: Duke University Press, 2005).

13. According to Mirowski, there have been "three regimes of twentieth-century American science organization" connected to specific historic contexts, i.e., "captains of erudition regime," "Cold war regime," and "Globalized privatization regime." Philip Mirowski, *Science-Mart: Privatizing American Science* (Cambridge, MA: Harvard University Press, 2011), 92–95.

14. For Boltanski and Chiapello, the lack of critique is paradoxically what threatens contemporary capitalism of a crisis. The objective of the authors is therefore to propose a critique that does not aim at destroying but at containing it. Luc Boltanski and Ève Chiapello, *The New Spirit of Capitalism* (London, Verso, 2005).

15. Cited in *L'Obs*, July 11, 2004: www.nouvelobs.com/culture/20040710.OBS2633/le-lay -nous-vendons-du-temps-de-cerveau.html.

16. Dating from 1967, Debord's influential essay *Society of the Spectacle* provides a prescient analysis of what he describes as the dissolution of critical sense as a result of the process of spectacularization. Guy Debord, *Society of the Spectacle*, trans. Ken Knabb (London: Black and Red, 2000).

17. Indeed, "to have values or not to have values: the question is always with us," writes Becker. But he adds that the alternative between being engaged and being neutral is a false one since it is impossible "to do research that is uncontaminated by personal and political sympathies." Whichever perspective we privilege is a side we take. Howard Becker, "Whose Side Are We On?," *Social Problems* 14, no. 3 (1967): 239–47, 239, 241 and 242.

18. For Mills, "it is now the social scientist's foremost political and intellectual task to make clear the elements of contemporary uneasiness and indifference." C. Wright Mills, *The Sociological Imagination* (New York: Oxford University Press, 1959), 13.

19. The study conducted by Agger covers the period from 1938 to 1988 but he extends his observation to the late 1990s. The turn to positivism is marked by the increase of the proportion of tables and figures compared to text, the standardization of the presentation of articles, the inclusion of literature reviews, and the length of the list of references. Ben Agger, *Public Sociology: From Social Facts to Literary Acts* (Lanham, MD: Rowman and Littlefield, 2007), 203, 210, and 229.

20. The presidential address delivered by Burawoy at the annual meeting of the American Sociological Association in 2004 is one of the most discussed texts of the discipline. Michael Burawoy, "For Public Sociology," in *Public Sociology*, ed. Dan Clawson, Robert Zussman, Joyra Misra, et al., 23–64 (Berkeley: University of California Press, 2007), 34.

21. Titled "Elegy," the first chapter gives the tone of this lament for a lost time when something was possible that soon after would be no more. Luc Boltanski, Rendre la réalité inacceptable: À propos de "La production de l'idéologie dominante" (Paris: Demopolis, 2008), 11–13 and 79–95.

22. The article has the form of an "Encyclopedia of preconceived ideas and commonplaces" of the "ideological labs" of the "dominant social philosophy." Pierre Bourdieu and Luc Boltanski, "Intellectual Field and Creative Project," *Social Science Information* 8, no. 2 (1969): 89–119, 9–10.

23. In his essay "A Tale of Two Sociologies," Thomas Bénatouïl develops this opposition, which involved of course various other sociologists: Jean-Claude Chamboredon, Jean-Claude Passeron, and Abdelmalek Sayad, among others, on the critical sociology side; Bruno Latour, Michel Callon, and Laurent Thévenot, on the pragmatic sociology side. Thomas Bénatouïl, "A Tale of Two Sociologies: The Critical and the Pragmatic Stance in Contemporary French Sociology," *European Journal of Social Theory* 2, no. 3 (1999): 379–96.

24. Not surprisingly, Walzer favors the second option, adding that critics "can't just criticize, they must also offer advice, write programs, take stands, make political claims" and "must look for a way of talking in tune with but also against their accompaniment." Michael Walzer, *The Company of Critics: Social Criticism and Political Commitment in the Twentieth Century* (New York: Basic Books, 2002), xix–xx and 25–26.

25. The argument of the "threshold of the cave" has been presented in several essays, notably in my defense and illustration of critique. Didier Fassin, "The Endurance of Critique," *Anthropological Theory* 17, no. 1 (2017): 4–29, 21–25.

26. Lukasz Hardt has reviewed the criticisms formulated against economics after the economic crisis of 2008 and targeting in particular its "unrealistic models," its "excessive mathematization," and its "overconfidence in its theoretical claims." Lucasz Hardt, "The Recent Critique of Theoretical Economics: A Methodologically Informed Investigation," *Journal of Economic Issues* 50, no. 1 (2016): 269–87, 269.

27. Joan Scott writes that "among historians, the search for security takes various forms: a renewed emphasis on empiricism and quantitative analysis, the rehabilitation of the autonomous willing subject as agent of history, the essentializing of political categories of identities by the evidence of 'experience,' the turn to evolutionary psychology for explanations of human behavior, the endorsement of the timelessness of universal values, and the trivialization and denunciation of the 'linguistic turn.'" Joan Scott, "History-Writing as Critique," in *Manifestos for History*, ed. Keith Jenkins, Sue Morgan, and Alun Munslow, 19–38 (New York: Routledge, 2007), 20.

28. Webb Keane suggests that the most profound tension in anthropology has been between "the epistemologies of estrangement and of intimacy," in other words, between the recognition of universals through comparison and the affirmation of particulars through ethnography, the trend having been in recent years toward the latter. Webb Keane, "Estrangement, Intimacy, and the Objects of Anthropology," in *The Politics of Method in the Human Sciences*, ed. George Steinmetz, 59–88 (Durham: Duke University Press, 2005), 62.

29. Although the French government decided to limit the celebration of this anniversary for political reasons, social scientists have produced a series of critical analyses of the

events and their aftermath, allowing a reopening of the debate about this period. Julie Pagis, *May '68: Shaping Political Generations* (Amsterdam: Amsterdam University Press, 2018).

30. In particular by Bruno Latour, whose famous article in *Critical Inquiry* has generated a flourishing of anticritique initiatives in the social sciences and humanities. Bruno Latour, "Why Has Critique Run out of Steam? From Matters of Fact to Matters of Concern," *Critical Inquiry* 30, no. 2 (2004): 225–48.

31. Dewey M. Clayton, "Black Lives Matter and the Civil Rights Movement: A Comparative Analysis of Two Social Movements in the United States," *Journal of Black Studies* 49, no. 5 (2018): 448–80.

32. Didier Fassin and Anne-Claire Defossez, "An Improbable Movement? Macron's France and the Rise of the Gilets Jaunes," *New Left Review* 115 (January–February 2019).

Bibliography

Agger, Ben. *Public Sociology: From Social Facts to Literary Acts.* Lanham, MD: Rowman and Littlefield, 2007.

Becker, Howard. "Whose Side Are We On?" *Social Problems* 14, no. 3 (1967): 239–47.

Bénatouïl, Thomas. "A Tale of Two Sociologies: The Critical and the Pragmatic Stance in Contemporary French Sociology." *European Journal of Social Theory* 2, no. 3 (1999): 379–96.

Boltanski, Luc. *Rendre la réalité inacceptable: À propos de "La production de l'idéologie dominante."* Paris: Demopolis, 2008.

Boltanski, Luc, and Ève Chiapello. *The New Spirit of Capitalism.* Translated by Gregory Elliot. London, Verso, 2005. French edition 1999.

Bourdieu, Pierre. "La production de l'idéologie dominante." *Actes de la recherche en sciences sociales* 2, nos. 2–3 (1976): 3–73.

Bourdieu, Pierre, and Luc Boltanski. "Intellectual Field and Creative Project." *Social Science Information* 8, no. 2 (1969): 89–119. French edition 1966.

Brown, Wendy. *Undoing the Demos: Neoliberalism's Stealth Revolution.* New York: Zone, 2015.

Burawoy, Michael. "For Public Sociology." In *Public Sociology*, edited by Dan Clawson, Robert Zussman, Joyra Misra, et al., 23–64. Berkeley: University of California Press, 2007.

Clayton, Dewey M. "Black Lives Matter and the Civil Rights Movement: A Comparative Analysis of Two Social Movements in the United States." *Journal of Black Studies* 49, no. 5 (2018): 448–80.

Debord, Guy. *Society of the Spectacle.* Translated by Ken Knabb. London: Black and Red, 2000. French edition 1967.

Dewey, John. "Context and Thought." In *The Essential Dewey*, vol. 1, *Pragmatism, Education, Democracy*, edited by Larry Hickman and Thomas Alexander, 206–16. Bloomington: Indiana University Press, 1998.

Fassin, Didier. "The Endurance of Critique." *Anthropological Theory* 17, no. 1 (2017): 4–29.

——. "Sure Looks a Lot Like Conservatism." *London Review of Books* 40, no. 13 (2018): 15–17, www.lrb.co.uk/v40/n13/didier-fassin/sure-looks-a-lot-like-conservatism.

Fassin, Didier, and Anne-Claire Defossez. "An Improbable Movement? Macron's France and the Rise of the Gilets Jaunes." *New Left Review* 115 (January–February 2019).

Foucault, Michel. "What Is Critique?" In *The Politics of Truth*, edited by Sylvère Lotringer, 41–81. Los Angeles: Semiotext(e), 1997.

Furet, François. *The Passing of an Illusion: The Idea of Communism in the Twentieth Century*. Chicago: University of Chicago Press, 1999. French edition 1995.

Harcourt, Bernard. *The Illusion of Free Markets: Punishment and the Myth of Natural Order*. Cambridge, MA: Harvard University Press, 2011.

Hardt, Lucasz. "The Recent Critique of Theoretical Economics: A Methodologically Informed Investigation." *Journal of Economic Issues* 50, no. 1 (2016): 269–87.

Keane, Webb. "Estrangement, Intimacy, and the Objects of Anthropology." In *The Politics of Method in the Human Sciences*, edited by George Steinmetz, 59–88. Durham: Duke University Press, 2005.

Latour, Bruno. "Why Has Critique Run out of Steam? From Matters of Fact to Matters of Concern." *Critical Inquiry* 30, no. 2 (2004): 225–48.

Mills, C. Wright. *The Sociological Imagination*. New York: Oxford University Press, 1959.

Mirowski, Philip. *Science-Mart: Privatizing American Science*. Cambridge, MA: Harvard University Press, 2011.

Pagis, Julie. *May '68: Shaping Political Generations*. Amsterdam: Amsterdam University Press, 2018. French edition 2014.

Sartre, Jean-Paul. "Preface." In *The Wretched of the Earth*, by Franz Fanon, translated by Richard Philcox, xliii–lxii, New York: Grove, 2004. French publication 1961.

Savio, Mario. *The Essential Mario Savio: Speeches and Writings that Changed America*. Edited by Robert Cohen. Berkeley: University of California Press, 2014.

Scott, Joan. "History-Writing as Critique." In *Manifestos for History*, edited by Keith Jenkins, Sue Morgan, and Alun Munslow, 19–38. New York: Routledge, 2007.

Steinmetz, George. "Positivism and Its Others in the Social Sciences." In *The Politics of Method in the Human Sciences*, 1–56. Durham: Duke University Press, 2005.

Traverso, Enzo. *Left-Wing Melancholia: Marxism, History, and Memory*. New York: Columbia University Press, 2016.

Walzer, Michael. *The Company of Critics: Social Criticism and Political Commitment in the Twentieth Century*. New York: Basic Books, 2002 [1988].

CHAPTER 2

CRITIQUE AS A POLITICAL PRACTICE OF FREEDOM

LINDA M. G. ZERILLI

W hat does it mean to think about critique as a *political* practice? The answer to this question may seem at first obvious: insofar as critique aims at exposing forms of unjust power, critique is political. Is critique political, however, if it arises not in public spaces and in relation to different and often conflicting points of view but in private or institutional spaces where opinions tend to converge? Thinking about such questions, I aim not at an analytic definition of critique, as if critique meant one thing or happened in one kind of space. Rather, my goal is to retrieve the origins of critique in the public space as a practice of freedom, that is, of speaking and acting with citizens and strangers about matters of common concern.

A political genealogy of critique is all the more important today, when the practice of critique in advanced capitalist liberal democracies such as the United States seems to be mostly restricted to the activity of "professional thinkers" and the space of the academy, which is at once charged with preserving the tradition of critical thought and maligned for harboring an arrogant intellectual elite. But the academy, as both Michel Foucault and Hannah Arendt in their different ways will show us, is not the original home of critique; it is the place to which critique retreats when it loses its footing in the political realm. Critique was born not inside the relatively sheltered intellectual spaces of the academy but in this public space, where it took the form of opposition to the tenacious idea of politics as rule, according to which the few have natural governing authority over the many. Grasping this inaugural task of critique can help make sense of our contemporary predicament, in which even the more limited conception of critique as academic freedom is under siege. Rather than settling for what is ultimately an illusory safe harbor in the academy at the price of indifference to the political realm, Arendt and Foucault invite us to reorient our thinking around forms of critique that contest the politics of rule and engage the always contingent and uncertain realm of human affairs.

Critique as the Art of Not Being Governed Thusly

In his writings on Kant and enlightenment, Foucault describes critique as "the art of not being governed" in a particular way and by particular people.[1] Critique is neither the anarchic refusal of all modes of governance nor the acceptance of whatever mode of governance may contingently arise. Foucault connects the emergence of critique to the historical development of what he calls "governmentalization" and its particular modern form of rationality. Alongside the developing "art of governing men and the methods of doing it," he argues, arose a question: "how not to be governed?"[2] Critique is a quotidian skill cultivated in continuous interplay with hegemonic arts of governing, which originated in doctrines of the reason of the state in sixteenth-century Europe through the advent of liberalism in the eighteenth century up to the neoliberalism of the present day.

I seek to retrieve what is specifically political or—more precisely—politically public in Foucault's idea of critique as a practice of not being governed (in a certain way). To do this, I shall distinguish the *political* idea of critique from two related ideas, both of which have been widely discussed in the secondary literature: the *philosophical* idea of critique as an "ontology of ourselves" or "ontology of the present," on the one hand, and the *ethical* idea of critique as "self-transformation," on the other hand. I contrast my reading with the well-known interpretations of John Rajchman and Judith Butler, each of whom offers, respectively, insightful accounts of the philosophical and ethical conceptions. My aim is to tease out the strand of Foucault's thinking that concerns a politically public practice of critique, which may or may not be articulated with these other conceptions. Because Foucault himself often folds the political conception of critique into either philosophical or ethical conceptions, my interpretation tries to reconstruct the political conditions under which critique as an art of not being "governed thusly, like that, in this way" could gain traction.[3]

In his lecture "What Is Critique?," delivered in 1978 to the French Society of Philosophy, Foucault sets out the basic parameters of his rereading of the Kantian inheritance, specifically the relationship between the demand of *Aufklärung* (*Sapere Aude!*) and the idea of critique (the limits to knowledge). According to John Rajchman, the lecture "is notable in at least two ways":

First, in addressing this Society (rather than, for example, later debating with the social historians), Foucault was taken with the rather dramatic notion that French philosophers ... might assume "responsibility" for a new lumière "breaking through the academic window," which would allow them to play a distinctive role in a larger European and international debate; secondly, at the same time, in putting the accent on the political stakes in this larger debate, Foucault introduces the notion of governmentality through which Kant's own idea of "man's release from his self-incurred tutelage" would be linked to the refusal "to be governed like that"—precisely the passages in which Foucault talks of a "politics of truth."[4]

In Rajchman's telling, "What Is Critique?," like all of Foucault's "lectures on enlightenment,. . . [is] tied up with the problem of the 'public use of reason' or the 'intellectual' vocation or role of philosophy."[5] But this reading—though valid in important respects—risks unduly prejudicing our understanding of Foucault's return to Kant as an attempt "to rethink the very idea of critique in philosophy," to cite Rajchman, with politics as that which is partly at stake in this rethinking but not the site of the rethinking itself.[6] Although this interpretation might at first seem perfectly plausible—Kant after all was himself a philosopher who rethought critique—it can lead to an attenuated understanding of what it might have meant for Kant to use one's reason publicly (Arendt, as we shall see, has a quite different reading) and, more important, what it might mean for us. Consequently, the second "notable" aspect of Foucault's lecture, "the refusal 'to be governed like that' and the entire question of counter arts of governing," could appear as if it were synonymous with a (philosophical) practice of intellectual elites.

The point here is not to deny that Foucault was interested in "the problem of post-war French philosophy," as Rajchman notes.[7] After all, he was addressing a philosophical society and beyond that specific context may well have been engaged in a broader attempt "to invent a new style of critique, a new kind of critical philosophy," that could hold its own against "Post-Kantian German critical thought."[8] Dominated by the towering figure of Jürgen Habermas, the German reception of Kant had come increasingly to understand its mission as one of rescuing enlightenment and the Kantian inheritance from the so-called nihilism of Foucault and other French so-called poststructuralist thinkers. Nevertheless, we also know that Foucault was skeptical of elites and of anyone who claimed to have keys to the kingdom of critique and social transformation. We need instead to consider how an "agonistic collectivity in critical thought," to invoke Rajchman's evocative phrasing of Foucault's project, arises in and through a specific and at times fraught relation to the political realm.[9]

The political basis of intellectual critique is confirmed in Foucault's account of governmentalization and responses to emerging modes of governance. Alongside the developing sixteenth-century "art of governing men and the methods of doing it" he observes in "What Is Critique?" arose the question "how not to be governed?"[10] Historically speaking, the critique of unjust power and the wish "not to be governed *like that*" took at least three forms: (1) questions regarding "what sort of truth the Scriptures told" and the authority of the Church to interpret them;[11] (2) claims to "universal and indefeasible rights to which every government . . . will have to submit";[12] and (3) demands for valid reasons for any truth-claims advanced by secular and ecclesiastical authorities.[13]

Critique as an "art of not being governed" is not a refusal of all governance but a differentiated relation to various forms of power. Foucault explains: "I do not mean that governmentalization would be opposed, in a kind of face-off by the opposite affirmation 'we do not want to be governed and we do not want to be governed at all.' I mean that, in this great preoccupation about the way to govern, . . . we identify a perpetual question which would be: 'how not to be governed *like that*, by that, in the name of those principles, with such and such an objective in mind, and by means of such procedures, not like that, not for that, not by them.'"[14]

Critique does not aim to reinstate an illusory prepolitical freedom, then, but points to the need to refigure political relations in ways that foster collective resistance to unjust power. "Not to want to be governed like that also means not wanting to accept these laws because they are unjust because . . . they hide a fundamental illegitimacy," Foucault writes.[15] Critique faces off arts of governing as an "act of defiance, as a challenge, as a way of limiting these arts of governing and sizing them up, transforming them, of finding a way to escape from them or, in any case, a way to displace them."[16] Critique as "the art of voluntary insubordination," he summarizes, "would essentially insure the desubjugation of the subject in the context of . . . the politics of truth."[17] The question is how insubordination can be practiced and defended as a *political* claim, a claim to not be governed in *these* ways, on the one hand, and to *other* possibilities for being governed, or, as I prefer to put it, other modes of being politically in common, on the other hand.

Critique as an Ethical Practice of Desubjugation and Self-Transformation

Distinguishing between "the will not to be governed at all" and "the will not to be governed thusly, like that, by these people, at this price," Foucault rejects the idea of freedom as "an originary aspiration."[18] Nevertheless, in answer to questions, Foucault also hesitates to rule out an originary freedom. "I was not referring to something that would be a fundamental anarchism, that would be like an originary freedom, absolutely and wholeheartedly resistant to any governmentalization. I did not say it, but this does not mean that I absolutely exclude it," he remarks.[19]

One could proceed here to argue along now familiar lines that Foucault needs recourse to origins to rescue the idea of human freedom from his "totalizing" conception of power. Although the genealogist and certainly the archaeologist Foucault appears at times to have such recourse, I would agree with Rudi Visker that, for Foucault, "there is no power without the possibility of resistance, and this resistance is guaranteed by the freedom present in every power relation. Power can only be exerted over free subjects and can only be exerted insofar as they are free. If this freedom disappears, then we must speak, rather, of violence: a slave in chains is not being subjected to power but to physical compulsion."[20] That said, granting freedom as the very condition of power does not answer to the problem of the legitimacy of any *particular* form of resistance. The question is whether this problem can only be solved, as Habermas and like-minded critics hold, through recourse to the normative "foundations" posited by (moral) philosophy.

In her commentary on Foucault's lecture, Judith Butler creatively struggles with just these issues of normativity and the recourse to origins. "Foucault finds a way to say 'originary freedom,' and I suppose that it gives him great pleasure to utter these words, pleasure and fear. He speaks them, but only through staging the words, relieving himself of an ontological commitment, but releasing the words themselves for a certain use. Does he refer to originary freedom here? Does he seek recourse to it? Has he found the well of originary freedom and drunk from it?"[21]

Rather than attempt to ground his claim to originary freedom, as proponents of universal rights historically have done (ontologically) and as many neo-Kantians continue to demand we do (epistemologically), Foucault takes what Butler calls the "oddly brave" risk of a speech act whose validity can have no epistemological or ontological guarantee.[22] Absent any "foundational anchor," freedom is affirmed "by the artful performance of its release from its usual discursive constraints, from the conceit that one might only utter it knowing in advance what its anchor must be," she observes. Foucault calls into question "the regime of truth" in which he, qua subject, has been formed and performs critique as "desubjugation" by way of his utterance.[23] His claim to an originary freedom is an attempt to posit a value that he, qua subject, "knows" he cannot philosophically ground. Like Nietzsche's performative account of the origin of morals, Foucault's "speech act inaugurates the value, and becomes something like an atopical and atemporal occasion for the origination of values," asserts Butler.[24]

To make sense of Butler's capacious freedom-centered interpretation of Foucault's speech act, we need to grasp the idea of critique that she advances in his name. In her account, the philosophical conception of critique (i.e., the "ontology of ourselves" or "of the present") meets an ethical conception of critique (i.e., "desubjugation" qua "self-transformation"). Foucault is not concerned with the normative question that dominates the Frankfurt School idea of critique: "the primary task of critique will not be to evaluate whether its objects—social conditions, practices, forms of knowledge, power, and discourse—are good or bad, valued highly or demeaned, but to bring into relief the very framework of evaluation itself," she observes.[25] For Foucault, "the relation [to this framework and its norms] will be 'critical' in the sense that it will not comply with a given category, but rather constitute an interrogatory relation to the field of categorization itself, referring at least implicitly to the limits of the epistemological horizon within which practices are formed." Critique, then, is "the very practice that exposes the limits of that epistemological horizon itself," explains Butler. "Moreover, the critical practice in question turns out to entail self-transformation in relation to a rule of conduct [and] self-transformation lead[s] to the exposure of this limit."[26]

It is through acts of "self-stylization" and "self-transformation," then, that Butler's Foucault practices critique; he forms himself as an ethical subject whose actions cannot be subsumed under inherited rules of conduct. This process is imbricated with but also different from the philosophical conception of critique or "ontology of ourselves," by which the subject identifies the limits to being and knowing as they are set out by certain regimes of truth. The limits themselves are revealed according to Butler in the very act of their transgression by which the subject gives shape to itself as ethical.[27] "To gain a critical distance from established authority means for Foucault not only to recognize the ways in which the coercive effects of knowledge are at work in subject-formation itself, but to risk one's very formation as a subject" by means of the suspension of "judgment," she writes.[28] Released from the demands of judgment, which "subsum[es] a particular under an already constituted category," Foucault forms himself as an *ethical subject* against but also within a regime of truth. This "politics of desubjugation" is the more "fundamental meaning" of Foucauldian critique according to Butler.[29]

Butler's interpretation provides a response to the (Habermasian) charge that Foucault lacks normative grounding for critique. But what might we risk overlooking when we fold the idea of critique into an ethical act of self-transformation in relation to given categories of identity (e.g., "What counts as a person? What counts as a coherent gender? What qualifies as a citizen?"). We need to probe more closely into the worldly conditions of an act of desubjugation (here figured as the claim to an originary freedom). What does such an act take for granted?

The Political Conditions of Desubjugation and Self-Transformation

The question (from Jean-Louis Bruch) that prompts Foucault at once to deny and retain the possibility of an originary freedom also elicits a more explicitly political conception of critique as a way of making collective claims in a public space. Bruch's question focuses on the difference between two interlocutions in Foucault's lecture: "the decision-making will not to be governed" and "not being governed *like that*."[30] When asked by Bruch whether "the decision-making will not to be governed" needs to be "the object of an investigation, a questioning that would be, in essence, philosophical," Foucault replies

> This dimension of critique . . . seems to me to be so important because it is both part of, and not a part of, philosophy. If we were to explore this dimension of critique, would we not then find that it is supported by something akin to the historical practice of revolt, the non-acceptance of a real government, on the one hand, or, on the other, the individual experience of the refusal of governmentality?
>
> Should we not now investigate what the will not to be governed thusly, like that, etc., might be both as an individual and a collective experience? It is now necessary to pose the problem of the will. . . . However, since this problem of the will is a problem that Western philosophy has always treated with infinite precaution and difficulties, let us say that I have tried to avoid it as much as possible. Let us say that it was unavoidable.[31]

Describing critique as both "an individual and collective experience," I would argue, only makes sense as a "*politics* of desubjugation," as Butler put Foucauldian critique, if we insist on the conjunctive "and."[32] Indeed, we would miss what is distinctive about this political conception of critique as collective action if we were to fold it into desubjugation as an individual act of will. What facilitates such an act and makes it more than a subjectively isolated expression of resistance? Does not Foucault's individual claim to an originary freedom need to be connected to a political idea of critique as collective action to have any worldly traction?

The fraught place of an originary freedom in Foucault's text points to the aporia of the will when it comes to freedom. In Arendt's view, the problem with claiming an originary freedom is the problem of thinking about freedom as an inner state, a conception of freedom that has exerted tremendous influence upon the Western tradition of philosophical thought. In this tradition, she observes, "free will and freedom became synonymous notions, and the presence of freedom was experienced in complete solitude."[33] Other people immediately turn this idea of freedom as free will into a problem and a mirage. The part of critique that "is both part of, and not part of philosophy," as Foucault put it, is what Arendt calls the transformation of the "I-Will" into the "I-Can."[34] Whereas "philosophical freedom," focused on the self's relation to itself, requires no more than an I-will, "independent of circumstances and of attainment of the goals the will has set," writes Arendt, "political freedom . . . consists in being able to do what one ought to will."[35] For the few Enlightenment thinkers such as Montesquieu who retain the political conception of freedom, she notes, "it was obvious that an agent could no longer be called free when he lacked the capacity to do—whereby it is irrelevant whether this failure is caused by exterior or by interior circumstances."[36] To be felicitous, then, a claim to freedom must involve more than a subject engaged in a willful act of desubjugation, for the I-will inevitably relies on an I-can and so on others in political community.

An adequate response to Arendt would have to take up the late Foucault's complex relation to Greco-Roman Stoicism, in which the modern problem of the will is radically rethought in relation to his understanding of freedom as a practice of self-care. In this essay, I shall only note that in the writings on critique, Foucault presupposes but does not really explore its mutually imbricated individual and collective nature. Consequently, critique can at times sound, as Butler's reading shows, as if it turned solely on the subject's individual ability to elude the presumably limiting power of concepts and categories of identity—and yet it is also Foucault who gave us a political and public account of critique in the sense of the historical practice of revolt animated by the desire not to be governed thusly.

The politically public conception of critique that I am trying to tease out of Foucault becomes more visible in his posthumously published essay "Kant on Enlightenment and Revolution" (1986). Here, Foucault argues that *Aufklärung* calls forth two distinct forms of critical thinking: an "analytic of truth" that focuses on the limits of cognition and the rules for proper reasoning as exemplified in Kant's first *Critique*, on the one side; and "another kind of questioning, another mode of critical interrogation," that concerns "the contemporary field of possible experience" as exemplified in Kant's response to the French Revolution, on the other side.[37] Foucault describes his reading of Kant as reflecting the "philosophical choice" to pursue critique as an "ontology of the present, an ontology of ourselves" rather than an analytic of truth, and this ontology takes as its object Kant's account of political revolution.[38] It does so, moreover, by seeking the genealogy of critique in the phenomenon of revolutionary enthusiasm and its transmission in what Arendt, reading Kant on the same world-historical event, describes as a practice of public reason and reflective judgment.

In Foucault's telling, Kant's response to the Revolution is not to decide about "what part should be retained and set up as a model" for future political revolt.[39] That would accord with the subsumptive model of judgment that Kant called determinative and that Butler rightly rejects as having any role to play in Foucauldian critique. Kant's response is an attempt to make sense of the will to revolution and the enthusiasm that gripped spectators like Kant himself, though they might not—as Kant did not—condone insurrection as a principled act. The question to which the Revolution was (for Kant) an answer was whether one could speak of the "progress of the human race." The answer, however, came not in the form of the Revolution itself as "a noisy, spectacular occurrence," writes Foucault.[40] Rather, "what is significant is the way the Revolution operates as spectacle, the way it is generally received by the spectators who do not take part in it but watch it, witness it, and for better or worse, allow themselves to be swept along by it."[41] It is their "enthusiasm for the Revolution," observes Foucault, "that is [for Kant] the sign of a moral disposition of humanity; this disposition manifests itself in two permanent ways: the right of every people to provide itself with the political constitution which appears good to the people itself; and the lawful and moral principle of a constitution framed in such a way as to avoid . . . war."[42]

Put otherwise, critique is figured not as the event, the actual historical revolt against arbitrary power that was at issue in Foucault's response to Bruch, but as the *relation* to the event that harbors a judgment: the right of a people to decide the question of which art of governance is appropriate for them. It is a judgment based on neither the success nor the failure of the Revolution, which characterizes historicist and determinative forms of judgment, but on radical contingency: the Revolution did not have to happen. Yet it did happen and—moreover—it could happen again: "For this event is too important . . . not to be recalled to memory by the peoples at the occasion of each favourable circumstance, so that they would then be aroused to a repetition of new attempts of this kind," comments Foucault.[43] The event becomes a story for Kant, to cite Arendt's reading, "whose importance lies precisely not at its end but in its opening up new horizons for the future."[44]

What breaks apart sedimented ways of being and acting, then, is not the willful act of an individual subject claiming an originary freedom and suspending judgment tout court; it is "the relation that they [the spectators] themselves experience with this Revolution of which they are not themselves active agents," as Foucault put it. To see this relation in its proper political register, however, we need to foreground the public character of spectators in Kant's account. Publicity is at the center of Arendt's reading: "What constituted the appropriate public realm for this particular event were not the actors but the acclaiming spectators," she writes.[45] To see what is public here, she observes, we need to distinguish Kant's revolutionary spectator from the tradition's ideal of spectatorship based on "the superiority of the contemplative way of life." That ideal is "as old as the hills; it is, in fact, among the oldest, most decisive notions of philosophy," remarks Arendt.[46]

Historically first realized in Plato's Academy, where the "cave of opinions" could be left behind in search of "the truth of things that are everlasting," it is an ideal for which "meaning (or truth) is revealed only to those who restrain themselves from acting" and, indeed, from any involvement in the contingent and messy realm of human affairs. It is an ideal of contemplative spectatorship that underwrites "a turning away from the polis, an *a-politia*, so to speak, or indifference to politics," she writes, as the condition of all genuinely critical thought.[47]

"Kant's view is different: one withdraws also to the 'theoretical,' the onlooking standpoint of the spectator, but this is the position of the Judge," whose standard of judgment is progress, observes Arendt.[48] Progress, we have seen, is not a rule that can be applied but an example that opens up horizons for the future. Kant's spectator is no philosopher in his study, shutting out the world of human affairs, but a member of the reading and writing public. Spectators exist in the plural. Foucault sees this plurality too, but his interpretation leaves open the question of how plural spectators relate to each other through the event and how their shared enthusiasm indicates a practice of spectatorship that departs from a merely contemplative (philosophical) form. To answer this question we need first to grasp what Kant understood by the *"public use of one's reason."*[49]

The distinction between the private and the public uses of reason is examined by both Arendt and Foucault, though Foucault does not really probe what makes reason public (rather than, say, not private).[50] In "What Is Enlightenment?," for example, he follows Kant's famous essay to open the fundamental problem: "that of knowing how the use of reason can take the public form that it requires."[51] Kant's answer, he argues, proposes a sort of contract between the sovereign and his subjects, which renders the duty to obey consistent with universal reason. "Let us leave Kant's text here," Foucault advises, in order to open the more pressing question of what the Enlightenment can mean *for us*, namely, "the permanent reactivation of an attitude—that is, of a philosophical ethos that could be described as a permanent critique of our historical era."[52] "In what is given to us as universal, necessary, obligatory, what place is occupied by whatever is singular, contingent, and the product of arbitrary constraints?"[53] That is what Foucault calls "philosophy as the problematisation of a present-ness," and characterizes as the lasting legacy of Kant.[54]

Arendt would remind us that the critical stance celebrated by Foucault holds only insofar as critique is practiced beyond the solitary confines of the philosopher's study and in dialogue with the opinions of other citizens. For Kant, she observes, reason is public rather than private not only when we think beyond the confines of our social roles, what Kant called being a mere "cog in a machine." We must also think beyond the confines of the philosophical ideal of spectatorship. "Critical thinking [for Kant] is possible only where the standpoints of all others are open for inspection. Hence, critical thinking, while still a solitary business, does not cut itself off from all others." On the contrary, "the more people participate in it, the better."[55] "By the force of imagination it makes the others present and thus moves in a space that is potentially public, open to all sides."[56] The individual practice of critique is not separate from but irreducibly connected to this potentially public space. Arendt explains:

Freedom of speech and thought, as we understand it, is the right of an individual to express himself and his opinion in order to be able to persuade others to share his viewpoint. This presupposes that I am capable of making up my mind all by myself and that the claim I have on the government is to permit me to propagandize whatever I have already fixed in my mind. Kant's view of this matter is very different. He believes that the very faculty of thinking depends on its public use; without "the test of free and open examination," no thinking and opinion-formation are possible. Reason is not made "to isolate itself but to get into community with others."[57]

The idea of critique that Arendt would have us retrieve, then, is not that of the epistemological Kant who would expose the limits of our knowledge; it is the political Kant who would remind us of the public conditions of critical thinking. Foucault too recognizes that the key legacy of Kant lies in the idea of critique as a genuine "political problem."[58] For Kant, he observes, "the use of reason must be free and public. Enlightenment is thus not merely a process by which individuals would see their own personal freedom of thought guaranteed. There is Enlightenment when the universal, the free, and the public uses of reason are superimposed on one another."[59] The "critical tradition" that Foucault traces back not to the "analytics of truth" and so to the epistemological Kant but to a different—Arendt would say political and aesthetic—Kant, however, cannot take hold in the absence of the public use of reason.

Such use involves what Kant called the "enlargement of the mind," writes Arendt, citing Kant, which is "accomplished by 'comparing our judgment with the possible rather than the actual judgment of others, and by putting ourselves in the place of any other man.'" Arendt famously calls the Kantian practice of public reasoning "representative thinking," imaginatively thinking from standpoints not one's own.[60] It is only then, from standpoints not our own, that we can see the contingency of our own and engage in the ontology of ourselves, only then that we can see that which is given to us as universal, necessary, obligatory as "singular, contingent, the product of arbitrary constraints," and only then that we can take up the Enlightenment with Foucault as "the problematisation of a present-ness."[61]

* * *

For "the problematization of a present-ness" to be more than "an empty dream of freedom," as Foucault observes, "this historico-critical attitude must also be an experimental one":

I mean that this work done at the limits of ourselves must, on the one hand, open up a realm of historical inquiry and, on the other, put itself to the test of reality, of contemporary reality, both to grasp where change is possible and desirable, and to determine the precise form this change should take. This means that the historical ontology of ourselves must turn away from all projects that claim to be global or radical. In fact, we know from experience that the claim to escape from the system of contemporary reality so as to produce the overall programs of another society, of another way of thinking, another culture, another vision of the world, has led only to the return of the most dangerous traditions.[62]

Foucault departs from the utopian Enlightenment tradition, which sought solace in moralized and ultimately unrealistic forms of critique that "skip the political aporia," to borrow Reinhardt Koselleck's phrase.[63] Realistic practices of critique, it seems to me, need to resist the move outside the political realm in the search for what Arendt and Foucault show to be an illusory freedom. According to Arendt, we recall, Plato's founding of the Academy outside the walls of ancient Athens, largely as a response to what he saw as the tenuous status of philosopher-citizens after the trial and execution of Socrates, continues to influence "our idea of academic freedom today."[64] By restricting the exchange of opinions to "a sphere that is populated by the few rather than the many," the Academy effectively introduced "a new concept of freedom into the world," one that is hostile to plurality and as such intended as "a fully valid substitute for the marketplace, the agora, the central space for freedom in the polis."[65] This turning away from politics, however, comes to haunt the freedom of critical thought for which it appears to be the condition.

Freedom from politics or retreat to a space outside politics as the condition of genuine critique remains important for our own understanding, insofar as it both casts suspicion on the opinions of the many as a vital source of critical thought and makes it difficult for us to grasp politics as the original home of both freedom *and* critique. On the contrary, we tend to see politics as the *object* of critique, which can be practiced only from wholly *outside* politics. This way of thinking leads often enough to a moralized and unrealistic conception of critique whose public basis is occluded; or it leads to a philosophical conception of critique that stands opposed to the unpredictable and contingent world of human affairs.[66] It leads us to think that the way to secure the future of critique is to shore up the boundaries of whatever intellectual home we may inhabit. Freedom to criticize is then understood to be that which it is the job of politics to secure: namely, the real freedom of spaces of critical thinking outside of politics such as the university into which many of us have indeed retreated today.[67]

The original separation of politics and critique that Arendt identifies with the Academy and finds characteristic of the modern university, however, does not sustain but endangers critical thought. Endangers, because the indifference, if not hostility, to politics that characterizes our academic spaces and under-standing of critique leads us to lose track of the worldly conditions of such thought, which both Foucault and Arendt have shown to be irreducibly politi-cal. By "political" I do not mean politicized in the way that the heated debates about so-called political correctness assume. For these debates presuppose that ideally the university should be a space of critical inquiry that is free to the extent that it has wholly divorced itself from the political realm.[68] Such a uni-versity would just extend the politics of rule that was the original target of cri-tique, albeit in the protected form of an academic elite, sheltered from the vicissitudes of politics and the opinions of the many. Current debates, then, do not belie but confirm the problem I have described.

"The few, whenever they have tried to isolate themselves from the many—be it in the form of academic indifference or oligarchic rule—have manifestly ended up depending on the many, particularly in all those matters of commu-nal life requiring concrete action," warns Arendt.[69] Written in the 1950s, these prescient words capture what is to my mind the genuine dilemma faced today by those of us worried about the future of critique and the limits of a defense of academic freedom that is blind to critique's original home and continuing condition in the political realm.

Notes

1. Michel Foucault, "What Is Critique?" (1978), in *The Politics of Truth: Michel Foucault*, ed. Sylvére Lotringer, trans. Lysa Hochroch and Catherine Porter (Los Angeles: Semiotext[e], 2007) 41–82, 45.
2. Foucault, 44.
3. Foucault, 75.
4. John Rajchman, "Enlightenment Today: Introduction to *The Politics of Truth*," in Fou-cault, *The Politics of Truth*, 9–28, 19.
5. Rajchman, 21.
6. Rajchman, 21.
7. Rajchman, 19.
8. Rajchman, 21.
9. Rajchman, 13.
10. Foucault, "What Is Critique?," 44.
11. See Foucault, 45–46.
12. Foucault, 46.
13. See Foucault, 46–47.
14. Foucault, 44.
15. Foucault, 46.
16. Foucault, 45.
17. Foucault, 47.
18. Foucault, 75.
19. Foucault, 75.

20. Rudi Visker, *Michel Foucault: Genealogy as Critique*, trans. Chris Turner (New York: Verso, 1995), 103.

21. Judith Butler, "What Is Critique? An Essay on Foucault's Virtue," http://eipcp.net /transversal/0806/butler/en, 1–14, at 11.

22. Butler, 12.

23. Butler, 12.

24. Butler, 10.

25. Butler, 3.

26. Butler, 4.

27. Butler, 13, 6.

28. Butler, 12.

29. Butler, 2.

30. Foucault, "What Is Critique?," 75.

31. Foucault, 75.

32. Foucault, 76.

33. Hannah Arendt, "What Is Freedom?," in *Between Past and Future: Eight Exercises in Political Thought* (New York: Penguin, 1993), 143–71, 158.

34. Arendt, 160.

35. Arendt, 161.

36. Arendt, 161.

37. Michel Foucault, "Kant on Enlightenment and Revolution," trans. Colin Gordon, *Economy and Society* 15, no. 1 (February 1986): 88–96, 96.

38. Foucault, 96.

39. Foucault, 95.

40. Foucault, 93.

41. Foucault, 93.

42. Foucault, 93.

43. Foucault, 94.

44. Hannah Arendt, *Lectures on Kant's Political Philosophy*, ed. Ronald Beiner (Chicago: University of Chicago Press, 1992), 56.

45. Arendt, 61.

46. Arendt, 55.

47. Hannah Arendt, "Introduction *Into* Politics," in *The Promise of Politics*, ed. Jerome Kohn (New York: Schocken, 2005), 93–200, 133.

48. Arendt, 55–56.

49. Arendt, *Lectures on Kant's Political Philosophy*, 39.

50. Arendt and Foucault agree that the private use of reason obtains for Kant when man remains in his strictly social role and is (to cite Kant) a mere "a cog in a machine." See Arendt, *Lectures on Kant's Political Philosophy*, 39; Foucault, "What Is Enlightenment?," in *The Politics of Truth: Michel Foucault*, ed. Sylvére Lotringer, trans. Lysa Hochroch and Catherine Porter (Los Angeles: Semiotext[e], 2007), 97–120, 102.

51. Foucault, "What Is Enlightenment?," 103.

52. Foucault, 103, 111.

53. Foucault, 113.

54. Foucault, "Kant on Enlightenment and Revolution," 89.

55. Arendt, *Lectures on Kant's Political Philosophy*, 39.

56. Arendt, 39.

57. Arendt, 39–40.

58. Foucault, "What Is Enlightenment?," 103.

59. Foucault, 103.

60. Hannah Arendt, "Truth and Politics," in *Between Past and Future: Eight Exercises in Political Thought* (New York: Penguin, 1993), 227–64, 241. I discuss both Arendt and Kant on public reason in *A Democratic Theory of Judgment* (Chicago: University of Chicago Press, 2016), chap. 1.

61. Arendt, "Truth and Politics," 113; "Foucault, "Kant on Enlightenment and Revolution," 89.

62. Foucault, "What Is Enlightenment?," 114.

63. Reinhardt Koselleck, *Critique and Crisis: Enlightenment and the Pathogenesis of Modern Society* (Cambridge, MA: MIT Press, 1998). Koselleck argues that the enlightenment idea of critique as the total rational power to put all into doubt begins from a place outside politics and develops in an increasingly utopian register. According to him, critique arose in the eighteenth century as an art of moral and cultural opposition to monarchy, but also to political society generally. "Politically powerless as a subject of his sovereign lord, the citizen conceived himself as moral, felt that the existing rule was overpowering, and condemned it proportionally as immoral since he could no longer perceive what is evident in the horizon of human finiteness" (11). Unable or unwilling to put forward practical alternatives to existing institutions, Enlightenment "morality skips the political aporia" and comes to be wholly in the grip of an unrealistic and antipolitical conception of critique (11).

64. Arendt, "Introduction *Into* Politics," 133.

65. Arendt, 131.

66. The moralization of critique and its utopian character go hand in hand, but their historical condition has been political exclusion. As Koselleck argues, the Absolutist State banished morality to the private realm in its effort to restore political order in the wake of the destruction wrought by religious wars. But by excluding citizens from the official public realm, it also created the breeding ground for utopianism. "Inevitably, citizens will come into conflict with a State that subordinates morality to politics, adopts a purely formal understanding of the political realm and thus reckons without developments peculiar to the emancipation of its subjects. For their goal will be to perfect themselves morally to an extent that will permit them to know, and let every man know himself, what is good and what is evil. Each one becomes a judge who knows, on grounds of his enlightenment, that he is authorized to try whatever heteronomous definitions contradict his moral autonomy. Once implemented by the State the separation of morality and politics hence turns against the State itself; it is forced into standing a moral trial for having achieved something, i.e., to have created a space in which it is possible (for the individual) to survive." Koselleck, *Critique and Crisis*, 11. Controversial though Koselleck's account of the Enlightenment may be, he raises a problem that persists in contemporary liberal democratic society, namely, the tendency to exercise critique from a moral position that is both outside and hostile to politics and especially to the formal political realm.

67. Koselleck, 134–35. For a fascinating study of how this retreat led to the so-called canon wars over the literary curriculum at the modern university, see John Guillory, *Cultural Capital: The Problem of Literary Canon Formation* (Chicago: University of Chicago Press, 1993).

68. Critical accounts of the politicization of the university, which have exploded in recent years, can be traced back to the acrimonious debate over multiculturalism in the 1980s, when the demand for fair representation in the curriculum on the part of women and racial and ethnic minorities was seen as the triumph of cultural identity and

particularism over academic neutrality and universality. More recent accounts focus on the debate over free speech, microagressions, rape culture, and so on. See Frank Furedi, *What's Happened to the University?: A Sociological Account of Its Infantalisation* (New York: Routledge, 2017); Bradley Campbell, *The Rise of Victimhood Culture: Microaggressions, Safe-Spaces, and the New Culture Wars* (New York: Palgrave MacMillan, 2018); Laura Kipnis, *Unwanted Advances: Sexual Paranoia Comes to Campus* (New York: Harper, 2017).

69. Kosselleck, 132, 133.

Bibliography

Arendt, Hannah. "Introduction *Into* Politics." In *The Promise of Politics*, edited by Jerome Kohn. New York: Schocken, 2005.

——. *Lectures on Kant's Political Philosophy.* Edited by Ronald Beiner. Chicago: University of Chicago Press, 1992.

——. "Truth and Politics." In *Between Past and Future: Eight Exercises in Political Thought.* New York: Penguin, 1993.

——. "What Is Freedom?" In *Between Past and Future: Eight Exercises in Political Thought.* New York: Penguin, 1993.

Butler, Judith. "What Is Critique? An Essay on Foucault's Virtue," 2001. http://eipcp.net /transversal/0806/butler/en.

Campbell, Bradley. *The Rise of Victimhood Culture: Microaggressions, Safe-Spaces, and the New Culture Wars.* New York: Palgrave MacMillan, 2018.

Foucault, Michel. "Kant on Enlightenment and Revolution." Translated by Colin Gordon. *Economy and Society* 15, no. 1 (February 1986).

——. "What Is Critique?" In *The Politics of Truth: Michel Foucault*, edited by Sylvére Lotringer, translated by Lysa Hochroch and Catherine Porter. Los Angeles: Semiotext(e), 2007.

Furedi, Frank. *What's Happened to the University? A Sociological Account of Its Infantalisation*, New York: Routledge, 2017.

Guillory, John, *Cultural Capital: The Problem of Literary Canon Formation.* Chicago: University of Chicago Press, 1993.

Kipnis, Laura. *Unwanted Advances: Sexual Paranoia Comes to Campus.* New York: Harper, 2017.

Kosselleck, Reinhardt. *Critique and Crisis: Enlightenment and the Pathogenesis of Modern Society.* Cambridge, MA: MIT Press, 1998.

Rajchman, John. "Enlightenment Today: Introduction to *The Politics of Truth.*" In *The Politics of Truth: Michel Foucault*, edited by Sylvére Lotringer, translated by Lysa Hochroth and Catherine Porter. Los Angeles: Semiotext(e), 2007.

Visker, Rudi. *Michel Foucault: Genealogy as Critique.* Translated by Chris Turner. New York: Verso, 1995.

CHAPTER 3

CRITIQUE WITHOUT A POLITICS OF HOPE?

AYŞE PARLA

When I hoped I feared
Since I hoped I dared.

—Emily Dickinson, Fr. 594 (1861–65)

In his essay "On Stuckedness" (2015), Ghassan Hage writes that critique, understood in part as the exposition of the unsustainability of capitalism and the proposition for alternative models of organizing life, once hinged on hope. Hope was central to critique via a mediating term: crisis. If economic and political crises were endemic to and not exceptional in capitalism, crisis itself became a source of hope. Hage proceeds to argue that from the mid-twentieth century onward, however, and in particular with the rise of fascism, the hope that hitherto animated critique began to dissipate. The reason was a shift in the understanding of the mediating term, crisis: once viewed as an opportunity for seeing through the veil of capitalist ideology and for working toward social transformation, crisis increasingly came to be perceived as yet another mechanism for ensuring the reproduction of capitalist economy and society. At this point comes Hage's twist to the so-far-familiar narrative: this shift resulted in "a depressed and depressing form of critique," one in which the belief in social change and in the revolutionary subject were given up.[1] The crisis of critique for Hage, therefore, is tantamount to a crisis in hope.

In a piece written a decade earlier, "Hope, Critique and Utopia," Craig Browne identifies a similar shift concerning the aspirations of critique with regard to the end of capitalism but with a diametrically opposed diagnosis with regard to the role played by hope. Browne, too, discerns within critical social theory a move away from the more radical goals of transformation and toward the more modest goals of revision, or as he specifies it, "from Marxist projects of emancipation to Habermasian projects of democracy."[2] This shift, Browne states, is the result of a decline in the faith in utopian projects. But Browne differs from Hage in his assessment of how hope articulates with the crisis-critique nexus. Unlike Hage, Browne does not see a concomitant wane in hope in relation to critique. To the contrary, he observes a boom in hope, one that occurs "against the intentions of critical social theory.... Hope is embraced because of the loss of utopian alternatives and a lack of confidence in the value of transformation."[3]

Browne's starting point is to take hope as a suspicious category, one that is less politically reliable than, for example, desire. For Browne, this is at least in part because of hope's theological associations with passivity and resignation, therefore rendering hope short of the kind of active energy that utopian thought requires.[4] In the rest of his essay, Browne rescues hope from what he takes to be its damning theological connotations and insists that hope is still a useful category for critique. But the important point for my purposes is not how Browne salvages hope.[5] Rather, I am interested in the striking difference between what two contemporary theorists take hope to be, before whatever gloss they might then put on hope. For Hage, hope is inherently productive of transformative energies and its loss results in a depressing and depressed form of critique. Whereas for Browne, hope is at least initially complicit in the status quo and therefore in "blunting the utopian thrust of critical thinking."[6]

This essay takes its inspiration from two such widely divergent presuppositions about both the diagnosis and the assumptions about hope even for those who agree on its centrality to critique. But I want to shift the question precisely away from whether one should have hope or not—hope, at least in some minimal form, is necessary to the act of living, as basic psychological wisdom, if not life itself, teaches us. My goal here is to foreground instead the uneven social distribution of *political* hope and to interrogate the repercussions of such differentiation for critique. Through pulling into the conversation alternative legacies of thinking about hope by philosophers and activists who speak and act not from positions of privilege but from positions of persecution or marginalization, I attend to the ways in which structural and historical privilege impacts the political imagination of hope, especially as it pertains to visions of a nation's future. More specifically, I rethink the relationship between hope and critique by emphasizing a backward-looking hope and one that takes seriously the refusals of disenfranchised citizens to join the summons for political hopeful-ness, even when such appeals get made in the name of progressive politics.

An important caveat concerns the ways in which hope often gets tossed around as a blanket category of analysis and experience. In various contempo-rary takes on hope, whose popularity as a category of analysis is soaring (so much so that the *Stanford Encyclopedia of Philosophy* felt compelled to include its very first entry on "hope" in March 2017), different kinds of hope and differ-ent conditions for hoping are too easily collapsed onto one another or appealed to simultaneously as if they are substitutable. But, for example, when Cheryl Mattingly writes about hope as a resource among people struggling to live with chronic illness in the face of the unlikelihood of recovery, her explication is quite different from the hope that David Graeber urges us to recover against the erasures of capitalist modes of organization.[7] If it is somewhat sloppy from an analytic standpoint to invoke hope as a shorthand to refer to vastly diver-gent lifeworlds and resources, it seems presumptuous from the point of view of lived experience to assume parallels between the daily practices imbued with hope among those severely ill and the daily practices of citizens who cultivate hope for the society's future.

In what follows then, I limit myself to an exploration of the politics of hope. My motivation for such delimitation derives from an insistence on contextual-izing and historicizing hope rather than considering it in the abstract. It is informed as well by an ethnographic sensibility, one that requires us to under-take more conceptual labor in thinking through, rather than simply assuming the connections between, on the one hand, the role of the personal/familial in sustaining hope and, on the other hand, the landscape of politics and its incite-ments to hope toward change on a collective scale. The specific context from which my theoretical intervention begins is the depiction of a recent vote in Turkey, where, despite the grim outlook of the political state of affairs, the pol-itics of hope dominated the public scene of dissent. I draw on this case to rethink hope's temporalities and to highlight the structural and historical con-ditions of its uneven distribution.

Hoping in a Compromised Election

In April 2017, a referendum was held in Turkey to move from a parliamentary to a presidential system. The envisioned presidential system would grant sweep-ing executive powers to the country's president, one whose already rapid rise in worldwide rankings as an authoritarian ruler gained further momentum with the declaration of a state of emergency after a failed coup attempt in July 2016.[8] Ostensibly declared in response to the failed coup attempt of July 2016, these consecutive states of emergency have continued to function as a justification for a nationwide purge, including the sacking and imprisonment of more than a hundred thousand public employees, politicians, journalists, academics, and ordinary citizens. They serve, in short, to suppress any and all dissent against the current government, the Justice and Development Party (AKP), and its heady mix of neoliberal, conservative, neo-Ottomanist, and religious rule.

The most obvious concern surrounding the legitimacy of the referendum in 2017, intended to seal the former party head and current president Recep Tayyip Erdogan's leadership until 2027, was that it was held under a state of emergency. But beyond the shadows of doubt cast by the state of emergency on fair voting conditions, one could also argue, as Yetvart Danzikyan, the editor-in-chief of the weekly Armenian newspaper *Agos* did, that the referendum had already lost all legitimacy when the ruling government, together with the consent and collaboration of the most sizeable opposition party, the center-left Republican People's Party (CHP), lifted the constitutionally protected immunity of members of parliament a few month prior to the elections.[9] This was a decisive— and, for Turkey's already flawed democracy, disastrous—move that authorized the arrests of Kurdish politicians who belonged to the Democratic Party of the People (HDP), the party that predominantly and historically represents Turkey's historically oppressed Kurdish minority and the party that was posing the most significant threat to AKP's monopoly on power. Departing from its image as the sole representative of the Kurdish vote, HDP's popularity across the board had soared, reaching proportions unprecedented in the Republic's entire history: even devoted CHP voters, increasingly discontent with their party's decades-long inertia and disarmed by HDP copresident Demirtaş's inclusive rhetoric, environmental and human rights sensibilities, extraordinary wit, and musical charms, were leaning in favor of HDP. In early 2015, in what may have been the shortest speech in Turkey's parliamentary history, Selahattin Demirtaş, who is known affectionately as "Selo Başgan" (Chief Selo) in local parlance and dubbed "the Kurdish Obama" in international media, repeated the same sentence three times with dramatic effect: "We won't let you become an executive president." This prescient allusion referred to President Erdoğan's plans for a presidential regime. Demirtaş's taunt proved more prophetic than Erdoğan himself may have credited at the time: HDP achieved a historic breakthrough in the June 2015 elections. Not only was a pro-Kurdish party passing the formidable and structurally unjust 10-percent election threshold for the first time in Turkey's voting history, but HDP also dealt a severe blow to the AKP's majority rule, in effect since 2002, by gaining eighty seats. In the absence of consensus for a coalition-formed government and the sudden and suspicious eruption of violence and fatal bombings across the country, AKP moved to snap elections in November 2015. At those elections, also tainted by rumors of electoral fraud, the AKP restored its parliamentary majority and weakened the Democratic Party of the People by reducing their representation in parliament. But it could not get rid of HDP entirely as the latter still managed to pass the 10-percent threshold and, even if in diminished numbers, retained its seats in parliament, obstructing AKP's designs for absolute majority and for the shift to the presidential system. And so AKP dealt the final, decisive blow by putting behind bars both Selahattin Demirtaş and copresident Figen Yüksekdağ, along with a sizable number of the party membership. They remain imprisoned still.

Such were the considerably compromised conditions under which the referendum to consolidate President Erdoğan and his party's rule was to take place. Furthermore, the two sides were not remotely equal in campaign opportunities, with the "Yes" campaign dominating print and airwave in the virtually government-controlled media and the "No" supporters being bullied at campaign events and facing detentions. Despite all, however, the landscape of dissent in Turkey was nonetheless awash with hope. The ubiquitous proclamations of hope among the no-sayers were most immediately tied to a specific object: a No-outcome. The hope for a No-outcome also included broader desires on the part of the No-sayers: hope for a better future for Turkey, one in which the increasing tyranny of the current regime would come to a halt or at least abate. Activists, politicians, columnists, and social media commentators reiterated with ever-intensifying gusto the necessity for holding on to hope. It increasingly seemed not enough to cast a No-vote. It also became necessary, among the vocal opposition, to proclaim, constantly and loudly, that one had hoped.

What to make, then, of the insistence on hope in an election that was rigged from the start? Was such insistence on hope admirable as a tactical move to overcome lethargy? Was a politics of hope commendable on the more radical principle that hope in the face of improbability is precisely the worthwhile kind of hope to nurture?[10]

Ümit Kıvanç, a leftist writer, columnist, film director, and prominent public intellectual, was an emblematic figure in propounding this politics of hope with simultaneous sophistication and belligerence. In an op-ed piece he wrote after the No-vote lost by a narrow margin—the loss most likely the result of electoral fraud at the last minute—Kıvanç (2017) vented his anger at those who had voiced criticism of the hope discourse. Kıvanç depicted the critics of the hope discourse as a uniform chorus, attributing to them a condescending and flippant attitude. "Come on, darling, you are telling me you still have hope?," the critics of hope taunt the hopeful No-sayers in Kıvanç's satirical personification of the former. Against what he deems to be the irresponsible cynicism of the critics of hope, one that is purely motivated by calculations of failure or success, he insists, Kıvanç extols the ethical commitments of the proponents of a politics of hope: The latter "cannot bear injustice and wrongfulness. They cannot continue to comfortably get on with their lives. . . . They feel pangs piercing into their hearts as they sit to dinner, go to bed, or hug their loves ones if their spouses, comrades, friends have been fired, imprisoned." Having thus unveiled the truth about the true intentions of both sides as well as having properly meted out their respective moral worth, Kıvanç concludes his diatribe with an address to the critics of hope that starts as a challenge and ends as a command: "Fine. There is no chance of success. Are you content? What the hell will you do now? Since there is no hope, who cares if they imprison so and so? Go ahead, say that. But what do you want from people who fight against injustice? Why do you demoralize (us)? *You* may not need justice, but others do! . . . So stop screaming! Shut up. Don't try to dissuade people from their struggle, don't make them feel like their pursuit is meaningless."

Kıvanç's tone is abrasively polemical and his vision of political citizenship Manichean, one in which subscribing to the politics of hope becomes the absolute arbiter for sorting out the morally virtuous who care about injustice in the world from the morally indifferent who spray their nihilist venom. Written in more amicable spirit, an intervention by Alyanak and Üstek-Spilda articulates similar concerns.[11] Being critical of the hope in the elections may be a "productive intellectual exercise," the authors concede. But that acknowledgment of the potential intellectual value of the critique of hope instantly follows with an accusatory plea: "For those of us who have nothing else but hope to ponder on, a critique of hope comes as a sinister blow to our very lifeline." There is also a warning: "Losing hope in hope itself risks leaving us to wallow in apathy." No matter how compromised the elections may have been and how bleak the political agenda in Turkey in the preceding years, the authors conclude that "giving up hope in and on Turkey does not help."

The common concern across the board when met with challenges to a politics of hope may be summed up in two related propositions: (1) those who were critical of the politics of hope, the argument goes, speak from positions of privilege and comfort and, as such, they are merely flexing intellectual muscle and (2) the challenge to a politics of hope was tantamount to apathy, inaction, and even nihilism. I want to argue that both propositions in fact operate on a false dichotomy. They reduce the options either to a hopeful campaign for a no vote in the referendum or to inaction or despair. Beyond the Turkish context and more broadly, the exclusive grounding of doing politics only in hope reinscribes, as insightfully identified by Jessica Greenberg, a further set of binaries that radically diminish the field of activism and action: hope and hopelessness; apologia and utopia; moral purity and compromise.[12] I now turn to a vignette from the election landscape in Turkey to complicate these dichotomies and to unsettle the assumption that the critique of the politics of hope is a frivolous exercise at the disposal of the indifferent or privileged intellectual.

Who Dares Kill Hope?

On the day of the referendum, a woman who identified as an Armenian citizen of Turkey asked in a social media post what hope she could have of Turkey's future. The school in which she had cast her ballot—a No-vote, she made clear—was named the Talat Pasha Elementary School. For the great majority of the Turkish public, there is nothing unusual in the fact that a school is named Talat Pasha. It is part and parcel of the violent ordinary that Talat Pasa, the chief commander who signed off on the Armenian Genocide, thus occupies public space in Turkey through elementary schools and countless streets that are named after him in most cities across the country. What is unthinkable in postgenocide Germany, for example—imagine having schools or streets named after Adolf Hitler—is an unmarked, ordinary occurrence in postgenocide Turkey.

The protest of this particular voter not only exposed the monstrous extraordinary and its normalization. It also punctured a particular narrative version of hope by challenging, if not collapsing, hope's temporalities. Even if the outcome had been a No, what hope for the future could a descendant of the genocide have in a country where the violence of the past continues to be inflicted on her in the present, and indeed in the very movement in which she partakes in the dissident act that is supposed to usher in the hopeful future? The voter's outcry was heard by some. But the social commentary it elicited was predominantly marked by the impatience among those calling for hope: Was it really the time to kill hope by clinging to the past when the times demanded prioritizing action in the hopes of a better future?

When does insistence on a politics of hope begin to turn tyrannical and be detrimental to critique that chooses not to partake in the "collective" expression and effervescence of the politics of hope? Why is a pessimistic assessment labeled as the antithesis of both hope and critique? Do we have to choose between, on the one hand, an overconfident and defensive politics of hope and, on the other hand, the retreat into resignation, passivity, cynicism? What follows then might be read as an exercise in suspending that knee-jerk response to an unhopeful analysis or protest: "But where is the hope?" or the more accusatory "How dare you kill hope?" Subscribing to the politics of hope during the Turkish referendum, while initially an act of dissidence, became hegemonic in its impulse to censure those who resisted waxing hopeful about Turkey's future because they had suffered the most at the hands of its genocidal past. The politics of hope being propounded by the No-campaigners demanded participation in a hopeful future for Turkey, without reckoning with why certain citizens, speaking from positions of dispossession, would hesitate or refuse to partake in that particular political hope. The critique embodied in that refusal—the critique of the legacy of state violence, of the unequal distribution of the grounds for political hope and the limited inclusiveness of the hoped-for future—fell on deaf ears in an election landscape that would not tolerate any challenges to its buoyant political hopefulness.

Only Hope Did Not Escape Pandora's Box

Given the contemporary refascination with a politics of hope, revisiting the checkered trajectory of the history of philosophical engagements with hope offers a sobering reminder of what has been a dizzying spectrum of appraisals. In ancient Greek philosophy, Vogt argues, hope was primarily associated with inadequate knowledge of facts or with wishful thinking and was thus seen as likely to lead to detrimental action.[13] Perhaps one of the strongest negative pronouncements on hope is to be found in Nietzsche's interpretation of the myth of Pandora in which he designated hope as the worst of all evils because it "prolongs the torments of man."[14] Schopenhauer, too, in his *World as Will and Representation*, tended to view hope as a fundamentally flawed relationship to the world characterized by the inability to withstand hardships at the heart of existence.

Even if they did not come down so hard on hope, most philosophers seem to have recognized it as a fundamentally ambivalent emotion. For Spinoza, the philosopher who perhaps most thoroughly pondered the ambivalence of hope, it is doubt that distinguishes hope from confidence. In a justly famous formulation Spinoza defines hope as an "inconsistent pleasure" that he contrasted with fear, which, in turn, he described as "inconsistent pain." The operative word for both hope and fear in Spinoza's grammar of affect is "inconsistent." It is a term that captures the presence of a certain element of doubt intrinsic to both hope and fear.[15] Whether identified as "doubt" by Spinoza or "despair" (Mattingly) or "fear" (Seneca), the moving antonyms of hope point to the ambivalence at the core of hope that was captured in the myth of Pandora's box: unlike all the other vices that escaped, did hope remain in the box because it was the one virtue or because it would go on to plague humankind throughout the rest of time?

Such equivocal approaches to hope sought to capture its ambiguities: hope has the potential to enable and disable or to inspire and to veil, depending on the context. But there is a contemporary strand of critical theory and leftist politics that summons us to unconditionally reclaim hope and to do so especially in these dark times. Recall Barack Obama's best-selling *Audacity of Hope*—and public intellectuals and thinkers such as David Harvey (2000) or Barbara Ehrenreich (2000) who have recently posited that the lack of hope or some form of optimism is the biggest barrier to progressive politics.[16] *Hope in the Dark* by Rebecca Solnit, who has created her niche as the alternative to pessimistic activists and academics, may be considered a paradigmatic example. Solnit takes stock of the past five decades and concludes that despite "hideous economic inequality, attack on civil liberties, and climate change," there is inevitable proof of major victories and progress. These include "tremendous human rights achievements" as well as forms of resistance, such as the antiglobalization demonstrations in Seattle and the worldwide marches against war in Iraq, forms of resistance that entail "new and exhilarating alliances across distance and difference."[17] Solnit's cheerful assessment of the historical record is supplemented by what she identifies as the power of the altruistic, idealistic forces already at work in the world. "Most of us would say, if asked, that we live in a capitalist society, but vast amounts of how we live our everyday lives—our interactions with and commitments to family lives, friendships, vocations, membership in social, spiritual and political organizations—are in essence non-capitalist or even anti-capitalist, made up of things we do for free, out of love and on principle."[18] Solnit's faith in hope, then, is premised on the abundance of noncapitalist relations at work even within capitalist society.

The anthropologist and activist David Graeber has stated similar sentiments. In his manifesto from 2008, "Hope in Common," Graeber assures us that "Hopelessness is not natural. It needs to be produced, and we only need to look closer at our everyday lives, and we would start noticing all the ways in which everyday life contains acts of cooperation." Hopelessness is an ideologically induced condition, and we can see beyond the layers of mystification to discover hope as the real state of affairs. Much of this contemporary strand of thinking on hope as a horizon of possibility that is utopian and emancipatory draws on the formidable legacy of Ernst Bloch.

The Unbearable "Buoyancy" of Blochian Hope

In his magnum opus, *The Principle of Hope* (1986), Bloch posits hope as the core of humankind. If for Marx, the act of labor is what defines our species-being, for Bloch, our distinguishing characteristic is the act of hoping. According to Bloch, humans possess an ontologically prospective orientation that automatically produces "hoping" because the act of living itself is about striving, and because striving is necessarily oriented toward the future. However, even as hope constitutes the essence of mankind, something goes fundamentally wrong with the way we hope. In the spirit of the Marxist tradition that locates the alienation of species-being as alienation from its own labor in class-stratified societies, Bloch believes that the bourgeois class is guilty of having contaminated hope by emptying out its prospective and revolutionary potential. Hope, in its bourgeois guise, has been reduced to petty daydreams. However, this is still no cause for despair. Because hoping is the very basis of being and striving, even in petty daydreams, there remains extractable that other part, which is "provocative, is not content just to accept the bad which exists, does not accept renunciation. It can be extricated from the unregulated daydream and from its sly misuse, can be activated undimmed."[19]

Not hiding his irritation with Bloch's "excessive cheerfulness," Terry Eagleton finds the kind of ontologizing Bloch enacts of hope to be ultimately antithetical to the historical materialism that Bloch fervently avowed adherence to. In Bloch's universe, writes Eagleton (2015), hope takes on a cosmic quality; Bloch finds "hope in the world as if there is uranium." On the face of it, this assessment could also be applied to Lauren Berlant's psychoanalytic explication of optimism (2011) as an objective relation to the world, one that enables us to go on getting up in the morning and getting though the day. But there is a crucial difference: Berlant goes on to demonstrate how optimism becomes cruel given the compromised conditions on which it rests, particularly in late capitalism. Bloch, on the other hand, is assured that this objective dynamic of hope, in Eagelton's words again, "has the backing of the universe in unfolding its inherent purpose towards perfection" and "is one that no mere empirical defeat could rebuff."

Here we reach, perhaps, one central question in relation to what gets designated as critique. There may be general agreement that critique "tends to imply a questioning of a certain state of the world that is underlain by a dissatisfaction of what it is, whether from a political or moral viewpoint or from an epistemological or a theoretical view point."[20] But as Didier Fassin goes on to elaborate, following the categorization made by David Owen, the two main traditions associated with critique significantly diverge after that shared dissatisfaction with the given state of affairs. One school of critical theory, in the vein of Marx and the Frankfurt School, would assert not only that becoming cognizant of all the layers of deception caused by ideology is possible but that such awareness portends emancipation. By contrast, the genealogical tradition would limit such awareness to only a greater recognition of what counts as true and what as false without the subsequent promise of emancipation. More pertinently for my purposes here, Fassin then provides a striking assessment about not just the content but also the different *affective* tone of these two traditions and their orientation: critique in its critical theory strand is more about "indignation," Fassin writes, while critique in its genealogical strand is more about "astonishment."

Revisiting Fassin's distinction between indignation (in critical theory) and astonishment (in genealogy) with regard to the role hope plays in each offers a way out of the binary of either unequivocally embracing hope or giving it up. One may continue to be astonished by the unfairness of the world, without the easier comforts that indignation offers through its concomitant promise of an obvious, permanent "fix." Despite their tempting effervescence, Blochian incitements to hope exude indignation not just about the state of the world with all its rampant injustices. They also smuggle in indignation against those who dare to try to take hope away.

An alternative to the "indignant" stance may also be found in the anthropologist Peter Redfield's evocative ethnography of the humanitarian work of members of the Médecins Sans Frontière (MSF). Redfield identifies the trademark of the stance of MSF workers as its moral minimalism, a stark contrast to the untarnished optimism of the Blochian universe. MSF workers diverge from the maxim that has acquired the status of scripture in leftist praxis and much of contemporary Western public culture, namely that "action demands hope and hope demands optimism if not a fully articulated utopia" (229). Instead, they operate with a disillusioned awareness of the immediate limits of humanitarian deeds when measured against the structural injustice that pervades the world. Such awareness does not result in a total abandonment of hope (or action). But it does require what Redfield describes as a major modification to the category of hope, which he captures in his brilliantly evocative phrase "residual hope."

Trimming grand gestures and injecting more minimalism into our moral claims, whether as activists or critical theorists, might be a welcome antidote to the triumphalism that is characteristic of various dissident political imaginaries, whether in the philosophical universe of Bloch or the political activism of the Turkish referendum. The No-sayers in Turkey went on drumming the beat of hope regardless of the reality of experience in the present: that the elections were held under severely compromised conditions including a state of emergency and an incarcerated leadership of the party that posed the most serious threat. The mere satisfaction of waxing lyrical on hope presided over the uneasy facts of indifference among radicalized or lethargic Kurdish citizens who had no faith in the vote in the first place—indeed, a fraction of the HDP proposed boycotting the elections, a proposition that was vehemently shot down—or among the wary Armenian citizens for whom the very act of voting in an institutionalized setting reenacted the denial of genocide.

The triumphalism of the No-campaign in Turkey was thus not only futuristic at the expense of duly taking stock of the present, namely, the compromised conditions under which the referendum took place. It was also presentist in its inadequate confrontation with the past. The outcry that marked the protest of the Armenian voter, a protest that cannot be reduced to a preoccupation with the past—as the criticism often goes. The outcry also constitutes a critique of continuing disenfranchisement in the present. Perhaps the notion of hope could instead be thought as the less indignant and more minimal belief that our political condition is not "natural" or the belief that critique is about exposing the history of the present, its contingency, and the paths not taken.

A Backward-Looking Hope

In contrast to the Blochian focus on the glorious possibilities the future portends, there are different legacies of reckoning with the temporalities of political hope. One such alternative is the Benjaminian genealogy that insists on placing the emphasis on the momentous weight of the past: "For historical materialism it is a question of holding fast to a picture of the past, just as if it had unexpectedly thrust itself, in a moment of danger, on the historical subject. . . . The only writer of history with the gift of setting alight the sparks of hope in the past, is the one who is convinced of this: that not even the dead will be safe from the enemy, if he is victorious. And this enemy has not ceased to be victorious."[21]

One would not need to embrace the Messianic overtones in this oft-quoted passage to take from it the idea of political hope without a teleological thrust. Benjamin's discontentment with the progressivist vision of history stems from the latter's reliance on the guarantee of a better future as well as its inadequate confrontation with the catastrophic nature of the past. Like Benjamin, who refused to attenuate the horrors that haunt civilized Europe and their implication for visions of the future, the feminist legal scholar Patricia Williams rearticulates the past-future nexus through the historically compromised conditions in which blacks in the United States are able to hope:

> The individual unifying cultural memory of black people is the helplessness of living under slavery or in its shadow. I grew up living in the past: the future, some versions of which had only the vaguest possibility of happening, was treated with respect of the already-happened, seen through the prismatic lenses of what had already occurred. . . . What hope would there be if the assignment were to pour hope into a timeless, formless futurism? The desperate psychological and physical oppression suffered by black people in this society makes such a prospect either unrealistic (experienced as unattainable) or other worldly (as in the false hopes held out by many religions of the oppressed).[22]

The sense of a future always already inflected through the knowledge of a violent past presents us with a different politics of hope, the very first requirement of which seems to be to call into question its seemingly self-evident invocations. In *Between the World and Me* (2015), Ta-Nehisi Coates warns his son to not forget that "in America, it is traditional to destroy the black body—it is heritage." In contrast to a forward-looking James Baldwin, who, in *The Fire Next Time* (1963), assured *his* fifteen-year-old nephew of the possibility of the dream of "making America what it must become," Coates offers little by way of comfort and is resolutely oriented to the past and its legacy of violence. He catalogues recent shootings of black kids by law enforcement as some of the most recent reinstatements of the brutal legacy of violence that "dislodges brains, blocks airways, rips muscle, extract organs, cracks bones, breaks teeth." And immediately after recalling this archive of broken flesh, Coates goes on to recall the host of a news show who, after listening to him, showed the picture of an eleven-year-old black boy tearfully hugging a white police officer. The news show host then turned to ask Coates about "hope." At that moment, Coates tells his son and his readers, "I knew I had failed."

Prioritizing the gaze into the past rather than an orientation to a hopeful future is the austere thread that binds together Walter Benjamin, who only escaped the Holocaust by recourse to suicide, Patricia Williams, who as a lawyer and established professor can hardly rely on the semiformal codes of mutual trust her white colleagues take for granted in everyday transactions, Ta-Nehisi Coates, who refuses to offer easy comfort to his son's disillusionment when the officer who shot the twelve year old is exonerated; and the descendant of genocide in Turkey, who has to cast her vote in a school named after the perpetrator. It is not a coincidence that each in different ways are wary of a "formless futurism," as Williams puts it. The question then is not about who has or does not have hope in terms of being personally hopefully disposed to the world. Rather, it is for whom a politics of hope can seamlessly and effortlessly become a rallying cry and for whom such politics is more strained and troubled.

At the 2017 "Speaking Power to Justice" public salon event of the Association for Political and Legal Anthropology, in response to the question posed by Jennifer Curtis on whether "the weight of history—from enslavement, exploitation, dispossession, disenfranchisement and state/elite sanctioned murder—has pushed hope out of the range of political options for some Black activists," the anthropologist Orisanmi Burton responded, based on his research on black radical politics: "The people I study, talk to, look up to, read—they don't talk about hope. That word doesn't come up. I'd like to suggest substituting the word strategy."[23]

Burton's rendition of black activists' insistence on struggle and strategy is a sobering corrective to the charge that challenging the politics of hope condemns one to inaction. The charge that critical analyses that refuse to strike a hopeful note disable political struggle has also been leveled at the recent and eclectic school of thought labeled "Afro-pessimism." Afro-pessimism posits the history of slavery as a defining, singular event that continues to render blackness and black suffering a structure of being that is unique. The corollary is that anti-blackness is a form of racism that cannot be reduced to or compared with other kinds of racism.[24] In its insistence on the continuing relevance of slavery to the conditions of blacks in the United States today and its refusal to accept any analogies to black suffering, Afro-pessimism is also skeptical of coalitional politics to the extent that it merely alleviates white guilt or advances the agendas of other marginalized groups while leaving intact the structural oppression of blacks.

Some of the fury Afro-pessimism has unleashed, including among progressive intellectuals and academics of a liberal bent, replicates the criticisms directed at Ta-Nehisi Coates and his "unhopeful" political vision. The emphasis on the singularity of slavery, the criticism goes, reifies white supremacy instead of its historically contingent character. Moreover, insisting on the defining relevance of the past to the present diminishes the sense of what is possible, robbing people of the capacity for action and instead forever binding them to their "singular" suffering.

As problematic as Afro-pessimism's ontologization of blackness and its concomitant refusal of analogy may be, I am wary of the disproportionately hostile dismissals of Afro-pessimism as "conservative," as "debilitating," or, as Sexton has recently captured with sardonic gloss, as a "morbid fixation on the depredations of slavery." I take to heart those criticisms of Afro-pessimism that call out the latter's dangerous potential for essentializing and its inattentiveness to the gendered dynamics of blackness. However, it seems to me to be at least in part Afro-pessimism's resistance to the celebratory politics of hope that triggers the defensive posture. The dismissive gesture that reduces Afro-pessimism to a school of thought that kills hope and incites inaction undermines the larger legacy of black radical thought it draws on. Instead of seeing in Afro-pessimists "the diagnosticians of their own society," as Saidiya Hartman characterizes them,[25] such dismissals miss the resistance work of Afro-pessimism against the celebratory antiracist rhetoric that is not willing to give up the "metanarrative thrust towards an integration into the national project."[26]

Quite some time before it became fashionable to write about hope in anthropology, Ghassan Hage had already begun developing a unique and distinctively Bourdieusian analysis of the differential distribution of hope.[27] My approach to political hope in this chapter has been deeply indebted to Hage's concern with the differential distribution of hope. But my particular intent has been to capture some forms of political hopefulness for the imagination of national futures that get monopolized by the already privileged and foreclosed to historically dispossessed groups.

✳ ✳ ✳

In his *Pessimism: Philosophy, Ethic, Spirit*, Joshua Dienstag asks why the word *pessimist* "functions so well as a gesture of dismissal" and "as a casual intellectual put-down."[28] As a partial answer, he suggests that critics of pessimism tend to too quickly collapse description with an affective stance as if those offering bleak descriptions of the state of affairs "rejoiced at the decline or decay they described." He goes on to say that "Rather than hiding from the ugliness of the world, perhaps we can discover how best to withstand it."[29]

Critics of pessimism may retort by saying that it is precisely the politics of hope that would aid us in "withstanding the ugliness of the world." In this piece, I have tried to point toward a path away from what threatens to become an intolerant politics of hope. I have instead reclaimed historical and contemporary expressions of "a depressed and depressing form of critique," to return to Ghassan Hage's depiction that I opened the essay with. I have done so, however, not in order to lament what despair does to critique but rather for what it opens up for critique.[30]

My goal in rethinking the relation between hope and critique has been to move the issue beyond different individual temperaments, affective makeup, or capacities for tolerating or not tolerating melancholia. What I have done, instead, is to call attention to different subject positions, situated differently vis-à-vis access to and participation in political imaginations of better futures. To do so, I have forged a path alongside Benjamin and Williams: a path that meanders into the past instead of rushing into the future. Didier Fassin has taken that Benjaminian path to show how the emotion of *ressentiment* on the part of those oppressed by South African apartheid needs to be considered as a resistance to national projects of reconciliation.[31] As such, *ressentiment* is not just about the past but about the irruption of the past into the present. What that Benjaminian path entails for the political context of Turkey, I would argue, is an insistence on dwelling in the genocidal past and its afterlives, its continuing effects in the present. It entails not being outraged at or dismissive of those refusals of political hope by those who are the most vulnerable targets of that violent past.

This essay has been an invitation, then, to pause on that threshold between the explanatory-analytical and the anticipatory-utopian. Rather than a cursory nod to history, can we dare dwell longer in the threshold of what the catastrophic nature of the past implies for the present before we leap onto the future that assures the consolation of transcendence? A politics of hope to be salvaged seems to require an asymmetry in terms of hope's relation to temporality: full acknowledgment of the horrific certainties of the past and partial/cautious expectation in the possibilities of the future. Without such asymmetry in configuring the politics of hope,[32] that quintessential motto of prefigurative politics, "another world is possible," might remain as the conceit of the already privileged that masquerades as hope. Or, as a colloquial Turkish saying goes, hope will function merely as the "bread of the poor," providing them with enough subsistence to keep them just exactly where they are.

Notes

The interactions with every single "Crit" in what was an intense and joyful year at the Institute were invaluable. I would like to thank especially Lori Allen, Karen Engle, and David Kazanjian for their close engagement with the text through its several iterations.

Jennifer Curtis gave momentum to the original idea when she solicited a piece on the referendum for PoLAR and I have benefited from her supportive and brilliant feedback. I am grateful to Jessica Catellino for inviting me to speak on this topic at UCLA's Anthropology Lunch Seminar Series, where the engagement of an amazing audience helped me sharpen my arguments, and I thank especially Can Açıksöz, Akhil Gupta, Sondra Hale, Gail Kligman, Zeynep Korkman, Ruken Şengül, and Anoush Suny. Ahmet Faik Kurtulmuş and Nora Tataryan provided most generous feedback on the final draft. I am grateful to Didier Fassin for recalling the lines by Emily Dickinson used for the epigraph for this piece. Above all, I am indebted to Didier Fassin and Bernard Harcourt for their sharp insights and excellent suggestions along the entire process, even as I have not been able to do justice to all the wonderful challenges they posed.

1. Ghassan Hage, "On Stuckedness: Critique of Crisis and Crisis of Critique," in *Alter-Politics: Critical Anthropology and the Radical Imagination* (Melbourne: Melbourne University Press, 2003).

2. Craig Browne, "Hope, Critique, and Utopia," *Critical Horizons* 6, no. 1 (2005): 63–86, 72.

3. Browne, 68.

4. This is a partial and to my mind inadequate interpretation of the varieties of theological hope. St. Thomas Aquinas's explication of hope as one of the three fundamental virtues of Christianity, for example, offers a more complex understanding of hope that is also based on rationality and immediate action in the world.

5. Browne charts the territory that Ernst Bloch also did through his key distinction between petty (bourgeois or religious) hope versus true, revolutionary hope.

6. Browne, "Hope, Critique, and Utopia," 71.

7. Cheryl Mattingly, *The Paradox of Hope: Journeys Through a Clinical Borderland* (Berkeley: University of California Press, 2010); David Graeber, "Hope in Common," 2008, https://theanarchistlibrary.org/library/david-graeber-hope-in-common.

8. States of emergencies have been renewed ever since, with the sixth consecutive state of emergency in effect as of the writing of this piece in April 2018.

9. Yetvart Danzikyan, "Referandum Yok Hükümde Olmalı," April 20, 2017.

10. The conditions for the kind of radical hope which the philosopher Jonathan Lear has recently and eloquently articulated were not present in the Turkish context—namely conditions of extreme epistemological loss that shakes one's ways of knowing the world and being in the world to the very core and out of which a radical hope for reanchoring and reimagining one's self (and community) may then flourish. Jonathan Lear, *Radical Hope: Ethics in the Face of Cultural Devastation* (Cambridge, MA: Harvard University Press, 2008).

11. Oguz Alyanak and Funda Ustek-Spilda, "Is It Over: On the Melancholy of Lost Hope," *Political and Legal Anthropology Review*, May 11, 2017, https://politicalandlegalanthro .org/2017/05/11/is-it-over-on-melancholy-of-lost-hope.

12. Jessica Greenberg, "Being and Doing Politics: Moral Ontologies and Ethical Ways of Knowing at the End of the Cold War," in *Impulse to Act: A New Anthropology of Resistance and Social Life*, ed. Othon Alexandrakis (Bloomington: Indiana University Press, 2016).

13. Katja Maria Vogt, "Imagining Good Future States: Hope and Truth in Plato's *Philebus*," in *Selfhood and the Soul*, chap. 2 (Oxford: Oxford University Press, 2017).

14. Friedrich Wilhelm Nietzsche, *Human, All Too Human: A Book for Free Spirits*, trans. R. J. Hollingdale (1878; Cambridge: Cambridge University Press, 1986).

15. Baruch Spinoza, *Ethics*, ed. and trans. G. H. R. Parkinson (Oxford: Oxford University Press, 2000), 215.

16. See David Harvey, *Spaces of Hope* (Berkeley: University of California Press, 2000).

17. Rebecca Solnit, *Hope in the Dark: Untold Histories, Wild Possibilities* (New York: Nation, 2004), xiv.

18. Solnit, xvii.

19. Ernst Bloch, *The Principle of Hope*, vol. 1, trans. Neville Plaice, Stephen Plaice, and Paul Knight (Boston: MIT Press, 1995), 4.

20. Didier Fassin, "The Endurance of Critique," *Anthropological Theory* 17, no. 1 (2017): 4–29, 10, https://doi.org/10.1177/1463499616688157.

21. Walter Benjamin, *Illuminations: Essays and Reflections* (New York: Random House, 2007).

22. Patricia Williams, *The Alchemy of Race and Rights* (Cambridge, MA: Harvard University Press, 1992), 154, 163–64.

23. APLA hosted its 2017 salon, "Speaking Justice to Power: Anthropology Responds to the New World Disorder," on November 30, 2017, during the AAA annual meeting in Washington, DC.

24. Jared Sexton, "Afropessimism: The Unclear Word," *Rhizomes: Cultural Studies in Emerging Knowledge* 26 (2016), www.rhizomes.net/issue29/sexton.html; Frank B. Wilderson, III, *Red, White and Black: Cinema and the Structure of U.S. Antagonisms* (Durham: Duke University Press, 2010).

25. Saidiya Hartman and Frank B. Wilderson, III, "The Position of the Unthought," *Qui Parle* 13, no. 2 (2003): 183–201.

26. Saidiya and Wilderson, 185.

27. Ghassan Hage, *Against Paranoid Nationalism: Searching for Hope in a Shrinking Society* (Annandale: Pluto, 2003).

28. Joshua Dienstag, *Pessimism: Philosophy, Ethic, Spirit* (Princeton: Princeton University Press, 2006), x.

29. Dienstag, x.

30. Indeed, as Perry Anderson has argued in *Considerations of Western Marxism* (New York: Verso, 1996), there was always a melancholic vein to Western Marxism. In contemporary scholarship, Ann Chectkovic, along with other members of the "public feelings" project, has pioneered a more embracing approach to what are often avoided in politics and schools of political thought as "negative feelings." Against Wendy Brown's critique of melancholy as emblematic of impasse in her critique of left-wing melancholia, Chetkovic ponders how melancholy itself can be productively recuperated for politics.

31. Didier Fassin, "On Resentment and Ressentiment: The Politics and Ethics of Moral Emotions," *Current Anthropology* 54, no. 3 (2013): 249–67, doi:10.1086/670390.

32. I am indebted to Ahmet Faik Kurtulmuş for his astute diagnosis of this asymmetry.

Bibliography

Alyanak, Oguz, and Funda Ustek-Spilda. "Is It Over: On the Melancholy of Lost Hope," *Political and Legal Anthropology Review*, May 11, 2017, https://politicalandlegalanthro.org/2017/05/11/is-it-over-on-melancholy-of-lost-hope.

Anderson, Perry. *Considerations of Western Marxism*. New York: Verso, 1996.

Aquinas, Thomas. *Thomas Aquinas on Faith, Hope, and Love*. Edited by Christopher Kaczor. Washington, DC: Sapientia Press, Ave Maria University, 2008.

Benjamin, Walter. *Illuminations: Essays and Reflections.* New York: Random House, 2007. Originally published in 1968.

Berlant, Lauren. *Cruel Optimism.* Durham: Duke University Press, 2011.

Bloch, Ernst. *The Principle of Hope.* Vol. 1. Translated by Neville Plaice, Stephen Plaice, and Paul Knight. Boston: MIT Press, 1995.

Brown, Wendy. "Resisting Left Melancholy." *boundary 2* 26, no. 3 (1999): 19–27.

Browne, Craig. "Hope, Critique, and Utopia." *Critical Horizons* 6, no. 1 (2005): 63–86.

Burton, Orisanmi. Association for Political and Legal Anthropology Salon. "Speaking Justice to Power: Anthropology Responds to the New World Disorder." November 30, 2017, AAA annual meeting, Washington, DC (with Laura Nader, Sara Schneiderman, Ayse Parla, organizers: Eric Harms, Jennifer Curtis, Heath Cabot).

Coates, Ta-Nehisi. *Between the World and Me.* New York: Random House, 2015.

Cvetkovic, Ann. *Depression: A Public Feeling.* Durham: Duke University Press, 2012.

Danzikyan, Yetvart. "Referandum Yok Hükümde Olmalı." *Agos: Armenian Biweekly*, April 20, 2017, www.agos.com.tr/tr/yazi/18295/referandum-yok-hukmunde-olmali.

Dienstag, Joshua. *Pessimism: Philosophy, Ethic, Spirit.* Princeton: Princeton University Press, 2006.

Eagleton, Terry. *Hope Without Optimism.* Charlottesville: University of Virginia Press, 2015.

Fassin, Didier. "The Endurance of Critique." *Anthropological Theory* 17, no. 1 (2017): 4–29, https://doi.org/10.1177/1463499616688157.

——. "On Resentment and Ressentiment: The Politics and Ethics of Moral Emotions." *Current Anthropology* 54, no. 3 (2013): 249–67, doi:10.1086/670390.

Gibson-Graham, J. K. *A Postcapitalist Politics.* Minneapolis: University of Minnesota Press, 2006.

Graeber, David. "Hope in Common," 2008, https://theanarchistlibrary.org/library/david -graeber-hope-in-common.

Greenberg, Jessica. "Being and Doing Politics: Moral Ontologies and Ethical Ways of Knowing at the End of the Cold War." In *Impulse to Act: A New Anthropology of Resistance and Social Life*, edited by Othon Alexandrakis. Bloomington: Indiana University Press, 2016.

Hage, Ghassan. *Against Paranoid Nationalism: Searching for Hope in a Shrinking Society.* Annandale: Pluto, 2003.

——. "On Stuckedness: Critique of Crisis and Crisis of Critique." In *Alter-Politics: Critical Anthropology and the Radical Imagination.* Melbourne: Melbourne University Press, 2003.

Hartman, Saidiya, and Frank B. Wilderson, III. "The Position of the Unthought." *Qui Parle* 13, no. 2 (2003): 183–201.

Harvey, David. *Spaces of Hope.* Berkeley: University of California Press, 2000.

Kivanc, Umit. "Ay Sizin Hala Umudunuz mu var cilik." *Yeşil Gazete*, May 6, 2017, https:// yesilgazete.org/blog/2017/05/06/ay-sizin-hala-umudunuz-mu-varcilik-umit-kivanc/.

Lear, Jonathan. *Radical Hope: Ethics in the Face of Cultural Devastation.* Cambridge, MA: Harvard University Press, 2008.

Mattingly, Cheryl. *The Paradox of Hope: Journeys Through a Clinical Borderland.* Berkeley: University of California Press, 2010.

Nietzsche, Friedrich Wilhelm. *Human, All Too Human: A Book for Free Spirits.* Translated by R. J. Hollingdale 1878; Cambridge: Cambridge University Press, 1986.

Redfield, Peter. *Life in Crisis: The Ethical Journey of Doctors Without Borders.* Berkeley: University of California Press, 2013.

Sexton, Jared. "Afropessimism: The Unclear Word." *Rhizomes: Cultural Studies in Emerging Knowledge* 26 (2016), www.rhizomes.net/issue29/sexton.html.

Solnit, Rebecca. *Hope in the Dark: Untold Histories, Wild Possibilities.* New York: Nation, 2004.

Spinoza, Baruch. *Ethics.* Edited and translated by G. H. R. Parkinson. Oxford: Oxford University Press, 2000 [1677].

Vogt, Katja Maria. "Imagining Good Future States: Hope and Truth in Plato's *Philebus.*" In *Selfhood and the Soul*, chap. 2. Oxford: Oxford University Press, 2017.

Wilderson, Frank B., III. *Red, White and Black: Cinema and the Structure of U.S. Antagonisms.* Durham: Duke University Press, 2010.

Williams, Patricia. *The Alchemy of Race and Rights.* Cambridge, MA: Harvard University Press, 1992.

CHAPTER 4

THE USEFULNESS OF UNCERTAIN CRITIQUE

PETER REDFIELD

Anthropology would plead in vain for that recognition to which its out-standing achievements in the realm of theory otherwise entitle it, if in this ailing and troubled world of ours, it did not first endeavor to prove its usefulness.

—Claude Lévi-Strauss

At the end of an essay on the enduring value of critical thinking, Didier Fassin quotes Claude Lévi-Strauss's observation about the need to demonstrate anthropology's utility beyond its theoretical prowess. Answering this ancestral challenge, Fassin writes: "There are many ways to understand what it is to be 'useful' for anthropologists and how to 'prove' it. In a world that is undoubtedly still 'ailing and troubled,' I would argue that the most crucial remains critique."[1] The allusion and response provide a satisfying conclusion to his meticulous argument, a nod to an unanticipated iconic source, while offering disciplinary validation.

But how exactly might critique prove useful? This abstract question arises constantly in mundane but eminently practical moments of recognition in academic life: seeking funding, filling out reports, presenting the value of critical thinking to undergraduates or donors. The contemporary university—particularly beyond its most elite and well-endowed branches—exhibits

diminishing patience for the intrinsic value of contemplation, let alone potentially awkward inquiries, even as it expects demonstrated productivity and
constant evidence of continued utility. What might skeptical and combative
modes of thinking accomplish beyond sowing disharmony or doubt (terms
unlikely to find favor within institutional frameworks)? One standard answer
in social science would be to reveal the politics of the situation, to call back into
question things otherwise hidden or obscured. However, this too translates
poorly in contexts where value derives from practical application, or where the
scale of transformation appears historically unlikely or utopian.

In what follows I pursue the question of usefulness through two examples,
both of which unsettle the certainty of critique and the ethnographic tradition
of anthropology, if in different ways. My first example derives from continuing
efforts by anthropologists and others to inject a greater dose of critical reflection
into the expanding behemoth known as "global health," and the varieties of
resistance encountered. In global health, both critique and ethnography struggle against a tide of moral certainty about the definitions of health, as well as
the hegemony of quantitative conceptions of truth-claims. In a worldview
defined by metrics and rigorous "studies"—evidence-based and increasingly
defined against an ideal model of the randomized controlled trial—traditions
of critical thinking struggle for traction, and ethnographic methods appear too
small, slow, and particularistic to be of value, producing mere "anecdotes." It
thus grows difficult to raise concerns in any authoritative way. At the same time,
the topic of health defies simple dismissal or categorical opposition, given that
most progressive critics ultimately *favor* improving human well-being. As with
human rights (see Karen Engle's essay in this volume), the would-be critic of
global health faces the challenge of navigating contradictory impulses, and balancing theory and practice.

My second example stems from recent interest in humanitarian forms of
design, and the proliferation of innovative devices to respond to basic human
needs in what are euphemistically glossed as "resource-poor settings." Like
health, innovation and attempts to ameliorate disaster and poverty prove complex topics for critical social science. However, in contrast to global health,
design centrally incorporates attenuated elements of critique and ethnography
into its reflexive routine, effectively systematizing an anecdotal approach
directly into its method. By emphasizing prototypes, feedback, and iteration,
design thinking invites commentary and user input, and typically pursues a
rapid form of fieldwork in its practice. It embraces stories and experiential life
at the level of individual users. At the same time, however, these commitments
remain attenuated and tightly bound to a specific goal. The result threatens to
tame both critique and ethnography into anodyne pursuits, with results that
fit onto a post-it note. Thus, the legacy of critique beloved by political theorists
and admired by engaged ethnographers can appear superseded and empty

through partial embrace as well as preemptive rejection. It is not simply enough to be partially included in a narrowly restrictive way. While design may offer different opportunities, it ultimately proves no more reassuring to critical thinking than global health.

How then to appear "useful" as a critical ethnographer, particularly when confronting both a troubled and ailing world and stridently instrumental forms of reason? In the third section of the essay I turn from the present moment to follow an attempt by the idiosyncratic twentieth-century pedagogue Abraham Flexner to justify the pursuit of "useless" knowledge. Although Flexner ultimately emphasizes the value of basic research in terms of its potential economic and technical impact, he does so by reminding his readers that action and effect do not always fall in a simple line, and that the temporality of insight proves hard to predict. His essay thus affirms the value of recognizing uncertainty. At a moment when modes of evidence and experimentation define common-sense conceptions of pragmatic worth, uncertainty may offer strategic possibilities to modify a frame of discussion, a mode of critique in a minor key. Critical responses to global health and humanitarian design, I suggest, should neither simply reject the question of use out of hand nor presume the historical privilege of detached elite traditions or an intoxicating, romantic dream of radical realignment that ignores material habits. Rather, the contemporary project of critique in actually existing institutions becomes one of continual translation, partial realignments, and agitation in modest forms with mundane questions. An essential move in this direction is to insist on widening conceptions of "use" beyond immediate utility—particularly the calculable sort incorporated into utilitarian valuation—and recognizing the modest but reliable value of remaining open to unexpected possibility. My goal in exploring the usefulness of critique thus is less to offer any definitive endorsement than to insist on the enduring value of reminders of uncertainty, particularly when engaging bureaucratic audit and demands for instrumental justification, or, more uncomfortably, our own ethical commitments and political desires.

Pursuing Critique in a Moral Empire of Evidence

My first case stems from an evolving series of engagements with a central front in the new university: the imperial rise of an institutional phenomenon known as "global health" and attempts by medical anthropologists to grapple with it. A phrase largely unknown just two decades ago now appears across an expanding research and education industrial complex. Displacing earlier formulations such as tropical medicine and international health, the new moniker now authorizes a range of projects and adorns multiple programs, particularly in the United States. This shifting vocabulary for a wider terrain of medical practice implies different semantic associations. The first two elements map reasonably well onto successive regimes of political vision: tropical medicine named a growing endeavor during the later phase of European empire, followed by the emergence of international health during decolonization and the postwar geopolitical system of nation-states, exemplified by the fledgling World Health Organization.[2] But where to fit global health?

As Fassin notes in another essay, global health is something of an obscure object in intellectual terms, tailor-made for the illumination of critique.[3] At first glance it might appear simply another variation on international health, a more fashionable upgrade, if you will, better suited for the times. However, on closer inspection certain features stand out: shifting epidemiological profiles; increasingly mobile populations; a growing focus on pharmaceuticals, transnational institutions, and forms of care; transnational social networks formed around infectious diseases, particularly HIV/AIDS; a heightened reliance on research trials and data analytics; and a moral emphasis on an imperative to "save lives" within a frame that emphasizes humanity rather than citizenship. Indeed, global health has proved sufficiently troubling enough to anthropologists and fellow travelers that its critical analysis has become a pressing project for a number of prominent figures in the field.[4] Here I will gesture toward this literature, underscoring findings that bear on the question of use.

On the one hand, the growth of global health transformed the subfield of medical anthropology, both intellectually and demographically. An increasing focus on biomedical forms of healing (as opposed to distinctively varied folk practices and alternative traditions), along with crusades inspired by HIV/AIDS and the prominence of charismatic figures such as Paul Farmer, has posed new problems related to suffering, and recast what had been a relatively specialized field into a moral project working to advance health equity. Medical topics appeared newly relevant, and politically significant. Swelling undergraduate enrollments offset declines elsewhere in the discipline, while an expanding array of nonacademic NGOs and research contractors such as RTI International ("An independent nonprofit research institute dedicated to improving the human condition")[5] implied employment prospects. Anthropology could speak to the moment, associate itself with a form of justice, and prove *useful*.

On the other hand, the emerging norms of global health proved more fraught for the qualitative end of the discipline, particularly its critical edge. The heightened role of nonstate actors in the health sector raises questions about accountability and sustainability, as well as its association with neoliberal economic theories and patterns of privatization. The technical focus and impersonal, homogenized logic of biomedical care often fail to recognize cultural difference within its moral project, overlooking the effects of its own paternalistic triumphalism.[6] Deeper structural roots of inequality and injustice remain untouched by the many earnest clinical and educational projects; medicine, after all, offers no direct treatment for poverty or the side effects of capitalist production, imperial expansion, or racism. Most frustratingly, at a methodological level global health provides relatively little room for slower, longer efforts to achieve understanding exemplified by the anthropological tradition of ethnography. Research in large, well-funded projects moves on a detached plane of quantified results, frequently indifferent to place. Good numbers have become essential to any argument, and the randomized controlled trial (RCT) increasingly serves as the gold standard for truth-claims.

The current emphasis on data is not simply a reanimation of distinctions between quantitative and qualitative approaches, or even divides between technocratic and social priorities. As Vincanne Adams points out, the expansion of the RCT experimental approach and an associated focus on constant measurement has not only reoriented health projects around data production, but also displaced older quantitative methods, such as simple accounting of vaccines or patient visits, familiar to a wide range of health systems and agendas.[7] Adjectives like "evidence-based," "experimental," and "cost-effective" have grown increasingly indispensable in efforts to sway both public and private policy. All anticipate the generation of quantitative data, presented in standardized modes ready to be translated across space and time. Nothing is truly established until tested—and then tested again. The emphasis on discrete, time-bounded studies effectively minimizes the significance of history or singular empirical encounters (dismissed as "anecdotal"), posing a challenge to all who would pursue older or slower forms of knowledge generation. Although the purveyors of stories and experience still play a role, they swim against a powerful current generated by an insatiable need for good numbers. A study without sufficient prospect of producing good data can face the possibility of abandonment, underscoring the blindness that can accompany the great power of statistical insight.

The result of these trends narrows the scope for critically minded social science in methodological terms. At the same time the moral force of claiming life-saving efficacy renders global health relatively immune from critical questioning, as those striving to advance a more critical vision frequently point out. João Biehl and Adriana Petryna note that "global health players can become impervious to critique as they identify emergencies, cite dire statistics, and act on their essential duty of promoting health in the name of 'humanitarian reason' or as an instrument of economic development, diplomacy or national security."[8] Health, after all, has grown into a quasi-sacred value. "How can anyone take a stand against health?" Jonathan Metzl asks at the outset of a critical collection titled *Against Health*. He hastens to reassure the reader that "anyone who feels ill before, during or after reading this book should seek immediate medical attention."[9] Moreover, he adds, no one should doubt that the contributors all adhere to a catechism of biomedical precepts: from the germ theory of disease and the importance of hand washing to penicillin, the promise of stem cell research, and the significance of social determinants to relative health. Rather, their target is the very moralism that resists critical attention, the manner in which it has grown difficult, if not impossible, to raise questions that challenge the frame of reverence surrounding well-being. Metzl's recognition of the rhetorical need to reassure the reader (reiterated by the various authors of subsequent chapters) reflects the tension inherent in undertaking such a project. For the faithful, such an approach would appear not just sacrilegious, but also a waste of time.

My own encounter with a similar tension occurred within a multiyear working-group project at my home institution that sought to pursue "critical conversations" around global health. The University of North Carolina boasts a strong profile in the health sciences, with one of the top schools of public health in the country, a lively department of social medicine in the medical school, and a dense network of institutions and corporations in the neighboring Research Triangle Park. Undergraduate enrollments in medical anthropology have surged in recent years, and the subspecialty represents an area of potential rapprochement between cultural and biological wings of the discipline. At the same time, the rise of service-learning initiatives has sent an ever-increasing number of students, undergraduate and medical alike, into global adventures, often with little preparation in language, history, or culture in the form favored by anthropology. For these reasons, a loose working group of faculty and graduate students organized around the theme of "Moral Economies of Medicine" thought it would be useful to devote ourselves to a collective investigation of all that global health had come to embody, inviting internal and external visitors to engage in episodic dialogue.

Even at the organizational stage of our conversation series, it quickly grew apparent that the term *critique* itself presented issues, as it held strongly negative connotations for some colleagues, especially those with close ties to practitioners and experimental method. To them, a "critical" form of global health would represent a purely negative enterprise, the form of its opposition contributing little to advance knowledge. As a consequence, the project required some delicate rhetorical positioning, a feat perceptively encapsulated by the title of one visitor's presentation: "Steps Toward a Constructively Critical Anthropology of Global Health."[10] To be constructively critical, of course, implies a shared faith in the validity of the larger endeavor. The fact that this needed articulation and emphasis at the very outset of a discussion revealed tension evoked by the very terms of critique itself: within this domain any critical thought should not stray beyond the parameters of shared value. Otherwise it might venture into a danger zone of conflict and potential rupture. At stake was the very possibility of conversation itself. Veering in a strongly critical direction threatened to alienate an important constituency, the one most directly invested in the current form of the global health enterprise and most suspicious of the value of agonistic thinking. Promising a positive contribution in advance helped allay these general fears enough to permit a discussion, one that could include critical points at a more specific level. At the same time the rhetorical ground remained fragile, and the scope of challenge circumscribed. To keep conversation alive required periodic assertions of faith.

Fassin proposes the threshold as the key site for critical engagement, particularly with quasi-sacred moral projects like humanitarianism and global health.[11] But it requires considerable art to stand on such a liminal space and not close a door, keeping a foot in the room. The practice of international research can entail navigating public secrets that a wide array of actors uphold.[12] The heroic truth of *parrhesia*—risky, undomesticated critique—unsurprisingly receives little support, as the residents of this particular cave have little interest in learning it might have a limit. Insights traveling the other direction, for example, ethnographic reports related to the experiences and frustrations of those directly affected by health projects, may enjoy greater institutional traction, but only inasmuch as they appear to speak to potential amelioration of the problem at hand. The risk here is disciplinary and not simply individual in scope. If anthropology (especially in its qualitative form) needs to justify itself through use, and medical anthropology is one of its most practical means to do so, then the art of presenting a "constructive" mode of critique for global health appears increasingly vital to maintaining a place in the university. The question then becomes what such an engagement might produce, limit, or sustain.

Downsizing Utopia, by Design

My second case derives from a longer research project on humanitarian design, looking both at the modest (yet wildly innovative) devices it produces to respond to basic human needs—e.g., water, sanitation, shelter—and the general mode of engagement it seeks. These devices, which embody small, realist utopian dreams, frequently and properly encounter critics who distrust their mix of hyperbolic claims and limited ambitions. They thus offer an additional opportunity to probe traditions of critique for their embedded assumptions about modernist social-technical forms and infrastructure alongside egalitarian principles. At the same time design, like global health, has created new conditions of potential nonacademic employment for anthropologists. Here, however, the methodological tradition of ethnography serves as the explicit asset, when reconfigured and applied to consumer research and product development. In an era when "design thinking" plays a significant role in Silicon Valley versions of capitalist enterprise and "innovation" has become a keyword in business discourse, design and ethnography lie entangled in a new and unexpectedly passionate embrace. In the right light, elements of anthropology can indeed appear useful, even essential.

The potential attraction of ethnography for design grows clearer after recognizing that it offers a method to examine users in the wild, exploring what people actually do with systems and things. Prominent strains of design theory now stress the importance of taking a "user-centered" or "human-centered" approach. Moreover, the predominance of prototyping means that potential solutions to any given problem circulate out of a laboratory and into a field, as it were, at a core stage of their development.[13] However fast-paced, contemporary design is an extended, reiterative practice that involves continued interaction with situated actors and everyday life worlds. It remains open-ended and open-minded in its attention to detail. Rather than strict control, it seeks imaginative input and invites continual response. Once adjusted to a different rhythm of engagement and specific, practical goals, ethnography can play a role in product production—or any other planned intervention. At the same time, design practitioners have adopted elements of language dear to anthropologists' hearts: participation, empathy, unbounded problems. Like any good match, they seem to listen.

Just as with global health, however, the new enthusiasm for design has also generated unease and acquired critical attention. Writing after a long career in the heart of California's innovation frontier beginning with Xerox PARC, Lucy Suchman calls for "less a reinvented anthropology as (or for) design than a critical anthropology of design."[14] A key aspect of such an endeavor would be to attend to Silicon Valley hubris ("The future arrives sooner here"), both identifying the limits of design practice and recognizing the degree to which its efficacy depends on things that exceed them. In extending this genealogical project Keith Murphy notes, "when design is considered comprehensively as form, action, and effect all at once, questions regarding the morality of social engagement tend to emerge."[15] Such is certainly the case when designers pursue projects intended to achieve social good.

Humanitarian design explicitly rejects a focus on products driven by raw consumerism, submitting even its aesthetic impulse to the goal of ameliorating the world. To quote a statement from an influential Smithsonian exhibit: "The *Design for the Other 90%* exhibition and book are intended to draw attention to a kind of design that is not particularly attractive, often limited in function, and extremely inexpensive. It also has the inherent ability to transform, and in some cases, actually save human lives."[16] Or in the words of another well-known advocate of the approach, humanitarian design seeks "beautiful solutions to ugly problems" with "small stories and the user as paramount."[17] The result has been a remarkable array of artifacts, many displaying impressive ingenuity and potential utility, if not always a firm attachment to actual use.[18]

For example, concern over the provision of clean drinking water has inspired an astonishing array of projects, none more likely to seduce academics than The Drinkable Book. A paper-based water filtration system, its pages infused with silver and copper nanoparticles that purify liquid poured through them, the book combines public health advocacy and practice into a single object. Developed by a young chemist named Theresa Dankovich as a handcrafted volume with educational messages printed on tear-out half pages, the initial prototype received considerable press attention in 2015 following field trials in Bangladesh, Ghana, Haiti, and South Africa. Dankovitch subsequently cofounded a company called Folia Water, which seeks to scale the concept into "the world's first water filter that costs pennies, not dollars."[19] Whether or not the effort ultimately achieves its goals, it typifies the approach taken by this genre of innovation, offering a small material fix for a large sociotechnical problem. Any greatness this book might achieve would stem from the most literal application of its pages, use value in the most immediate sense of the term.

Design practice represents a moving target for anthropological critique in that it emphasizes process, while embracing elements of an ethnographic approach. The importance of creating and field-testing prototypes reflects a core tenant of engaging with experience. Rather than reflecting a universal template (a common complaint of anthropologists with standardized technology), objects should fit into a given locale, incorporating input from everyday users. For example, consider the approach of a Norwegian-Ugandan venture called Design Without Borders to generate a modest health intervention in the form of an improved commodity. When seeking to create a "locally adapted" motorcycle helmet for *boda-boda* drivers, a popular but risky mode of transport through Kampala's chaotic traffic, the group defined both problem and proposed solution in situated terms. Observing patterns of behavior and interviewing potential customers, they focused on factors affecting demand and resistance to helmet wearing before coming up with a cheaper, lighter-weight alternative that featured better visibility and ventilation as well as styling. They exhibited the result at the New York iteration of *Design for the Other 90%* in 2011. Although promising and generating positive feedback, the concept remained stalled at a familiar barrier to actual use: production. A member of the team clarified the problem for me, while dusting off a prototype five years later in Kampala: "Design showcases ideas. But if you want to make useful things and not just beautiful things then you need to understand local manufacture. That's why so many designs end up in the drawer: it's not clear how to produce them at scale or with the right price point in mind. People are used to certain prices, and if you want to compete you have to match them. These are *local* and not global ideals (even if the operation is not simply local)."

The same logic, he added, applied to the organization itself. Originally a nonprofit institute, Design Without Borders now sought to become a commercial Ugandan enterprise that could survive on its own without Norwegian subsidies. The helmet was only one of an array of projects, which included the very effort to foster design itself as a form of development. This dream of localization also appeared stubbornly elusive, as, he noted ruefully, Ugandans were not accustomed to the idea of paying for design. But beyond the question of humanitarian designers' relative ability to cajole users to turn their products into daily habits rather than exotic curiosities, their activities raise other issues about the scope of intervention, and the parameters of imagination.

To explore this scale of vision, I turn to the other end of the humanitarian sector known as water and sanitation to delve a little deeper into technical detail. The Peepoo is a "personal single-use toilet" designed for use in poor urban settings and under emergency conditions. Created by a Swedish architect, and subsequently developed and distributed by a small Swedish social enterprise known as the Peepoople, it offers a modest upgrade to the plastic bag toilet common in urban slums, a simple means to dispose of human waste, neutralize its pathogens, and transform it into fertilizer, all in one go. Modeled on the "flying toilet" method of using plastic bags—an all-too-real phenomenon of urban slum life—the Peepoo consists of a double-layered sack of biodegradable plastic with a small pouch of urea inside. As explained on the Peepoople website, the addition of this common fertilizer effects a magical transformation: "When the urea in Peepoo comes into contact with feces or urine, a breakdown into ammonia and carbonate takes place, driven by enzymes that naturally occur in feces. As the urea is broken down, the pH-value of the material increases and sanitization begins. Disease-causing microorganisms, are inactivated after four weeks. Because dangerous bacteria are inactivated, there is no methane gas development from the feces inside Peepoo."[20]

Since the bag itself is fully biodegradable ("a mixture of aromatic co-polyesters and polylactic acid . . . with small additives of wax and lime") and urea is a nonhazardous chemical, the eventual result is a safe and valuable bundle of nutrients for farming. In a miracle of modern alchemy, the Peepoo transforms waste into a potential commodity. Accepting the addition of fluid or toilet paper, it can handle the product of both "washers" and "wipers" equally well.

However minimalist, it thus holds an eco-utopian promise of closing a circle even as it fulfills a humanitarian ambition of satisfying a vital human need. If incorporated into a microenterprise of fertilizer production, it might even offer possibilities for income, and a modest means for economic development.

At the same time, it requires neither water nor permanent space; it is fully mobile and can adjust to circumstances. At this conceptual level the Peepoo is not simply a better plastic bag, then, but a serious engagement with a set of nested problems. One might even see it as utopian, if in a highly attenuated and realist form. And yet, it also appears a pitiful substitute for a progressive vision. Would such a small dream suffice?

Like health, "innovation" arouses anthropological suspicion, without lending itself to complete opposition. This is particularly true in domains like humanitarian aid and international development, both pervaded by a sense of moral mission and haunted by a perception of continued failure of the current status quo. Who could be against trying some potential improvement, particularly when confronted with obvious and continuing suffering? Nonetheless, when novelty combines market enthusiasm with a narrow technical focus, it invites critical response from anthropologists and fellow travelers. As fetishized by contemporary capitalism and university administration, the possibility that something new might enter the world chronically promises more than it delivers, and overlooks counterbalancing concepts like maintenance and repair. As Tom Scott-Smith observes in a caustic appraisal, the current design mode of innovation overestimates the technical power of "tiny improvements wrapped in hyperbole," too often driven by the interests and imaginations of professionals and further distancing them from those they would help.[21] He worries about the humanitarian embrace of the private sector, and its further retreat from oppositional politics. If human suffering ultimately derives from the structural inequality of the global political economy, then it seems unlikely to be resolved by small fixes, particular ones that rely on profit motive to sustain them. The problem to which humanitarianism responds, Scott-Smith stresses, ultimately remains a question of politics.

Just as humanitarian design displays limited political ambitions, it rarely achieves major material impact. In material terms the Peepoo is unlikely to provide a durable "solution" to the problem of mass sanitation. The bag has struggled to find a stable niche beyond emergency applications and has confronted problems in balancing demand and production. Its main Kenyan project has always required subsidies and now depends on a Stockholm-based Christian NGO called International Aid Services (IAS), which has taken over the Peepoople's operations. Even if successfully brought to scale, its minimalism would horrify potential users who expect more than a plastic bag. Its own producers have seen it as a stopgap for a bad situation, "a meantime product" as one of them once described it to me. In keeping with Scott-Smith's observation, this minimal form of sanitation offers the tiniest of improvements imaginable, wrapped in a hyperbolically playful name. Generations of criticism about technological efforts to foster development would cast its purpose into doubt: this could be the smallest antipolitics machine.[22]

And yet the Peepoo stubbornly offers something more. Its limits and likely failure notwithstanding, it enlarges technical questions commonly disregarded by political critique: What to do about horrendous sanitation in global slums? The modernist impulse would be to sweep away political blockages and extend sewer lines, delivering the promise of hygiene equally to all. Anything short of that would fail to achieve justice. The flush toilet, however, requires a reliable and steady flow of water to operate, something not always simple to guarantee in many settings and subject to ecological doubt on a global scale. Ecological realism complicates modernist projects. In an era of increasing water shortages, then, what might a material politics of sanitation look like? Even with its stark minimalism and limited impact, this simple plastic bag thus opens a small but stubborn query for political thought, an arena of productive uncertainty: How much do our technopolitical expectations still derive from modernist infrastructure? If the modernizing project has indeed stalled, if ecology represents a legitimate concern, then how to craft alternative visions? What might justice look like if it started to attend to technical details?

Writing in an enthusiastic and laudatory vein, Bruno Latour celebrates precisely this capacity of design to reopen modernist assumptions:

> If it is true that the present historical situation is defined by a complete disconnect between two great alternative narratives—one of emancipation, detachment, modernization, progress and mastery, and the other, completely different, of attachment, precaution, entanglement, dependence and care—then the little word "design" could offer a very important touch stone for detecting where we are heading and how well modernism (and also postmodernism) has been faring. To put it more provocatively, I would argue that design is one of the terms that has replaced the word "revolution!" To say that everything has to be designed and redesigned (including nature), we imply something of the sort: "it will neither be revolutionized, nor will it be modernized."[23]

Design, in other words, is far from revolutionary in either mode or outlook. By eschewing rupture, agonistic struggle, and dramatic transformation, it ultimately describes an incremental project of responding to a given world rather than conjuring up a radically new one. Entangled by attachment, it seeks to be useful, in a most immediate way. Critique, by contrast, has often served as a reservoir of grander dreams, and consequently remains impatient with technical questions. When cast directly in this revolutionary tradition it foregrounds questions of justice over utility, assuming the possibility of progress through detachment and mastery. The dominant leftist lineage, after all, emerged in tandem with industrialization, and pursued a vision of progress wedded to mass infrastructure. For Latour, such residual modernism appears a fatal flaw. Without adopting all elements of his larger program, one can still recognize a point of tension for disciplines attached to the practice of critique. Dismissing modest, partial engagements, then, may not only complicate claims to usefulness, but also threaten to resurrect unexamined traces of past forms. At the same time, however, a key critical complaint remains: failing to recognize the narrow ambitions of such projects threatens to endorse a world of endless minor increments and limited utilitarian objects.

Questioning Use and the Value of Uncertainty

But do we even know with any certainty what is and is not useful? In October 1939, even as war engulfed Europe, Abraham Flexner published an untimely essay in *Harper's Magazine* with the provocative title "The Usefulness of Useless Knowledge." It seemed a singularly inauspicious moment to advocate for the free expression of knowledge and curiosity, championing "the fearless and irresponsible thinker."[24] Flexner, however, was not the sort of person to allow a mere world crisis to get in the way of a good vision. An idiosyncratic scholar and self-made educational authority, he had directed the establishment of the Institute for Advanced Study and overseen its early growth. The topic of useless knowledge was not new to him; indeed, he had labored over the same theme for some time, both in print and in institutional practice.

Flexner's essay examines the question of utility from two points of view, which he labels "scientific" and "humanistic or spiritual." The bulk of the text focuses on examples in which insights from basic science eventually prove of practical worth, recalling, for example, that the invention of the radio depended on earlier work in electromagnetism, which had never anticipated such an application. This general point about basic science would grow all the more convincing with the wartime advent of nuclear weapons, developed through what had previously appeared as abstract research in theoretical physics. In this sense the essay's title might well have been "The Potential Usefulness of Knowledge Without Immediate Purpose." However, Flexner gestures beyond this utilitarian frame of application: "I am not for a moment suggesting that everything that goes on in laboratories will ultimately turn to some unexpected practical use or that an ultimate practical use is its actual justification. Much more am I pleading for the abolition of the word 'use,' and for the freeing of the human spirit."[25] A generous reading of his claim, along with the surrounding essay, would underscore its deeper recognition of uncertainty relative to knowledge. One never fully knows where any insight might lead, or what any discovery might do, prior to investigation. The very term *use* itself implies a preordained and fixed field of function, a given understanding of what will count as a purpose or need. By putting the designation of "uselessness" into question, Flexner effectively unsettles any easy assumption of use value, and with it questions of utility.

Flexner himself was an unlikely historical figure, whose path to prominence would appear to exemplify the uncertain and unpredictable trajectory he wished to foreground. Although now largely forgotten outside of medical pedagogy, he unexpectedly proved remarkably influential in that domain. The son of an immigrant Jewish peddler in Kentucky, he managed to turn himself into a pre-eminent expert of higher education, thanks in part to critical assistance from an older brother (who sent him to Johns Hopkins) and then from his wife (a former pupil who became a successful playwright and socialite), producing a series of works on pedagogy. The most vital of these took the form of a critical survey of medical education in the United States and Canada. Commissioned by the Carnegie Foundation, the "Flexner Report" (as it informally came to be known) would prove a watershed document leading to significant moderniza-tion, regulation, and reform in medical training. In many respects it deserves ancestral recognition in the establishment of biomedical norms in the back-ground of global health. It was undeniably useful in the highest degree—few "studies" have enjoyed such sweeping influence. However, its effects proved a double-edged sword: by emphasizing scientific training and advocating the closure of poorly resourced and ill-equipped institutions, the report limited training opportunities for African American physicians. Although relatively accepting of women's equality, Flexner readily subscribed to racial stereotypes and envisioned a segregated future. Thus this tireless advocate of curiosity also proved an enthusiastic participant in structural racism, to apply the judgment of one retrospective review.[26] Being useful also carries uncertain dangers, the possibility of unintended consequences as well as planned outcomes. Even an avowed critic of simplistic conceptions of practicality—which Flexner surely saw himself to be (his first book was titled *The American College: A Criticism*)—can eagerly launch an effective crusade with profound effects and varied results.

Complications and all, Flexner's thought and biography provide a poten-tial opening for a strategic response to the question of usefulness and a note of warning about utilitarian demands. Although it appears unlikely that any frontal assault on the concept of use would have much effect at this historical moment, suffused by constant evaluation and measures of impact, smaller ques-tions that call attention to the uncertainty surrounding it might offer open-ings and opportunities. Like the history of science, the ethnographic tradition lends itself to following loose ends, and tugging on threads that might unravel. Precisely where critique grows difficult it also becomes most essential; confront-ing domains like global health or humanitarian design may entail new strate-gies for engagement and disciplinary survival. Rather than facing irrelevance or co-optation, critical anthropology might reimagine itself as uncertainly use-ful, and pursue a project of being usefully uncertain.

Flexner's own legacy recalls the significance of contingency and unintended consequences for particular historical threads. As the author of the famous Carnegie report, he became a leading expert on medical education, without possessing any formal degree or the slightest conventional qualification. When approached by Louis Bamberger and Caroline Bamberger Fuld to help found a medical school in New Jersey, he convinced them to fund the Institute for Advanced Study instead. A thoroughly elitist, Utopian project of academic privilege, it unexpectedly benefited from the rise of fascism in Europe, which generated a wave of prominent European intellectuals suddenly eager to emigrate. Without initially intending to, the institute ended up sheltering a generation of refugee scholars. And following several abortive attempts, four decades later it became home to the School of Social Science, which would nurture projects of critical theory, including this volume.

* * *

If the world looked both "ailing and troubled" and concerned with use to Lévi-Strauss six decades ago, it only seems more so now. The pressure to appear useful pervades all aspects of university self-presentation and accounting, even as it permeates the atmosphere of secondary schools. Many initiatives—flush with a modernizing, revolutionary zeal akin to that of Flexner's famous report— seek to upend education in an effort to realign it with new technologies and market needs. By contrast his later essay in defense of curiosity claims fewer heirs. For all the rhetorical commitment to "risk-taking" in innovation and entrepreneurship, perceptions of what counts as practical have narrowed such that only knowledge promising direct translation into commercial purpose signifies certain value. Beyond elite settings, sustained by private endowments, the liberal tradition that once underwrote critical thinking as a hallmark of educational attainment as well as class distinction continues to erode. The intellectual disciplines of classic humanities and nonremunerative basic sciences appear less pragmatic, and hence less viable, to a generation of funders, administrators, and students alike. This perspective may be far from new, but has become newly all-encompassing, particularly at public institutions, powered by a heightened capacity for monitoring and measurement and reinforced by widespread perceptions of economic precarity.[27]

How might critique fit into such an anxiously hyperutilitarian ethos? And conversely, what might attention to use reveal about critique? Neither question proves simple. However capacious and vague a concept, usefulness permits no absolute opposition for anyone wishing to engage the world of experience to discernable effect. Like efficiency, it describes a technical good—a relational quality that acquires specific meaning within given parameters, such as the proverbial (or Heideggerian) hammer and nail. At the same time, the demand to demonstrate use value in given terms, narrowly defined and known beforehand, moves it from specific, defined engagements into abstraction. Once there it quickly transmutes into a discursive assumption, easily deployed to restrict other avenues of inquiry and perpetuate a given order. The question of use, then, produces something of a double bind for critique, with contradictory imperatives. To echo Karen Engle's reprise of Gayatri Spivak's phrase in this volume, being useful is both something a would-be critic "cannot not want"—at least in the long run—and also something to arouse continuing suspicion, especially when the terms of use are dictated in advance. The real question always remains "useful to *what end*?"

In pursing this inquiry, I have focused on trends in anthropology, both as a disciplinary thread of connection to my chosen references and as an illuminating example within the frame of academia, the home of institutionalized forms of critique. Although far from the only venue for critical impulse, and ever circumscribed by institutional pressures, the university has intermittently served as a space for reflection, and hence a repository of possibility for critical interrogation. In the current conjuncture, anthropology finds itself looking both utterly useless and potentially useful, depending on venue and form. When focused on its classic, open-ended quest to catalogue and analyze human difference it seems distinctly antiquarian and impractical. Attached to projects of health interventions and innovative product design, however, it can appear relatively sensible and potentially levelheaded. The rise of global health has reoriented one possibility for medical inflections of the discipline, provided any critical impulse remains properly constructive. The emergence of design likewise offers practical opportunities for ethnographic engagement, as long as it accepts a foreshortened, application-driven mode of practice. Both hold potential dangers as well as opportunities. A novice anthropologist thus faces a wider array of options to appear useful and sporadically achieve effects than, say, a political theorist awaiting the total relevance of a revolutionary moment. And here might lie a possibility for thinking critically along the edges of critique.

Use assumes a known end point, a defining purpose against which to measure any given activity. As Flexner astutely observes in his essay, however, such end points often take shape retroactively: the invention of the radio recasts the physics of electromagnetism as a practical endeavor, but only after the fact. Other end points remain abstract, and sometimes phantom goals, such as a utopian society or a condition of economic stability. Both "health" and "innovation"—the end points of examples given—describe open-ended pursuits, hard to oppose in principle but infinitely questionable in practice. Writing with regard to global health, and the difficulties of adjusting ethnographic methods to its expectations, Stacy Pigg strikes a similar note to Flexner.[28] She suggests that an overemphasis on "doing" can lead to a false sense of certainty about how decisions unfold in practice, rushing to achieve predetermined goals. She advocates ethnographic "sitting" as an alternative mode of engagement, one that attends to small, awkward stories and offers the possibility of critical reflection about the political stakes embedded in defined goals. This reflection may fail to achieve a direct impact on policy, being predictably ignored in the urgency to act. But it can nonetheless serve as a reminder of the ambiguity of use and goals, a modest site of exchange for alternative possibilities. Anthropology's weakness could also prove its potential strength: a fluid, open-ended approach can reopen endpoints to their proper state of uncertainty. If enrollment into practical endeavors such as global health and product design threatens to narrow ethnographic engagement into a utilitarian channel, it may conversely, even inadvertently, reveal unexpected eddies and leaks in the very channel itself.

The modest vision of uncertain critique I sketch here remains focused on life within institutions, the world of those who might record, investigate, or interpret, or even coproduce with others beyond, but remain attached to professionalized forms of knowledge. It interprets "construction" in a material sense, recognizing engagement and alteration as a long and slow endeavor, rather than a certain quest for defining moments of rupture. In this sense it combines the spirit of dissatisfaction associated with revolution with a mode of intervention borrowed from design. That is, it refuses to simply accept what is given, but also never forgets to keep the question open, time and time again. It advocates continued curiosity about how to actually achieve any given project, anticipating side effects, and tries to be useful in situated ways even as it resists the apotheosis of usefulness as its own end. Such uncertain critique may not always be constructive in the sense of being complacently cheerful, but it need not be intentionally destructive either, or even overtly confrontational or agonistic in its approach. Rather, it remains rigorously open to the unexpected, and the possibility of surprise. From this perspective critique may have many modes, not all of which need announce themselves as such. At certain moments innocent questions, patient inquiries, and modest interventions may all prove *useful* in a larger, more indeterminate sense of prying open efforts to foreclose thought and introducing sufficient doubt to allow for discussion. In practical terms, this means telling smaller stories, the ones that never quite fit, retaining awkward numbers, preserving puzzling bits of evidence—the elements that may not define a situation, but leave it slightly unsettled. Anthropology is good at all these things. As its practitioners struggle to appear instrumentally useful in institutional terms, they should not forget the critical potential of uncertainty. If Fassin is correct in identifying the threshold as a liminal space of opportunity, and a natural habitat for critical ethnography, then positioning is all important. To extend the metaphor beyond caves: finding a threshold requires keeping some door ajar.

Notes

1. Didier Fassin, "The Endurance of Critique," *Anthropological Theory* 17, no. 1 (March 2017): 23.
2. For a revealing snapshot of this shifting vocabulary in English, compare the frequency of the terms *global health* vs. *international health* vs. *tropical medicine* between 1900 and 2008 in Google Books Ngram Viewer.
3. Didier Fassin, "The Obscure Object of Global Health," in *Medical Anthropology at the Intersections: Histories, Activisms, and Futures*, ed. Marcia Inhorn and Emily Wentzell, 95–115. Durham: Duke University Press, 2012.
4. See, e.g., Vincanne Adams, ed., *Metrics: What Counts in Global Health* (Durham: Duke University Press, 2016); and João Biehl and Adriana Petryna, eds., *When People Come First: Critical Studies in Global Health* (Princeton: Princeton University Press, 2013).
5. "About RTI," www.rti.org/about-us.
6. See Lisa Stevenson, *Life Beside Itself: Imagining Care in the Canadian Arctic* (Berkeley: University of California Press, 2014) on anonymous care, and also Johanna Crane, *Scrambling for Africa AIDS, Expertise, and the Rise of American Global Health Science* (Ithaca: Cornell University Press, 2013).
7. Vincanne Adams, "Metrics of the Global Sovereign: Numbers and Stories in Global Health," in *Metrics: What Counts in Global Health*, ed. Vincanne Adams, 19–54 (Durham: Duke University Press, 2016), 32, 36.
8. João Biehl and Adriana Petryna, "Critical Global Health," in *When People Come First: Critical Studies in Global Health*, ed. João Biehl and Adriana Petryna (Princeton: Princeton University Press, 2013), 7.
9. Jonathan Metzl, "Introduction," in *Against Health: How Health Became the New Morality*, ed. Jonathan Metzl and Anna Kirkland (New York: New York University Press, 2010), 1.
10. Presentation by Peter Brown to UNC Moral Economies of Medicine Working Group, February 2015.
11. Didier Fassin, "The Endurance of Critique," *Anthropological Theory* 17, no.1 (March 2017): 24. For a critical reflection on global health that explicitly adopts the Christian moral framework of sins and virtues, see Catherine Panter-Brick, Mark Eggerman, and Mark Tomlinson, "How Might Global Health Master Deadly Sins and Strive for Greater Virtues?," *Global Health Action* 7, no. 1 (March 2014).
12. P. Wenzel Geissler, "Public Secrets in Public Health: Knowing Not to Know While Making Scientific Knowledge," *American Ethnologist* 40, no. 1 (February 2013): 13–34.
13. See Anke Schwittay and Paul Braund, "Iterate, Experiment, Prototype," *Limn* 9 (2018), https://limn.it/iterate-experiment-prototype/?doing_wp_cron=1519006854.11757397 65167236328125 for cogent summary.
14. Lucy Suchman, "Anthropological Relocations and the Limits of Design," *Annual Review of Anthropology* 40 (2011): 3.
15. Keith Murphy, "Design and Anthropology," *Annual Review of Anthropology* 45 (2016): 440.
16. Barbara Bloemink, "Foreword," in *Design for the Other 90%* (New York: Cooper-Hewitt, Smithsonian Institution, 2007), 5.
17. Emily Pilloton, "Introduction: Design Can Change the World," in *Design Revolution: 100 Products That Are Changing Peoples Lives* (London: Thames and Hudson, 2008), 45–46.
18. When brought to scale, many visions falter, e.g., the PlayPump or One Laptop per Child. See Michael Hobbes, "Stop Trying to Save the World: Big Ideas Are Destroying

Development," *New Republic*, November 17, 2014, https://newrepublic.com/article/120178/problem-international-development-and-plan-fix-it.

19. See the home page of Folia Water, www.foliawater.com. See also the NPR Goats and Soda blog presentation of the Drinkable Book, August 19, 2015: www.npr.org/sections/goatsandsoda/2015/08/19/432854450/this-is-one-book-that-you-want-to-get-all-wet.

20. Peepoople Frequently Asked Questions, www.peepoople.com/information/faq/.

21. Tom Scott-Smith, "Humanitarian Neophilia: The 'Innovation Turn' and Its Implications," *Third World Quarterly* 37, no. 12 (May 2016): 2239–40.

22. James Freguson, *The Anti-Politics Machine: "Development," Depoliticization and Bureaucratic Power in Lesotho* (Cambridge: Cambridge University Press, 1990).

23. Bruno Latour, "A Cautious Prometheus? A Few Steps Toward a Philosophy of Design (with Special Attention to Peter Sloterdijk)," September 3, 2008, in *Proceedings of the 2008 Annual International Conference of the Design History Society*, 2.

24. Abraham Flexner, *The Usefulness of Useless Knowledge* (Princeton: Princeton University Press, 2017), 78.

25. Flexner, *The Usefulness of Useless Knowledge*, 71.

26. Ann Steinecke and Charles Terrell, "Progress for Whose Future? The Impact of the Flexner Report on Medical Education for Racial and Ethnic Minority Physicians in the United States," *Academic Medicine* 85, no. 2 (February 2010): 236–45; Abraham Flexner, "Medical Education in the United States and Canada: A Report to the Carnegie Foundation for the Advancement of Teaching," Carnegie Foundation Archive online document.

27. See, e.g., Max Weber's famous appraisal of the American academy in 1919: Max, Weber, "Science as a Vocation," in *From Max Weber: Essays in Sociology*, ed. H. H. Gerth and C. Wright Mills, 129–56 (New York: Oxford University Press, 1946); and Anne Allison's commentary regarding the contemporary sense of a precarious present. Anne Allison, "Precarity: Commentary by Anne Allison," Curated Collections, *Cultural Anthropology* website, September 13, 2016, https://culanth.org/curated_collections/21-precarity/discussions/26-precarity-commentary-by-anne-allison.

28. Stacy Leigh Pigg, "On Sitting and Doing: Ethnography as Action in Global Health," *Social Science and Medicine* 99 (December 2013): 127–34.

Bibliography

Adams, Vincanne. "Metrics of the Global Sovereign: Numbers and Stories in Global Health." In *Metrics: What Counts in Global Health*, edited by Vincanne Adams, 19–54. Durham: Duke University Press, 2016.

Allison, Anne. "Precarity: Commentary by Anne Allison," Curated Collections, *Cultural Anthropology* website, September 13, 2016, https://culanth.org/curated_collections/21-precarity/discussions/26-precarity-commentary-by-anne-allison.

Biehl, João, and Adriana Petryna. "Critical Global Health." In *When People Come First: Critical Studies in Global Health*, edited by João Biehl and Adriana Petryna, 1–20. Princeton: Princeton University Press, 2013.

Bloemink, Barbara. "Foreword." In *Design for the Other 90%*, 5–8. New York: Cooper-Hewitt, Smithsonian Institution, 2007.

Crane, Johanna. *Scrambling for Africa AIDS, Expertise, and the Rise of American Global Health Science*. Ithaca: Cornell University Press, 2013.

Fassin, Didier. "The Endurance of Critique." *Anthropological Theory* 17, no. 1 (March 2017): 1–26.

——. "The Obscure Object of Global Health." In *Medical Anthropology at the Intersections: Histories, Activisms, and Futures,* edited by Marcia Inhorn and Emily Wentzell, 95–115. Durham: Duke University Press, 2012.

Ferguson, James. *The Anti-Politics Machine: "Development," Depoliticization and Bureaucratic Power in Lesotho.* Cambridge: Cambridge University Press, 1990.

Flexner, Abraham. "Medical Education in the United States and Canada: A Report to the Carnegie Foundation for the Advancement of Teaching." Carnegie Foundation Archive online document, 1910, http://archive.carnegiefoundation.org/pdfs/elibrary/Carnegie _Flexner_Report.pdf.

——. *The Usefulness of Useless Knowledge.* With companion essay by Robbert Dijkgraaf. Princeton: Princeton University Press, 2017.

Geissler, P. Wenzel. "Public Secrets in Public Health: Knowing Not to Know While Making Scientific Knowledge." *American Ethnologist* 40, no. 1 (February 2013): 13–34.

Hobbes, Michael. "Stop Trying to Save the World: Big Ideas Are Destroying Development." *New Republic,* November 17, 2014, https://newrepublic.com/article/120178/problem -international-development-and-plan-fix-it.

Latour, Bruno. "A Cautious Prometheus? A Few Steps Toward a Philosophy of Design (with Special Attention to Peter Sloterdijk)." September 3, 2008, in *Proceedings of the 2008 Annual International Conference of the Design History Society,* 1–13, www.bruno-latour .fr/sites/default/files/112-DESIGN-CORNWALL-GB.pdf.

Metzl, Jonathan. "Introduction." In *Against Health: How Health Became the New Morality,* edited by Jonathan Metzl and Anna Kirkland, 1–11. New York: New York University Press, 2010.

Murphy, Keith. "Design and Anthropology." *Annual Review of Anthropology* 45 (2016): 433–49.

Panter-Brick, Catherine, Mark Eggerman, and Mark Tomlinson. "How Might Global Health Master Deadly Sins and Strive for Greater Virtues?" *Global Health Action* 7, no. 1 (March 2014): 23411, http://dx.doi.org/10.3402/gha.v7.23411.

Pigg, Stacy Leigh. "On Sitting and Doing: Ethnography as Action in Global Health." *Social Science and Medicine* 99 (December 2013): 127–13.

Pilloton, Emily. "Introduction: Design Can Change the World." In *Design Revolution: 100 Products That Are Changing Peoples Lives,* 10–47. London: Thames and Hudson, 2008.

Schwittay, Anke, and Paul Braund. "Iterate, Experiment, Prototype." *Limn* 9 (2018), https: //limn.it/iterate-experiment-prototype/?doing_wp_cron=1519006854.1175739765167236 328125.

Scott-Smith, Tom. "Humanitarian Neophilia: The 'Innovation Turn' and Its Implications." *Third World Quarterly* 37, no. 12 (May 2016): 2229–51.

Steinecke, Ann, and Charles Terrell. "Progress for Whose Future? The Impact of the Flexner Report on Medical Education for Racial and Ethnic Minority Physicians in the United States." *Academic Medicine* 85, no. 2 (February 2010): 236–45.

Stevenson, Lisa. *Life Beside Itself: Imagining Care in the Canadian Arctic.* Berkeley: University of California Press, 2014.

Suchman, Lucy. "Anthropological Relocations and the Limits of Design." *Annual Review of Anthropology* 40 (2011): 1–18.

Weber, Max. "Science as a Vocation." In *From Max Weber: Essays in Sociology,* edited by H. H. Gerth and C. Wright Mills, 129–56. New York: Oxford University Press.

CHAPTER 5

HUMAN RIGHTS CONSCIOUSNESS AND CRITIQUE

KAREN ENGLE

It is difficult to name a single instance in which critical theory has killed off a progressive political project. Critical theory is not what makes progressive political projects fail; at worst it might give them bad conscience, at best it renews their imaginative reach and vigor.

—Wendy Brown

For some time now, critical scholars and human rights advocates alike have approached human rights not only as a progressive political project, but as one in need of protection from critique. When critical legal theorists in the United States challenged rights discourse in the 1980s, for example, they largely gave human rights a pass. The few scholars who started to bring insights of critical legal theory to human rights law and discourse during that time were generally ignored by human rights scholars and advocates (two groups that overlapped a good deal in those days), who apparently saw the critiques as unworthy of engagement.

Nonetheless, the number of critical approaches to human rights has grown over time, and some critiques have taken hold in both the scholarly discourse about and the practice of human rights. Some critiques have even been mainstreamed within international and regional human rights institutions. For example, early radical feminists pointed to the exclusive attention of human rights to acts committed by states, arguing that human rights law and discourse were structurally biased against women in their exclusion of the so-called private sphere, where they claimed women were most likely to experience unequal treatment and violence because of their gender. After initial significant resistance, mainstream international human rights advocacy absorbed the critique in a remarkably short time, calling for states to be held accountable for their inaction on certain rights violations by nonstate actors. Institutions and legal doctrine followed suit, acknowledging the duty of states, as a matter of human rights law, to investigate, prosecute, and punish those nonstate actors, as part of what I have elsewhere called the "turn to criminal law in human rights."[1]

While feminists, including some who identify as radical feminists, continue to criticize human rights law and discourse, they rarely engage in the type of structural critique with which many began. Indeed, human rights law, including its reliance on criminal enforcement, is today a dominant vehicle for achieving many feminist goals. Thus, like many liberal human rights advocates, feminists challenging human rights are likely to call for broader application or improved enforcement of law that they generally support.

I am primarily interested here in critiques of human rights that I see as in line with those of the early radical feminists. They come from the perspective that Wendy Brown and Janet Halley have identified as "the state of the art of 'left internal critique' focused on law reform."[2] For Brown and Halley, "a left political orientation begins with a critique—not necessarily a rejection—of liberalism itself as well as an explicit focus on the *social* powers producing and stratifying subjects that liberalism largely ignores."[3] Regarding rights, they note that while leftists do not "*necessarily* oppose rights . . . they are wary of liberalism's generally more sanguine equations between rights and liberty, equal rights and equality."[4] A great deal of recent critical scholarship on human rights expresses that wariness.

Critical human rights scholarship has become more common, more tolerated, and even more heeded in the twenty-first century than in earlier eras. Nevertheless, a certain reticence can be found in much of the left critical work on human rights. Authors are often reluctant to reject liberalism or rights outright, as Brown and Halley suggest is the case more generally among left internal critics. More importantly for my purposes, they often betray a concern that critique might destroy the human rights project or perhaps, more aptly, be seen as attempting to destroy it. They manage that concern in a variety of ways. I offer here a phenomenological account of some of those ways, which include different couplings of belief in and doubt about both human rights and the critique of them.

I begin by drawing upon some of my own experiences as a left critical scholar, building upon concerns expressed to me about my own work, to illustrate the strength of the fear among human rights scholars and advocates that critique poses a threat to a progressive political project. Next, I identify four ways in which left critical human rights scholars and activists have internalized, or attempted to manage, this perceived threat. These are (1) professing a commitment to human rights, even while critiquing them; (2) confessing an inability to let go of rights as something that one "cannot not want"; (3) accepting and perpetuating a split between critique and advocacy; and (4) absorbing and responding to critique as part of the human rights advocacy profession. Each of these approaches represents different—if overlapping—manifestations of rights consciousness in contemporary international society. I aim to gain a better understanding of that consciousness by exploring the ways in which these four approaches have been deployed.

Finally, I entertain a conundrum—namely that, despite all the concern about protecting human rights from critique and all the effort expended to do so, human rights discourse is no longer necessarily the lingua franca of emancipatory political struggles. Not only have other discourses emerged to address issues like economic inequality and climate change, but human rights language itself is often deployed—and, some would say, co-opted—by powerful state and nonstate entities for antiemancipatory ends. Further, among the resurgence of right-wing populism in many parts of the world, human rights are sometimes outwardly repudiated. How should we think about the future of critique in a world that has signaled to many, albeit for different reasons, the "end" of human rights?

Fear of Killing a Progressive Political Project

In October 2009, I received an email from a European colleague, inviting me to participate in a conference on the Universal Declaration on the Rights of Indigenous Peoples (UNDRIP) of 2007. The conference would be the starting point of the drafting of a collaborative commentary on UNDRIP. Eager to be involved, I said yes and sent him a copy of the introduction to my then-soon-to-be-published book on indigenous rights. In the book, I caution indigenous rights advocates not to build their legal and political strategies around a human right to culture or around other rights, such as the right to property, that rely on essentialized conceptions of culture. Though such strategies have resulted in some victories for some groups, particularly in Latin America, I argue, they set an impossibly high bar for most indigenous groups to achieve recognition, much less control, of their heritage, land, and economic development.

Sending my colleague the introduction turned out to be a mistake. Shortly thereafter, I received the following email from him:

> Thanks, Karen for your interesting introduction. Your critique is a foundational one—the effort to protect peoples is seen as emanating from a social movement

propelled by a supposedly ill-designed or potentially even dishonest "strategic essentialism." As with any good critical scholar, you have a good time proving, and probably you are correct, that indigenous peoples are not all wedded to the traditional ways of life as they are made out to be. Your work remains at that level of critical deconstruction. . . . [The conference] is designed to provide a commentary to the 2007 Declaration and to cement, so to say, the very fragile architecture of rights that after so many years the UN has been able to achieve. So, let us postpone this debate to another forum.

The other forum he proposed was a scholarly conference, which—to his credit—he did follow up on. Yet, having my work labeled appropriate for theory, but not for politics, was frustrating. Calling it merely "critical deconstruction" functioned to separate it from the work of indigenous rights activists that I engage with in the book and deny the extent to which many of them were also unhappy with the compromises wrought by the UNDRIP.

The crux of the message was its concern with the "fragile architecture" of the UNDRIP. It was because it was fragile that we should "cement" it. Not only was I failing to cement it, I was arguably making it more fragile by suggesting that "indigenous peoples are not all wedded to the traditional ways of life as they are made out to be." I apparently showed that well, since he conceded "probably you are correct," but perhaps I showed it too well. And I definitely had too good of a time doing it, which is what one who is a "good critical scholar" does.

Importantly, my colleague did not claim I was wrong, even about an argument I was not making—that there was ill will, or "potentially even dishonest 'strategic essentialism.'" Rather, the problem for him was that I might be right. He feared that by articulating a compelling critique, I would only make matters worse. In effect, my colleague was asking me to heed Bruno Latour's call for a new type of critic, "not the one who lifts the rugs from under the feet of naïve believers" but "the one for whom, if something is constructed, then it means it is fragile and thus in need of care and caution."[5]

After my book was published in 2010,[6] I had a similar encounter, this time about the potential effects of the scholarly intervention. I was invited to make a presentation on it to a law faculty with a significant number of critical scholars (not in the United States). The person who invited me was also a respondent at the talk, and she spoke favorably about the book in public. Over a couple of drinks after the talk, however, this same scholar confessed deep discomfort with my position, or perhaps her attraction to it. She was convinced by it, on one level, she insisted. But "I'm just not ready to see indigenous people die," she told me. (She did say "people," not "peoples.") When I asked why she thought my book would lead to such dire consequences, she replied that I was taking away the only legal avenue available to indigenous peoples and individuals. She might have even said that I was pulling the rug out from under them.

I responded by saying that I thought she had imbued my work with a striking amount of power. I also reminded her that the legal avenue she was concerned about preserving was not immune to manipulation and disappointment. But I added that, even were my work to be taken seriously—in scholarship, advocacy, or policy—my hope was that it would lead advocates to consider the possible long-term distributive effects of their advocacy. Doing so might lead to better, more creative legal and political avenues for a larger group of people and peoples. She replied that she was not sure she was willing to wait for that result.

I do not think that either of my interlocutors would see themselves as critical legal scholars (though the second seemed more tempted than the first). They might identify as "progressive," but, for the most part, they are committed to liberal law reform, which they believe my work threatens. Nevertheless, neither stated that my position (however understood) was necessarily wrong. It was just not something they would be willing to pursue in their own scholarship or advocacy.

In the anecdotes I just recounted, my thought was respected. It was the *expression* of it, at least in particular settings, that was suspect. In an earlier day, the critical thought about human rights was itself seen as the threat. Perhaps the first critical scholarship on the contemporary human rights movement was David Kennedy's article "Spring Break," published in 1985, about his participation in a human rights mission sponsored by a number of scientific and medical associations.[7] Kennedy, along with a medical doctor and a writer, went to Uruguay to visit medical students who were being held as political prisoners, in what turned out to be the final months of a military dictatorship. The mission's stated aim was to assess the student prisoners' health.

Kennedy published a keen and edgy self-reflective narrative that focused largely on the team's personal and professional encounters with both male and female prisoners, as well as with prison and other governmental officials. It both considered and demonstrated the difficulty of defining boundaries between the personal and the professional. It also called into question the human rights movement's ability to maintain the neutral, or antipolitical, stance it claimed.

Today, narrative accounts of human rights and humanitarian enterprises, as well as other more traditional scholarly critiques of human rights law and discourse, are plentiful. But in 1985, Kennedy's account was unique and provocative. Indeed, the *Harvard Law Review* initially agreed to publish the piece, but then became reluctant because, as Kennedy later put it, "there was something unseemly about uncertainty in the face of suffering. To write about moral ambiguity risked sacrilege."[8] Further, Kennedy drew ire for his observations of the gender dynamics at play in visiting sex-segregated prisons. Reflecting back on one such line from "Spring Break"— "I feared that my desire to see the women prisoners, to cross the boundary guarded by these men, shared something with [the guards'] prurient fascination for our [female] guide"—Kennedy later asked,

"Was it wrong to think that?. . . In the intensity of identity politics, the flash of feminist anger that shot through the campus in the following years, I was told I should not have thought it."[9]

Had Kennedy written an analytical piece in the mid-1980s about the indeterminacy of human rights, or even about rights more generally, it would have been less, or at least differently, controversial. After Kennedy refused to make changes demanded by the *Harvard Law Review*, the *Texas Law Review* accepted the article for publication. But the editors asked Kennedy to write an appendix that would contextualize "Spring Break" in contemporary legal scholarship. The appendix situated the work not in international law or human rights, but within Critical Legal Studies (CLS) and its critique of the indeterminacy of rights. Though controversial, the latter was at the time a recognizable and acceptable critique to engage. Ironically from today's vantage point (two decades after the proclaimed death of CLS),[10] CLS gave Kennedy cover for his otherwise threatening exposure of the politics of antipolitics and the (mere) humanity of those engaged in human rights work.

As the example of my first interlocutor made clear, things seem to have changed since those early days in which it was sacrilege to question human rights, even if only in one's own mind. Kennedy concurs. As he put it in 2009, "in subsequent years, as the bloom came off the rose of human rights, whenever I taught ['Spring Break'], our trip seemed to foreshadow what many then were discovering about the dark sides of human rights advocacy."[11] If my anecdotes are representative, the bloom coming off the rose might mean that human rights scholars and advocates often *think* what Kennedy and other left critical scholars have articulated, and even are willing to admit that they do. It remains controversial, however, to act upon or publish those thoughts, particularly in moments perceived as fragile—during a military dictatorship, as with Kennedy's work, or shortly after the passage of a long sought and highly contested international document, as with my book.

Contemporary Human Rights Consciousness

At the same time that scholars not self-identifying as left critical scholars nevertheless acknowledge their critical thoughts, many left critical human rights scholars—consciously or not—suggest ambivalence about, rein in, or otherwise defend their critiques against the fear that they are dooming a progressive, or even liberal, human rights project. Some have internalized that fear. Even for those who have not internalized it, the need to respond to the fear often guides strategy.

Before I detail some of the ways that critical scholars have managed this fear, let me offer a brief summary of the scholarly critiques of human rights that have emerged over the past twenty-five years, borrowing from extensive conceptual mapping already done by David Kennedy and Frédéric Mégret.[12] Among the critiques Kennedy and Mégret identify are those about the indeterminacy of rights; the colonial history and legacy of human rights; the presumed neutrality of human rights; the ways in which human rights have occupied the field of emancipatory projects; the inability of human rights to provide the emancipation they promise; the tendency of human rights to narrow, generalize, and essentialize; the legitimating power of human rights; the overly legalized practice of human rights; and the governance power of human rights. Many of these critiques are aimed at the negative, often unintended consequences of human rights advocacy.

Although my summary does not do justice to the breadth or depth of the critiques Kennedy and Mégret discuss, it provides some background for understanding the types of works that populate my own map of the ways that critical human rights scholars and advocates respond to the fear of dooming a progressive political project.[13] Sometimes they express a commitment to human rights, even while sowing doubt, as a tactical matter—to get more people to listen to their critiques, or even join in their projects outside of human rights. Other times they seem unable or unwilling to tolerate the very paradoxes or other conclusions their critiques have illuminated or produced.

I have chosen examples that I myself have deployed in some form, or that have given me solace in my own uncertainty about how to respond to the concerns (by others or internalized) that I might be endangering a progressive political project—whether by my thought, academic writing, advocacy, or teaching. (I confess that such concerns are the toughest when they apply to advocacy, particularly as I codirect an interdisciplinary center—"at the intersection of academics and advocacy"—on human rights and justice.) I have therefore chosen the work of people whose approaches and perspectives I most share. Indeed, I am in direct conversation with many of them.

I do not claim that the list I give is fully representative of the ways that left human rights critics manage the tensions between belief and doubt, for themselves or others. It certainly is not. But I hope the list will provoke questions about and provide insight into contemporary human rights consciousness, and perhaps rights consciousness (and even unconsciousness) more broadly. I also hope it will be useful for those who consider the application of left internal critique to other law reform efforts.

Assertion of Commitment to Human Rights Regardless

Human rights critics sometimes offer statements that they support the human rights movement or believe it has done significant good, alongside analyses that suggest the opposite. Support for human rights is common, of course, but here I am interested in the juxtaposition of support and critique, without any hand-wringing or suggestion of ambivalence.

I convey such support implicitly in nearly all of my writing, simply by using a professional title that makes clear my connection to a university human rights center. Sometimes I am more explicit. When my invitation to participate in the meeting about the commentary on UNDRIP was revoked, for example, I responded with an email that invoked my commitment to human rights practice. Although I insisted that I did not believe that "advocacy and theory should be divorced from each other," I sent links to reports I had helped author through my human rights center to show that I was committed to "the cause."

Kennedy similarly deploys a professional commitment to human rights in his article "The International Human Rights Movement: Part of the Problem?," published in 2002.[14] More traditional in form than "Spring Break," the piece sets forth what Kennedy calls "an incomplete and idiosyncratic list" of concerns and questions about the human rights movement, many of which I included earlier, and which together might suggest that the movement is "more part of the problem in today's world than part of the solution."[15] In the article's conclusion, he calls upon his readers to stop "treating the human rights movement as a frail child, in need of protection from critical assessment or pragmatic calculation."[16]

Although the article is filled with convincing arguments that the human rights movement is part of the problem, Kennedy opens the piece with an assertion that his earlier work lacked: "There is no question that the international human rights movement has done a great deal of good."[17] He also announces his loyalty to the cause (although he avoids saying that he is part of the human rights movement directly). Indeed, as early as the second paragraph, he situates himself "as a well-meaning internationalist and, I hope, compassionate legal professional."[18] Soon thereafter, he names his audience as "other well-meaning legal professionals."[19]

In a response to "Part of the Problem?" written shortly after its publication, Hilary Charlesworth contends that Kennedy's professional performance in the piece differs from much of his other work, which aims "to destabilize the idea that international lawyers have a common set of values from which the best answers to the issues of international law can be derived."[20] She sees his "self-identification as 'well-meaning' and 'compassionate'" as performing a number of functions. For my purposes, the most important one is that it "preempts the charge that this is just another soulless deconstruction of a substantive area of law."[21] Of course, human rights are not just any other substantive area of law. Critique of human rights calls for such a preemption in ways that critiques of other areas of law, whether domestic or international, might not. Indeed, I do not believe that it is coincidental that it was in the context of human rights that Kennedy chose to express his allegiance to what many see as a progressive, or at least well-meaning, political project. I think it is also relevant that he did so at a moment when critique was gaining traction in the field. The attribution of well-meaning aims to both himself and his audience might also have served to make the critiques more acceptable to engage with and more persuasive.

A similar gesture can be seen in Samuel Moyn's book *The Last Utopia*, published in 2010, which challenges dominant historical narratives that proclaim the natural, progressive ascendancy of human rights over a period of centuries. Moyn argues that human rights instead emerged in the 1970s as a result of the collapse of other utopias and political projects, such as revolutionary communism and nationalism. Although human rights "were born as an alternative to grand political missions—or even as moral criticism of politics," Moyn claims, they have turned into a problematic maximalist project of "providing a global framework for the achievement of freedom, identity, and prosperity."[22] It is problematic in part because of the many political movements, particularly redistributive ones, displaced by human rights. In the prologue to the book, Moyn suggests the breadth of his challenge to the orthodox, common-sense view of the history of human rights. He also makes an appeal to believers in human rights by expressing appreciation for their object of devotion: "To give up church history is not to celebrate a black mass instead. I wrote this book out of intense interest—even admiration for—the contemporary human rights movement, the most inspiring mass utopianism Westerners have had before them in recent decades."[23]

In much of his writing since then, Moyn has pursued an argument begun in *The Last Utopia*: while human rights might be well equipped for certain types of limited interventions, they are not suited to the maximalist agenda for which many have touted them. In more recent work on the "drastic mismatch between the egalitarian crisis and the human rights remedy," Moyn argues for human rights not to be replaced, but to be supplemented by a redistributive project. He reaches this conclusion after stating: "To be absolutely clear, this is not to contradict the moral significance and possibly even historical success of human rights when it comes to their core uses in combating political repression and restraining excessive violence."[24]

Perhaps Moyn believes that a stripped-down version of human rights can exist alongside and even be improved by his larger political aims. But, as Wendy Brown has argued, even minimalist ideas of human rights are maximalist, in that they prioritize certain issues and approaches that can hinder redistributive aims.[25] Nevertheless, the question that remains is why Moyn insists here that he is not contesting the moral significance or historical success of human rights, and, in particular, why he needs to make this "absolutely clear."

The statement reads, and functions, much like Kennedy's assertion that the good of human rights is "beyond question." Whom are they hoping to convince, and of what?

Would Kennedy's and Moyn's critiques have been less or more convincing without these assertions? Mégret contends that, because human rights critiques are often pragmatic, they "must also recognize the huge capital of sympathy from which human rights benefit, and the positive uses that capital can be put to." Thus, a part of the critical project is concerned with "how to actualize both the project and practice of human rights in ways that avoid or at least minimize some of the dangers that have historically beset human rights."[26] If Moyn's and Kennedy's aims were "to actualize" human rights, Mégret's rationale might explain their avowed support for human rights or well-meaning professionalism. But in fact, their projects are *not* human rights projects. Rather, their goal is largely to try to convince human rights advocates to focus their efforts elsewhere.

While neither Moyn nor Kennedy seems preoccupied with the potential death of a progressive political project, perhaps they both want to distinguish themselves from those on the right who in fact have that aim. They might also hope to assuage the concerns of their potential followers. One convinced by Moyn, for example, could then turn to the project of "supplementing" (rather than "substituting") human rights, with the belief that the core they are supplementing would stay intact.

Deployment of the Double Negative

In his survey of critical approaches to human rights law, discourse, and practice, Mégret describes the "project" of the critique of human rights as "a project committed to paradoxical thinking, willing to live to the full the contradictory promise of rights, and accept the ambivalence inherent to them." Although Mégret is right that some critics claim to be committed to paradoxical thinking, many of those same critics retreat from it. While they do express ambivalence, they are likely to resolve that ambivalence in favor of rights. Some invoke the work of Gayatri Chakravorty Spivak, saying that rights are "that which we cannot not want."

In its original instantiation, this double negative appears in Spivak's argument that the deconstructive stance entails the persistent critique of "a structure that one cannot not (wish to) inhabit."[27] By framing the activity of desire, the "wish to," in parentheses, Spivak evokes a distinction between those who already inhabit the structure in question and those who may only be able to desire it. Adopting the stance of deconstruction involves recognizing and critiquing the predicament faced by those who do *not* occupy the space, but cannot *not* want it. As she puts it at another point: "Claiming catachreses from a space that one cannot not want to inhabit and yet must criticize is, then, the deconstructive predicament of the postcolonial."[28]

Spivak has used other versions of this statement in a variety of places, generally dropping the parentheses along with the reference to deconstruction. She has also applied it to rights, contending, for example, that what makes an American is, in part, the desire to participate in the "We the People" of the Constitution and in the civil rights it grounds. Americans (and those on the margins who desire to participate in the "We") are thereby constrained by an identity that is conditioned by the need for, and desire of, rights. Because of that constraint, she argues, even the "radical" cannot take a position directly against civil rights: "One way or another, we cannot not want to inhabit this great rational abstraction."[29]

A number of scholars have taken up versions of Spivak's expression in the context of human rights more broadly. In doing so, they have tended to rely more on the desire or allure of rights than on the compulsion to critique included in Spivak's original version. Wendy Brown, for example, opens her essay "Suffering Rights as Paradoxes" by declaring: "This paper does not take a stand for or against rights."[30] She relies upon one version of Spivak's expression to justify that refusal.[31] Brown then essentially sets forth a critique of rights, specifically considering the value of rights language for women and outlining the "deeply paradoxical" nature of such language. She notes, for example, that rights "must be specific and concrete in order to reveal and redress women's subordination, yet potentially entrench our subordination through that specificity"; "they emancipate us to pursue other political ends while subordinating those political ends to liberal discourse"; and "they promise to redress our suffering as women but only by fracturing that suffering—and us—into discrete components, a fracturing that further violates lives already violated by the imbrication of racial, class, sexual, and gendered power."[32] Recognition of such paradoxes, she asserts, can threaten to paralyze political strategy.[33]

Brown's savvy critique culminates in a paragraph of questions that are meant to suggest the emancipatory possibilities of attention to paradox. The penultimate sentence (and question) of the essay asks, "how might the paradoxical elements of the struggle for rights in an emancipatory context articulate a field of justice beyond 'that which we cannot not want'?" The final sentence/question that then follows seems like a retreat from much of the essay's critique, especially if it is meant to suggest an answer to the question that precedes it. In that final line, Brown asks, "what form of rights claims have the temerity to sacrifice an absolutist or naturalized status in order to carry the possibility?"[34] While Brown's articulation of the paradoxes certainly demonstrates that rights are neither absolute nor natural, it does not take temerity to embrace that idea. Indeed, notwithstanding absolutist rhetoric at times, most rights advocates are as aware as anyone that rights are contested, and they do not see such contestation as politically paralyzing.[35]

Brown's use of the double interrogatory at the end of the essay, then, suggests a need to hold on to the potential of rights. It supports her claim that she is taking a stand neither for nor against rights, though the final sentence tends toward a vote "for" over much of the essay's tendency "against." More importantly, it demonstrates her hesitation to abandon the very object of her critique.

If Brown ultimately seeks a way to get "beyond" Spivak's double negative through a particular form of rights, others have deployed the double negative in ways that temper their own critiques of rights. For example, in an essay on *Lawrence v. Texas*, the US Supreme Court case striking down sodomy law, Teemu Ruskola critiques the decision's focus on "intimate sexual conduct" for the respectability it demands of gay people.[36] Toward the end of the essay, he calls upon gay rights advocates to "focus not on the love but on the acts that dare not speak their names."[37] Immediately after issuing that call, he inserts a paragraph on the limits of rights discourse. He then offers a critique of the liberal rights on which the court relies, including that "they impose their own normalizing discipline on subjects," but he goes on to contend that "they are surely preferable to a regime of homophobic violence sanctioned by sodomy laws." He continues, "As Gayatri Spivak observes with artful ambivalence, liberal rights are something that 'we cannot not want': without them one has no legal and political existence."[38]

Ruskola's description of Spivak as ambivalent seems like projection here; it provides a way for him to express his own ambivalence. It serves to temper his critique of the decision (it is better than what preceded it) and as a caveat or qualification to his own call for moving away from a logic of respectability. It is a reminder of what might happen in the absence of a progressive, or even liberal, political project. That said, he also deploys his own double negative after the colon, careful not to say that liberal rights are in fact sufficient for legal and political existence.

Neville Hoad also critiques the norm of respectability in the deployment and recognition of gay rights, in the context of teaching an African novel to students in a course on sexual orientation and human rights. In a chapter for a book on human rights pedagogy in literary and cultural studies, he too deploys Spivak's double negative. While he is perhaps truer to Spivak's commitment to deconstructive critique, he nevertheless also uses the double negative to soften or limit the critique he seems willing to offer his students.

Hoad guides his readers through his method of teaching what is known as the first gay novel from Nigeria to a classroom of undergraduate students in Texas. The first half of the piece engagingly introduces the novel, as well as how Hoad provides students with the background they need to read it and how he teaches a particular passage that raises issues about homosexuality and religion.

In the second half of the piece, however, the students largely disappear, as Hoad begins to read the novel critically for the "not-so-hidden norms" in its use of gay rights and as he draws a comparison to gay rights in South Africa.[39] As a fellow teacher of human rights, in this second half I find myself eager to learn how much of the critique he will attempt to teach his students, and how much of it he might attempt to elicit from them. But his only suggestion of a response does not appear until the final paragraph, when he writes: "In relation to the question of a human right to sexual orientation, I find myself once again returned to Gayatri Spivak's definition of deconstruction as 'the critique of a structure that you cannot wish not to inhabit.' That is my position. I certainly do not expect it to be my students."[40]

In context, the paragraph expresses Hoad's commitment to critique and to an understanding of the double bind, especially for postcolonial subjects, that Spivak exposes. At the same time, he seems reticent to share it with his students. Perhaps he is concerned more about the fragility of his students than human rights. Might he be afraid of pulling the rug out from under them?

Split of Critique from Advocacy

Since many human rights scholars also engage in human rights advocacy, left critical scholars often find themselves confronting questions about whether and how they might use some of the very tools in practice that they have critiqued in theory. However much they might like to bring critique to advocacy, they must navigate the risk that engagement with advocacy will dull their critique—both inside and outside of the advocacy. One way some of them manage that risk is by compartmentalizing. They pursue left critique in scholarship but continue to use—although perhaps also attempt to tweak—the tools that they have critiqued as problematic in advocacy. They sometimes characterize this approach as "strategic" (as in "strategic essentialism")[41] or as necessary compromise, and it is often motivated by a stated fear that critique would be damaging at worst and unhelpful at best to the political project. As my interlocutor in my opening anecdote encouraged me to do, they keep critique in the scholarly realm. Rather than staying out of the advocacy realm altogether, they engage, but they do so in a way that my colleague feared I would not.

In anthropology, "activist research" has provided a way for some to split critique from advocacy. One of the principal proponents of activist research, Charles Hale, distinguishes it from "cultural critique" as follows: "Cultural critique strives for intellectual production uncompromised by the inevitable negotiations and contradictions that these broader political struggles entail. Activist research is compromised—but also enriched—by opting to position itself squarely amid the tension between utopian ideals and practical politics."[42]

He makes another distinction as well, encouraging activist researchers to keep one foot "firmly planted in the rarified space of cultural critique" and the other "cautiously, but confidently, [in] law, demographics, statistics, human ecology, geographic information systems, and other technologies of objective (no quotation marks allowed) social science."[43] In short, Hale calls on the activist researcher to "deploy positivist social science methods [in activism] and subject them to rigorous critique [outside of it] while acknowledging with acceptance the cognitive dissonance that results."[44]

Hale applies his theories about activist research to his own participation in what turned out to be a seminal case before the Inter-American Court of Human Rights. In 2001, the court ruled on behalf of the Awas Tingni in their indigenous land rights claim against Nicaragua. Hale notes that, despite the difficulty of making indigenous claims that do not "reinforce internal rigidities or create criteria that other subaltern communities would be unable to meet," he approached the case "in hopes of contributing useful and persuasive expert testimony; the idea of carrying out a critique of the problematic notion of culture underlying the community's claim could not have been further from my mind."[45] Hale's semicolon speaks volumes; the critique of the cultural claim could not in any way contribute useful and persuasive expert testimony.

Although I believe Hale accurately describes many of the tensions experienced by academics engaged in human rights advocacy and by advocates engaged in academia, he also perpetuates dichotomies that we should try to break down—in both theory and practice. As a legal academic and advocate, I am particularly troubled by his distinction between cultural critique and law, because it suggests that bringing cultural critique to law would inappropriately challenge law's utility. It is also troubling in its failure to recognize the extent to which *not* deploying cultural critique participates in the production of legal rules that cannot accommodate the everyday messiness and contradictions in many human rights claims, especially those based on culture. At the end of the day, if indirectly, Hale calls for a self-consciously anticonstructivist account of law that tolerates an essentialized view of culture.

I believe we need to resist both the anticonstructivist account of law and the essentialized view of culture. I also believe that the resistance needs to take place in both scholarship and advocacy. At some level, Hale might not disagree (double negative intended). He might be fine with my writing, with my scholarly hat on, that we should resist those accounts—even resist them in advocacy—as long as I do not actually *try* it out in practice. But, of course, if I write it, I want it to make its way into practice. And that is what he, and those like my second interlocutor, fear. Hale's approach depends upon critique and advocacy occupying separate silos, but that in turn assumes that you always know whether you are in the realm of critique or advocacy, and that your audiences only read what you intend for them.

Absorption of Critique Into Practice

At the same time that some critics split critique from their advocacy, some human rights advocates have absorbed and often responded to critique. Some have even generated critique, making it a part of their job.

I opened this essay with discussion of how mainstream human rights organizations and institutions responded to the critiques by radical feminists about the public/private distinction in human rights, in part by finding states accountable for investigating, prosecuting, and punishing certain nonstate actors. More recently, Susan Marks has written about how several UN human rights reports and analyses now include discussion of "root causes" of human rights violations, largely as a response to the critiques of human rights professionals' failure to address structural causes of those violations. She argues that these attempts to address root causes are inadequate for a variety of reasons, mostly stemming from their inability to recognize that human rights violations have beneficiaries.[46] This argument leads Marks to call attention to the "planned misery" that even the root-cause investigations conceal. Although she concludes that "the international system of human rights protection, at least as currently configured," is incapable of attending to alternative explanatory causes of human rights violations,[47] she shows through a number of concrete examples that human rights actors have in fact absorbed and responded to, if insufficiently, earlier critiques about the need to consider root causes.

For Kennedy, expertise is partly the reason for this ability to absorb critique. In reflecting on how the human rights field has changed since the "bloom came off of the rose of human rights," he contends that, as the field became professionalized, advocates began to "remind one another to analyze, strategize, keep our powder dry, weigh and balance."[48] While it might seem counterintuitive, given the call for splitting critique from advocacy that we just considered, professionalization facilitates the ability of human rights advocates not only to have critical thoughts, but to articulate them and include them as professional practice. As Kennedy puts it, "modern human rights professionals are often the first to know and to admit the limits of their language, their institutional practices, their governance routines. They know there are darker sides; they weigh and balance and think shrewdly and practically."[49] In contrast to Hale's experience of advocacy, critique makes its way into practice here as technique. Still, there are limits to what human rights professionals can internalize or absorb into their work. At the end of the paragraph quoted earlier, Kennedy takes into account arguments like those made by Hale, acknowledging that "the dark side is as readily denied as admitted. In the field, it is denied in the name of the pragmatic, at headquarters in the name of ethical commitment."[50]

Kennedy has continued to explore some of these ideas in a book on expertise. There he contends that human rights professionals operate strategically between two types of vocabularies: denunciation (speaking truth to power) and pragmatism (attempting to engage authority). They are able to do so, in part, because they "speak in the shadow of, evoke, and imagine themselves contributing to the requirements of universal ethics."[51] A common sense, it seems, has developed that allows for contestation from the inside, but still within relatively well-defined boundaries. Kennedy suggests that the strategic play is always operating against the threat of more forceful critiques—of "idolatry, enchanted tools, loss of practical sense," on the denunciation side, and "instrumentalization and loss of ethical moorings," on the pragmatic side.[52]

In both accounts, human rights professionals have a more nuanced understanding than Hale's activist researchers of the indeterminacy of their tools. Nonetheless, they have consented to limits on the scope of their critical activity. Unlike Hale, they have no place to step outside of their professional sphere and engage what is beyond such limits; indeed, real danger lies outside. As Kennedy puts it, "to associate human rights with injustice or bad outcomes both betrays the community of the faithful . . . and is bad strategy. . . . To affirm the downsides can only delegitimate law and retard progress toward a better world."[53] It could, in other words, doom a progressive political project.

Critique and the "End" of Human Rights?

My account thus far suggests a preservationist tendency within much human rights critique. Whether they are actually afraid of killing off a progressive project or simply hope to convince others that doing so is not their aim, many of the critics I examined demonstrate both a drive to critique and—as in Spivak's observation—an inability to let go of the desire for rights, especially for those who can merely desire them.

Given that even most critics tend to be preservationists, we might think that human rights would continue to hold the grip on our emancipatory imagination. In fact, though, human rights discourse does not provide the only or even the principal avenue of attempted political emancipation today; it has lost political salience for many on the left. New left political discourses have emerged that do not necessarily rely on rights and perhaps do not even seek to incorporate them. Emancipatory political struggles today are as likely to sound in the register of economic inequality, climate change, or corruption as in that of human rights.

Human rights advocates have responded to this change in two ways, both of which also suggest some attentiveness to left internal critiques. Some insist on the necessity, even centrality, of human rights as a means of responding to economic inequality, climate change, and corruption—all of which they acknowledge as among some of our greatest social justice challenges today. They call for an expansion of human rights, through the type of maximalism that Moyn rejects. Other advocates recognize the differences between human rights and other discourses and, rather than trying to make human rights do everything, call for a "more in-depth form of collaboration that responds to the need to bring diverse knowledge and activism together in a way that is, to some extent, extraordinary," as Martin Abregú, Vice President of the Ford Foundation, stated in his explanation of the restructuring of the foundation that led to the elimination of its human rights division in 2017.[54]

In a different vein, much has been written of the "end" of human rights in recent years. Those who pronounce the near-death of human rights echo some of the critiques about the indeterminacy of rights, as they often point to ways that human rights have become instrumentalized—used by public and private actors alike to justify oppressive institutions and policies, from neoliberalism to military intervention. In the process, they argue, human rights have failed. The human rights movement, in particular, has lost any potency it might have had to respond to injustice.

While liberal and some left advocates of human rights (critical and not) have long been concerned about governmental and neoliberal uses of human rights law and discourse, they have largely seen those uses as co-optation, suggesting that there is some less adulterated form of human rights that can and should be recovered.[55] In contrast, those who pronounce the "end" generally base their diagnosis on what they see as the difficulty of wresting rights from the hegemonic uses to which they have been put. Yet, even Costas Douzinas, who is often associated with "the end of human rights" discourse because of his book from 2000 by that title, calls for human rights to be allowed to "reclaim their redemptive role in the hands and imagination of those who return them to the tradition of resistance and struggle against the advice of the preachers of moralism, suffering humanity and humanitarian philanthropy."[56] Others, such as Stephen Hopgood with his book titled *The Endtimes of Human Rights*, have been less insistent on salvaging them, at least in a maximalist form.[57] Makau Mutua, in a recent piece on the topic, questions the assumption that there ever was an age of rights worth returning to.[58]

The recent resurgence of right-wing populism in Europe, the United States, and Latin America arguably presents a challenge to the diagnosis of instrumentalization and co-optation. The concern motivated by these political developments is not that human rights are being put to bad use by states or powerful private actors, but that they are being openly repudiated. As Philip Alston put it in a speech from 2017 titled "The Populist Challenge to Human Rights": "The populist agenda that has made such dramatic inroads recently is often avowedly nationalistic, xenophobic, misogynistic, and explicitly antagonistic to all or much of the human rights agenda." As a result, he contends, "the challenges the human rights movement now faces are fundamentally different from much of what has gone before."[59] Alston uses this challenge to call for what he has long advocated—greater attention to economic and social rights—albeit in a way that will better attend to the issue of distribution. He also uses it to call for some changes in the human rights movement, such as its becoming more local and, somewhat surprisingly perhaps, more engaged with corporate actors.

Alston also calls for critical scholars "to take account of the unintended consequences" of their critique. In doing so, he intentionally borrows a line from critical scholars who, in part through the critiques I have enumerated and described here, have long called for human rights advocates to attend to the unintended consequences of their work. In particular, Alston cautions against "unenlightening dead-end scholarship which simply leads us to despair and does no favor to our students, let alone our fellow humans."[60] He derides "one of the world's leading international legal scholars" who gave a talk at NYU about the contingency and subjectivity of human rights, only to leave in distress a student who came to law school to promote human rights. The anecdote demonstrates that critique is capable of killing progressive impulses, if not the entire political project. Alston's reaction resonates with Hoad's ambivalence about sharing his critique with his potentially fragile (my addition) students. It also calls into question the extent to which Hale's splitting might apply to the classroom or to engagement with students more broadly. When the topic is human rights, are students coded as activists rather than academics?

Alston is not alone in his wariness of critique, especially in a moment in which, as his opening line declares, "The world as we in the human rights movement have known it in recent years is no longer."[61] Yet, he does not totally reject it. In a move that is strikingly parallel to Kennedy's and Moyn's attesting their commitment to human rights, he expresses his commitment to critique. "This is not for a moment an attempt to diminish the importance of critical scholarship," he insists. Indeed, he continues, "many of my own ideas have been drawn from the best of that scholarship."[62]

In his failure to dismiss critique fully, notwithstanding its unintended consequences, Alston suggests that the critiques of human rights might be an important tool to combat right-wing populism. Even his own turn to issues of economic inequality in his role as Special Rapporteur on Extreme Poverty and Human Rights reflects some internalization of the critique that human rights have not dealt sufficiently with issues of distribution (if not with the critique that it tries to do too much).[63]

If I began this essay with the precarity of critique and the reluctance of many critics to abandon human rights, I have ended it with the precarity of human rights and a reluctance to abandon critique. Perhaps we are in a time when human rights no longer provide the structure for that which one cannot not wish to inhabit (no parentheses necessary). If emancipatory struggles are operating on new planes, maybe we need to be willing to move to those planes. But we should not make them immune from critique. Indeed, as Spivak herself notes, even in moments of liberation, the "productive unease of a persistent critique" should not be left behind.[64]

Notes

Many thanks to the other authors in this collection for their participation in the year-long seminar that made it possible. From the seminar, I am especially grateful to Lori Allen, Didier Fassin, Vanja Hamzić, and Bernard Harcourt for their comments on the chapter at various stages. I also benefited greatly from comments by Janet Halley and David Kennedy, the research assistance and feedback of Simone Gubler and Regina Larrea Maccise, and the editing of Anne Quaranto.

1. Karen Engle, "Anti-Impunity and the Turn to Criminal Law in Human Rights," *Cornell Law Review* 100, no. 5 (2015): 1069–128.
2. Janet Halley and Wendy Brown, eds., *Left Legalism/Left Critique* (Durham: Duke University Press, 2002), 4.
3. Halley and Brown, 6.
4. Halley and Brown, 7.
5. Bruno Latour, "Why Has Critique Run out of Steam? From Matters of Fact to Matters of Concern," *Critical Inquiry* 30, no. 2 (2004): 225–48, 246.
6. Karen Engle, *The Elusive Promise of Indigenous Development: Rights, Culture, Strategy* (Durham: Duke University Press, 2010).
7. David Kennedy, "Spring Break," *Texas Law Review* 63, no. 8 (1985): 1377–424.
8. David Kennedy, *The Rights of Spring* (Princeton: Princeton University Press, 2009), 9.
9. Kenney, 17–18.
10. One of the founders of CLS, Duncan Kennedy, wrote in 1997 that "there was once a 'movement' called CLS; there still exists a CLS 'school' and a 'theory of law' called CLS; and there is from time to time a media 'factoid' called CLS." Duncan Kennedy, *A Critique of Adjudication: Fin de Siècle* (Cambridge, MA: Harvard University Press, 1997), 9.
11. Kennedy, *Rights of Spring*, 97.
12. Frédéric Mégret, "Where Does the Critique of International Human Rights Stand?," in *New Approaches to International Law*, ed. José María Beneyto and David Kennedy, 3–40 (The Hague: TMC Asser, 2012); David Kennedy, "The International Human Rights Movement: Part of the Problem?," *Harvard Human Rights Journal* 15 (2002): 101–26.
13. I have not considered whether and how those ways might map onto particular types of critiques, which might be a project for another day. For now, however, I do not see an obvious correlation between the types of critiques made and the ways their authors manifest and manage their unease.
14. Kennedy, "International Human Rights Movement."
15. Kennedy, 101.
16. Kennedy, 125.
17. Kennedy, 101.
18. Kennedy, 101.
19. Kennedy, 102.
20. Hillary Charlesworth, "Author! Author! A Response to David Kennedy," *Harvard Human Rights Journal* 15 (2002): 127–32, 129.

21. Charlesworth, 128.
22. Samuel Moyn, *The Last Utopia: Human Rights in History* (Cambridge, MA: Harvard University Press, 2010), 9.
23. Moyn, 8–9.
24. Samuel Moyn, "Human Rights and the Age of Inequality," *OpenGlobalRights*, October 27, 2015, www.openglobalrights.org/human-rights-and-age-of-inequality/. In his most recent book on inequality and human rights, he is perhaps less hopeful about (or more demanding of) supplementation, noting that "local and global economic justice requires redesigning markets or at least redistributing from the rich to the rest, something that naming and shaming are never likely to achieve, even when supplemented by novel forms of legal activism." He also repeats the "moral significance" and "historical success" of language, replacing "to be absolutely clear" with "there is no contradicting it." Moyn, *Not Enough: Human Rights in an Unequal World* (Cambridge, MA: Harvard University Press, 2018), 218.
25. Wendy Brown, "'The Most We Can Hope For . . .': Human Rights and the Politics of Fatalism," *South Atlantic Quarterly* 103, nos. 2–3 (2004): 451–63.
26. Mégret, "Critique of International Human Rights," 25.
27. Gayatri Chakravorty Spivak, "Constitutions and Culture Studies," *Yale Journal of Law and the Humanities* 2, no. 1 (1990): 133–47, 147.
28. Gayatri Chakravorty Spivak, *Outside in the Teaching Machine* (New York: Routledge, 1993), 64.
29. Spivak, 279.
30. Brown, "Suffering Rights as Paradoxes," *Constellations* 7, no. 2 (2000): 208–29, 230.
31. Brown, 230, quoting Spivak, *Teaching Machine*, 45–46.
32. Brown, "Suffering Rights as Paradoxes," 238.
33. Brown, 239: "Paradox appears endlessly self-canceling, as a political condition of achievements perpetually undercut, a predicament of discourse in which every truth is crossed by a counter-truth, and hence a state in which political strategizing itself is paralyzed."
34. Brown, 240.
35. Susan Marks makes a similar argument when she quotes a British human rights advocate responding to then-Prime Minister David Cameron's attribution of the riots in August 2011 to an underlying moral collapse by those who believe that they have "rights without responsibilities." For the advocate, the "idea that [human rights law] somehow provides unfettered and limitless rights without any corresponding responsibilities is patent nonsense—respect for the rights of others is inbuilt into [human rights law] and rights can be limited for a number of legitimate reasons including public safety and national security." Susan Marks, "Four Human Rights Myths," in *Human Rights: Old Problems, New Possibilities*, ed. David Kinley, Wojciech Sadurski, and Kevin Walton, 217–35 (Cheltenham, UK: Edward Elgar, 2013), 218.
36. Teemu Ruskola, "Gay Rights Versus Queer Theory: What Is Left of Sodomy After *Lawrence v. Texas*?," *Social Text* 23, nos. 3–4 (2005): 235–49, 241–43.
37. Ruskola, 244.
38. Ruskola, 244.
39. Neville Hoad, "Sexual Orientation and Human Rights: *Walking with Shadows* in Nigeria," in *Teaching Human Rights in Literary and Cultural Studies*, ed. Alexandra Schultheis Moore and Elizabeth Swanson Goldberg, 168–77 (New York: Modern Languages Association, 2015), 176.
40. Hoad, 177.

41. In the introduction to the book that caused the revocation of my invitation to the UNDRIP conference, I discuss the implicit and explicit use of "strategic essentialism" (a term also attributed to Spivak, but used in ways she has distanced herself from) by many indigenous rights advocates. Indeed, much of my discussion here on the split between critique and advocacy was first articulated there. Engle, *Indigenous Development*, 11–14.

42. Charles R. Hale, "Activist Research v. Cultural Critique: Indigenous Land Rights and the Contradictions of Politically Engaged Anthropology," *Cultural Anthropology* 21, no. 1 (2006): 96–120, 100.

43. Hale, 115.

44. Hale, 113.

45. Hale, 112, 97.

46. Marks argues that the discourse of root causes halts the investigation too soon, treats effects as though they are causes, and often identifies causes simply to put them aside. Susan Marks, "Human Rights and Root Causes," *Modern Law Review* 74, no. 1 (2011): 57–78, 74.

47. Marks, 71.

48. Kennedy, *Rights of Spring*, 98.

49. Kennedy, 96.

50. Kennedy, 96.

51. David Kennedy, *A World of Struggle: How Power, Law, and Expertise Shape Global Political Economy* (Princeton: Princeton University Press, 2016), 143.

52. Kennedy, 144.

53. Kennedy, 251.

54. Martín Abregú, "What Strengthening Human Rights Has to Do with Challenging Inequality," *Equals Change Blog. Ford Foundation*, May 22, 2017, www.fordfoundation .org/ideas/equals-change-blog/posts/what-strengthening-human-rights-has-to-do -with-challenging-inequality/.

55. See, for example, Balakrishnan Rajagopal, "Counter-Hegemonic International Law: Rethinking Human Rights and Development as a Third World Strategy," *Third World Quarterly* 27, no. 5 (2006): 767–83, 775 (noting the association of human rights with "hegemonic international law," claiming that the protagonists of that vision of human rights "are undermining the future of human rights itself").

56. Costas Douzinas, *Human Rights and Empire: The Political Philosophy of Cosmopolitanism* (New York: Routledge, 2007), 293. For the earlier book, see Costas Douzinas, *The End of Human Rights* (Oxford: Hart, 2000).

57. Stephen Hopgood, *The Endtimes of Human Rights* (Ithaca: Cornell University Press, 2013).

58. Makau Mutua, "Is the Age of Human Rights Over?," in *The Routledge Companion to Literature and Human Rights*, ed. Sophia McClennen and Alexandra Schultheis Moore, 450–58 (London: Routledge, 2016).

59. Philip Alston, "The Populist Challenge to Human Rights," *Journal of Human Rights Practice* 9, no. 1 (2017): 1–15, 2–3.

60. Alston, 13.

61. Alston, 1.

62. Alston, 13.

63. See Philip Alston, *Report of the Special Rapporteur on Extreme Poverty and Human Rights*, Human Rights Council, Twenty-Ninth Session, Agenda item 3, UN Doc. A/ HRC/29/31, May 27, 2015.

64. Spivak, *Teaching Machine*, 46.

Bibliography

Abregú, Martín. "What Strengthening Human Rights Has to Do with Challenging Inequality." *Equals Change Blog. Ford Foundation,* May 22, 2017, www.fordfoundation.org/ideas/equals-change-blog/posts/what-strengthening-human-rights-has-to-do-with-challenging-inequality/.

Alston, Philip. "The Populist Challenge to Human Rights." *Journal of Human Rights Practice* 9, no. 1 (2017): 1–15.

——. *Report of the Special Rapporteur on Extreme Poverty and Human Rights.* Human Rights Council, Twenty-Ninth Session, Agenda item 3, UN Doc. A/HRC/29/31, May 27, 2015.

Brown, Wendy. *Edgework: Critical Essays on Knowledge and Politics.* Princeton: Princeton University Press, 2005.

——. " 'The Most We Can Hope For . . .': Human Rights and the Politics of Fatalism." *South Atlantic Quarterly* 103, nos. 2–3 (2004): 451–63.

——. "Suffering Rights as Paradoxes." *Constellations* 7, no. 2 (2000): 208–29.

Charlesworth, Hillary. "Author! Author! A Response to David Kennedy." *Harvard Human Rights Journal* 15 (2002): 127–32.

Douzinas, Costas. *The End of Human Rights.* Oxford: Hart, 2000.

——. *Human Rights and Empire: The Political Philosophy of Cosmopolitanism.* New York: Routledge, 2007.

Engle, Karen. "Anti-Impunity and the Turn to Criminal Law in Human Rights." *Cornell Law Review* 100, no. 5 (2015): 1069–128.

——. *The Elusive Promise of Indigenous Development: Rights, Culture, Strategy.* Durham: Duke University Press, 2010.

Hale, Charles R. "Activist Research v. Cultural Critique: Indigenous Land Rights and the Contradictions of Politically Engaged Anthropology." *Cultural Anthropology* 21, no. 1 (2006): 96–120.

Halley, Janet, and Wendy Brown, eds. *Left Legalism/Left Critique.* Durham: Duke University Press, 2002.

Hoad, Neville. "Sexual Orientation and Human Rights: *Walking with Shadows* in Nigeria." In *Teaching Human Rights in Literary and Cultural Studies,* edited by Alexandra Schultheis Moore and Elizabeth Swanson Goldberg, 168–77. New York: Modern Languages Association, 2015.

Hopgood, Stephen. *The Endtimes of Human Rights.* Ithaca: Cornell University Press, 2013.

Kennedy, David. "The International Human Rights Movement: Part of the Problem?" *Harvard Human Rights Journal* 15 (2002): 101–26.

——. *The Rights of Spring.* Princeton: Princeton University Press, 2009.

——. "Spring Break." *Texas Law Review* 63, no. 8 (1985): 1377–424.

——. *A World of Struggle: How Power, Law, and Expertise Shape Global Political Economy.* Princeton: Princeton University Press, 2016.

Kennedy, Duncan. *A Critique of Adjudication: Fin de Siècle.* Cambridge, MA: Harvard University Press, 1997.

Latour, Bruno. "Why Has Critique Run out of Steam? From Matters of Fact to Matters of Concern." *Critical Inquiry* 30, no. 2 (2004): 225–48.

Marks, Susan. "Four Human Rights Myths." In *Human Rights: Old Problems, New Possibilities,* edited by David Kinley, Wojciech Sadurski, and Kevin Walton, 217–35. Cheltenham, UK: Edward Elgar, 2013.

——. "Human Rights and Root Causes." *Modern Law Review* 74, no. 1 (2011): 57–78.

Mégret, Frédéric. "Where Does the Critique of International Human Rights Stand?" In *New Approaches to International Law*, edited by José María Beneyto and David Kennedy, 3–40. The Hague: TMC Asser, 2012.

Moyn, Samuel. "Human Rights and the Age of Inequality." *OpenGlobalRights*, October 27, 2015, www.openglobalrights.org/human-rights-and-age-of-inequality/.

——. *The Last Utopia: Human Rights in History*. Cambridge, MA: Harvard University Press, 2010.

——. *Not Enough: Human Rights in an Unequal World*. Cambridge, MA: Harvard University Press, 2018.

Mutua, Makau. "Is the Age of Human Rights Over?" In *The Routledge Companion to Literature and Human Rights*, edited by Sophia McClennen and Alexandra Schultheis Moore, 450–58. London: Routledge, 2016.

Rajagopal, Balakrishnan. "Counter-Hegemonic International Law: Rethinking Human Rights and Development as a Third World Strategy." *Third World Quarterly* 27, no. 5 (2006): 767–83.

Ruskola, Teemu. "Gay Rights Versus Queer Theory: What Is Left of Sodomy After *Lawrence v. Texas*?" *Social Text* 23, nos. 3–4 (2005): 235–49.

Spivak, Gayatri Chakravorty. "Constitutions and Culture Studies." *Yale Journal of Law and the Humanities* 2, no. 1 (1990): 133–47.

——. *Outside in the Teaching Machine*. New York: Routledge, 1993.

CHAPTER 6

CRITIQUE AS SUBDUCTION

MASSIMILIANO TOMBA

C ritique as practice and theory is always grounded in a specific conception of history and time. I look at critique from the standpoint of history in order to raise a different question: What kind of conception of history should we embrace for the critique to be adequate to our contemporaneity? What I call *subduction*, borrowing this term from geology, refers to the sliding of historical layers sinking under one another. The image of history as an overlapping of historical-temporal layers stands in opposition to the unilinear image of historical time. The latter has produced the image of history as an inevitable development passing through necessary phases.

The pluralization of historical temporalities responds to the need to understand and intervene in a globalized world—a need that involves, besides provincializing Europe,[1] also overcoming the provincialism of time, which imposes the linear trajectory of European history as normative for the rest of the world. From this perspective, critique has the task of disclosing new possibilities, which are enclosed in the multitemporal layered present.

The singularization of the concept of history in universal history is intrinsically Eurocentric and colonial. It puts European civilization at the top of the historical-temporal vector, judging the enormous variety of non-European political and economic forms as precapitalist or premodern. This conception of history allowed for Mill's colonial liberalism, which, by operating in the disjuncture between universalism and its actualization, considers despotism the appropriate political form for backward states of society populated by "nonage" races.[2] The concept of universalism, not unlike other "isms" such as nationalism, liberalism, and even socialism, operates as a temporalized and temporalizing arrow-concept. Modern political concepts are presented as universal, operating as temporal vectors that, as bearers of a unifying need, produce historical-temporal differentiations and gradations of historical time that become stages in the arrow of unilinear historical time.

Movements for decolonization reacted against this conception of history.[3] In a letter of October 24, 1956, that he wrote to Maurice Thorez, at that time the General Secretary of the French Communist Party, Aimé Césaire denounced the paternalism of the Communist Party members, "their inveterate assimilationism; their unconscious chauvinism; their fairly simplistic faith, which they share with bourgeois Europeans, in the omnilateral superiority of the West; their belief that evolution as it took place in Europe is the only evolution possible, the only kind desirable, the kind the whole world must undergo."[4] Finally, denouncing the "emaciated universalism" that suppresses the multiplicity of particular and alternative paths of development, Aimé Césaire presented an alternative vision of universalism, based on solidarity that respects the particulars. With that letter Aimé Césaire announced his resignation from the Party.

The least one can expect from critique today is the rejection of the unilinear conception of historical time and the Western "emaciated universalism." In the 1950s, looking at the anticolonial struggles, Ernst Bloch developed an idea, counter to the unilinearity of historical time, of a "broad, flexible and thoroughly dynamic 'multiverse.' . . . A unilinear model must be found obsolete if justice is to be done to the considerable amount of non-European material. It is no longer possible to work without curves in the series; without a new and complex time-manifold (the problem of 'Riemannian time')."[5] Ernst Bloch, pretty well unheeded, tried to build a theoretical and political bridge between the anticolonial struggles and the Western labor movement. Today, the project to provincialize Europe has largely been accomplished. Two interconnected tasks remain: provincializing historical time and deprovincializing Europe after its provincialization.

The self-representation of modernity as a monolith and nontranscendable era is also, and above all, the result of the destruction and annihilation of many historical alternatives that have emerged in the last five hundred years. I have chosen this timeframe in the sense given by the indigenous movements on the five hundredth anniversary of the conquest of America. Indeed, in the first Article of the Gathering "500 Years of Indian Resistance" indigenous peoples rejected "the Quincentennial celebration" and aimed to turn that date into a struggle toward liberation, self-determination (Art. 2), defense of indigenous "forms of spiritual life and communal coexistence" (Art. 3), traditional exercise of Common Law (Art. 7), and the right to land (Art. 8).[6] These declarations were echoed in the first Zapatista Declaration: "We are the product of 500 years of struggle."[7] In saying this, it ties into a different trajectory of modernity, which is rooted in the forms of self-government and communal possession of land. At the same time, one has to emphasize that a similar history was fought in Europe. It was the history of the Diggers for the defense of the commons, of the German peasants' insurgency for the defense of communal possession in 1525, of the numerous peasant revolts and insurgencies that have dotted all of modern history. If we want to be fair toward the many struggles that have tried to bring about an alternative to modern Western colonization, we must deprovincialize Europe and also be fair toward the many insurgencies that have tried to give a different direction to Western modernization. Europe is not monolithic; its history is stratified by trajectories that are alternative to the nation-state, to the capitalist mode of production, and to private property. There is a legacy that has its roots in those struggles, but it is not just the expression of resistance against oppressive power. It is a different legacy that indicates a different trajectory of modernity. It is a history not of victims, but of political practices and possibilities opened up in the tension between different historical temporalities. What these experiments share is not the condition of being victims, but the *factum of freedom*. If we start from the victims, the discourse stops at power, be it the evil power that creates victims or the benevolent power that should protect them. It is a discourse in which victims are passive subjects not capable of political agency and always in need of protection. At most it leads to human rights and their "emaciated universalism." But those subjects, in the moment of their action, are not victims; they are agents in a multiplicity of experiments with politics. What they share is a political practice that exceeds the present reality. This excess has to do with the way in which freedom and democracy are concretely experienced and tested beyond the constitutional shell of the state and its procedures. This excess is always risky. But it is this risk of politics that human beings have in common. There is no universalism or essentialist definition of the human that preexists that risk. The human is what we share when we experience that excess and take the risk of politics.

The Time of Critique and the Critique of Time

"Critique is the crisis (*die Kritik ist die Krise*)," wrote Bruno Bauer in 1842.[8] According to Bauer, critique has in the crisis the condition of its own possibility and, in the very act of comprehending, it produces the crisis, elevating it to the categories of the self-representation of the age. This conception of both critique and crisis is anchored in a specific philosophy of history in which the epochal function of critique consists in the devaluation of the categories through which the existing reproduces itself. By doing this, the critique creates room for something new. This conception of history is still Hegelian and unilinear: when an epoch comes to an end, the task of criticism is to bring this end to consciousness so as to create the conditions of possibility for real change. Bruno Bauer's intellectual and political trajectory shows how this conception of critique has been shared by both progressive and conservative streams. The difference between them can be represented by the algebraic sign that one puts before the historical arrow: positive for a progressive conception of history, negative for a declining one. In the former case, it is a question of accelerating processes of democratization and equality, in the latter, of restraining and resisting the increasing atomization and leveling of society. Both these paths would be beaten in the intellectual parabola that goes from Hegel to Nietzsche and would carry on politically in the twentieth century.

However, there are other ways to look at history and therefore at critique. If Bloch abandoned unilinear time for the historical multiverse, Walter Benjamin introduced the idea of the "differential of time." What the dominant historiography considers deviations, which "disturb the main line of inquiry," are for Benjamin the basis of his understanding of history.[9] According to Benjamin, the task of the real historical materialist is not just explaining the past, reconstructing it from its dark side, but turning it into something unfinished, which has the possibility of being oriented in a different way.

For Reinhart Koselleck historical research is "of many forms of time superimposed one upon the other."[10] Latter-day Koselleck worked on a pluralization of temporalities without recurring to the empty periodization of old and new. Paying attention to the simultaneity of multiple historical times, he observed that the spatializing metaphor has the advantage of pluralizing the concept of time: "temporal strata" (*Zeitschichten*) refer, as in the geological model, to multiple layers of time (*Zeitebenen*) of different lengths and from different places, but that are nonetheless simultaneously present and active.[11]

Finally, Marx, in his later years in dialogue with the Russian populists, devised a geological conception of history in which different layers overlap. In this new vision, as Marx learned from Chernyshevsky, historical jumps were possible, and Russia did not have to go through the process of capital accumulation that had taken place in Europe. On the contrary, the Russian agrarian commune could have been the basis for new collective forms of land ownership.[12] Marx observed that the capitalist mode of production incessantly encounters preexisting forms and it "encounters them as antecedents, but not as antecedents established by itself, not as forms of its own life process."[13] The result of this encounter, as Harry Harootunian points out, gives rise to "a heterogeneous mix rather than the destruction of one made by another."[14] This "heterogeneous mix" of temporalities, in which archaic forms coexist and overlap with new forms, gives rise to social and political conflicts, whose outcomes are not predefined by any law of history. These unpredictable results are

demarcated by the political struggle for the orientation of new historical trajectories. In the examples given, the modern conception of universal history is
rearticulated into a plurality of historical temporalities. What I intend to do in
these pages is to present how these different temporalities are interwoven and
in friction with one another, and how the tension between different temporalities shapes a field of possibilities in which new political trajectories can be
generated.

A new conception of history as multiverse requires a different conception of
time. There is need for an elastic time, as Ernst Bloch suggested, borrowing the
idea of space conceived by the mathematician Bernhard Riemann. Or, again borrowing other concepts from mathematics, a topological time, thus as a circle
drawn on a handkerchief, then crumpled and wrinkled and in which the distance between points becomes variable and the past can overlap the present.[15]
In other words, there is no longer need for a time that is absolute and Newto-
nian, but rather relativistic. A time that, just as in relativistic physics, is bent by
gravity so too, in history, is bent by the density of events. There exists a chron-
ological time that always goes by in the same way, without quality and indifferent to any qualitative change. Its absolutism leads one to say that if a civilization has remained "backward" it is because it used its time poorly. But there is
no such thing as having used time well or poorly. Time is used in a different way,
and this qualitative difference impresses upon time a rhythm and a direction: a
temporality. Global, social, and political space must be interpreted as entirely
temporalized: there are different rhythms, speeds, and legacies that run parallel,
intersect, and conflict when one temporality imposes itself as dominant and tries
to synchronize the others. These conflicts act as prisms that refract the white
light of universal history in the colors of the different temporalities.

Empty and homogenous time is purely abstract, but it has real effects. It is
the time of capital or, more precisely, it is the time of socially necessary labor
that, through the world's stock markets, marks the rhythm of the production
of goods in the world market.[16] Its real effects can be observed in the differentiation of levels of exploitation around the globe. The empty and homogenous
time also works in the violent processes of construction and reproduction of
national homogeneity. It regulates the disciplining of a nation through the regulation of the rhythms of life, from school to retirement, from work to national
holidays. This empty and homogenous time, which is not located anywhere in
real space, collides with the heterogeneous time of many forms of life. The latter is not constituted by the survival of remainders but rather it is the plot of
the times of the postcolonial world, which constitutes most of the populated
modern world.[17]

The encounter between temporal trajectories does not produce the subsump-
tion of heterogeneous temporalities into homogenous time. On the contrary,
that tension recombines existing temporalities and produces new ones. These,

in turn, are sedimented in temporal-historical layers that slide over one another. This image can be productively developed in geological terms. From the friction generated by the sliding between temporal-historical layers the pressure and temperature rise and, in the tension between different layers, new political and social configurations become possible. These are subduction phenomena in which metamorphic rocks are formed and, in our case, new, unprecedented configurations of preexisting legal, political, and economic material are generated. These new configurations become possible and real when elements of what-has-been are reactivated in a constellation of the present. It is with this clash between temporalities that a critical historiography works. To give an example within European history, this does not draw a straight line from the Middle Ages to the modern age, but sees in the enormous medieval juridical, political, and economic material a shrub of possibilities that not the historian but the agents in a specific insurgency have from time to time reactivated.

This way of looking at history also changes the way we understand and use our concepts. If political concepts are considered as historically stratified, then at any historical moment, different layers are, or may be, activated. Political concepts do not evolve in a linear manner, according to an outline that is dear to the history of ideas. Rather, they are political words crossed by many semantic layers that have historically sedimented and that, in particular situations, emerge on the surface, recombining into a new configuration of the present. In other words, there are particularly weighty political terms, such as *democracy, freedom, equality*, which carry semantic stratifications that, in different conceptual constellations, can trigger different political meanings and work as catalysts that can produce change. An example, in our present, is the term *democracy* for how it has been reactivated by the movements of the Indigenous Peoples, in the Arab Spring and the global Occupy, and the many bridges between them.[18] What is at stake in these movements is not a demand for new democratic procedures to legitimize a representative democratic state in crisis, but another way of practicing democracy.

When Barack Obama celebrated the Egyptian insurgency of 2011, calling for a "peaceful transition into democracy,"[19] what was implied by the democracy he was talking about was the political form of the modern Western nation-state—as if this constituted the goal of a universal history traced from the trajectory of the modern West. At the same time, on a poster exhibited during a demonstration of the Occupy movement in London, one could read, "Democracy is an illusion." If President Obama was trying to bottle the democratic excess that emerged in the insurgency by enclosing it in the constitutional shell of the state, the anonymous London protester denounced the procedural idea of democracy as an illusion.

Tertium semper datur. There is another possibility. In 2013, in the Indignados movement in Spain, statements like "Our democracy is kidnapped by the parliament" and "Democracy is in the street and not in parliament"[20] could be read. The dissatisfaction with the real existing democracy was expressed in the intention not to fix representative democracy, but to practice democracy in a different way. The difference between *las calles*, the streets, and *el congreso*, the parliament, is not only spatial, but also and above all temporal. One of the criticisms aimed at the Occupy movement concerned the slow lengths of time of the decision-making process, a criticism that essentially reproduced the arguments used in the early modern age to legitimize the monopoly of state power and its rapid decision-making against the lengthy decision-making time of the imperative mandate. Two temporal dimensions intertwine here. One relative to the different decision-making speed, the other to the reactivation of a nonmodern institution: the imperative mandate and its reactivation in a new democratic context.[21]

There is not a single democratic trajectory to be implemented through democratic procedures. If democracy is an experiment with politics, this experiment is open to possibilities other than those of modern Western representative democracy. It is time to extract concepts not from newly coined words, but from old and present-day practices that experiment and anticipate new institutional forms and ways of life. These practices take place starting from a double interruption of the dominant modernity. On the one hand, they take place in the penumbra of the state, subverting one of its cardinal principles: the monopoly of state power. On the other hand, the subjects acting democracy in *las calles* reactivate institutions that from the point of view of dominant modernity would be awkward or even premodern, but in the hands of the insurgents are nonmodern institutions that, reconfigured in the present, disclose new possible futures. From here it emerges that (1) critique should be articulated around the duo of history and power, showing the need to pluralize both; (2) historiographical work is a research field related to possibilities, trajectories, and paths opened in an insurgency. It is the insurgents who operate as historians when they reconfigure archaic institutions in the present, making them not only contemporary, but also, and above all, full of topicality and future.

Subduction and Other Trajectories

During the Paris Commune of 1871, the Communards began an experiment with democracy that split sovereignty into a plurality of authority organized around the reactivation of medieval institutions. The individual/sovereignty binary structure, typical of the modern state, was disassembled and rearticulated in a plurality of forms in which the people gave themselves organization and voice, i.e., clubs, associations, popular organizations, and so on, which exercised power in their political practices.[22] What the Communards shared was a political space, and not an abstract national belonging. This belonging always needs the identity/exclusion couple, whereas the Communards were experimenting with new ways of universal access to politics, ways not based on that binary opposition. A different conception of citizenship emerged from this experiment, not based on the privilege of birth in a given nation and not even abstractly defined in cosmopolitan terms but articulated through participation and political practice at local assemblies. The democratic excess liberated in the practice of the Communards was redefining the concepts of politics starting from new political and social practices. It was the same *excès de démocratie* practiced by the sansculottes in the continuous convocation of the primary assemblies and sections, which intimidated Robespierre, who saw them as a threat against the national sovereignty represented by the Convention.[23]

In their political practice, the Communards show us that the temporality constituted by nonmodern institutions, which they extracted from the Middle Ages, encompasses a rich multiplicity of futures that have gone unfulfilled. Here, an alternative trajectory of modernity is experimented with by activating historical layers and nonmodern political traditions, based on a plurality of authorities and their mutual limitation. But to grasp this interweaving of historical temporalities, one must look at history in a new way. Indeed, from the perspective of the Communards, the vast medieval juridical, political, and social structure liberated enormous legal and political material for new possible configurations.

We can find an echo of this insurgent democracy in the numerous practices that in our day redefine the politics of citizenship in terms of agency that starts from the neighborhood, not as an abstract place, but "concrete, territorialized and rooted."[24] The issue is not finding explicit references to the Paris Commune. What unites different insurgencies is a common experiment with politics and with oneself, which begins in the penumbra of the state. The modern nation-state, from this perspective, was itself an experiment. What is wrong with the modern state is the universalization of its political categories that have made it a normative goal for the whole of humanity.

In *Thomas Müntzer als Theologe der Revolution*, published in 1921, Ernst Bloch responds to the defeat of the German councils by reactivating a long-standing alternative tradition of modernity dating back almost half a millennium, to the wars of the German peasants of 1525. He, in turn, taps into a tradition, reactivating the gesture made by Friedrich Engels, who had published his volume *The Peasant War in Germany* following the Revolution of 1848 and then again, in a second edition, after the defeat of the Commune. The topicality of the parallel derives from the defeat, but primarily from the need to keep an alternative tradition to capitalist modernity alive.

What emerged in 1919 was the democratic excess that was already practiced in the sansculottes assembly. The emergence of this excess caused a violent political and intellectual reaction. On the one hand, Carl Schmitt, in his book on dictatorship, published in the same year as Bloch's book on Müntzer, wanted to channel and neutralize the political excess of the councils in the sovereign decision of the state. With his book *Dictatorship*, which was born "in the unfavorable external circumstances of our time,"[25] Schmitt sought a solution to political chaos by hindering the road to the alternative that had been delineated with the council republic. Schmitt shared in the liberal mind-set of the fear of falling into a state of nature, the obsession of neutralizing conflict, and closing the "deviation"[26] that had begun in 1793 and reemerged in a long series of insurgencies that dotted the nineteenth and twentieth centuries. For Schmitt, the idea of 1793 was advocated by a legacy that, "starting from Babeuf and Buonarotti and leading up to Blanqui," would reach the insurgency of 1919. In this tradition, Schmitt argues, the dictatorship of the proletariat "presupposes the concept of a sovereign dictatorship, just in the form it stands at the root of the theory and practice of the National Convention."[27] The year 1793 is Schmitt's *annus horribilis.* It is, literally, with this date that the book *Dictatorship* ends. But with this date, Schmitt does not just end his own book; he also intends to end an alternative legacy of modernity by flattening it on the concept of the sovereign dictatorship of the modern state.

Schmitt was wrong. For him there was only one historical temporality dominated by a monolithic political modernity. The alternative to Schmitt, not only theoretical, but above all practical, was rather in the paths interrupted and brutally repressed by state sovereignty. The political alternative of the sansculottes, articulated in a plurality of assemblies and political authorities, was not a prelude to the Terror, but was crushed by it, that is to say, by the sovereign power of the state in the name of unity of the French nation. The same unity that Schmitt wanted to defend.

Similarly, the Spartacist experiment was militarily suppressed by the Social Democrat Gustav Noske with the help of the right-wing Freikorps, who opened the way to National Socialism. The Spartacist experiment was resumed in Bavaria in 1919 when the insurgents transferred the administration of the city into the hands of the factory councils, planned a reform of the educational system, facilitated the socialization of property, and began to design a system for the abolition of paper money. This experiment was also interrupted when the Social Democratic president Friedrich Ebert arranged the military repression of the Soviet Republic.

To understand what was interrupted by the brutality of the nation-state, it is useful to look at an alternative constitutional draft that precedes the Weimar Constitution (1919). A draft constitution drawn up by Gustav Landauer in November 1918 states that council democracy "as self-determination of the people, and of individual groups among the people, is something entirely different to the nonsense of elections, which means abdication of power by the people and governing of an oligarchy."[28] This alternative political trajectory, which does not take the avenue of the national representative state, has its own legacy that Landauer, like the Communards of 1871 before him, does not hesitate to reconnect with medieval institutions. Landauer wrote: "Our revolution has already begun returning to the true democracy we can find in the medieval constitutions of municipalities and provinces, in Norway and in Switzerland, and especially in the meetings of the sections of the French Revolution."[29] This return (*zurückkehren*) to true democracy is anything but nostalgic. It refers to the alternative tradition of 1793 and to the many experiments that tried to give a different direction to Western modernity but were left interrupted. Landauer, not unlike the *Sans-culottes* in 1793 and the Communards in 1871, wrote that the "imperative mandate will be crucial, not only in the fields of government and legislation but regarding all motions presented to the people by executive bodies."[30] This, in fact, characterizes the imperative mandate: at its base there are not "atomized voters abdicating their power," but "municipalities, cooperatives, and associations determining their own destiny in big assemblies."[31] In other words, sovereignty is not displaced in the unity of the people-nation, but it is articulated in groups and associations. A similar perspective can be found in the manifesto of the Spartacus League from 1918: "Right of immediate recall by the local workers' and soldiers' councils and replacement of their representatives in the central council, should these not act in the interests of their constituents. Right of the executive council to appoint and dismiss the people's commissioners as well as the central national authorities and officials."[32] The right to recall by the local workers' and soldiers' councils is, first of all, an expression of a different way of understanding politics: based not on the monopoly of the power of the nation-state, but on a plurality of authority articulated in councils and associations. It is in this form that democratic excess emerges, not as chaos, but as an institutional fabric alternative to the sovereignty of the modern state. These institutions do not take over the sovereignty of the state or aim to crash it. Instead, they reconfigure the entire political and social fabric, in which the state ceases to represent the unity of the nation and becomes one unit among units. It is a question of working with a different theory of institutions, which the insurgents created by building bridges between the present and a multiplicity of nonmodern and non-Western institutions, as Mariategui did when he related the *ayllus*, the Indigenous local forms of self-government, with Russian *mir*, and the Soviets.[33] Bloch also works with these bridges in his book on Müntzer. Ernst Bloch wants to release the democratic excess that was experimented with in 1919, and presents another way that brings together Thomas Müntzer and the sixteenth-century peasant wars with the revolutionaries of the 1920s.

In the declaration of the German peasants of 1525, called the "Twelve Articles," a manifesto printed in twenty-five thousand copies in just two months, the peasants defended communal possession of land in an antifeudal sense, oriented toward a nonhierarchical communalism; they supported the imperative mandate as a practice of community power, universal equality and brotherhood as a way of being.[34] Here, forms of democratic self-government, universal equality, and communal possession of land were organized through the reinvention of institutional forms inherited from the Middle Ages. Müntzer showed a trajectory of modernity that diverged from the one taken by another Thomas, the Englishman Hobbes, and his anthropological assumption of the fear of violent death, which is what individuals experience in a situation where power is not concentrated in the hands of a single sovereign. Müntzer's historical antagonists were the German princes and Martin Luther, who, similarly to what Hobbes affirmed, wrote that in the absence of a single authority "any man might become judge over another. Then authority, government, law, and order would disappear from the world; there would be nothing but murder and bloodshed."[35] The German peasants, the killing of whom Luther encouraged as if they were "a mad dog," and later the German insurgents of 1919 and numerous other insurgents of modernity, were not only experimenting with new institutions but, as it were, they were also experimenting with themselves. Just as they were dismantling the state, so too they were dismantling their own subjectivity by testing a different political anthropology, a more mature one because it could handle the anxiety that comes from the instability of politics. Drawing from mystical tradition, Müntzer tried to harmonize the external event of salvation with the process of salvation of the inner person.[36] Eventually, he tried to translate this project into a social and political plan.

Critical Memory

In his book on Thomas Müntzer, Bloch observed that history is not kept alive through memory (*Erinnerung*), but rather through "the productive method of remembrance (*Eingedenken*),"[37] which allows the dead to return to act in a new context of meaning (*Sinnzusammenhang*), which shows the new. It is the alternative trajectories of modernity that are reactivated and made present again in the "context of meaning" of an insurgency, in which they become even more present than they were in their historical present. These contexts of meaning are not activated in an archive by the historian, but in a struggle, by the collectivity of insurgents. It is the German Spartacists who cite the Russian Revolution, the institutions of the Paris Commune, the common use of land defended by the peasants in 1525, and go back in history as far as the slave revolt against Rome in the first century BC. The sansculottes of 1793, the Communards of 1871, the Spartacists of 1919 all cite the medieval institution of the imperative mandate without hesitation, because for them history does not proceed from the Middle Ages to modernity along a straight line, but rather has the shape of a shrub, in which there are possibilities, interrupted branches, and alternative routes. It is the insurgents, and not the historian as an individual, who extract and reactivate from the rich, nonmodern historical material alternatives to state and capitalist modernity. For critical history all that remains is to show these alternative ways. This is what Benjamin would call "a solidarity with dead brothers."[38] In a double sense. First is the solidarity with insurgents and their legacy. But it is also the solidarity that links an insurgency to a multiplicity of interrupted experiments, to revive and bring to fulfillment in the present what was not possible then.

Walter Benjamin borrowed from Bloch the idea of remembrance (*Eingedenken*) and turned it into the key to unlocking these blocked futures. Benjamin must be taken seriously when he writes that remembrance "can make the incomplete (happiness) into something complete, and the complete (suffering) into something incomplete."[39] The conception of the incompleteness (*Unabgeschlossenheit*) of the past constitutes the scandalous and often largely misunderstood assumption introduced by Walter Benjamin in his reflections on the concept of history.[40] Max Horkheimer attacked the idealistic, religious nature of incompleteness: "The slain are really slain. . . . If one takes the lack of closure entirely seriously, one must believe in the Last Judgment."[41] It is possible to find a bifurcation in the conception of critique here. The idea of incompleteness is not, as Habermas would suggest, a ploy to virtually reconcile, in some communicative context, a past injustice that otherwise could not be repaired.[42] It is not the historian who makes the past incomplete, but the insurgents. They transform the past into an arsenal full of possibilities from which to draw to shape the present. And it is the insurgents, in their political experiment, who continue what was interrupted and, in their struggle, bring the dead back to life. As the Spartacus League did with the name of the Thracian gladiator, protagonist of the slave uprising against Rome.

What makes it difficult, or even impossible, to understand the nature of incompleteness is this change of perspective that decentralizes the subject of historical knowledge, placing it at the center of historical action. In his thesis 12 on the concept of history, Benjamin wrote: "the subject of historical knowledge is the struggling, oppressed class itself."[43] Emphasis should be placed not only on the oppressed class, but also and above all on the present participle "struggling." It is not a matter of making history from the point of view of some oppressed subject or victim, because it is the agency of historical subjects that makes the past intelligible and incomplete. The historian, as an individual, has little to do. Indeed, very little. The historian *is called* on to participate and show how the insurgents, in their action, extract the raw material from the past to transform the present and give shape to the future. The sense of this calling, which for Horkheimer was religious, is above all ethical. It is a duty toward those who died in order to put an end to centuries of oppression.

In order not to let the dead die again, or be embalmed in a museum, a political historiography is needed that, reproducing in theory what has been anticipated in practice in an insurgency, is charged with bringing to light the contexts of meaning that are disclosed when different temporalities collide with one another. Ernst Bloch's book on Müntzer was not written in order to remember the suffering of the German peasants and their defeat, but as a remembrance of the insurgency of 1525 as a possibility of a different life, a possibility that calls into question our present and, above all, awaits completion. This reminder not only invests the present generation with ethical-political responsibility toward a past generation but provides an orientation for thinking about what seems to be today more and more difficult to think about: a real alternative to state and capitalist modernity. It is not a matter of inventing a new political form ex nihilo to be implemented. This was the typically modern attitude introduced by Descartes in philosophy and by Hobbes in politics. Rather, it is about digging into so-called premodern and protomodern forms to extract nonmodern material and to think of it as it was reconfigured into an insurgency of modernity.

Remembering Müntzer means making the insurgency of 1525 something incomplete. It was the German insurgency of 1918–19 that showed Bloch that the road of 1525 was still open and not suppressed by the triumphal march of *Weltgeschichte*; it showed that particular past as full of possible futures; it showed, finally, how different temporal layers are mixed. This is the meaning of remembrance. In other words, it is the democratic excess experienced in the insurgency of 1918–19 that shows how the insurgency of 1525 is incomplete—because it is part of the same experiment.

Five hundred years ago, Thomas Müntzer pointed his finger toward a configuration of property relations, power, and anthropology that retied the paths of medieval mysticism, the tradition of local self-government, and communal lands in an original way. In the mystical language that Müntzer inherited from Meister Eckhart, to achieve this condition, the human being must make room for God, that is, he must create space inside himself and stop being what has been done to him. This process, in German *Entwerden*, is the way toward inner change and thus also the condition for a new order. *Entwerden* could be translated today, albeit improperly, as the interweaving of desubjectification and resubjectification toward a change that comes about not only from external circumstances but, above all, from within man. We are faced with a tradition that, by blending together mysticism and communal possession of land, indicates the direction toward a different trajectory of modernity, a tradition that indicates a different individuation, alternative to that which has become dominated by the centrality of the ego and possessive individualism.

It is possible to give critique a different direction by pivoting on the idea of remembrance (*Eingedenken*), which indicates the passage from "I think" to a "we" as the subject of historical knowledge that, in the act of a concrete struggle, opens the present up to new possibilities that connect and orient toward an incomplete past. In other words, as we have seen for the Communards and the German peasants of 1525, it is the struggling oppressed class that in the insurgency, through an act of remembrance, recalls a past legacy and reactivates anachronistic institutions in an entirely new configuration. This legacy does not keep us tied to the past but, on the contrary, it is what allows us to identify alternatives to a present that tends to represent itself as ahistorical and project its shadow on a future that, as depicted in recent cinematography, is often portrayed in apocalyptic terms, as if the end of the world were the only alternative to the historical present. Instead, there are countless futures stuck in what-has-been that show, in nonmodern material, alternatives to state and capitalist modernity. Without any romanticism, the insurgents disclose futures that were encapsulated in the past, which now reemerges on the surface as a layer of time full of new possibilities. It is their insurgent critique that brings about a subduction capable of showing the incompleteness of the past and calls "us" to accomplish what was left incomplete then. Here, insurgency ceases to be opposition to power and becomes the art of practicing an alternative trajectory of modernity constituted by a multiplicity of experiments with the democratic excess. Critique becomes both an ethical and political attitude, a way of thinking and acting, or, one could say, the art of governing and being governed in a different way. These alternatives constitute the many temporal layers of our present, which recombine in the moment of an insurgency, when anachronistic institutions merge together, thereby freeing incomplete futures from the past. These experiments build unexpected bridges between Western experiences and those of the global South.

Notes

1. Dipesh Chakrabarty, *Provincializing Europe: Postcolonial Thought and Historical Difference* (Princeton: Princeton University Press, 2000).
2. John Stuart Mill, *On Liberty, and Other Writings* (Cambridge, MA: Cambridge University Press, 1989), 13; Uday S. Mehta, *Liberalism and Empire: A Study in Nineteenth-Century British Liberal Thought* (Chicago: University of Chicago Press, 1999).
3. Gary Wilder, *Freedom Time: Negritude, Decolonization and the Future of the World* (Durham: Duke University Press, 2015).
4. Aimé Césaire, "Letter to Maurice Thorez," *Social Text* 28, no. 2 (2010): 145–52, 149.
5. Ernst Bloch, "Differentiations in the Concept of Progress" (1955), in *A Philosophy of the Future*, 112–44 (New York: Herder and Herder, 1970), 143.
6. "Delcaration of Quito, Ecuador," July 1990 in http://unpfip.blogspot.com/2012/09/declaration-of-quito-1990.html. See Anne-Claire Defossez and Didier Fassin, "La colère des Indiens de l'Équateur," *Le Monde diplomatique*, August 1990, 3.

7. "First Declaration of the Lacandona Jungle," January 1, 1994, in http://enlacezapatista
   .ezln.org.mx.
8. Bruno Bauer, *Die gute Sache der Freiheit und meine eigene Angelegenheit* (Zürich: Verlag des literarischen Comptoirs, 1972), 204. On the relation between crisis and critique, see Reinhart Koselleck, *Critique and Crisis: Enlightenment and the Pathogenesis of Modern Society* (Cambridge, MA: MIT Press, 2000).
9. Walter Benjamin, *The Arcades Project* (Cambridge, MA: Harvard University Press,
   1999), 456.
10. Reinhart Koselleck, *Futures Past: On the Semantics of Historical Time* (New York:
    Columbia University Press, 2004), 2.
11. Reinhart Koselleck, *Zeitschichten* (Frankfurt: Suhrkamp, 2001), 9; Reinhart Koselleck,
    Vom Sinn und Unsinn der Geschichte (Frankfurt: Suhrkamp, 2010), 96–114.
12. Teodor Shanin, ed., *Late Marxism and the Russian Road: Marx and "the Peripheries
    of Capitalism"* (New York: Monthly Review Press, 1983), 97–126.
13. Marx, *Theories of Surplus Value* (Amherst, NY: Prometheus 2000), 3:468.
14. Harry Harootunian, *Marx After Marx: History and Time in the Expansion of Capital-
    ism* (New York: Columbia University Press, 2015), 206.
15. Michel Serres, with Bruno Latour, *Conversations on Science, Culture, and Time* (Ann
    Arbor: University of Michigan Press, 1995), 60: "If you take a handkerchief and spread
    it out in order to iron it, you can see in it certain fixed distances and proximities. If
    you sketch a circle in one area, you can mark out nearby points and measure far-off
    distances. Then take the same handkerchief and crumple it, by putting it in your
    pocket. Two distant points suddenly are close, even superimposed. If, further, you tear
    it in certain places, two points that were close can become very distant. This science
    of nearness and rifts is called topology, while the science of stable and well-defined
    distances is called metrical geometry."
16. Massimiliano Tomba, *Marx's Temporalities* (Leiden: Brill, 2013), 159–86.
17. Partha Chatterjee, *The Politics of the Governed* (New York: Columbia University Press,
    2004), 8.
18. Rebecca Manski of Occupy Wall Street acknowledged the Zapatista influence after vis-
    iting Oventic. She said: "As soon as I arrived I saw that many of the principles, lan-
    guage, themes and ways of organizing Occupy Wall Street had been taken straight
    from Zapatista philosophy." See www.aljazeera.com/indepth/features/2014/01/are
    -mexico-zapatista-rebels-still-relevant-20141183731812643.html.
19. Natasha Mozgovaya, "Obama: Egypt Must Begin Peaceful Transition Into Democracy
    Now," *Haaretz*, February 2, 2011, www.haaretz.com/1.5116631.
20. Matthew Johnson and Samid Suliman, *Protest: Analysing Current Trends* (New York:
    Routledge, 2015).
21. Massimiliano Tomba, "Who's Afraid of the Imperative Mandate?," *Critical Times* 1,
    no. 1 (2018), https://ctjournal.org/index.php/criticaltimes.
22. Martin Phillip Johnson, *The Paradise of Association: Political Culture and Popular
    Organizations in the Paris Commune of 1871* (Ann Arbor: University of Michigan Press,
    1996), 89.
23. *Archives Parlementaires*, June 14, 1793, vol. 66, p. 530, in *Archives parlementaires de 1789
    à 1860: recueil complet des débats législatifs & politiques des Chambres françaises* (1862–
    1913). Paris: Librairie administrative de P. Dupont.
24. Sian Lazar, *El Alto, Rebel City: Self and Citizenship in Andean Bolivia* (Durham: Duke
    University Press, 2008), 63; James Holston, *Insurgent Citizenship: Disjunctions of
    Democracy and Modernity in Brazil* (Princeton: Princeton University Press, 2008), 252.

25. Carl Schmitt, *Dictatorship: From the Origin of the Modern Concept of Sovereignty to Proletarian Class Struggle* (Cambridge: Polity, 2014), xlv.

26. François Furet and Denis Richet, *La revolution française* (Paris: Hachette, 1986), 9.

27. Schmitt, *Dictatorship*, 179.

28. Gustav Landauer, "The United Republics of Germany and Their Constitution," in *All Power to the Councils?: A Documentary History of the German Revolution of 1918–1919*, ed. Gabriel Kuhn (Oakland, CA: PM Press, 2012), 200.

29. Kuhn, *All Power to the Councils?*, 200–201.

30. Kuhn, 201.

31. Kuhn, 201.

32. Rosa Luxemburg, "What Does the Spartacus League Want" (December 1918), in *Selected Political Writings of Rosa Luxemburg*, ed. Dick Haward (New York: Monthly Review Press, 1971), 373.

33. Jose Carlos Mariategui, *Seven Interpretative Essays on Peruvian Reality* (Austin: University of Texas Press, 1971).

34. Tom Scott and Bob Scribner, *The German Peasants' War: A History in Documents* (New York: Humanity Books, 1991), 252–57; Peter Blickle, *Die Revolution von 1525* (Munich: Oldenbourg, 2004), 321–27.

35. Martin Luther, *An Admonition to Peace: A Reply to the Twelve Articles of the Peasants of Swabia* (1525), in *Luther, Selected Political Writings*, ed. J. M. Porter (Eugene, OR: Wipf and Stock, 1974), 76.

36. Hans-Jürgen Goertz, *Thomas Müntzer: Apocalyptic Mystic and Revolutionary* (Edinburgh: T and T Clark, 1993), 103.

37. Ernst Bloch, "Differentiations in the Concept of Progress" (1955), in *A Philosophy of the Future*, 112–44 (New York: Herder and Herder, 1970), 18.

38. Walter Benjamin, *Über den Begriff der Geschichte* (Frankfurt: Suhrkamp, 2010), 38.

39. Walter Benjamin, *The Arcades Project* (Cambridge, MA: Harvard University Press, 1999), 471.

40. Benjamin, 471.

41. Benjamin, 471; see also Max Horkheimer, "On Bergson's Metaphysics of Time," *Radical Philosophy* 131 (2005): 9–19.

42. Jürgen Habermas, "Modernity's Consciousness of Time and Its Need for Self-Reassurance," in *The Philosophical Discourse of Modernity: Twelve Lectures* (Cambridge, MA: MIT Press, 1999), 15. See also Axel Honneth, "Kommunikative Erschließung der Vergangenheit. Zum Zusammenhang von Anthropologie und Geschichtsphilosophie bei Walter Benjamin," *Internationale Zeitschrift für Philosophie* 1 (1993): 3–19.

43. Walter Benjamin, "On the Concept of History," in *Walter Benjamin: Selected Writings*, vol. 4, *1938–1940*, ed. Howard Eiland and Michael W. Jennings (Cambridge, MA: Harvard University Press, 2006), 394.

Bibliography

Bauer, Bruno. *Die gute Sache der Freiheit und meine eigene Angelegenheit.* Zürich: Verlag des literarischen Comptoirs, 1972 [1842].

Benjamin, Walter. *The Arcades Project.* Cambridge, MA: Harvard University Press, 1999.

——. "On the Concept of History." In *Walter Benjamin: Selected Writings*, vol. 4, *1938–1940*, edited by Howard Eiland and Michael W. Jennings. Cambridge, MA: Harvard University Press, 2006.

——. *Über den Begriff der Geschichte*. Frankfurt: Suhrkamp, 2010.

Blickle, Peter. *Die Revolution von 1525*. Munich: Oldenbourg, 2004.

Bloch, Ernst. "Differentiations in the Concept of Progress" (1955). In *A Philosophy of the Future*, 112–44. New York: Herder and Herder, 1970.

——. *Thomas Müntzer als Theologe der Revolution*. Munich: Kurt Wolff, 1921.

Césaire, Aimé. "Letter to Maurice Thorez." *Social Text* 28, no. 2 (2010): 145–52.

Chakrabarty, Dipesh. *Provincializing Europe: Postcolonial Thought and Historical Difference*. Princeton: Princeton University Press, 2000.

Chatterjee, Partha. *The Politics of the Governed*. New York: Columbia University Press, 2004.

Defossez, Anne-Claire, and Didier Fassin. "La colère des Indiens de l'Équateur." *Le Monde diplomatique*, August 1990, 3.

Furet, François, and Denis Richet. *La revolution française*. Paris: Hachette, 1986.

Goertz, Hans-Jürgen. *Thomas Müntzer: Apocalyptic Mystic and Revolutionary*. Edinburgh: T and T Clark, 1993.

Habermas, Jürgen. "Modernity's Consciousness of Time and Its Need for Self-Reassurance." In *The Philosophical Discourse of Modernity: Twelve Lectures*. Cambridge, MA: MIT Press, 1999.

Harootunian, Harry. *Marx After Marx: History and Time in the Expansion of Capitalism*. New York: Columbia University Press, 2015.

Haward, Dick, ed. *Selected Political Writings of Rosa Luxemburg*. New York: Monthly Review Press, 1971.

Holston, James. *Insurgent Citizenship: Disjunctions of Democracy and Modernity in Brazil*. Princeton: Princeton University Press, 2008.

Honneth, Axel. "Kommunikative Erschließung der Vergangenheit. Zum Zusammenhang von Anthropologie und Geschichtsphilosophie bei Walter Benjamin." *Internationale Zeitschrift für Philosophie* 1 (1993): 3–19.

Horkheimer, Max. "On Bergson's Metaphysics of Time." *Radical Philosophy* 131 (2005): 9–19.

Johnson, Martin Phillip. *The Paradise of Association: Political Culture and Popular Organizations in the Paris Commune of 1871*. Ann Arbor: University of Michigan Press, 1996.

Johnson, Matthew, and Samid Suliman. *Protest: Analysing Current Trends*. New York: Routledge, 2015.

Kant, Immanuel. "An Answer to the Question, 'What Is Enlightenment?'" In *Toward Perpetual Peace, and Other Writings on Politics, Peace, and History*. New Haven: Yale University Press, 2006 [1784].

Koselleck, Reinhart. *Critique and Crisis: Enlightenment and the Pathogenesis of Modern Society*. Cambridge, MA: MIT Press, 2000.

——. *Futures Past: On the Semantics of Historical Time*. New York: Columbia University Press, 2004.

——. *Vom Sinn und Unsinn der Geschichte*. Frankfurt: Suhrkamp, 2010.

——. *Zeitschichten,* Frankfurt: Suhrkamp, 2001.

Kuhn, Gabriel, ed. *All Power to the Councils? A Documentary History of the German Revolution of 1918–1919*. Oakland, CA: PM Press, 2012.

Lazar, Sian. *El Alto, Rebel City: Self and Citizenship in Andean Bolivia*. Durham: Duke University Press, 2008.

Luther, Martin. *An Admonition to Peace: A Reply to the Twelve Articles of the Peasants of Swabia* (1525). In *Luther, Selected Political Writings*, edited by J. M. Porter. Eugene, OR: Wipf and Stock, 1974.

Mariategui, Jose Carlos. *Seven Interpretative Essays on Peruvian Reality*. Austin: University of Texas Press, 1971.

Marx, Karl. *Capital*. Vol. 1. London: Penguin, 1992.

——. *Theories of Surplus Value*. Amherst, NY: Prometheus 2000.

Matheson, Peter, ed. *The Collected Works of Thomas Müntzer*. Edinburgh: T and T Clark, 1988.

Mehta, Uday S. *Liberalism and Empire: A Study in Nineteenth-Century British Liberal Thought*. Chicago: University of Chicago Press, 1999.

Mill, John Stuart. *On Liberty, and Other Writings*. Cambridge, MA: Cambridge University Press, 1989.

Mozgovaya, Natasha. "Obama: Egypt Must Begin Peaceful Transition Into Democracy Now." *Haaretz*, February 2, 2011, www.haaretz.com/1.5116631.

Schmitt, Carl. *Dictatorship: From the Origin of the Modern Concept of Sovereignty to Proletarian Class Struggle*. Cambridge: Polity, 2014.

Schumpeter, Joseph A. *Capitalism, Socialism and Democracy*. London: Routledge, 1994.

Scott, Tom, and Bob Scribner. *The German Peasants' War: A History in Documents*. New York: Humanity Books, 1991.

Serres, Michel, with Bruno Latour. *Conversations on Science, Culture, and Time*. Ann Arbor: University of Michigan Press, 1995.

Shanin, Teodor, ed. *Late Marxism and the Russian Road: Marx and "the Peripheries of Capitalism."* New York: Monthly Review Press, 1983.

Tomba, Massimiliano. *Marx's Temporalities*. Leiden: Brill, 2013.

——. "Who's Afraid of the Imperative Mandate?" *Critical Times* 1, no. 1 (2018), https://ctjournal.org/index.php/criticaltimes.

Wilder, Gary. *Freedom Time: Negritude, Decolonization and the Future of the World*. Durham: Duke University Press, 2015.

CHAPTER 7

WHAT'S LEFT OF THE REAL?

VANJA HAMZIĆ

How might one theorize the *limits* of one's knowledge without merely acknowledging that such limits are contingent upon one's ways of *learning-in-the-world*? And what if one's ways of learning—often disciplined into a *discipline* such as anthropology or philosophy—are prefigured so as to always reflect a type of (academic) reality, a system of knowing with its defined histories, methodologies, and goals? What's left behind, that is, beyond such disciplinary knowledge? And to what end? Can the unknowable be defined, and if so, how? Can its *existence*, its ontological possibility, form a constitutive element of the human condition? Relatedly, if the unknowable is recognized as an element of the everyday, of our social and disciplinary practices, how will its existence relate to critical theory and the project(s) of the left? To wit, will we know more, or better, about the world, our disciplines, and ourselves by conceding our intrinsic "failure" to know all? If so, can the unknowable be *structured* within our theories and methodologies of knowing, or does our perception of the unknowable suggest that purely structural approaches to *knowing-in-the-world* cannot succeed?

The unknowable, often loosely described as that which is left behind (and yet remains) once we have chartered our lifeworlds, or lifeworlds of others we seek to know, is by no means a new concept. As I show in this essay, the unknowable has resurfaced as an idea in social anthropology and has found renewed salience in continental philosophy. Its application to political theory, on the other hand, holds the promise of resistance to the notion that politics is (ever) an ontology. In an eclectic survey of each of these fields of inquiry, I will endeavor to demonstrate that the unknowable is typically seen as a condition of reality—*it's a thing* in that it is thinkable as thing or, for some, as things. My choice of authors and their disciplinary leanings is guided by their theoretical reliance on thing(s) *and* a certain cross-disciplinary structuralist tradition that regards reality as consisting of definable clusters—including the cluster of the unknowable. Perhaps this should be said right away: to me, a critique of the unknowable makes sense precisely inasmuch as it can reveal the failures of structuralism to account for reality's ostensible clusters. Reality is messy and so is the unknowable. And, because of this, our disciplines are ultimately unable to deal with the unknowable in a structured, premeditative way. That's not a bad thing. Instead, this simply shows that our disciplines are ripe for reimagination and our critical pursuits in need of recalibration toward a much messier understanding of what can and what cannot be known.

Three Disciplinary Proposals: An Overview

In social anthropology, the unknowable has made a notable comeback within the purview of the so-called ontological turn. Here the unknowable appears not as a thing, but as things—and things to *think with* at that. The editors of a seminal anthology titled *Thinking Through Things* thus call for a renewed attention to things with a view to divesting them from any preconceived anthropological knowledge of what they might *be*. The proposed move is distinctly ontological in that it insists on replacing "thing-as-analytic" with "thing-as-heuristic": the ethnographer is invited to suspend the familiar meanings of things so as to make space, cognitive and otherwise, for the unfamiliar meanings of things—those imparted by the ethnographer's interlocutors—to *be* on their own terms.[1] At issue, of course, is the problem of representation—that is, of the consequences of anthropological interpretations of things, people, cultures, through an always already Euro-American ontological matrix. To counter such epistemic violence and allow for other worldings—the worldings of the encountered others—to appear *meaningfully*, the ethnographer is to concede at the outset that much of such ways of being-in-the-world is to remain unobservable, unknowable, ontologically disparate. Thinking through things, it seems, implies thinking things through while realizing, even perhaps a priori, the limits of one's knowledge.

In philosophy, the ontological domain of the unknowable has reappeared within the various strands of continental materialism and realism that make up the so-called speculative turn. Of those, one stands out as most avowedly structuralist, precisely because it finds its origin not in a philosophical project per se but in that of Jacques Lacan's structuralist psychoanalysis. Its colorful proponent, Slavoj Žižek, relies on Lacan's lifelong preoccupation with the Real (*le réel*), which, along with the Symbolic and the Imaginary, formed in Lacan's works the very topology of "human reality" (*réalité humaine*)—a topology that Lacan theorized as interlocking its three constitutive elements into a type of Borromean knot.[2] For Lacan, then, the Real was that-which-is-unknowable in both the symbolic and the imaginary registers of human psyche,[3] that whose presence ultimately serves to confirm reality's own limitation. Or, as Žižek puts it, "it is not part of reality but a kind of inexistent point of reference with no place in reality which, *in its absence*, structures reality."[4] Being both present *as such* but constitutively absent from reality, the Real is a paradox, "the 'impossible' point of the coincidence of opposites: the Real is the In-itself external to (symbolized) reality, but it is simultaneously the obstacle that makes the In-itself inaccessible."[5] This is how the unknowable prefigures both outside the Symbolic and the Imaginary, as a kind of specter of reality's never-quite-completeness.[6]

Finally, in political theory, the Real as the specter of the unknowable could be understood as an antidote to Realpolitik inasmuch as it introduces an external to the political (*le politique*) and, by extension, to what might be called everyday politics (*la politique*). The result, as averred by Susan Buck-Morss: "politics is not an ontology" or, even more provocatively, "the ontological is never political." To arrive at this conclusion, Buck-Morss retraces the transformation of Karl Marx's initial ontological philosophy toward an engagement with the nascent social sciences—including anthropology, psychology, sociology, and economics—"understood not in their positivist, data-gathering or abstract mathematical forms" but as sciences of (material) history proper. A critical potential immanent in this turn meant for Buck-Morss not a return of the kind of political philosophy that presumes an ontological primacy—the return of the political—but the birth of "social theory done reflectively—that is, critically": the advent of critical theory. Hence, argues Buck-Morss, "when Marx said thinking was itself a practice, he meant it in this sense. He did not then ask: What is the ontological meaning of the *being of practice*? Instead, he tried to find out as much as he could about the socio-historical practices of human beings in his time." For Buck-Morss, then, the ontological divorce between the two differently gendered forms of politics opens up a space for experimentation—a Benjaminian *Spielraum*—in which, ultimately, "the world can be otherwise."[7] The specter of the unknowable is no longer just dreadful and abject—it recuperates some of the Lacanian possibility that the reality of human psyche, inclusive of that which is constitutively external to it, can be not always already traumatic.

On the pages that follow, I offer a preliminary assessment of these three strands of the unknowable—in anthropology, continental philosophy, and political theory—and, in so doing, consider how they might relate to one another. At stake is the potential salience of acknowledging the conceptual and methodological boundaries not only of a particular discipline, but also of *meaningfully* taking into account the limits and conditionality of disciplinary knowledge. This, I propose, is an important consideration for critical theory—not least because critique features prominently in such interrogations of the unknowable.

Each of the three disciplinary endeavors grapples with critique, either as its preferred modus operandi or as an estranged praxis—the latter sometimes being described as a "postcritical" stance[8] or even an antithesis to critique. Note that, for example, the ontological turn in anthropology has been derided as both anticritical and apolitical—a depiction that has since been challenged by some of its leading proponents.[9] Besides, it has also been asserted that "ontology" might be just another word for "culture" or, even worse, just another word for "colonialism."[10] I begin by revisiting some of these debates from the perspective of the unknowable—my "critical object" proper. Against this backdrop, however, while acknowledging the endurance of critique,[11] I focus, to the extent possible, on the critical potentials of the ontological turn, rather than plotting its outright dismissal. What does it mean, for instance, that the proponents of this turn so often caution that their investment is *primarily* methodological?

With respect to Žižek's appropriations of the Lacanian Real, I center on Judith Butler's seminal poststructuralist critique of it,[12] which reveals, among other things, that at least certain deployments of the Real, in both Žižek and Lacan, appear to suffer from patriarchal bias. This, in turn, exposes the fallacy of structuralist thinking in both continental philosophy and social anthropology.

Finally, I return to Buck-Morss's radical proposal that the ontological is never political, especially with respect to the specter of the unknowable. I suggest an approach that is, in a way, a synthesis of my previous observations with regard to anthropology and philosophy. This is not to rehearse the distinction between *le politique* and *la politique*,[13] but to ask what appears to me to be a crucial question: In what way are diverse worldings salient for critical theory and the left project? And, relatedly, to what extent does it matter that such worldings—such ways of being-in-the-world and knowing-in-the-world—may be at least partly (although rarely ever fully)[14] mutually unknowable?

The Unknowable and the Ontological Turn in Anthropology

Since its foremost articulation in *Thinking Through Things*, published in 2007, the ontological turn in anthropology has been exposed to an extraordinary amount of criticism, coming from nearly all other strands of current anthropological thought. Small wonder, then, that its proponents have produced an equally remarkable body of responses of varying coherence and clarity. A recent addition to this literature, Holbraad and Pedersen's *The Ontological Turn: An Anthropological Exposition*, stands out for its conceptual clarity as well as the authors' stated ambition to provide a comprehensive guide to the ontological turn's genealogy and fundamental claims. That is, in part, why I find the book valuable for the purposes of this essay, even if it fails to encompass the many diverse substrands of the ontological turn and becomes, instead, an exposition proper of Holbraad and Pedersen's stakes in this turn. At the same time, their volume reads as a compendium of caveats about the ontological turn—a necessity, perhaps, given the relentless debates about the many dangers of an ontologically oriented anthropology. How, then, does the unknowable bode in this particular iteration of the ontological turn?

With its tripartite focus on reflexivity, conceptualization, and experimentation as analytical practices, the main claim of the turn, as Holbraad and Pedersen see it, still seems to be that it is strictly *methodological*, i.e., its concern is decidedly not with "what the 'really real' nature of the world is" but, rather, with posing "ontological questions to solve epistemological problems." If this appears confusing that is just fine because, according to Holbraad and Pedersen, "it so happens that epistemology in anthropology has to be about ontology, too." However, an ontology is not even gestured at in *The Ontological Turn*, for to do so would be to acknowledge that a "really real" of sorts exists as such. Instead, one is guided toward a set of techniques aimed at "*freeing thought* from all metaphysical foundationalism—whether substantive or methodological, normative or pluralistic." This remarkable objective, if at all feasible, should help the fieldworker (with whom it is primarily concerned) not so much to see differently as to see different *things* in the field, for it is no longer *through* them but *from* them that thinking should be done. Having "detheorized" the thing by getting rid of its presupposed analytical connotation—a move proposed by *Thinking Through Things*—one is now presumably ready to follow *The Ontological Turn*'s instruction in filling the thing back up, albeit only contingently, "according to its own ethnographic exigencies." The point is to allow the thing to *become* the empirical source of "conceptualization"—to let it, as it were, differentiate *itself*. But if the thing, so self-differentiated, *can be* free "from any ontological determination whatsoever," as Holbraad and Pedersen would have it, then the thing in and of itself points to its (radical) unknowability. The thing's very "conceptual affordances" seem to be *coming* from an epistemic abyss where the humanly unknowable reigns. Moreover, although this move is billed as distinctly posthumanist, the (radical) unknowability of the thing is always in relation to humans.

The unknowable also appears front and center in another important feature of the ontological turn—its reliance on the *inherent* multiplicity of meaning. Having chartered an intellectual map of their turn that includes not only the obvious (e.g., Eduardo Viveiros de Castro) but also somewhat speculative candidates (such as Roy Wagner and Marilyn Strathern, neither of which explic-itly centered their work on the ontological), Holbraad and Pedersen provide a detailed exploration of the techniques and terms of art used by the (ostensibly) like-minded anthropologists to account for the problem of translation across the different conceptual regimes that the fieldworker and those "in the field" are likely to inhabit. Invention, obviation, relation, postplural abstraction, perspectivism, and other such concepts—all are arrived at by observing what Viveiros de Castro calls "equivocation": an inevitable series of "errors" that befall any attempt to "successfully" translate between two or more *ontologically* different conceptual regimes. But, neither for Viveiros de Castro nor for Hol-braad and Pedersen is this failure to understand necessarily undesirable: talk-ing past each other, if "controlled," can result in new conceptualizations, espe-cially if it causes long-held anthropological assumptions to transform by the power of contradicting ethnographic materials. This is also why, we are told, ontologically informed anthropological analyses are destined to fail, and in so doing lay bare the largely tacit criteria of anthropological evidence. At issue is, however, the "problem" of ontological disparity that not only confounds trans-lation but so presumed mutual unknowability of people (and things) in con-versation, too. If meanings are always already multiple so that cross-ontological understanding is at best unlikely, the unknowable appears as a necessary con-dition of one's ontologically informed knowledge about the other. And, it occu-pies a spectral position not at all unlike to that of the Lacanian Real: in its paradoxical, constitutive absence-presence it reveals reality's own limitation—at least inasmuch as a *potential* reality can be observed in the field *as* a concep-tual regime.

It is in this mode of critique that the ontological turn approaches anthropo-logical inquiry and, with it, the presumptive conceptual limits of such terms of art as *politics* and *critique* itself. "If, anthropologically speaking, we can (must) desist from deciding in advance what, say, 'self-determination,' 'peoples' or 'world' might be," write Holbraad and Pedersen, "then surely we should do the same with the very notion of 'politics,' which motivates this endeavour." The trouble is not in the motive, described as a relentlessly reflexive investment in noncompleteness as an anthropological resolve, which imbues "politics" with "a manifold of potentials for *how things could be*." It is the ontological turn's professed strand of the political that necessitates "a postcritical distortion of the concept of politics itself." The distortion is performed as a sort of "reversed deconstruction" that turns things into "what they could be, but still are not," by taking the world "too seriously" and by "adding to it"—thus making it "more" or "differently real." This is achieved by divesting from critique performed in the "hegemonic" mode of "sceptical debunking."[15] Instead of thinly veiled "cul-tural critique" reduced to "sceptical distance" in anthropology, Holbraad and Pedersen's is a call for a "critique of critique"[16] that is postcritical in its reliance on experimentation and "inherently uncertain grounds for research engagements and interventions"[17]—a fieldwork-based Foucauldian "counter-science" proper that puts *everything* in question.

But just how is this thoroughgoing reformation program supposed to be accomplished, if it is emptied of just about every term of art that suggests (and not just to "us") syndicated political action, or at least its analysis (in the field)?[18] Surely, an ontological orientation should not prevent anthropologists from engaging with the domains of critique and the political that analyze and contemplate resistance to such "scaled-up" phenomena (or, if you like, things) as "capitalism," "neocolonialism," "fascism," "nationalism," "sexism," and so on while taking seriously ontological disparities that might become apparent along the way? Or, do such concepts by sheer weight of their "isms" fall outside an ontologically minded anthropological inquiry? Relatedly, to what end is the critique immanent to the ontological turn prefixed with a sinister "post," when it is hardly not known to almost anyone, Holbraad and Pedersen included, that there exist (if I may say so) numerous iterations of critique other than "sceptical debunking"—in anthropology and beyond? Such shortsightedness is surprising for a turn that Holbraad and Pedersen modestly describe as "the most theoretically reflexive project that anthropology has produced" to date (which, to be sure, betrays the very possibility of a "purely methodological" turn).[19] Besides, the directive of putting everything into question does not quite square with the turn's professed antimetaphysical stance, even if that stance is defended as strictly methodological.[20]

Still, one cannot deny the critical potential of the ontological turn in particular with respect to its thing-driven manner of conceptualization: for *how things could be* matters precisely inasmuch as it can dislodge entrenched epistemological truisms and expose the unknowable—seemingly never quite dissimilar to the Lacanian Real—in their midst. If anthropology is imbued with the potential to contemplate ontological disparity as an epistemological issue, then its "counter-scientific" work in the field could unearth an untold number of "differently real" ways of being-in-the-world, which of course *may be* a matter of critical and political concern, too.

The Lacanian Real and the Speculative Turn in Philosophy

Needless to say, the becoming of objects (things) in and of themselves has also been a preoccupation of a number of exponents of the so-called speculative turn in continental philosophy, and even the very possibility of an empirically grounded disparity of things can sometimes take center stage in thinking "difference" as such. As early as in *Différence et répétition*, Gilles Deleuze posits that "the difference 'between' two things is only empirical, and the corresponding determinations are only extrinsic. However, instead of something distinguished from something else, imagine something which distinguishes itself—and yet that from which it distinguishes itself does not distinguish itself from it." For him, one such thing is lightning, which "distinguishes itself from the black sky but must also trail it behind, *as though* it were distinguishing itself from that which does not distinguish itself from it." The possibility of *unilateral* distinction is what, ultimately, makes difference (as such) possible. The method of extrapolating difference in its conceptual and metaphysical primacy is strikingly similar to that of thinking *from* things in anthropology, although the very stakes of doing so are avowedly disparate: Deleuze interrogates the so-called univocality of Being while anthropologists, presumably, take no specific ontological stance.[21]

The most explicit connection between ontological difference and the unknowable *as* the Lacanian Real is, however, made in Slavoj Žižek's works. For Žižek, the Real—that specter of reality's never-quite-completeness—appears precisely as an insurmountable parallactic gap (and note his focus on vision and observability of things): "the parallax of ontological difference, of the discord between ontic and transcendental-ontological (one cannot reduce the ontological horizon to its ontic 'roots,' but one also cannot deduce the ontic domain from the ontological horizon, i.e., transcendental constitution is not creation), [is] the parallax of the Real."[22]

Defined as a discord in the "order" of Being—and of primarily that-which-is-observable-about-Being—ontological difference in Žižek is of a decidedly structuralist nature. This, of course, is not surprising, given Lacan's own structuralism, which he inherited, for the most part, from the father of structural anthropology, Claude Lévi-Strauss.[23] Specifically, Lévi-Strauss's writing in the early stages of the development of his theory of structural transformation presupposes, for example, a "psychic unity" of humankind.[24] Žižek's theory of the Real thus comes full circle, with Lévi-Strauss's early structuralism *also* significantly foregrounding the oeuvre of Viveiros de Castro—that ontologically minded anthropologist par excellence.

The foundational feature of Žižek's theory of the Real—which, at the same time, makes his work anthropologically relevant—is that it constitutes a limit to the observability both of the thing and, mutatis mutandis, of the human. Here, to observe is to know and to know is to observe—a proposition not at all unattractive to ontologically oriented anthropologists who deal in epistemological quandaries. Even if one (so oriented anthropologist) might ask whither the field(work) in Žižek, it is obvious that his observations on reality's ultimate incompleteness make sense precisely with respect to how ontoepistemic limits are understood—in the field, or elsewhere.

However, in anthropology and in continental philosophy alike, structuralism has many critics. For our purposes, it is instructive to recall Judith Butler's critique of the Real in Žižek from a decidedly poststructuralist (and feminist) perspective to address his *discursive* failure to totalize what she calls "the social field." In fact, writes Butler, any attempt to totalize this field should be read as a symptom, revealing the trauma of the Real in its full potential of "disrupting and rendering contingent any discursive formation that lays claim to a coherent or seamless account of reality." At issue, if you will, is the very order of things and its totalizing assumptions—Lacan's and Lévi-Straussian "laws" of Being and Žižek's mostly tacit adoption of them. That order, fears Butler, can hardly be free from heteronormative underpinnings with distinctly *political* consequences: "Here it seems crucial to ask whether the notion of a lack [qua the Real] taken from psychoanalysis as that which secures the contingency of any and all social formations is itself a presocial principle universalized at the cost of every consideration of power, sociality, culture, politics, which regulates the relative closure and openness of social practices."

Butler demonstrates, for example, how the Lacanian proposition *la femme n'existe pas* ("Woman does not exist"), unproblematized by Žižek, reveals that what is traumatic is the nonexistence of Woman, "that is, the fact of her castration." If symbolization is denied precisely at this "fissure"—that is, if the Real manifests itself exactly at *this* presupposed limit of *what could be*—might it not reveal something altogether different, a patriarchal social order that both Lacan and Žižek seem to inhabit unproblematically? Thus, quips Butler, "we might well ask why the conversation about the castration of woman must stop here. Is this a necessary limit to discourse, or is it imposed in order to ward off a threatening set of consequences? And if one raises a question about this necessary limit, does one inadvertently become the threat of castration itself? For if woman did exist, it seems that, by this logic, she could only exist to castrate."

Dangerous, then, is the very operation of ontological structuralism, which vests an outside to the socially intelligible with ostensibly preideological "laws," thereby precluding the possibility of politicizing the relation between, say, discourse and the Real. This is because such "laws" of necessity *posit themselves* as resistant to critique. At issue is the fixity of relations within the presumed ontological structure, which leads to "a prepolitical pathos that precludes the kind of analysis that would take the [R]eal/reality distinction as the instrument and effect of contingent relations of power."[25] To call for unfixing of such relations, as Butler does, is not to deny the unknowable, but to make *some* of its discursive deployments politically accountable.

The Specter of Commonist Ethics in Political Theory

Much as with other conceptual regimes,[26] it is difficult for political theory, even at its most experimental, to contemplate an external to itself, that is, an outside to its core element of study. Susan Buck-Morss's conceptualization of her "commonist" ethics is all the more remarkable for attempting to do just that: to theorize an outside to both the political (*le politique*) and daily politics (*la politique*), albeit not without an explicit rejection of ontology. Here is how she reasons:

> With all due respect to Marcel Gauchet, Chantal Mouffe, Giorgio Agamben, and a whole slew of others, the attempt to discover within empirical political life (*la politique*) the ontological essence of the political (*le politique*) leads theory into a dead end from which there is no return to actual, political practice. . . . The post-metaphysical project of discovering ontological truth within lived existence fails politically. It fails in the socially disintegrated Husserlian-Heideggerian mode of bracketing the *existenziell* to discover the essential nature of what "the political" is. And it fails in the socially critical, post-Foucauldian mode of historicized ontology, disclosing the multiple ways of political being-in-the-world within particular cultural and temporal configurations.

What's peculiar for this rejection is that "the multiple ways of political being-in-the world" are not denied; rather, Buck-Morss's project seeks to divest political philosophy from an urge to search for the "ontological essence" within empirical political life—precisely because of the likely political consequences of such a mission: "Existential ontology is mistaken in assuming that, once 'the character of being' (Heidegger) is conceptually grasped, it will return us to the material, empirical world and allow us to gather its diversities and multiplicities under philosophy's own pre-understandings in ways adequate to the exigencies of collective action, the demands of actual political life. In fact, the ontological is never political. A commonist (or communist) ontology is a contradiction in terms."

The point is that our ways of being-in-the-world, replete as they are with many categories of personhood, "do not fit neatly into our politics"—whatever our professed political orientation(s). For the same reason, Realpolitik can be rejected as "all too real" precisely for its inability to grasp these pluralities. One can presume, then, that the unknowable serves to de-essentialize any conceptualization of the political, for it provides for an externality to such efforts, where things are not necessarily known, where alliances are not always straightforward. This, in turn, opens up an experimental space in which, politically, the world *could be* otherwise.

Startlingly, this antiontological stance bears an uncanny resemblance with the ontological turn in anthropology, precisely inasmuch as it introduces a crisis of the ontological as a political (and ethical) act (although it could *also* be described as a methodology), intent to dispel a priori ontological assumptions.

One can presume that this positionality also shares in a Butlerian poststructuralist concern with contingent relations of power in the world, especially since Buck-Morss explicitly tasks critical theory with *doing* social theory *reflexively*.[27] Nothing quite *is* for Buck-Morss prior to thoroughly experimental materialist collective politics and, with it, prior to life's many ostensibly "ontic" forms. The unknowable, in particular, with its potential for perpetual externalization, renders ontology politically redundant, if not outright dangerous.

Is it then apt to account for an ontoepistemic "messiness of life" with respect to all three of our conceptual regimes (anthropology, continental philosophy, and political theory) especially since the specter of the unknowable seems to make relatively similar appearances—and, crucially, perform cognate functions—across these fields? And, after all, is such an insight salient for critique and the left in their contemporary material pluralities?

✳ ✳ ✳

There can be little doubt that one of critical theory's chief impulses has been to *know more* and to *know better*. Yet the mechanics of such knowledge-making praxis have varied just as much as the objects of critical study. In this essay, my intention has been to account for three disciplinary traditions that have introduced an additional dimension, or problem, to this task by drawing our attention to the unknowable. But how is this helpful?

Perhaps one can know *even* better if one takes a cue from the anthropological turn's attention to the ways *things could be* that rejects epistemological "truths" and works "counter-scientifically" toward accounting for "differently real" things—and people—in the world. This would require a critical theory and politics beyond any singular ontology—a praxis that at its core rejects the primacy of the Euro-American knowledge-production system by exposing its many disciplinary limitations as to what or who is, and what or who is not, knowable.

Perhaps one could also know *even* more by conceding, along with Butler and Buck-Morss, that our knowledge and our political and social realities do not fit neatly into any preconceived ontological structure and are not bound by any ostensibly preidological "laws." This is not to deny the effects of contingent relations of power, but, quite the opposite, to expose them further by laying bare the fallacies of ontological structuralism, which prefigures the Real as *prepolitical* and, indeed, *precritical*. Instead, the Real could be understood as a kind of destabilizer of that-what-seems-to-be-knowable, an externalizing ingredient to a knowledge-producing practice that questions the boundaries and categorical "truths" of such practice—in short, a critical object and object of critique proper. The existence of the unknowable, then, could be seen as an invitation to reimagine, over and over again, how we know-in-the-world—a call for a renewed attention to critique of our epistemic practices and their political implications—a reminder, that is, of the core promise of the left project: that the world could and must be otherwise.

Epilogue: Spillages of the Real

It may seem odd that one can think from anywhere/anyone but oneself and that the direction of one's thought, if such can be, is always projecting outside, thereby co-constituting not only the possibility of oneself but the selves and other discernible *things* of the world. Entangled in this existential drama, the self *survives* in its presumed centrality to life. But to think from the other, whether it be recognized as animate or inanimate or something altogether *different*, seems to introduce an additional crisis in one's living, and perhaps one's studies of *what could be* within/other than oneself.

It is doubtful that even the most "self-externalized" or "self-pluralized" fieldworker, let alone a philosopher or a political theorist, can so *discipline* oneself in worldings of the other that one's own worldings—one's being-in-the-world and one's knowing-in-the-world—recede into nothingness. Rather, it seems obvious that worldings flood into one another, co-constitute each other further and further, even if they are not *meant* to do so. The "real world," then, may or may not *be*. Life and one's worldings continue. If this is taken but as a basic premise, it is pertinent to ask each of our three (imagined) disciplinary workers: just where[28] *is* your field?

While this may be taken as a purely methodological question, such a move might obfuscate the drama of mutual worldings. Neither is the anthropologist, whose fieldwork is so often posited as *elsewhere*, nor other workers of the "social" or the "political," whose dealings with the self sometimes seem more easily discernible, immune from the crisis that entails distinguishing a worlding of the other from that of one's own. It is in this—again, most basic—sense that elsewhere is political.[29] The challenge seems to be not only how or whether to "represent" and "translate" the other's worldings, but also how or whether to acknowledge that they have become (and continue to become) part and parcel of one's own being-in-the-world and knowing-in-the-world. While the ontological turn, Butler, and Buck-Morss all warn against certain hegemony, whether of representational or post- and superstructural nature, that is likely to manifest in the process, they do not sufficiently attend to what seems to be an elementary occurrence—that worldings spill over and flood the all-too-crude distinction between "me"-"us" and "you"-"them."[30] Moreover, not only does one (continuously) *become* with the other, but even one's own becoming—as Buck-Morss avers—is not only perpetual but also multidirectional. This is sometimes taken as a certain plurality of existence (of "worlds" and "us"-"them" in them), but it does not have to be described as such; it could be that "perspectives" are different and "connections" partial,[31] or that there are worldings that are not readily apparent to "us."[32] Be that as it may, spillages occur. They can be critical—in terms of the crises of what's knowable that they bring forth—and political—for they can summon some apparently disparate worldings together.

In *Cruising Utopia*, José Esteban Muñoz describes queerness as "that *thing* that lets us feel that this world is not enough, that indeed something is missing."[33] Note that the thing speaks of itself here and that it speaks to an imagined *us*.[34] It speaks of absence. Who are we? And, *how* is this world, since to us it is not enough? The absent something suggests an incompleteness, not just of *this* world but of our worlding in it. So we look for the other in that we search for that someone/something that the thing we know tells us is missing in a world we don't quite know (for it might not even be "ours" for all we know). The unknowable, then, spilling from elsewhere, can be critical and political, too.

Notes

I would like to thank Safet HadžiMuhamedović for continuously directing my sight toward all things ontological; his major contribution to this field of inquiry is certain to break new ground; see Safet HadžiMuhamedović, *Waiting for Elijah: Time and Encounter in a Bosnian Landscape* (Oxford: Berghahn, 2018). I am also grateful to my fellow revelers in all things critical at the Institute for Advanced Study, and especially Lori Allen, Fadi Bardawil, Nick Cheesman, Andrew Dilts, Karen Engle, Didier Fassin, Bernard Harcourt, David Kazanjian, Allegra McLeod, Juan Obarrio, Ayşe Parla, Peter Redfield, Massimiliano Tomba, and Linda Zerilli for their invaluable insights and suggestions. Didier and Bernard were relentless in their editorial rigor and intellectual generosity; for this, I thank them immensely.

1. Amiria Henare, Martin Holbraad, and Sari Wastell, eds., *Thinking Through Things: Theorising Artefacts Ethnographically* (London: Routledge, 2007), 5.
2. I tend to agree with Adrian Johnson that the designation of Žižek's (never quite nonambiguous) philosophical leanings as transcendental materialist makes sense *particularly* for the purposes of the present analysis, that is, for discerning certain aspects of Žižek's ontology; see Adrian Johnson, *Žižek's Ontology: A Transcendental Materialist Theory of Subjectivity* (Evanston, IL: Northwestern University Press, 2008). For Lacan's work on the Real, see, for example, Jacques Lacan and Wladimir Granoff, "Le fétichisme: Le Symbolique, l'Imaginaire et le Réel," in *L'objet en psychanalyse: Le fétiche, le corps, l'enfant, la science*, ed. Marc Augé, Monique David-Ménard, Wladimir Granoff, Jean-Louis Land, and Octave Mannoni (Paris: Denoël, 1986), 19–31. Finally, for a pertinent topological analysis, see Will Greenshields, *Writing the Structures of the Subject: Lacan and Topology* (Cham: Palgrave Macmillan, 2017), 203–63.
3. Lacan proposes the metaphor of the table to illustrate this point. The imaginary table is a kind of repository of the functions of the thing known as "table": one can eat on it, put a vase on it, and so on. The symbolic table is the word *table* that finds its meaning in discourse, in expressions such as *à table!* or *faire table rase* or *table des matières*. The Real is constituted of the rest, that is, what one doesn't know about the table.

4. Slavoj Žižek, *Disparities* (London: Bloomsbury, 2016), 67 (emphasis mine).

5. Žižek, 68. In-itself (*an sich*) is Hegel's term that denotes merely potential or implicit, something considered separately from other things that may or may not have a separate ontological standing. Actuality, for instance, for Hegel *requires* relations with other things.

6. Cf. Ben Woodard, "Interview with Slavoj Žižek," in *The Speculative Turn: Continental Materialism and Realism*, ed. Levi Bryant, Nick Srnicek, and Graham Harman (Melbourne: re.press, 2011), 407. The Hegelian overtones of this elucidation are characteristic for Žižek's ontological project: first, he accepts Hegel's distinction between reality and actuality (*Wirklichkeit*): "reality is contingent external reality, not fully rational, while actuality is a reality which actualizes a notion, a reality in which the inner necessity of Reason transpires"; then, he tells us, "from the Lacanian standpoint, we should introduce here another difference, the one between actuality and the Real, not reality: actuality is a reality which actualizes a notional possibility, reality at the level of its Notion, while the Real is . . . virtual": as a point of reference, as an "obstacle to the actualization of the potentials of an entity," and, finally, as a "contingent meaningless fact not grounded in any preceding notional possibility": Žižek, *Disparities*, 67–68. See also Slavoj Žižek, *Interrogating the Real* (London: Bloomsbury, 2005).

7. Susan Buck-Morss, "A Commonist Ethics," in *The Idea of Communism* 2, ed. Slavoj Žižek (London: Verso, 2013), 57, 60, 75 (emphasis in original).

8. For a recent exposition of such an approach in literary and cultural studies, see generally Elizabeth S. Anker, and Rita Felski, eds., *Critique and Postcritique* (Durham: Duke University Press, 2017), 2, where "post-critique" is described as "less concerned with hammering home a 'critique of critique' than with testing out new possibilities and intellectual alternatives."

9. See, for example, Martin Holbraad and Morten Axel Pedersen, "The Politics of Ontology," *Cultural Anthropology*, 2014, https://culanth.org/fieldsights/461-the-politics-of -ontology; Eduardo Viveiros de Castro, "Zeno and the Art of Anthropology: Of Lies, Beliefs, Paradoxes, and Other Truths," *Common Knowledge* 17, no. 1 (2011): 128–45; Morten Axel Pedersen, *Not Quite Shamans: Spirit Worlds and Political Lives in Northern Mongolia* (Ithaca: Cornell University Press, 2011); Miho Ishii, "Acting with Things: Self-Poiesis, Actuality and Contingency in the Formation of Divine Worlds," *HAU: Journal of Ethnographic Theory* 2, no. 2 (2012): 371–88; and Mario Blaser, "Ontological Conflicts and the Stories of Peoples in Spite of Europe: Toward a Conversation on Political Ontology," *Current Anthropology* 54, no. 5 (2013): 547–68.

10. See, for example, Soumhya Venkatesan, Michael Carrithers, Karen Sykes, Matei Candea, and Martin Holbraad, "Ontology Is Just Another Word for Culture: Motion Tabled at the 2008 Meeting of the Group for Debates in Anthropological Theory, University of Manchester," *Critique of Anthropology* 30, no. 2 (2010): 152–200; and Zoe Todd, "An Indigenous Feminist's Take on the Ontological Turn: 'Ontology' is Just Another Word for Colonialism," *Historical Sociology* 29, no. 1 (2016): 4–22.

11. Cf. Didier Fassin, "The Endurance of Critique," *Anthropological Theory* 17, no. 1 (2017): 4–29.

12. Judith Butler, *Bodies That Matter: On the Discursive Limits of "Sex"* (New York: Routledge, 1993), 181–222.

13. Which might be better resolved with a Žižekian attention to disparity, rather than difference, of things; cf. Žižek, *Disparities*.

14. Cf. David Bond and Lucas Bessire, "The Ontological Spin," *Cultural Anthropology*, 2014, https://culanth.org/fieldsights/494-the-ontological-spin.

15. Martin Holbraad and Morten Axel Pedersen, *The Ontological Turn: An Anthropological Exposition* (Cambridge: Cambridge University Press, 2017), 22, 68, 185–88, 197, 289, 293–95 (emphasis in original).

16. A call that they identify, also, with Latour's lamentation over critique having "run out of steam"; see Holbraad and Pedersen, 289; Bruno Latour, "Why Has Critique Run Out of Steam? From Matters of Fact to Matters of Concern," *Critical Inquiry* 30 (Winter 2004): 225–48.

17. Casper Bruun Jensen, "Experiments in Good Faith and Hopelessness: Toward a Post-critical Social Science," *Common Knowledge* 20, no. 2 (2014): 362, quoted and endorsed in Holbraad and Pedersen, *The Ontological Turn*, 289–90n3.

18. In reaction to an earlier exposition of Martin Holbraad, Morten Axel Pedersen, and Eduardo Viveiros de Castro, "The Politics of Ontology: Anthropological Positions," *Cultural Anthropology*, 2014, www.culanth.org/fieldsights/462-the-politics-of-ontology-anthropological-positions, which declared the ontological turn "'revolutionary' in every sense of the term," David Graeber has produced a list of words that make no appearance in their essays on ostensibly "revolutionary politics" of the turn: "serf, slave, caste, race, class, patriarchy, war, army, prison, police, government, poverty, hunger, inequality (I leave out 'gender' because the phrase 'tacitly gendered perspective' does appear in one)": David Graeber, "Radical Alterity Is Just Another Way of Saying 'Reality': A Reply to Eduardo Viveiros de Castro," *HAU: Journal of Ethnographic Theory* 5, no. 2 (2015): 32n46.

19. Holbraad and Pedersen, *The Ontological Turn*, 290n4. Elsewhere the authors announce that "the core aim of the ontological turn in anthropology is relentlessly to challenge, distort and transform all things, concepts and theories pretending to be absolute": Holbraad and Pedersen, 287. With such a credo, it feels as though the turn's already nearing its end.

20. Graeber notes that, whenever critics accuse the turn of imposing its own "meta-ontology," the turn's exponents repeat their insistence that the ontological turn is "not a theory, but a method": Graeber, "Radical Alterity," 34n50. Be that as it may, the very injunction to question everything appears inescapably philosophical—in the mode, say, of Kierkegaard's protoexistentialist *methodological* stance: *de omnibus dubitandum est* (everything must be doubted)—for to presume nothing at all at the outset is a philosophical position, too; Søren Kierkegaard, *Johannes Climacus, or, De omnibus dubitandum est, and A Sermon*, trans. T. H. Croxall (Stanford: Stanford University Press, 1958).

21. Gilles Deleuze, *Différence et répétition* (Paris: Presse universitaires de France, 1968), 43, 52 (emphasis mine). He writes—with reference to Duns Scotus, Heidegger, and others—that "there has only ever been one ontological proposition: Being is univocal. . . . A single voice raises the clamour of being (*clameur de l'être*)."

22. Žižek, *Interrogating the Real*, xx.

23. Arguably, Lévi-Strauss's "The Effectiveness of Symbols" and "Language and the Analysis of Social Laws" were particularly meaningful to Lacan, and they feature throughout his *Écrits*; see Claude Lévi-Strauss, "The Effectiveness of Symbols," in *Structural Anthropology*, trans. C. Jacobson and B. Grundfest Schoepf (London: Allen Lane/Penguin, 1968), 181–201; Claude Lévi-Strauss, "Language and the Analysis of Social Laws," *American Anthropologist* 53, no. 2 (1951): 155–63; and Jacques Lacan, *Écrits* (Paris: Éditions du Seuil, 1966).

24. Holbraad and Pedersen, *The Ontological Turn*, 169.

25. Butler, *Bodies That Matter*, 192, 202–3, 207.

26. For a meditation on an outside to law—*alegality*—and its inherent complexities, see Vanja Hamzić, "Alegality: Outside and Beyond the Legal Logic of Late Capitalism," in *Neoliberal Legality: Understanding the Role of Law in the Neoliberal Project*, ed. Honor Brabazon (Abingdon: Routledge, 2017), 190–209.

27. Buck-Morss, "A Commonist Ethics," 57, 59–60, 75.

28. It would be equally pertinent to ask, for example, *when is* your field, except that this essay does not explicitly deal with the temporality of critique or disciplinary temporalities.

29. For an exemplary study, see David Trend, *Elsewhere in America: The Crisis of Belonging in Contemporary Culture* (Abingdon: Routledge, 2016). Needless to say, *elsewhere* is always philosophical, too. Suffice it to mention Heidegger's own take on being-in-the-world (*in-der-Welt-sein*) and its coterminous *Dasein* (Being-there), which has its humanly aspect in *Mitsein* (Being-with), suggesting that the human being is always already with others (of its "kind"); see Martin Heidegger, *Sein und Zeit* (Tübingen: Max Niemeyer, 1927).

30. Note that it would be even cruder to use the slash (/) to describe this distinction (i.e., "me"/"us" and "you"/"them"), in denial of what seems to be a "dividual" aspect of (at least some) self-conception(s); cf. Marilyn Strathern, *The Gender of the Gift: Problems with Women and Problems with Society in Melanesia* (Berkeley: University of California Press, 1988), 13.

31. Cf. Marilyn Strathern, *Partial Connections*, updated ed. (Oxford: Altamira, 2004); Eduardo Viveiros de Castro, "Cosmological Deixis and Amerindian Perspectivism," *Journal of Royal Anthropological Institute* 4, no. 3 (1998): 469–88.

32. It is a little suspect that the exponents of the ontological turn in anthropology so often look for the examples of what I termed here as "ontological disparity" in lands and people that are all too often portrayed as physically (and in many other ways) *distant* from an imagined "us." It is equally suspect that continental philosophy and, sometimes, political theory rely on a reverse move: abiding by a "tradition" that is ostensibly "ours" in ways more than one.

33. José Esteban Muñoz, *Cruising Utopia: The Then and There of Queer Futurity* (New York: New York University Press, 2009), 1 (emphasis mine).

34. Jacques Lacan, "La chose freudienne," in *Écrits* (Paris: Éditions du Seuil, 1966), 408.

Bibliography

Anker, Elizabeth S., and Rita Felski, eds. *Critique and Postcritique*. Durham: Duke University Press, 2017.

Blaser, Mario. "Ontological Conflicts and the Stories of Peoples in Spite of Europe: Toward a Conversation on Political Ontology." *Current Anthropology* 54, no. 5 (2013): 547–68.

Bond, David, and Lucas Bessire. "The Ontological Spin." *Cultural Anthropology*, 2014, https://culanth.org/fieldsights/494-the-ontological-spin.

Buck-Morss, Susan. "A Commonist Ethics." In *The Idea of Communism* 2, edited by Slavoj Žižek, 57–75. London: Verso, 2013.

Butler, Judith. *Bodies That Matter: On the Discursive Limits of "Sex."* New York: Routledge, 1993.

Deleuze, Gilles. *Différence et répétition*. Paris: Presse universitaires de France, 1968.

Fassin, Didier. "The Endurance of Critique." *Anthropological Theory* 17, no. 1 (2017): 4–29.

Graeber, David. "Radical Alterity Is Just Another Way of Saying 'Reality': A Reply to Eduardo Viveiros de Castro." *HAU: Journal of Ethnographic Theory* 5, no. 2 (2015): 1–41.

Greenshields, Will. *Writing the Structures of the Subject: Lacan and Topology.* Cham: Palgrave Macmillan, 2017.

HadžiMuhamedović, Safet. *Waiting for Elijah: Time and Encounter in a Bosnian Landscape.* Oxford: Berghahn, 2018.

Hamzić, Vanja. "Alegality: Outside and Beyond the Legal Logic of Late Capitalism." In *Neoliberal Legality: Understanding the Role of Law in the Neoliberal Project,* edited by Honor Brabazon, 190–209. Abingdon: Routledge, 2017.

Heidegger, Martin. *Sein und Zeit.* Tübingen: Max Niemeyer, 1927.

Henare, Amiria, Martin Holbraad, and Sari Wastell, eds. *Thinking Through Things: Theorising Artefacts Ethnographically.* London: Routledge, 2007.

Holbraad, Martin, and Morten Axel Pedersen. *The Ontological Turn: An Anthropological Exposition.* Cambridge: Cambridge University Press, 2017.

——. "The Politics of Ontology." *Cultural Anthropology,* 2014, https://culanth.org/fieldsights /461-the-politics-of-ontology.

Holbraad, Martin, Morten Axel Pedersen, and Eduardo Viveiros de Castro. "The Politics of Ontology: Anthropological Positions." *Cultural Anthropology,* 2014, www.culanth.org /fieldsights/462-the-politics-of-ontology-anthropological-positions.

Ishii, Miho. "Acting with Things: Self-Poiesis, Actuality and Contingency in the Formation of Divine Worlds." *HAU: Journal of Ethnographic Theory* 2, no. 2 (2012): 371–88.

Jensen, Casper Bruun. "Experiments in Good Faith and Hopelessness: Toward a Postcritical Social Science." *Common Knowledge* 20, no. 2 (2014): 337–62.

Johnson, Adrian. *Žižek's Ontology: A Transcendental Materialist Theory of Subjectivity.* Evanston, IL: Northwestern University Press, 2008.

Kierkegaard, Søren. *Johannes Climacus, or, De omnibus dubitandum est, and A Sermon.* Translated by T. H. Croxall. Stanford: Stanford University Press, 1958.

Lacan, Jacques. "La chose freudienne." In *Écrits,* 401–36.

——. *Écrits.* Paris: Éditions du Seuil, 1966.

Lacan, Jacques, and Wladimir Granoff. "Le fétichisme: Le Symbolique, l'Imaginaire et le Réel." In *L'objet en psychanalyse: Le fétiche, le corps, l'enfant, la science,* edited by Marc Augé, Monique David-Ménard, Wladimir Granoff, Jean-Louis Land, and Octave Mannoni, 19–31. Paris: Denoël, 1986.

Latour, Bruno. "Why Has Critique Run Out of Steam? From Matters of Fact to Matters of Concern." *Critical Inquiry* 30 (Winter 2004): 225–48.

Lévi-Strauss, Claude. "The Effectiveness of Symbols." In *Structural Anthropology,* translated by C. Jacobson, and B. Grundfest Schoepf, 181–201. London: Allen Lane/Penguin, 1968.

——. "Language and the Analysis of Social Laws." *American Anthropologist* 53, no. 2 (1951): 155–63.

Muñoz, José Esteban. *Cruising Utopia: The Then and There of Queer Futurity.* New York: New York University Press, 2009.

Pedersen, Morten Axel. *Not Quite Shamans: Spirit Worlds and Political Lives in Northern Mongolia.* Ithaca: Cornell University Press, 2011.

Strathern, Marilyn. *The Gender of the Gift: Problems with Women and Problems with Society in Melanesia.* Berkeley: University of California Press, 1988.

——. *Partial Connections.* Updated ed. Oxford: Altamira, 2004.

Todd, Zoe. "An Indigenous Feminist's Take on the Ontological Turn: 'Ontology' Is Just Another Word for Colonialism." *Historical Sociology* 29, no. 1 (2016): 4–22.

Trend, David. *Elsewhere in America: The Crisis of Belonging in Contemporary Culture.* Abingdon: Routledge, 2016.

Venkatesan, Soumhya, Michael Carrithers, Karen Sykes, Matei Candea, and Martin Hol-
    braad. "Ontology Is Just Another Word for Culture: Motion Tabled at the 2008 Meeting
    of the Group for Debates in Anthropological Theory, University of Manchester." *Critique
    of Anthropology* 30, no. 2 (2010): 152–200.
Viveiros de Castro, Eduardo. "Cosmological Deixis and Amerindian Perspectivism." *Jour-
    nal of Royal Anthropological Institute* 4, no. 3 (1998): 469–88.
——. "Zeno and the Art of Anthropology: Of Lies, Beliefs, Paradoxes, and Other Truths."
    Common Knowledge 17, no. 1 (2011): 128–45.
Woodard, Ben. "Interview with Slavoj Žižek." In *The Speculative Turn: Continental Mate-
    rialism and Realism*, edited by Levi Bryant, Nick Srnicek, and Graham Harman, 406–15.
    Melbourne: re.press, 2011.
Žižek, Slavoj. *Disparities*. London: Bloomsbury, 2016.
——. *Interrogating the Real*. London: Bloomsbury, 2005.

PART II

CRITIQUE IN PRACTICE

CHAPTER 8

SUBALTERN CRITIQUE AND THE HISTORY OF PALESTINE

LORI ALLEN

H istoriography of a particular kind can be a form of critical practice. The language games and epistemological struggles that
drive power/knowledge in different directions are historically
variable, and therefore understanding them requires a nimble historical tracing. Critical history in the genealogical mode, as inspired by Foucault and others, has been a productive method of nudging at the epistemological status
quo, an important goal of critique. Genealogical historicizing furrows the
grounds for novel thinking about political assumptions, and ideologies become
exposed. In so digging, the processes of historicity that have gone in to the
silencing of resistant voices and actors can be retrieved, as can the subaltern
narrative itself. What can be mined from evidentiary fragments of the past is a
view of what Michel-Rolph Trouillot dubbed historicity 1 and historicity 2. These
were the terms that Trouillot—anthropologist, historian, public intellectual,
and political critic—used to connote history as material process and history's
narration, processes that are at every stage marked by power. Unearthing these
processes and the silencings they entail allows a finer-grained analysis of the
workings of power itself, and of the possibilities of critique within it.

Along with history, anthropology's insistence on recording, respecting, and
making sense of other ways of knowing and being is also a mode of critical
practice. By relativizing categories of thought and activity through cultural
comparison, and by understanding events and individuals in their cultural contexts, the contingencies of knowledge and the power-laden forces of knowledge production can be made apparent. Indeed, one of anthropology's signal

contributions to social science has been its insistence on identifying other people, the "primitives" and Others of elsewhere, as logical, rational beings. The discipline has moved on to allow a concern with identifying points of shared perspective and common modes of thinking across cultures, including others' critical modes of thinking and knowledge production. This is especially important when the alterity (which is in fact material and structural rather than ontological) of those others has underwritten their dispossession and political marginalization.

With a combined historical and anthropological perspective, it becomes clear that it is not only scholars who are able to identify categorical assumptions. Historical actors are sometimes even better positioned—and motivated—to analyze the contingency of epistemologies and relativize hegemonic ideologies, because those structures of thought are part of what has maintained their domination. Gramsci's attention to the relationship between knowledge, social groups, and political change offers a useful lens for the examination of critique production by the dominated in political context. His gradated conception of subalternity that is always marked by different degrees of partial knowledge or understanding[1] opens questions about the range of perspectives of differently positioned people within a subaltern social group, allowing a consideration of "subaltern elite" and the functioning of their forms of critique. Certain interpretations of Gramsci's concept of the subaltern have equated it with a particular class position and relation of exclusion to the mechanisms of states. According to Peter Thomas, however, Gramsci conceived the notion of the subaltern as a social group: "not as excluded from the modern state, nor as merely oppressed or subjugated by it. Rather, they are fundamentally transformed and reconstituted by its expansive logic, mobilized to participate in the projects of the dominant group in contradictory and frequently passive forms."[2] With this definition that encompasses more than James Scott's peasant and Gayatri Spivak's ur-victim, we can also recognize the anticolonial intellectual as subaltern critic. Those characters from subaltern social groups who have been able to identify the epistemologies that surround them, recognize the nature of the system that ensures their domination, and formulate critique in the credible terms of the dominant discourse draw attention to the problem of critique in politics. This is a question of the relationship of knowledge to political action, of subaltern critique to critique as practice.

The Palestinian case is particularly illustrative of the significance of the social position of critique's articulation—of epistemological alterity—to the course of critique. Through the work of institutions of knowledge production such as higher education and journalism, Palestinians have been dismissed as having a tenuous relationship to politically relevant knowledge, to truth itself, because of their ethnic and historical background. As Arabs, as predominantly Muslim, as opponents of the Israeli state that claims to represent the Holocaust's

Jewish victims, Palestinians have been entrapped within layers of Orientalist discourse and political structures that silence or ignore their claims and critiques, constituting them, in the anthropologist Amahl Bishara's words, as "epistemic others."[3] Their political experiences of subjugation by Israel and subjection by military occupation are seen to forever infect their knowledge production. As Israeli prime minister Ehud Barak opined: "They are products of a culture in which to tell a lie . . . creates no dissonance. They don't suffer from the problem of telling lies that exists in Judeo-Christian culture. Truth is seen as an irrelevant category."[4] As such an epistemic other, even so esteemed a scholar as Edward Said could be challenged by those who objected to his nomination to deliver the prestigious Reith Lectures. "I was accused of being active in the battle for Palestinian rights, and thus disqualified for any sober or respectable platform at all," he reported.[5] Not only the exclusion of Palestinians' experiences but also the obliteration of their own analyses of the causes of those experiences have reflected and enabled their material and political dispossession for over a century.

Tracing the role that subaltern understandings, performances, and experiences of critique played in Palestinian political struggle complicates academic conceptualizations and theorizations of critique. Palestinians' long history of systematically making sense of their own conditions, partially recovered here through the story of one politically engaged individual, the Palestinian anticolonial intellectual Fayez Sayegh, illustrates the diversity of what it means to stage a critique, and what critique tethered to political action can do. Snapshots from the prodigious output of Sayegh's critical writings bring into focus the political alliances, the antagonists vulnerable to critique, the tools for critique's amplification, material resources, and mass mobilization that are some of the puzzle pieces required to create a landscape of social change. History provides a standpoint from which to evaluate the long-term effects of critique, to judge when and how critique gains real purchase over time, and to examine whose critique can pry open new horizons of judgment and action in what contexts.

The Critique of Palestinians: Inability to Narrate

When the British Empire pledged their support of the Zionists setting up a national home in Palestine in 1917, and then built that pledge into their mandate for governing Palestine under the League of Nations, Arabs objected. The Zionist establishment of colonies in Palestine, a country occupied by Arabs who already had been demanding their autonomy within the Ottoman Empire, did not accord with Western powers' promises after World War I. With the statement of US president Woodrow Wilson that "nationalities which are now under Turkish rule should be assured an undoubted security of life and an absolutely unmolested opportunity of an autonomous development," Arabs believed their national independence to be practically guaranteed. Their critique of Zionism, and of the Western powers that facilitated its expansion into a state, was articulated within terms that resonated with the dominant discourses of international law. They framed their claims to independence in nationalist terms, citing their centuries-long presence as a distinctive people in Palestine. Their rights to Palestine were established, they believed, by international law's preservation of the principle of self-determination and liberal notions of representative self-government. These themes have remained central in Palestinians' self-defense and in their critique of Zionist counterclaims ever since.[6]

Despite this long history of indigenous critique of the unfulfilled promises of Western liberalism, there is a belief that the Arabs have historically demonstrated an inability (or lack of investment in or unwillingness) to propagate their own narrative and perspectives in the West. According to this assessment, their subsequent loss of the propaganda war with Zionists has led to their loss of wars, both diplomatic and real. There is political-ideological work that gets smuggled into this assertion that they have been inferior narrators. A muting function is performed by this criticism of the Arabs' inability to speak, dangerous for being more subtle than the outright dismissal of Palestinians and what they have to say simply because they are Palestinian and therefore "synonymous with violence, fanaticism, the killing of Jews."[7] The disparagement of Palestinians' communicative inabilities is another instance of blaming the victim, ignoring power, and merely reiterating the old canard that the Palestinians never lose an opportunity to lose an opportunity. The scorn for Palestinians' discursive underperformance also carries with it a supposition that, had the Palestinians explained their perspective better to decision makers and Western public opinion, had their critiques been more trenchant, their political demands for independence would have been realized, a historical counterfactual incapable of being proved or disproved.

Uncovering this assumption is important because of the ideological work that it does in driving the focus onto narrative facility and away from other elements necessary for political change, such as practical things like material resources and political access to diplomatic circles, and other obstacles like the occlusions produced by racism. The negative judgment of Palestinian diplomacy elides other nondiscursive features of the confrontation that have consistently coalesced to tip the scales in favor of Zionism's goals and the furtherance of Israel's settler-colonial project. Moreover, in placing "the Arabs" or "the Palestinians" as a block under the label of ineffectual critical communicators, it discounts the many individuals and moments exhibiting Palestinians' concerted efforts at explaining their position. It elides the many demands that were made in the terms and with the values that their Western interlocutors could understand. A different (more ethnographic and less Whiggish and elitist) approach to the archives reveals that representatives have in fact conveyed the Palestinian case to the international community throughout a long history of often rigorously organized public relations activities.[8]

The Critiques of Fayez Sayegh

As Gramsci recognized, the challenges to recovering subaltern history and moments of "individual initiative" are formidable, given that, as Kate Crehan summarizes it, "the major conceptual structures available to them are themselves inextricably bound up with the hegemonic narratives of the dominant classes."[9] As with other stateless groups, traces of Palestinian "initiative" must be discerned partially through the records and terms produced by their oppressors. Official political discourse does contain such critical interchanges, among them diplomatic memoranda, unpublished research for politicians, and embassy missives. Another source is the United Nations, the global institution that many Palestinians and others see as being responsible for the establishment of Israel and for the creation of the 750,000 Palestinian refugees who fled during that initial war in 1948, where they have voiced their demands for national and individual rights since its establishment. These are useful sources for locating critique in the archives. But even more, with the right approach, they draw attention to the many other factors that make a narrative or political claim audible. Such materials prompt questions about whose hearing matters. Recovering some of these instances of foreign diplomacy and public relations efforts, as the rest of this chapter does, is itself intended as a means of critique that challenges some of what have become the standardized categories and imaginaries through which the conflict in Palestine has come to be seen.

Fayez Sayegh had pinpointed the powerful role of colonial knowledge in maintaining colonial power over Palestine and Palestinians well before Edward Said's interventions in *Orientalism*, and well before postcolonial theory made the interrogation of representation and discourse a typical feature of critique. Sayegh, a well-educated intellectual from a poor family with a Protestant preacher for a patriarch, rose in the political ranks of Arab nationalism from a position as member of the Syrian National Party into the Executive Committee of the Palestinian Liberation Organization. He was not a fully marginalized subaltern in the sense that has become popularized by Gayatri Spivak and the Subaltern Studies Group. With a PhD in philosophy from Georgetown University, Sayegh founded and helped direct the Research Center of the Palestine Liberation Organization in 1965. He was influential in promoting anticolonial intellectual output during the 1960s, including his own writing, "and was a foundational member of the diplomatic leadership" of the Palestinian national movement.[10] He later became the Chargé d'Affaires of the Arab States

Delegations' Office at the United Nations. His critiques were published, aired on television, and recorded in the official transcripts of the United Nations. Among other positions, he was the UN's special rapporteur to the International Convention on the Elimination of All Forms of Racial Discrimination from 1968 until he died in 1980. From his position as a delegate of Kuwait at the United Nations Sayegh presented and helped pass the highly controversial United Nations General Assembly (UNGA) Resolution 3379, which declared Zionism to be a form of racism.[11]

As someone who sometimes spoke from respected institutional bases like the UN, Sayegh was not a subaltern as James Scott has used the term. He was not someone confined to expressing critique in "hidden transcripts" or the ephemera of sarcastic comments. He was subaltern nonetheless, as the partial hearings he was accorded demonstrate.

Although Sayegh's institutional bases shifted, his humanist commitment to Palestinian liberation remained consistent, as did his reliance on logic and reasoned argument. He believed that the United Nations represented "a progressive concept of world order . . . the only hope of mankind today." In his view, the demand for Israeli withdrawal from Arab territory after the 1967 war that saw the military occupation of the West Bank, Gaza Strip, East Jerusalem, Sinai, and Golan Heights was "the only rational demand, the only demand consistent with a system of law and order."[12] He voiced a critique of Zionism's racism as early as 1946 and unfailingly grounded Palestinian demands for independence in international law and universalizing conceptions of rights and justice.[13] Throughout the range of genres and contexts in which he intervened, it is clear that Sayegh's target was precisely the discursive domination of Palestine and Palestinians by the Zionist narrative. But this critique was only registered after an institutionalized critical mass could increase its volume. Among other venues, Sayegh presented his critical analyses of the Arab-Zionist conflict at the Anglo-American Committee of Enquiry in 1946, from his position as Senior Adviser to the Foreign Ministry of Kuwait, and at the United Nations across many years, most famously when he presented the Zionism Is Racism resolution.

Pausing at these three moments provides an opportunity to analyze subaltern critique in the archives as a means to disrupt some received notions of critique within academic writing. Some academics who read earlier versions of this chapter were unwilling to recognize Sayegh as a subaltern in any way (because he had an elite education, because he was "Westernized"), and could not see how his discursive challenges to Zionism and its American support were a form of critique (because they were political polemic). I do not equate Sayegh's writings with critique in practice as a heroic lionization of him (another criticism of this chapter's earlier draft), but rather to explore what insights a gradated notion of subalternity and a politically attentive analysis of critique in practice can offer to our understanding of how critique works. Recognizing Sayegh's interventions as a form of subaltern critique brings into focus the significance of the institutional context of critique to its political efficacy, and the particular functioning of critique when it is generated out of political engagement. These three moments, in which Sayegh's interventions gain increasing relevance and resonance as the United Nations becomes a venue for voluble Third World solidarity, highlight what politically motivated critique can and cannot do in different contexts.

Few among non–Middle East experts would recognize Sayegh's name, as little has been written about him until recently beyond a couple of laudatory obituaries.[14] One trace of him does appear in the memoirs of Rabbi Elmer Berger, published in 1978, who describes Sayegh as a lifelong friend. Berger, an opponent of Zionism, was longtime Executive Director of the American Council on Judaism and then founding director of American Jewish Alternatives to Zionism. They both became members on the Advisory Board of the International Organization for the Elimination of All Forms of Racial Discrimination, and wrote pamphlets for this NGO dedicated to upholding the 1965 General Assembly Resolution No. 2106 on that issue. Through these organizations Berger became a well-known anti-Zionist, active in the United States from the 1940s through the 1990s. His writings are an interesting place to pick up Sayegh's story because of how Berger compares him to what he thought was the standard Palestinian political style, and for his characterization of his own approaches to critique.

As he records butterflies of memory throughout his *Memoirs of an Anti-Zionist Jew*, Berger repeats the criticism of Palestinian self-representation, and contrasts their weakness in this field to his own concern with tailoring political messages to his audiences. Berger narrates the development in himself of a pragmatic kind of sensibility, as he learns something of the ways of the world and how to have the best chance of influencing it. Although by his own accounts Berger never shifted in his beliefs about the threat that Zionism, and then Israel, posed to American interests in the Middle East, or in his religious convictions about the meaning of Judaism and Zionism's inconsistency with it, his approach to political work did become more refined, molded by a sense of realism and strategy. In addition to his certitude about the venality and hypocrisy of politicians, built up out of many years of talking to their Janus-faces, among his other developed convictions was one about the importance of choosing critical words well, and his firm belief that the Arabs never managed to achieve such discursive efficacy, particularly not in the context of the American public sphere and public perception of Israel-Zionism/Palestine. With a tone of near-desperation he reiterates throughout his memoir a contention that Arab efforts to explain the Palestinian issue and critique Zionism were too little, too late. And when they did try, in Berger's view, they did so too emotionally, in ways that reduced their credibility.

Berger reserved more respect and praise, however, for Sayegh. In stark contrast to another Arab representative, Khalil Totah, whom Berger describes as having a tendency during debates with Zionists to become "an almost maniacal, emotional hunted animal, screaming and striking back with anything that came to his mind or to his saddened and despairing heart," Sayegh had an "intellectual coolness" that Berger "enjoyed."[15] This coolness was put into action throughout Sayegh's career as a professor and international presenter of Palestinian political claims. According to Berger, he and Sayegh shared a cerebral comradeship. The rabbi was a scholarly looking bespectacled man from the Reform tradition of Judaism, and Sayegh was handsome and dimple-chinned, with sparkling brown eyes, which he had in common with his many scholarly brothers and sister.

Berger and Sayegh both toiled with the tools of their formidable intellects and well-chosen words, with an indefatigable energy across decades of advocacy work and writing. They argued along similar lines against Zionist exclusionism, but from distinct stances. Berger recognized the injustice of what Zionism did to the Arabs, and was fully sympathetic to the plight of the Palestinian refugees living in desperate conditions after fleeing Zionist forces during the war that ended with Israel's establishment in 1948. But his opposition to Zionism was primarily based on his belief that Jewish nationalism was "a political fabrication" that had "no validity in Judaism."[16] Although the historian Jonathan Gribetz has dubbed him "the PLO's rabbi,"[17] Berger argued from the standpoint of, and professed self-identification as, a Jew and as an American, on behalf of what he thought it was to be a good Jew and an American with American interests at heart. Berger's identity already gave him a level of credibility in the eyes of those he tried to convince, and he underscored his honorable and patriotic motives to enhance it. His subject position did not prevent opponents from dismissing him as a self-hating Jew. But his starting point still gave him a privileged access to certain audiences and entre into audibility.

Sayegh, although he had impressive scholarly credentials and capabilities, had to find other grounds from which to try to make his interventions. In contrast to Berger's self-positioning as an American patriot and Jew, Sayegh spoke from the terrain of moral universals, as a humanist, and as someone who saw philosophy and logic as the means for arriving at justice and achieving liberation. Echoing Berger's praise, others who have recorded observations about Sayegh's performances have described him as a "masterful debater" who ran his Zionist interlocutors into the ground, his sharp mind eventually scaring his opponents off from trying to counter him in public forums. His presentations were articulated through points of evidence derived from historical fact, with rational arguments based on international legal principles, often in terms of humanitarian ethics and transhistorical values. Always mindful of his audiences' perspective and likely biases, he drew attention to the use he made of certain kinds of sources, particularly official Zionist sources that would be received as most credible.

Critical Analysis and Critique in Context

The different forms of critical analysis and critique that Sayegh sought to interject into the debate about Palestine offer a kind of diagnostic of the political and epistemological terrain on which he found himself. What he chose to respond to were nodal points in the dominant discourse of the eras in which he spoke and wrote: against the typical ways of narrating Palestinians out of political subjecthood, against the erasure of the unfair political dealings of the British and internationally sanctioned dispossession of the native inhabitants of Palestine, and against the standard understandings of Zionism as an economic boon to the Arabs. His targets and the different styles he mobilized to reach them draw attention to the fact that critique, like the condition of subalternity, exists within gradations. Neither total domination nor epoch-making revolution exhausts the range of their possibilities. The fact that overlapping epistemologies are in operation at any single time means that critique must pivot.

Many academic discussions of critique insist on a distinction between criticism that takes an object and critique that questions the conditions of possibility for the discursive production of an object (or problem or concept). Critique, in this view, is that which challenges an epistemological status quo. But, if we consider the epistemological scene as it functions in a concrete political context, it becomes apparent more as a mobile Venn diagram of truth-claims and the assumptions upon which they rest, with certain categories of thought being more or less relevant to the contest at hand. The nudging of one circle to dislodge a certain array of concepts may end up deepening the outline of another. It may be, according to Ann Stoler (glossing Judith Butler), that "critique is a way of disclosing those very spaces that are secluded from us," but we must remember that the vantage point of that "us" is essential to how the spaces become secluded and revealed.[18] The "us" toward which Sayegh often aimed his critiques was a mainstream American audience whose understanding of the Middle East was largely delimited by Orientalist stereotypes and Zionist goals.

Among his writings were responses to pronouncements and publications that spread misinformation about Palestine. Many of Sayegh's interventions focused on laying out basic facts about Palestinian history and the colonial roots of Zionism. In one, issued in 1969 by the Embassy of the State of Kuwait in Washington, DC, Sayegh takes apart, paragraph by paragraph, a background document that had been prepared for the Subcommittee on the Near East of the Committee on Foreign Affairs in the US House of Representatives. His rejoinder is explicit about the nature of the congressional study's bias, and his critique of the reigning discourse is sharp. Sayegh emphasizes, for example, that the government study characterized Arab resistance against British and Zionist aggression as "terrorism," and excluded any mention of organized Zionist terrorism perpetrated by the Jewish Agency's military wings. Critique of the ideological biases inherent in such labeling practices was typical of Sayegh's writing. He consciously crafted his critiques and correctives with a political purpose and with specific audiences in mind, including US legislators responsible for determining American foreign affairs. In the case of Sayegh's analysis of this fault-filled backgrounder, he deployed the accepted methodologies—reference to official UN and government documents—and undermined their assumptions to challenge the authorized discourse, destabilizing the political status quo that constructs Arabs as belligerents, and that obscures the violence of their Zionist opponents.

Sayegh developed a critique more recognizable as critique, obviously aimed at challenging "the conditions of possibility that make judgment possible," in "A Note on the Palestine Problem," a pamphlet that he prepared on behalf of the Syrian National Party and submitted to the Anglo-American Committee of Enquiry.[19] In 1945, the British and US governments charged this investigative committee with the task of studying the problem of the displaced persons in Europe after World War II. In his "Note," Sayegh deconstructs what he believed to be the standard approach to the problem of Palestine, seeking to shift the perspective of the investigating commissioners from one anchored by political expediency to one of fairness. Explaining how the conceptualization of the issue led "from an erroneous starting-point" to "fruitless" attempts at resolution that were "apriori doomed to failure," Sayegh criticizes the standard attitude to the problem that begins from the standpoint of "a politician desiring to mitigate an embarrassing perplexing situation." He implores the commissions to instead investigate as an arbitrating judge seeking justice. As Sayegh argued, it is from the standpoint of justice, not compromise, that a solution could come into view.

In this pamphlet Sayegh reprises historical fact as he would in his analysis of the US government study from 1969, again with reference to Western decrees, including the Balfour Declaration, which Palestinians had been protesting since the British formalized their promise to facilitate a Jewish homeland in Palestine in 1917. But here he does so from a different angle, more focused on how Palestine has been imagined and framed by distinctly British and Zionist concerns. The "erroneous conception" and "unfortunate blunder in the approach" to the problem that kept it tethered to the Balfour promise are what make it appear insoluble, not any "intrinsic insolubility," he explains. He asserts that the Balfour Declaration was politically and legally invalid, and underscores the Declaration's own internal incoherence insofar as it promised a national home in Palestine to the Jewish people while also offering reassurances that it would do nothing to prejudice the civil and religious rights of non-Jewish communities there, an impossibility from its inception. Rather than trying to square that circle, what Sayegh believed was required was an alternative perspective on the problem "as an *injustice* which the Palestinians have been made to suffer through the introduction, into their country, of an alien people, ambitious enough to look upon this country as their own, and to seek to transform it into a national home wherein they will be not only the numerical majority, but the ruling power of the state as well! For, indeed, it is *this* that is the problem; and it is from *this* angle that it has to be viewed."

As a politically engaged critique Sayegh's treatise could not stop at presenting these deconstructionist and critical insights. It also had to offer a constructive alternative scenario, which he did by concluding with a proposal for a "radical solution" for the just settlement of the Palestine Problem: the "establishment of a democratic system of self-rule."[20]

Despite the interventions of Sayegh and many others who sought to interject a different perspective into the deliberations of the Anglo-American investigators, throughout their discussions and the committee members' post-facto recollections, they emphasized the Jewish Displaced Persons' desire to go to Palestine. The concerns, criticisms, and political demands of the Palestinians, by contrast, were often glossed over, or explicitly dismissed as being the product of irritating and unhelpful "intransigence."[21] For the Westerners, "compromise" was the appropriate framework. And despite arguments against the Balfour Declaration such as those of Sayegh and others that collectively and for decades challenged its legal and moral legitimacy, its haphazard drafting proved a politically expedient way to get the Jews on the British side of World War I, which proved its logical incoherence. The Declaration remained an anchor for the arguments of some of the Committee members' recommendations in favor of Zionist demands, as well as of Truman's pro-Zionist position.

It is impossible to know whether Sayegh's pamphlet made any impression on the members of the Committee. There is no record of any discussion of it among them, and it was likely not singled out for consideration among the mountains of memos and testimonies they received. The members who left diaries or published memoirs of their time on the Anglo-American Committee give little impression of having been swayed away from their original opinions and sympathies at all. Sayegh's was one voice in a chorus of critique that did not ultimately persuade the political powers away from the Zionist project when the time came for momentous decisions to be made. US president Truman singled out the committee's call to open Palestine to one hundred thousand Jewish immigrants. What followed in 1948–49 is what Palestinians refer to as the "Nakba," or disaster, when Israel's establishment as a state produced 750,000 Palestinian refugees, among them Sayegh and his extended family. Despite this world shattering event, Sayegh continued to debate and publish in an attempt to persuade others to consider alternative perspectives on Palestine, and to act for justice. "A Note on the Palestine Problem," swallowed into the Anglo-American Committee's archives, was just one piece in a long bibliography of Sayegh's writings. Others of his writings have reverberated more loudly.

UN Resolution 3379: The Critique of Zionism as Racism

One such intervention was United Nations General Assembly (UNGA) Resolution 3379, which named Zionism as a form of racism. In the autumn of 1975, Sayegh, as representative of Kuwait at the Third (Social, Humanitarian, and Cultural) Committee and at the General Assembly, explained and argued for this resolution, which his delegation cosponsored. The Resolution had the title "Elimination of All Forms of Racial Discrimination." It linked Israel to "the racist regimes in Zimbabwe and South Africa," which had "a common imperialist origin," and was passed with seventy-two delegates voting in favor, thirty-two opposed, and thirty-five abstentions. Although it was overturned—nearly two decades later—in response to Israel's demands, Resolution 3379 highlights important aspects of critique, and how it registers among different audiences. What permitted Sayegh's critique to "stick" through Resolution 3379 had as much to do with the political context in which it was expressed, and with the sensitivities of the targets of the critique at that moment, perhaps more so, than it did with the message he delivered—which was one he had been presenting for a long time.

The United Nations in this period was a novel sort of place. Originally, the international institution brought together powerful states that were willing to join only because they risked nothing of their sovereignty in doing so. After some two decades of existence, these states were now outnumbered. The growing ranks of the recently decolonized states—the United Nations grew from fifty-one countries to 147 by 1975—had given the Third World a new weight at the United Nations. (In 1974 the United Nations granted the PLO observer status with a large majority vote.) Although the UN General Assembly was established by the Great Powers as a sop, nothing more than a place for "small nations to blow off steam," as US president Roosevelt described it, their steam was starting to scald.[22] With the greater presence of non-European representatives in the UNGA, racism started to come center stage, many years after the United States refused China's proposal to include racial equality as an element of the UN Charter. The UN General Assembly debate in 1962 focused on racial discrimination and religious intolerance. Calls for the drafting of the Convention on Elimination of All Forms of Racial Discrimination from Francophone African states helped set the agenda of this meeting, while racism in South Africa and the United States also shaped the debate.[23]

The UNGA had become an important place for countries to represent themselves as sovereigns of a particular character, through the passing and debating of resolutions. UNGA resolutions declare political positions, and in their discussions of them UN delegates often elaborate the moral and legal principles upon which those positions are based. Political stances and alliances were particularly acutely expressed in the debates over Resolution 3379. If the United Nations had become a stage for the performance of Third World solidarity, some also considered it an important forum for reasserting the power and prestige of the United States. The fear that the United Nations and the postcolonial states that were vocal within it had gotten out of control was widespread across the American elite. Daniel Patrick Moynihan, the US ambassador to the United Nations during this period, took up his post with a determination to restore American honor in front of what he saw as sustained Third World attacks against it. With the outraged timbre of a US nationalist, Moynihan warned, "The honor of American democracy was being impugned. . . . What has come over us? Forget about a slander on our honor?" He went into his post at the United Nations with gloves off, stiffening his spine with the certitude that the United States must do the same: "We are the most powerful culture in the world, I felt; we must somehow get our nerve back."[24] He saw as the source of criticisms of Israel not any actions of Israel toward the Palestinians, but resentment and intolerance for democracy. His defense of Zionism was a repudiation of what he believed was an emboldened assault on America and Western values. UN delegates argued over this resolution in a context of Cold War and postcolonial Third Worldist perspectives. Reading Sayegh's statements from the UN plenary, however, one gets the sense of someone who cannot understand why reason and facts were not enough to persuade and change the political order, someone struggling against the ingrained views defining the ideological and epistemological scene in which he sought for his arguments to take hold.

> Zionism, with which the draft resolution before us is concerned, is not a concept which has no precise definition. The draft resolution does not refer to a word of indeterminate meaning. Zionism is not an amorphous concept which lacks precise form or specific content. On the contrary, the "Zionism" to which the draft resolution refers is a specific political reality. It is a political movement launched at a precise moment in time (in August of 1897) in a precise place (Basle, Switzerland) at the inspiration of a specific man (Theodor Herzl)—a movement which took the form of a specific organization (the World Zionist

Organization), which has held twenty-eight regular Zionist Congresses which, in turn, have created specific legislative, executive and other institutions and have adopted a number of formal resolutions, constituting the official doctrine and the official program of Zionism. It is all this (and nothing else other than this) that the draft resolution speaks about. Any semantic play on words is entirely beside the point. We are not engaged in semantic games here, but in very serious business.

In recounting these snippets of history, Sayegh sought to ground the debate, and Zionism itself, in a field of concrete events and actions, where the problem space is governed not by emotion or myth or religion, but by verifiable facts derived from credible sources. He similarly reminded his audience that the United Nations had also agreed a definition of racial discrimination in the United Nations Declaration on the Elimination of All Forms of Racial Discrimination of 1963. He quoted it as defining racial discrimination in article 1 of the UN General Assembly Resolution 1904 (XVIII) as "discrimination between human beings on the ground of race, colour or ethnic origin." The resolution that Sayegh was proposing would bring the clarifying lens of this resolution on racial discrimination to view Zionism in a new light, through the simple juxtaposition of definitions: "we come to this Committee with its own, long established and universally-accepted definition of 'racial discrimination,' and ask it to judge whether or not Zionism, as defined by the Zionist movement itself, constitutes a form of racism and racial discrimination, as defined by the Committee itself long ago."[25]

A distinct discursive frame was deeply entrenched and still was able to corral the approach to the conflict, penning it in with assumptions about the impossibility of Palestinian refugees returning to their homes in what had become Israel, assertions about the inherently anti-Semitic basis of Arabs' opposition to the Zionist takeover of Palestine, and claims of Israel's benevolence toward the Arabs for whom the Israeli presence was supposedly beneficial. Long before this UN debate, Sayegh had made a habit out of cataloguing the themes such as these that were typical in Zionist claims. These were the recurrent leitmotifs that Israel and its supporters circulated to police the narrow boundaries of the conceptual space. Reflecting his meticulous style, Sayegh had counted a total of 437 statements that were propagated about the Palestine problem, with some two hundred being "lasting themes" that arose regularly, and nineteen being what he considered the "durable" core of Zionist propaganda.[26] By the time he proposed Resolution 3379, although there were few variations among these refrains, there was one crucial difference in how the epistemological frame was construed: a shift in the dominant consensus about colonialism and racism. Colonialism was no longer generally considered to be a noble, civilizing process, and overt assertions about the inherent, natural inferiority of nonwhites or non-Europeans could no longer plausibly justify it. Things had changed since 1897, when the first Zionist Congress openly declared as a means to achieve Zionist aims "the promotion, on suitable lines, of the colonization of Palestine by Jewish agricultural and industrial workers."

To maintain Israel's political arrangements at a time when colonialism and racism were no longer regarded as justifiable systems or ideologies, its supporters had to ensure that its actions and precepts were not labeled as such. Resolution 3379 was so threatening to Israel's established order because this declaration that deemed Zionism a form of racism was hooked in to that altered system of values and moral categories. It arose within a transformed political and ideological structure in which postcolonial countries were now dominant voices in the UNGA. The United Nations had already pronounced self-determination as an ideal and practical goal, enshrining the principal in General Assembly resolutions on decolonization and in human rights conventions. Human rights generally had become an integral feature of efforts establishing norms to guide international relations. Likewise, dependency theory was well developed and by 1974, just before Resolution 3379 came to the floor, the UNGA had established a strategy for achieving economic autonomy as articulated in the Declaration on the Establishment of a New International Economic Order. So the bounds of acceptable discourse had stretched and the context for Sayegh's critique embodied in the Resolution had a more fortuitous ground. With these new reference points, he could point to the gap between Zionist ideology and practice on the one hand, and the United Nations' normative principles on the other: "The ideological requirements of the cardinal Zionist principle of 'Jewish exclusiveness' have thus been given absolute precedence over the moral and legal requirements of inalienable human rights."[27]

Israel's representative, Chaim Herzog (who would go on to become that country's president), sought to relocate the debate within the old frame. He prefaced his statement in the UN debate of Resolution 3379 with the attention-grabbing assertion that the future existence of the United Nations was itself at stake in the vote on this resolution. Evoking the specter of Hitler, who "would have felt at home . . . listening to the proceedings in this forum and, above all, to the proceedings during the debate on Zionism," Herzog went on to flatten the resolution into a base expression of anti-Semitism, studding his speech with characterizations of the resolution as "wicked" and "evil." The Resolution was, he insisted, an attack on the Jewish people, who "have given to mankind much of what is great and eternal." It was not just an attack on those who had brought such benefits to the Arabs, but an attack on Judaism, which was a boon for humanity itself. It was an attack on the religious community that was the source of the Bible and Ten Commandments, great thinkers and artists, "and as high a percentage of Nobel Prize winners in the world, in the sciences, the arts and the humanities, as has been achieved by any other people on earth." Reverting to this ad hominem attack aimed at discrediting any criticism of Israel as anti-Semitic (one that Sayegh had identified as a "durable theme" long ago), Herzog sought to shift the debate back onto the familiar colonial terrain set in a progressive history that only the enemies of progress would oppose. The resolution was an attempt by some countries—those Herzog described as "drunk with the feeling of power inherent in the automatic majority" and motivated by the "two evils [of] hatred and ignorance" and "wickedness"—to drag civilization back to "the Middle Ages."[28] He reprised the colonizer's binary logic to cast his opponents in religious terms: "On this issue, the world as represented in this Hall has divided itself into good and bad, decent and evil, human and debased." But, while deploying this typical colonialist's civilizational discourse that denied the colonized a coeval position on the scale of progress, he also seemed to recognize that the winds had shifted. In an apparent attempt to speak in the terms that had wider resonance, he described Zionism as a noble example of freedom struggle, even a model of it: "one of the most noble liberation movements of this century, a movement which not only gave an example of encouragement and determination to the people struggling for independence, but also actively aided many of them during the period of preparation for their independence or immediately thereafter."[29]

Again anchored by the balustrade of history, in Sayegh's contributions to the debate over this resolution he called out the Zionist representative on his attempt to claim a position within their contemporary moment's anticolonial zeitgeist:

We have also been told that Zionism is a national liberation movement. In fact, this claim was first voiced in 1968 by the twenty-seventh Zionist Congress. It took Zionism seventy-one years to discover its purported identity!

When Zionism started, it did not hesitate to call itself a colonial movement. Herzl wrote to none other than Cecil Rhodes. (I would refer members to Volume IV of his Diaries, page 1193 onward.) He pleaded with Rhodes: Please make a statement that you have examined my program and found it appropriate. Why do I come to you, Mr. Rhodes, you will ask? Because my program is a colonial program.

At that time, when colonialism was in vogue, Zionism had no difficulty in recognizing its true identity as a colonial movement. It called its first bank the colonial trust company. It called its department of settlement the department of colonization. It called its settlements "colonies." It likened its settlers to the conquistadores. It likened them to the French colons in North Africa. This was the literature of Zionism. This was the recognition by Zionism of its colonial nature.

But now, in the 1970's, with national liberation movements the vogue of the day, Zionism also wants to jump on the bandwagon and call itself a liberation movement.[30]

"Words Do Hurt Us" and American Attempts to Silence

Moynihan, in contrast, was not marching with the times but digging his heels into the colonial past. His memoirs about his time at the United Nations in this period are littered with comments that many of today's readers might find shocking or laughable, as they sound the tones of imperial arrogance with such unabashed clarity. The erasure from his narrative of Palestinians and Arab perspectives on the issues is almost total. Moynihan would not even accept that Resolution 3379 was the initiative of the Arab states. Instead, reading it within the boilerplate imagination of a Cold Warrior, he insisted it was the creation of the Soviet Union looking for a way to promote the idea that Zionism was a US invention and Soviet Jews were a fifth column.

Despite his unwillingness to admit to hearing the Palestinian critique, Moynihan was worried. Totalitarianism, of leftist and communist kinds, was an expansive threat, Moynihan believed. And reputational strength was needed to push it back. He believed that the words of critique that were circulating with greater volume and velocity through the UNGA had an impact: "Words hurt. . . . Our reputation as a free country is fundamental to us."[31]

When the resolution was passed, because times had changed and different kinds of people with firsthand experience of racism and the brutalities of colonialism had a vote at the United Nations, those who were threatened pulled out all the stops to distract from the core issues underlined in Resolution 3379. Throughout Moynihan's memoirs, Palestinians and their allies appear only as raving lunatics who do things in a "frenzy" while "leering." They have no arguments, experiences, or evidence, only a propensity to bribe countries for votes against Israel, because their opposition to the country was rooted in anti-Semitism and resentment of its existence as a democracy. Moynihan's only recognition of an Arab with arguments comes in his recounting of a lunch he had with Fayez Sayegh, whose "rage was clear at the people who had overmastered his own, and sent so many into exile." Sayegh countered Moynihan's claim that Zionism could not be equated with racism because "we had never defined racism," by pointing out that the United Nations had defined racism in the International Convention on the Elimination of All Forms of Racial Discrimination of 1965.

This tracing of critique through history shows that what can provide the grounds for the constitution of other political possibilities is the practice of other politics. Sayegh's writings and presentations reveal the epistemological awareness that went in to his critical contributions. They illustrate the extent to which he conformed to the rhetorical demands of rational discourse, grounding in historical fact his logical presentation of evidence. But it has never been the rules of evidence alone that determine what becomes politically relevant critique, in the Palestinian context or any other. Although words may hurt, as

Moynihan believed they did, they can only be effective in specific contexts. In Moynihan's world the United States was vulnerable, and colonial arrogance was easier to slap down, at least rhetorically. The UNGA had become a forum in which comparisons of Israel to apartheid South Africa were becoming more common, and words of antiracist and anticolonialist critique could reverberate. The contexts in which Sayegh's critiques took hold or were ignored were not only of Palestinians' making. The diplomatic erasure of his pamphlet from 1946 demonstrates this just as much as the period of antiracist solidarity mobilized within the United Nations marked by Resolution 3379 does. The humanism and antiracism that ran through Sayegh's interventions are values that transcend time and space, and can be sources of critique that are as relevant to the present as they were to the heyday of anticolonial nationalism. As the fate of Palestinians shows, like that of many other imprisoned and oppressed people, the United Nations is no longer functioning as a context for the activation of politically relevant knowledge. The question is what kind of institutional, political, organized solidarity can turn critique into a tool of liberation today.

Notes

My sincere thanks for critical feedback and constructive suggestions go to Didier Fassin, Bernard Harcourt, Ayse Parla, Peter Thomas, Rosemary Sayigh, Yezid Sayigh, and Yasmin Moll. For institutional and material support for this project, further thanks are due to Bernard Harcourt and the Institute for Advanced Study.

1. Antonio Gramsci, *The Prison Notebooks: Selections*, trans. Quintin Hoare and Geoffrey Nowell-Smith (New York: International, 1971), 9. On degrees of subalternity, see Marcus Green, "Gramsci Cannot Speak: Presentations and Interpretations of Gramsci's Concept of the Subaltern," *Rethinking Marxism: A Journal of Economics, Culture and Society* 14, no. 3 (2002): 10.
2. Peter Thomas, "Refiguring the Subaltern," *Political Theory* (2018): 8–9.
3. Amahl A. Bishara, *Back Stories: U.S. News Production and Palestinian Politics* (Stanford: Stanford University Press, 2012).
4. Benny Morris, "Camp David and After: An Exchange (1. An Interview with Ehud Barak)," *New York Review of Books*, June 13, 2002.
5. His lectures went on nonetheless. Edward W. Said, *Representations of the Intellectual: The Reith Lectures* (New York: Vintage, 1996), x.
6. For an account of this long history of critique, see Lori Allen, *Investigating Liberals: International Law and Commissions of Inquiry in Palestine* (Stanford: Stanford University Press, forthcoming).
7. Said, *Representations*, xi.
8. Lori Allen, "Determining Emotions and the Burden of Proof in Investigative Commissions to Palestine," *Comparatives Studies in Society and History* 59, no. 2 (2017): 385–414.
9. Kate Crehan, *Gramsci's Common Sense: Inequality and its Narratives* (Durham: Duke University Press, 2016), 60.
10. Editors, "Zionist Colonialism in Palestine," *Settler Colonial Studies* 2, no. 1 (2012): 206.

11. Keith P. Feldman, *A Shadow Over Palestine: The Imperial Life of Race in America* (Minneapolis: University of Minnesota Press, 2015), 23–57.

12. Andrew I. Killgore, "25 Years After His Death, Dr Fayez Sayegh's Towering Legacy Lives On," *Washington Report on Middle East Affairs*, January 25, 2010, www .washingtonreport.me/2005-december/in-memoriam-25-years-after-his-death-dr. -fayez-sayeghs-towering-legacy-lives-on.html.

13. Fayiz Sayigh, Note on the Palestine Problem: Submitted to the Anglo-American Inquiry Committee, prepared on behalf of the National Party. Beirut, March 19, 1946. No publisher, 7.

14. That is until a recent small rush of attention to Sayegh's writings. His contribution to (post)colonial studies was somewhat reprised when an excerpt from his study, *Zionist Colonialism in Palestine* (Beirut: Research Center, Palestine Liberation Organization, 1965), was published in the journal *Settler Colonial Studies* 1 (January 1, 2012): 206–25. Yoav DiCapua, Keith Feldman, and Ann Stoler have recently discussed Sayegh's role as a politically committed intellectual.

15. Elmer Berger, *Memoirs of an Anti-Zionist Jew* (Beirut: Institute for Palestine Studies 1978), 97, 29.

16. Elmer Berger, *Judaism or Jewish Nationalism: The Alternative to Zionism* (New York: Bookman Associates, 1957).

17. Jonathan Marc Gribetz, "The PLO's Rabbi: Palestinian Nationalism and Reform Judaism," *Jewish Quarterly Review,* 107, no. 1 (2017): 90–112.

18. Ann Stoler, "Doing Concept Work: An Interview with Ann Stoler about the Institute for Critical Social Inquiry," *Savageminds*, https://savageminds.org/2014/12/19 /doing-concept-work-an-interview-with-ann-stoler-about-the-institute-for-critical -social-inquiry/.

19. Judith Butler, "The Sensibility of Critique: Reply to Asad and Mahmood," in *Is Critique Secular?: Blasphemy, Injury and Free Speech*, ed. Talal Asad et al. (Berkeley, CA: Townsend Center for the Humanities, 2013), 115.

20. Sayigh, Note, 3–5, 12.

21. In his diary and radio addresses, James McDonald, a Zionist supporter on the Committee, used this word tens of times to describe the Arabs, usually without offering any details about what the Arab spokespeople actually said. See also Richard Crossman, *Palestine Mission: A Personal Record* (London: Hamish Hamilton, 1947), 73.

22. Robert Normand, and Sarah Zaidi, *Human Rights at the UN: The Political History of Universal Justice* (Bloomington: Indiana University Press, 2008), 110.

23. Steven L. B. Jensen, *The Making of International Human Rights: The 1960s, Decolonization and the Reconstruction of Global Values* (Cambridge: Cambridge University Press, 2016), 105, 110, 126. After the Convention was adopted by the UNGA in December 1965, it became a regular reference point in subsequent UN debates.

24. Daniel Patrick Moynihan, with Suzanne Weaver, *A Dangerous Place* (Boston: Little, Brown, 1978), 30, 42.

25. Fayez A. Sayegh, Statement Made at the 2134th Meeting of the Third (Social, Humanitarian and Cultural) Committee of the General Assembly on October 17, 1975. In *Zionism: A Form of Racism and Racial Discrimination: Four Statements Made at the U.N. General Assembly* (New York: Office of the Permanent Observer of the Palestine Liberation Organization to the United Nations, 1976), 5–6.

26. Fayez A. Sayegh, *Zionist Propaganda in the United States: An Analysis*, ed. Arlene F. Sayegh and Samir Abed-Rabbo (Pleasantville, NY: Fayez A. Sayegh Foundation, 1983), 9.

27. Sayegh, Statement, 10.
28. "Speech by Israeli Ambassador to UN Chaim Herzog, in Response to 'Zionism Is Racism' Resolution," *Ha'aretz*, May 13, 2005.
29. United Nations General Assembly, Thirtieth Session, 2400th Plenary, November 10, 1975 A/PV.2400, 776, 775.
30. United Nations General Assembly, 791.
31. Gil Troy, *Moynihan's Moment: America's Fight Against Zionism as Racism* (New York: Oxford University Press, 2012), 63, 92.

Bibliography

Allen, Lori. "Determining Emotions and the Burden of Proof in Investigative Commissions to Palestine." *Comparatives Studies in Society and History* 59, no. 2 (2017): 385–414.
——. *Investigating Liberals: International Law and Commissions of Inquiry in Palestine.* Stanford: Stanford University Press, forthcoming.
Berger, Elmer. *Judaism or Jewish Nationalism: The Alternative to Zionism.* New York: Bookman Associates, 1957.
——. *Memoirs of an Anti-Zionist Jew.* Beirut: Institute for Palestine Studies, 1978.
Bishara, Amahl A. *Back Stories: U.S. News Production and Palestinian Politics.* Stanford: Stanford University Press, 2012.
Butler, Judith. "The Sensibility of Critique: Reply to Asad and Mahmood." In *Is Critique Secular? Blasphemy, Injury and Free Speech*, edited by Talal Asad et al., 95–130. Berkeley: Townsend Center for the Humanities, 2013.
Crehan, Kate. *Gramsci's Common Sense: Inequality and its Narratives.* Durham: Duke University Press, 2016.
Crossman, Richard. *Palestine Mission: A Personal Record.* London: Hamish Hamilton, 1947.
Feldman, Keith P. *A Shadow Over Palestine: The Imperial Life of Race in America.* Minneapolis: University of Minnesota Press, 2015.
Gramsci, Antonio. *The Prison Notebooks: Selections.* Translated by Quintin Hoare and Geoffrey Nowell-Smith. New York: International, 1971.
Green, Marcus. "Gramsci Cannot Speak: Presentations and Interpretations of Gramsci's Concept of the Subaltern." *Rethinking Marxism: A Journal of Economics, Culture and Society* 14, no. 3 (2002): 1–24.
Gribetz, Jonathan Marc. "The PLO's Rabbi: Palestinian Nationalism and Reform Judaism." *Jewish Quarterly Review* 107, no. 1 (2017): 90–112.
Jensen, Steven L. B. *The Making of International Human Rights: The 1960s, Decolonization and the Reconstruction of Global Values.* Cambridge: Cambridge University Press, 2016.
Morris, Benny. "Camp David and After: An Exchange (1. An Interview with Ehud Barak)." *New York Review of Books*, June 13, 2002.
Moynihan, Daniel Patrick, with Suzanne Weaver. *A Dangerous Place.* Boston: Little, Brown, 1978.
Normand, Robert, and Sarah Zaidi. *Human Rights at the UN: The Political History of Universal Justice.* Bloomington: Indiana University Press, 2008.
Said, Edward W. "Permission to Narrate." *Journal of Palestine Studies* 13, no. 3 (Spring 1984): 27–48.
——. *Representations of the Intellectual: The Reith Lectures.* New York: Vintage, 1996.
Sayegh, Fayez A. *An Analysis of "The Continuing Near East Crisis: Background Information."* J. Willard Marriott Library's Aziz A. Atiya Library, University of Utah, 1969.

——. *Arab Unity: Hope and Fulfillment*. New York: Devin-Adair, 1958.

——. Statement Made at the 2134th Meeting of the Third (Social, Humanitarian and Cultural) Committee of the General Assembly on October 17, 1975. *Zionism: A Form of Racism and Racial Discrimination; Four Statements Made at the U.N. General Assembly*. New York: Office of the Permanent Observer of the Palestine Liberation Organization to the United Nations, 1976.

——. *Zionist Colonialism in Palestine*. Beirut: Research Center, Palestine Liberation Organization, 1965.

——. *Zionist Propaganda in the United States: An Analysis*. Edited by Arlene F. Sayegh and Samir Abed-Rabbo. Pleasantville, NY: Fayez A. Sayegh Foundation, 1983.

"Speech by Israeli Ambassador to UN Chaim Herzog, in Response to 'Zionism Is Racism' Resolution." *Ha'aretz*, May 13, 2005.

Stoler, Ann. "Doing Concept Work: An Interview with Ann Stoler about the Institute for Critical Social Inquiry." *Savageminds*, 2014. https://savageminds.org/2014/12/19/doing-concept-work-an-interview-with-ann-stoler-about-the-institute-for-critical-social-inquiry/.

Thomas, Peter D. "Refiguring the Subaltern." *Political Theory* (2018): 1–24.

Troy, Gil. *Moynihan's Moment: America's Fight Against Zionism as Racism*. New York: Oxford University Press, 2012.

United Nations General Assembly, Thirtieth Session, 2400th Plenary, November 10, 1975 A/PV.2400.

CHAPTER 9

CRITICAL THEORY IN A MINOR KEY TO TAKE STOCK OF THE SYRIAN REVOLUTION

FADI A. BARDAWIL

They refuse to see us

—Yassin al-Haj Saleh

*We do not anticipate the world with our dogmas
but instead attempt to discover the new world
through the critique of the old*

—Karl Marx

The academic preoccupation with the vicissitudes of critique has done a good job at highlighting how conservative forces and those in power manage to hijack a critical arsenal associated with progressive causes and radical politics. Anthropologists have been drawing our attention for a while now to such processes as appropriations of feminist languages by Christian fundamentalists. They have also revealed the limits of formal left-liberal demands for representation, such as those for equal time, which are now requested by conservatives and granted by the media to climate change deniers. In the wake of the proliferation of such acts of appropriation and hijacking by the likes of conspiracy theorists, and powerful state actors,

Euro-American calls were issued to forgo the critical project, deemed exhausted, altogether.[1]

Yet the appropriation of critical moves—such as social constructionism—which are deemed to carry an a priori liberatory potential, by agents on the opposite of end of the political spectrum (say, by climate change deniers who wield it to cast doubt on the solidity of scientific evidence), is nothing new. Edward Said's *Orientalism*, a seminal text of critique, which transformed the academic landscape globally and whose insurrectionary fire bypassed the university's high walls, leaving its mark on the worlds of art and politics, was read by some nationalists and Islamists as an apology for the Arabs and Islam. In its travels back to the Arab world the critical edge of Said's work was appropriated by nativists who transformed it into ideological fuel for their anti-Western rhetorics. In an afterword written about a decade and a half after *Orientalism*'s publication, Said clarified his points and lamented the reception of the book in the Arab world, which equated the critique of Orientalist knowledges with a systematic defense of Arabs and Islam, or an endorsement of nationalist and religious politics. *Orientalism*, Said wrote, "almost in a Borgesian way, has become several different books."[2]

In revisiting *Orientalism*'s travels, I aim not simply to make a historical point—namely that there are precedents to the appropriations of critical works and that what is now taken as a recent development is not so new after all. Rather, I want to make the conceptual point that one cannot determine in advance the uses to which a critical work can be put. Actors, as different as secular Arab nationalists and Islamists, can appropriate critique and transform it into ideology and an instrument of power. Once one starts from the premise that there is no way to fix a priori the pragmatic effects of a critical work as it travels in time and space, and between different constituencies, the injunction to forgo critique because it is being hijacked loses its purchase. This premise is also a reflexive reminder that critique, particularly in its Olympian versions, must not forget its own worldliness. Just as it seeks to apprehend the world, the world too catches it in its webs.

The more interesting question as a result is not critique's appropriation by political forces on the opposite end of the spectrum. This is a risk that is always there. It is also not the question of whether critique is exhausted or not. In many parts of the world where intellectuals, artists, and activists are forced to flee, put in jails, and assassinated, critique, which is not practiced from within the secure walls of the academy, does not come with the guarantees of liberal democracies. It is a modality of parrhesiatic practice that flanks the critic's life with danger. Abandoning it is what those in power dream of. Rather, it is the question of how critical theories can lose their insurrectional spark, become routinized, and start operating like mythological frames that bestow a fixed meaning on the world, excluding in the process emergent practices from the domain of emancipatory politics.

This question is politically urgent today since the practices of emancipation of Arab revolutionaries (2011–), particularly the Syrian ones, have been hastily brushed off in certain Arab and metropolitan leftist circles, as not properly revolutionary. I focus on the Syrian revolution because unlike the initial celebrations after toppling the pro-Western Tunisian and Egyptian presidents (2011), the uprisings in Syria were met from the get-go by suspicious apprehension or support of the regime by certain quarters of the left. The practices of the revolutionaries who early on faced a ruthless war machine, which was not a client of Western powers, clashed with the theoretical first principles, primarily anti-imperialism, but also secularism, that guide these leftists' political alignments. The Syrian revolution posed a serious challenge to leftist political critique and critical theory, which divided both Arab and Euro-American leftists. The calls of the men and women, who risked everything in rising against the Assad dynastic rule, remained for the most part unheard, or deliberately shut out. These militants' collective political practices were banished from the domain of emancipatory politics and solidarity with them was withdrawn because they were deemed not to fit with leftist first principles.[3] Theory prevailed over practice. Moreover, this dismissal seems to have been vindicated by the tragic unfolding of events. The political defeats of the revolutions appear to confirm the truth of the theoretical judgment. There is, of course, a distinguished genealogy of the collapse of conceptual truth unto political victory on the left. "Little has eviscerated Marxism," Russell Jacoby wrote a while ago, in one his signature distilled sentences, "more than its acceptance of the judgment of history as truth itself."[4] "Victory," he reminds us, "is not proof of truth."[5]

My wager in what follows is simple: instead of adjudicating political practice, as it did in the case of the revolution, critical theory ought today to be rethought in light of practice. The moral and political failures, primarily of anti-imperialist transcendentalism, in the wake of the Syrian revolution demands, first, a rethinking of the vicissitudes of leftist political criticism and theories. As a second step, I reactivate critical kernels from the works of Hannah Arendt, Aimé Césaire, Frantz Fanon, and Edward Said to articulate a practice of critique for our times attuned to the irruption of events and historical emergences. This is a practice in a minor key, which steers away from an Olympian theoretical will to totality and a dogmatic attachment to ideological first principles.[6] It is also one that remains alert to the risks of detachment from the world critical theory is prone to through the logics of professionalization or its metamorphosis into a mythology.

The authors I draw on sought in different ways to rearticulate critical theory to apprehend emancipatory politics in urgent times, when the mediations between theory and practice is severed. I do not revisit their works to offer ready-made answers to present conundrums. Rather, I underscore how questions that Césaire, Fanon, and Arendt addressed on how theory can be complicit in erasing emancipatory struggles and how concepts ought to be translated, displaced, and stretched to articulate a critical theory attuned to the emergence of newness in the world are salient again. Having done that, I bring this essay to a close by revisiting Edward Said's work to sketch the contours of an ethos of critique in a minor key. Said was very attentive to the different traps of closures, particularly the professional kind that academic critical theory can fall into. More importantly, Said's theoretical practice steers away from an understanding of critical theory as an end in itself, say, the attempt to have the last word on the state of the world, but as an energetic performance and a strategic intervention in a problem-space.[7] All in all, I think there is a lot to be learned, in, and for, our present, from these thinkers' generous ethos, their closeness to the pulse of those who were struggling against domination and exploitation, and their craft-like skill at critical elaborations.

I

The Arab revolutions in general, and the Syrian in particular, put on the table again the thorny political and theoretical question of naming an event. The struggles against the authoritarian regimes, inherited for the most part from the age of decolonization, were from the beginning far from isolated, local events. They were world events. The revolutions, and their aftermaths, underscored and heightened the interconnected nature of our world. This interconnectedness increasingly muddies the borders between left-wing and right-wing political positions and forecloses the possibility of positing visions of revolutionary teleology. Moreover, it puts the revolutions at risk of being critically apprehended by overarching theories with a big appetite for totalizing accounts.

The popular uprisings unfolded at a fast pace and covered large swathes of the Arab world from Tunis to Yemen. The dramatic pace of the events took everyone by surprise including the Western patrons of some regimes, Middle East experts, social scientists, and public intellectuals. In the years preceding the revolutions much intellectual energy had been spent on accounting for political stasis and pinpointing the "deficits" plaguing the region. For instance, eminent academic specialists of Tunisian politics such as Béatrice Hibou, who borrowed "much of her conceptual framework from Michel Foucault, . . . suggested that institutions of power had turned Tunisians into active participants in their own subjugation, making revolt inconceivable."[8] The three Arab Human

Development Reports, written by a group of Arab scholars and experts, and published by the United Nations Development Program, are exemplars of the prerevolutions genre of "deficits" literature. "The key diagnosis of the first report," notes the UNDP administrator who penned the forward to third report, "that the Arab world is suffering three fundamental deficits—in political rights, in women's rights and in knowledge—that have, together, held back human development across the region has now become widely accepted."[9] The speed, geographical scope, and dramatic outcomes of the popular uprisings sidelined many of the regime-centric scholarly lenses that attempted to account for the endurance of political authoritarianism and the transnational dialects of international organizations, which enumerated the deficits facing human development and forestalling empowerment.[10]

The Arab revolutions did not only constitute a world event because of their scale, accelerated rhythms, and impact. The tragic aftermaths of the grassroots collective movements in 2011 reveal the increasingly interconnected character of our world. The military, political, and economic interventions of international and regional forces in Syria not only rendered them accountable for their actions abroad but also transformed the revolution into *internal*—say, Lebanese, Turkish, and German—affairs that could take many shapes. For instance, these internal affairs could take the form of whether and how to accommodate the influx of fleeing refugees or how to counter security threats on their own territories, and the rise of neofascist and ultranationalist forces. This is particularly true in the Syrian case, where the politics of mass population displacements is part and parcel of the regime's warfare arsenal. A Syrian family who is forced out and relocates to Germany, for instance, is transubstantiated at the border into "refugees," who belong to a cultural minority in need of integration to "European values." Former revolutionaries turned refugees overnight find themselves a "problem" in Europe. A "problem" incorporated into narratives of decline that preceded the revolutions and take migrants/refugees to be major causes in the twilight of Europe by the right and some leftists, or victims to be saved by humanitarians. The moment of emancipation of the Arab revolutions, which for a moment envisaged a better future, was very shortly engulfed by the European age of regression, which is at pains to imagine brighter times to come. These interconnections and imbrications make it difficult to hold on to clear demarcations of borders and boundaries, despite the fantasies of radical purity of nationalists who wish to fence themselves off. More and more, "foreignness," in Clifford Geertz's memorable phrase, "does not start at the water's edge but at the skin's."[11]

These interconnections, as the tragic predicament of the Syrian revolution reveals, also make it difficult to hold on to crystal-clear visions of revolutionary teleology. Let's pause for a minute and listen to the voice of the Syrian thinker, revolutionary, and former political prisoner Yasin al-Haj Saleh, who talks of a complex "Syrian question," which today characterizes our global political present. The Syrian question, al-Haj Saleh argues, is the response of the powerful on the local, regional, and international levels to the revolutions of the vulnerable. "The powerful," he adds, "tie many Gordian knots which the vulnerable spend a lifetime trying to undo. Posing questions is a strategy through which all the vulnerable people in the world are disciplined."[12] The Syrian national struggle against tyranny became entangled in the infranational webs of sectarian and ethnic solidarities from below and the geopolitical interests of regional and international powers. al-Haj Saleh enumerates the major forces that contributed to the creation of the Syrian question in this order: Russia; the United States; the Saudi and Iranian theocracies; Turkey, Jordan, and Lebanon; "secular European republics and kingdoms that prioritize Christian and other 'minority' refugees"; Israel; and "finally the two poles of the underground world—the terrorist jihadist groups (which are basically independent intelligence agencies run by fanatics) and the international intelligence agencies (which are essentially a torturing and murdering apparatus) (25). After noting the increasingly depressing and complex nature of our present, which seems to loose a sense of direction, al-Haj Saleh reckons that "the crisis is no longer a Syrian one. It is a crisis of the world" (26).

Our one world in crisis seems light years away from the worlds the radical left inhabited in the 1960s and 1970s, which conceived of the world revolution as a process unfolding in three *distinct* but dialectically correlated geographical spheres: anticapitalist in the first world, antibureaucratic in the world of really existing socialism, and anti-imperialist in the third world.[13]

Today the borders between certain quarters of the left and the right are getting harder and harder to discern. Parts of the lefts and the right in Europe are getting closer on several fronts: namely, under the rubric of a nationalism, at times virulent, which upholds national sovereignty against supranational institutions, such as the European Union, global economic processes, and migrants.[14] Other leftists and right-wingers are also united by an attachment to a staunch secularism that is wielded in the face of migrants and refugees, which loses its edge as a critique of religious conservatism as it increasingly becomes an ideological weapon of racialization of minorities. Moreover, the support of segments of the Euro-American and Arab left to the Syrian dictator Bashshar al-Assad, who also became an icon of white nationalists, is another indicator of both the increasing interconnectedness of our world and the increasing difficulty in distinguishing between certain ideological positions when it comes to Syria.[15] Not to mention that the Syrian "secular" regime could not have survived without the military, economic, and logistical support of the Islamic Republic of Iran and the radical Islamist and sectarian militias that revolve in its orbit. In brief, the Syrian revolution and its aftermaths reveal the limits of traditional leftist critiques that deploy first principles—anti-imperialism, and secularism—as an a priori guide of political judgment.

Moving beyond an assessment of the first principles that guide the left's political alignments, can our critical theories apprehend the event? In what way is the theoretical apprehension of the event, its naming, overdetermined by belatedness, i.e., its coming after revolutions from which the conceptual features of what defines a "revolution" are distilled? This belatedness, which is tightly woven with the dialects of Arab "deficits," cuts across scholarly and media discourses on the region. It often manifests itself in the form of leading questions: Where is the Palestinian Gandhi? Where is the Muslim Luther? Where is the Arab Lenin? The suggested negative answer to these three questions underscores assumptions about "Palestinian violence," which exists outside of the sphere of "civility," Islam as a "problem" in and for modernity, and the "non-revolutionary" nature of the Arab uprisings since they did not come hand in hand with their token revolutionary theorist.

Seasoned scholars of Arab political life who tried their hands at giving a critical account of the revolutions outside of Eurocentric, and statist, molds drew their analytical tools from a left theoretical toolkit that is critical of neoliberalism both as a reorganization of capitalism and a political rationality that remakes subjects. "The political clout of neoliberalism," Asef Bayat writes, "lies in its ability to serve as a form of governmentality, in its ability to structure people's thinking to internalize the methods of the market society, considering them to be a commonsense way of being and doing things, against which no concrete alternative is imagined or needed."[16] Bayat compared the Arab revolutions to the Third-Worldist revolutions of the 1960s and the 1970s, and concluded that today's militants were co-opted by neoliberal logics and therefore *lacked* the radical anti-imperialist and social justice visions of emancipations that animated earlier revolutionary movements. The revolutionaries themselves, it seemed, were not proper revolutionaries. "By the time the Arab uprisings occurred," Bayat writes, "most Islamists and secular counterparts alike had been conditioned by the neoliberal climate."[17] I have a few qualms with this critical account of the revolutions. This historical comparative exercise bears a family resemblance with the deficit pronouncements that account for the present predicament of Arab societies by underscoring the deficits in democracy, human rights, women's rights—you name it—that separate them from a Western liberal democratic norm. In this case, the interpretation of the revolutions is overdetermined by their belatedness vis-à-vis the Third-Worldist revolutionary moment. This comparative exercise overlooks the historical unfolding of the past century's revolutions that witnessed the transformations of anti-imperialist politics—whether secular or Islamist—and socialist ideologies from visions of emancipation to bludgeons of power in the hands of regimes and militant forces. It is as if the Syrian revolutionaries who have been dominated, killed, and tortured by the Assad regime for more than four decades are now asked why don't they reactivate the Arab socialist legacy of the Ba'ath party, in whose name the family-run regime ruled them. To point this out is not an argument for forgoing past and present anti-imperialist and socialist traditions in the Arab world. Rather, it is a reminder that the political conjunctures in which the revolutions unfolded are not ones that can be subsumed under a smooth global narrative of transition from the good past of radical internationalist socialism to the bad neoliberal present. These pasts are connected in more than one way to our present. Moreover, Bayat's account is articulated in a behavioralist idiom, which makes neoliberalism an overbearing climate, which conditions militants of various ideological shades. In a nutshell, what troubles me the most in his account is the attempt to critically apprehend the multiple interconnections of our present at the levels of the circulation of capital and the productivity of political rationalities in a *totalizing*-cum-behavioralist theoretical dialect that is marshaled to banish the militants from the domain of revolutionary politics. The will to totality this account performs is hard to square with the multiple political discourses, organizational forms, and collective initiatives in the Arab world. There is a particular ease with which the totalizing critical scholar delimits from his Olympian perch the parameters of the political game structured in advance by the transcendental force. The deployment of neoliberalism as a master key has become like the earlier recourse to the West as the transcendental omnipotent force that is assumed to make history and remake people, therefore leaving us only with two options: to welcome it as its heralds or oppose it as its victims.

The mass political movements across the Arab world that called for their dignity against the decades of humiliation by postcolonial regimes displaced the West from the center of Arab mass *emancipatory* political practice. What do twentieth-century anticolonial movements, which were fueled by visions of national liberation from colonial domination, Marxian emancipation, and Islamist/nativist politics of decolonization, all have in common? They are all opposed, whether politically, economically, or culturally, to Western domination and exploitation. In the post–Cold War era, when revolutionary movements in the Arab world had ebbed, metropolitan and Arab leftists were divided around the question of Western military interventions in the region. They were faced with the hard political choice of either supporting "national sovereignty" under authoritarian rulers or banking on the possibility of a "democracy" brought about by imperial sanctions and occupations, as epitomized by the US invasion and occupation of Iraq (2003). Of course, quiet a few leftists declared their opposition both to dictators and Western interventions. This double refusal though was not carried by a political force, which was able to materialize this slogan into a political program. It was a good, moral position, which was not translated politically. The Arab revolutions, one the other hand, both in their first moment of elation and the second moment of tragedy, broke this political deadlock by snatching political practice from a predominant preoccupation with the West. The revolutions breached the matrix of left politics and critical theory that could not overcome the Empire/Resistance binary. To say this is to point out that critical theories do not only fall short of apprehending events by active conceptual erasure and totalizing sweeps. At times critical theory falls short because the event falls out of its circumscribed terrains of operations, and remains invisible, as a result.

The metropolitan oppositional epistemology critique, which caught like wildfire in the wake of Edward Said's *Orientalism* (1978), did not develop critical conceptual tools to grasp the modalities of power at work in Arab and Muslim societies whose subject was not the West. Major crises in the region that did not revolve in the orbit of the West politically and culturally, such as the internecine waves of battles during the Lebanese civil and regional wars (1975–90), the Syrian regime's massacre in Hama (1982), and the Iran-Iraq war in the 1980s, remained invisible in theory. This defensive theoretical anti-imperialism performs well as long as its targets are Western, which belong to two categories: either discourses with universal aspirations—say, human rights, secularism, Marxism, liberalism, and feminism—or culturalist reifications about Islam and the "Arab mind." It works better still if these discourses are peddled by empires, international organizations, and NGOs. That said, it doesn't have much to say *conceptually* on practices of emancipation, such as the Arab revolutions, or logics of power, such as the modalities of rule of the Assad regime, which fall outside of the imperial orbit. This issue is not exclusive to "anti-imperialist" practices of epistemology critique. The critical bite of more than a few of our critical theories is circumscribed by the implicit delimitation of their own terrain of operation. Deconstructionism, for instance, was mostly dominant in "those spaces of the literary critical establishment where the textual objects of reading could be recognized as cultural artifacts of the same philosophical system to which it turned its critical eye."[18] The Frankfurt School of critical theory produced incisive and sweeping analyses of late capitalism, yet it never surrendered the West as its civilizational unit of analysis, Herbert Marcuse's allusions to anticolonial struggles notwithstanding.[19]

II

The foreclosure and rendering invisible of practices of emancipation in theory and the refusal to extend words and acts of political solidarity with the Syrian revolutionaries by some leftists bring out questions that earlier generations of revolutionaries and theorists struggled with. I now turn to recovering for our present critical kernels from the works of Aimé Césaire, Franz Fanon, and Hannah Arendt. These authors share an ethos of attunement to the world, which led them each in their own way to interrogate preexisting theories in light of events and to theorize political emergences. In doing so, they performed a rearticulation of the cardinal axes of power and emancipation outside of its agreed-upon reference points. Recovering their ethos and their critical practice is, I hope, an antidote to the current theorizing, and the political alignments which followed from it, in the wake of the Syrian revolution, and the Arab revolutions more generally.

A few years after the beginning of the Algerian revolution (1954–62), before the height of Third-Worldist solidarity, Aimé Césaire, who was a député for Martinique at the time, wrote a powerful letter of resignation from the French Communist Party addressed to Maurice Thorez, the party's secretary general. Let's listen to Césaire as he justifies why he quit the party. Césaire, who is tackling the question of the relationship of the colonial question to communist internationalism, begins by underlining the former's singularity, "which cannot be reduced to any other problem."[20] This singularity, for Césaire, is what preempts considering the colonial struggle a fragment of a more important whole, which is constituted by the struggle of the French worker against capitalism. Césaire draws our attention to how taking class struggle as the universal ground of critique and solidarity robbed the colonial question of its singularity, rendering it subordinate to it and contributing to rejecting, "a priori and in the name of an exclusive ideology, men who are nevertheless honest and fundamentally anticolonialist" (148). He goes on to point out that, despite their radical class politics, metropolitan communists, like their bourgeois compatriots, espouse a simplistic belief in the "omnilateral superiority of the West" (149). Both communists and colonialists share an attitude of paternalism, one that Syrian revolutionaries have recently complained of in their dealings with some practices of European solidarity with their cause.[21] Note though that Césaire's critique of French communists, unlike nativist critics, does not ground itself in cultural particularity. "There are two ways to lose oneself," he writes, "walled segregation in the particular or dilution in the 'universal'" (152). Instead of this oscillation, between segregation and dilution, which are reminiscent of colonial logics, and logics of power more generally, that either seek to erase difference or reify it, he proposes a notion of the universal as a "deepening and coexistence of all particulars" (152). Césaire ends his resignation letter by urging his readers to have "the strength to invent instead of follow," and to clear the path "of ready-made forms, those petrified forms that obstruct it" (152). As I read him, Césaire is clearly not arguing for forgoing alliances and solidarity. Rather, he is proposing that critical practice should be, like Edward Said argued after him, attuned to the world, by inventing new forms that enable solidarities. This inventive labor of critique can take the form of stretching a concept to encompass practices that previously fell outside of its purview. The feminist tradition, for instance, stretched the notion of the political to encompass the private sphere—the personal is political. The concept of work was also widened in the late twentieth century outside of its traditional association with labor movements. "Progressive advocates," Anna Tsing writes, "expanded the category of work—and thus the grounds for solidarity—arguing that housework, sex work, piece work, and more were also work."[22]

Critical invention can also take the form of stretching a tradition of critical thinking, particularly through labors of conceptual translation. If Césaire helped us think the question of the erasure of emancipatory struggle, Fanon, writing some five years after him, urges us to think about how the travels of revolutionary theory can flip its valence and recode its meaning, and the ensuing necessity of forging new concepts to capture the singularity of the situation. In *The Wretched of the Earth*, Fanon tackles the question of revolutionary practice in a situation where the mediation between revolutionary theory and practice is severed. For Fanon, nationalist parties and their base of urban voters benefit from the colonial system, and a large number of colonial subjects adhere to metropolitan political parties. "These colonial subjects are militant activists under the abstract slogan: 'Power to the Proletariat,'" he writes, "forgetting that in their part of the world slogans of national liberation should come first. The colonized intellectual has invested his aggression in his barely veiled wish to be assimilated to the colonizer's world."[23] Fanon's critical observation alerts us to the reifications of revolutionary theory, which is assumed to retain its critical bite regardless of where, when, and by whom it is deployed.

"Marxist analysis," Fanon suggests, "should always be slightly stretched when it comes to addressing the colonial issue" (5).[24] In opposition to the colonized militants dabbling in "abstract" slogans of power to the proletariat, Fanon elevates the "wretched of the earth," who are not assimilated to the colonial world and whose bodies bear its brunt, to the role of the primary revolutionary agent (23). The "wretched of the earth" were like Mao's peasants and Gramsci's subalterns, "part of the search for a revolutionary subject that was *not-the-proletariat* (in the absence of a large working class) [which] was itself an exercise in a series of displacements of the original term.[25] This process of conceptual displacement/translation took place not only by thinkers in the colonial world, but also by those who posited that mediation between theory and practice has been severed in industrial capitalist societies because the proletariat has been co-opted by the system. In the conclusion to *One Dimensional Man*, Marcuse operates a similar displacement, noting that under the "conservative popular base" lies the "substratum of the outcasts and outsiders, the exploited and the persecuted of other races and other colors, the unemployed and unemployable," the specter that haunts the system.[26] "They exist outside the democratic process," and their life, Marcuse adds, "is the most immediate and the most real need for ending intolerable conditions and institutions. Their opposition is revolutionary even if their consciousness is not."[27]

The invention of new forms, the stretching of traditions, and conceptual displacements and translations are all part of the toolkit of rewiring critical theory in response to emancipatory emergences that trouble its already existing articulations of theory and practice. Hannah Arendt, like Césaire and Fanon, knew quiet well that it is theory that ought to be rethought to accommodate political practice, rather than banishing the revolutionaries from the domain of the political because their acts are not legible in theory. Arendt emphasized the necessity of staying close to the events and to the concepts the revolutionaries used to think about their actions. In the epilogue to *The Origins of Totalitarianism*, Arendt posits that Soviet totalitarianism has to be assessed in light of the Hungarian Revolution (1956). "Events, past and present," Arendt writes, "not social forces and historical trends, nor questionnaires and motivation research, nor any other gadgets in the arsenal of the social sciences—are the true, the only reliable teachers of political scientists, as they are the most trustworthy source of information for those engaged in politics."[28] In light of this statement Arendt notes that if the Hungarian revolutionaries said during the event that they were fighting against imperialism then "political science must accept the term" (503). I do not read Arendt as driving a wedge between structural social analysis and events. Rather, I read her as urging the student of politics to learn form events and stay close to the pulse of the men and women who are engaged in political struggles. Arendt's comments are particularly productive in the aftermath of the Syrian revolution, which raised a serious question about the lack of our critical theories to address foreign interventions that are not Western, such as Russia's military involvement. Quiet a few leftists and the authoritarian Arab regimes collapse imperialism onto Western military, economic, and cultural interventions. While cultural critics make sure to call into question the universals that are enlisted by Western forces in their "civilizing mission," they may condemn politically, but cannot apprehend critically, the politics of intervention and extraction that does not deploy civilizing discourses with their missiles. In a memorable sentence on the Hungarian revolution that can be borrowed to describe the predicament of the Arab revolutions, Arendt writes: "This light—who would deny it?—is not steady, it flares and flickers; yet it is the only authentic light we have" (503).

III

I bring this essay to a close by revisiting Edward Said's critical practice and ethos of criticism, which are profitable for the labors of rearticulating a critical practice watchful to the multiple political and professional traps of closure. Edward

Said's critical theoretical work is significantly, but not exclusively, concerned with the question of the mediation between metropolitan power and its cultural products, as well as the resistances to them by thinkers from the periphery. The West, broadly speaking, is at the heart of his critical elaborations. It may then seem odd at first glance to turn to Said to conclude an argument about the necessity today to rearticulate critical theory in a minor key to apprehend practices of emancipation that do not necessarily revolve in the West's orbit. I turn to him because I think there is a lot to be learned from Said's practice and ethos in rethinking critique as a worldly, urgent, and strategic intervention. Critique in a minor key forgoes theory's Olympian aspirations, but as Said's practice clearly shows us, its capacity for a resonance in the world is certainly not muffled as a result. In fact, it is amplified.

"It is the critic's job," Said affirmed, "to provide resistances to theory, to open it up towards historical reality, toward society, toward human needs and interests, to point up those concrete instances drawn from everyday reality that lie outside or just beyond the interpretive area necessarily designated in advance and thereafter circumscribed by every theory."[29] Said's call to critical vigilance against the tendency of theory to close itself off from historical processes is in tune with his overall aversion to dogmas, conventions, and orthodoxies. Yet, this stance is simply not an affirmation of a personal proclivity against closure. Said's concern, particularly as it pertains to critical theory, is primarily related the different ways in which its insurrectionary fire can be extinguished and how its oppositional capacity can be neutralized. Fundamental to this process of co-optation of critique is the pervading logic of expertise and professionalism, which operates on different planes. On the discursive plane, a critical theory, such as Lukacs's critique of reification, Said observes, can move from constituting an act of insurrection against the bourgeois order to becoming part and parcel of a researcher's domain. Theory for Lukacs, Said argues, was a "revolutionary will completely committed to worldliness and change" (234). In the hands of Lucien Goldman, Lukacs's brilliant disciple, Said observes, theory's insurrectionary role is sapped. It becomes part and parcel of a researcher's domain, "the place in which disparate, apparently disconnected things are brought together in perfect correspondence: economics, political process, the individual writer, a series of texts" (235). In brief, Said alerts us to how critical theory can lose its fire through the logics of institutionalization, which turn it from an intervention in the world into a normalized academic paradigm, in the Kuhnian sense.

The critical intervention turned normalized paradigm not only loses touch with historical processes from which it has risen, but through the increased logic of division of labor turns those who are bound by the paradigm into narrow academic subspecialists. This form of professionalization comes with its own institutions—departments, journals, conferences, and specialized papers—which increase the authoritative status of the theory and give rise to particular interests, which contribute to driving critical-theoretical practices increasingly away from political and public life.[30] Critique is then either rendered irrelevant, or worse becomes part and parcel of producing and reproducing a hegemonic political order.

Despite spending most of his life as a professional academic, Said's conception of critique as always attuned to developments in the world endowed his writings with a sense of urgency that spoke to, and resonated with, wide audiences. "Beneath the carefully considered prose, the humorous language and the kindness of Said's writings," wrote the Barbadian historian Melanie Newton, "is a sense of urgency, which also animates the writings of so many writers and artists from the Caribbean."[31] Said's critical ethos combined a sense of urgency with a generosity that left his readers energized. Criticism, he said in a vitalistic tone, must be "life-enhancing" (29). Whether he was writing about the different levels of mediations that tie European novels to imperialist ventures or discussing the continuing dispossession of Palestinians, Said's writings were as far as possible from resentment and the multiple constellations of *passions tristes* surrounding it. Said, who was very much aware that critique cannot just be reduced to a rationalist discussion of ideas, described Jonathan Swift's writings as "energetic, powerful and effective," which he dubbed "local performances" (79–82). This description of Swift and his attention to the "deployment and disposition of energies" in writings are, I think, an apt description of Said's own critical labors. I am mentioning these points to underscore that in this perspective critique is not only a matter of producing an account of the world that is epistemologically superior to the layman's account of their own condition. Said through his own writings and example gives us a way to think critique as a performance that mobilizes ideas and energies to enact a strategic intervention in the present. Said's practice of critique, as worldly, urgent, and energetic, one that never falls back on the "unthreatening combativeness" (23) of academic prose and keeps a watchman's eye on the dialectical transformations of critical breakthroughs into traps, is a salutary one, for the task of rewiring critique today.

IV

The acts of the vulnerable Syrian men and women whose courage propelled them to face a murderous dynasty, which has been occupying a republic for nearly half a century now, have been rendered invisible in theory. The singularity and originality of the Syrian revolution were muffled by the repetitions of segments of the Arab and Western lefts, which in the wake of the loss of assurance in history's progressive march forward recentered their political alignments as acts of resistance against Western military and cultural imperialism. In some cases, this politics was coupled with a support of non-Western regimes that were not clients of Western powers, or a justificatory attitude toward their authoritarianism toward their own citizens. The revolutionaries were also erased by those on the left and the right who insisted on framing them exclusively through the lens of "culture" ("religious fanatics") not to mention the dialects of terrorism ("security threat") and humanitarianism ("victims") by state agencies and international organizations. The foreclosure of the emancipatory dimension of the event was undertaken in part before the revolution became entangled over time in the infranational webs of social solidarities—sectarian, regional, ethnic—and swallowed by the supranational geopolitical interests of regional and international powers. The revolution also posed difficult political and theoretical questions to the left: How do we mobilize and be in solidarity, without paternalism, across difference?[32] And how do we think simultaneously the singularity of emancipatory events and the increasingly interconnected yet unequal world?

As a first step toward remedying the theoretical foreclosure of the revolutionaries' practice, I proposed to articulate for our present a theoretical practice that resists making leftist ideology into transcendental principles and critical theory's inclination toward totalizing accounts. Rather, I reactivated kernels from the work of earlier generations of theorists to make an argument for a practice of critique in a minor key that stays attuned to the pulse of the world, through acts of conceptual stretching and translation, and seeks to energetically and strategically intervene in it rather than conceptually master it. In doing that I was guided by, and drew sustenance from, Aimé Césaire's deceptively simple yet penetrating words to Maurice Thorez, which I now borrow one last time to bring my essay to close. "What I want," Césaire wrote, "is that Marxism and communism be placed in the service of black peoples, and not black peoples in the service of Marxism and communism. That the doctrine and the movement would be made to fit men, not men to fit the doctrine or the movement."[33]

Notes

Didier Fassin, Bernard Harcourt, and Peter Redfield read and commented on earlier drafts. I am thankful for their incisive comments and helpful suggestions.

1. See Susan Harding, *The Book of Jerry Falwell: Fundamentalist Politics and Language* (Princeton: Princeton University Press, 2000); Timothy K. Choy, "Articulated Knowledges: Environmental Forms After Universality's Demise," *American Anthropologist* 107, no. 1 (2005): 5–18; Bruno Latour, "Why Has Critique Run out of Steam? From Matters of Fact to Matters of Concern," *Critical Inquiry* 30 (2004): 225–48; Rita Felski, "Introduction," *New Literary History* 47, nos. 2–3 (2016): 215–29.

2. Edward Said, *Orientalism* (New York: Vintage, 1994), 330. See Didier Fassin, "The Endurance of Critique," *Anthropological Theory* 17, no. 1 (2017): 7–8.

3. I engage the failures of the Metropolitan anti-imperialist left in "Forsaking the Syrian Revolution: An Anti-Imperialist Handbook," *al-Jumhuriya*, December 22, 2016, www .aljumhuriya.net/en/content/forsaking-syrian-revolution-anti-imperialist-handbook.

4. Russell Jacoby, *Dialectic of Defeat: Contours of Western Marxism* (Cambridge: Cambridge University Press, 1981), 3.

5. Jacoby, 3.

6. My thinking about the practice of critical theorization in a minor key, and much more, is greatly indebted to David Scott's work, particularly his illuminating conversations with, and readings of, Stuart Hall. See David Scott, "Politics, Contingency, Strategy: An Interview with Stuart Hall," *Small Axe* 1 (1997): 141–59; and David Scott, *Stuart Hall's Voice: Intimations of an Ethics of Receptive Generosity* (Duke: Duke University Press, 2017). In thinking of a critical theory that forgoes its will to totality I also drew sustenance from Wendy Brown, *Edgework: Critical Essays on Knowledge and Politics* (Princeton: Princeton University Press, 2005) and a conversation with Brown about her work at the Institute for Advanced Studies in Princeton (December 6, 2016).

7. A "problem-space," David Scott writes, "is meant first of all to demarcate a discursive context, a context of language, but it is more than a cognitively intelligible arrangement of concepts, ideas, images, meanings, and so on—though it is certainly this. It is a context of argument, and therefore one of intervention. A problem-space, in other words, is an ensemble of questions and answers around which a horizon of identifiable stakes (conceptual as well as ideological-political stakes) hangs." David Scott, *Conscripts of Modernity: The Tragedy of Colonial Enlightenment* (Durham: Duke University Press, 2004), 4.

8. Charles Kurzman, "The Arab Spring Uncoiled," *Mobilization: An International Journal* 17, no. 4 (2010): 377.

9. United Nations Development Program, *Arab Human Development Report 2004: Towards Freedom in the Arab World* (New York: Regional Bureau for Arab States, cosponsored with the Arab Fund for Economic and Social Development, 2004), i.

10. See Lila Abu-Lughod, "Dialects of Women's Empowerment: The International Circuitry of the *Arab Human Development Report 2005*," *International Journal of Middle Eastern Studies* 41 (2009): 83–103.

11. Clifford Geertz, *The Uses of Diversity: The Tanner Lectures on Human Values* (delivered at the University of Michigan November 8, 1985), 261, https://tannerlectures.utah .edu/_documents/a-to-z/g/geertz86.pdf.

12. Yassin al-Haj Saleh, *The Impossible Revolution: Making Sense of the Syrian Tragedy*, trans. Ibtihal Mahmoud (London: C. Hurst, 2017), 25. Hereafter cited parenthetically in the text.

13. See Enzo Traverso, *Left-Wing Melancholia: Marxism, History, and Memory* (New York: Columbia University Press, 2017), 12.

14. For instance, see Matt Qvortrup, "Germany's Radical Left is Fuelling Anti-Immigrant Sentiment," *CNN*, September, 7, 2018, www.cnn.com/2018/09/07/opinions/sahra -wagenknecht-opinion-intl/index.html; and Abel Mestre, "L'immigration continue de diviser La Gauche," *Le Monde*, October 2, 2018, www.lemonde.fr/la-france-insoumise /article/2018/10/02/la-question-de-l-immigration-au-centre-de-la-recomposition-de -la-gauche_5363100_5126047.html.

15. Liz Sly and Rick Noack, "Syria's Assad Has Become an Icon of the Far-Right in America," *Washington Post*, August 14, 2017, www.washingtonpost.com/news/worldviews

/wp/2017/08/13/syrias-assad-has-become-an-unexpected-icon-of-the-far-right-in
-america/?noredirect=on&utm_term=.b02d681224b2.

16. Asef Bayat, *Revolution Without Revolutionaries: Making Sense of the Arab Spring* (Stanford: Stanford University Press, 2017), 23.

17. Bayat, 26.

18. Rosalind C. Morris, "Introduction," in *Can the Subaltern Speak? Reflections on the History of an Idea*, ed. Rosalind C. Morris (New York: Columbia University Press, 2010), 13.

19. I develop this point in "Césaire with Adorno: Critical Theory and the Colonial Problem," *South Atlantic Quarterly* 117, no. 4 (2018). See also Edward Said, *Culture and Imperialism* (New York: Vintage, 1993); and Amy Allen, "Adorno, Foucault, and the End of Progress: Critical Theory in Postcolonial Times," in *Critical Theory in Critical Times: Transforming the Global and Political Economic Order,* ed. Penelope Deutscher and Christina Lafont (New York: Columbia University Press, 2017), 183–206. Marcuse wrote: "The truth is that this freedom and satisfaction are transforming the earth into hell. The inferno is still concentrated in certain far away places: Vietnam, the Congo, South Africa, and in the ghettos of the 'affluent society': in Mississippi and Alabama, in Harlem. These infernal places illuminate the whole." Herbert Marcuse, "Political Preface 1966," in *Eros and Civilization: A Philosophical Inquiry into Freud* (Boston: Beacon, 1966), xiii.

20. Aimé Césaire, "Letter to Maurice Thorez," *Social Text* 103, vol. 28, no. 2 (2010): 147. Hereafter cited parenthetically in the text.

21. "In other words," Yassin al-Haj Saleh writes, "solidarity conceals the reality that its provider is in fact a custodian, with the recipient in his custody, or under her protection. This is not a healthy and equitable relationship. And even if the recipient, or ward, is not expected to express gratitude openly, they are nonetheless in too weak a position to criticize the paternalist tendencies of their guardian, the cause's manufacturer. That is, unless they leave the relationship, or revolt against it." Yassin al-Haj Saleh, "A Critique of Solidarity," *al-Jumhuriya*, trans. Alex Rowell, July 16, 2018, www.aljum huriya.net/en/content/critique-solidarity.

22. Anna Tsing, "Is There a Progressive Politics After Progress?," *Dialogues, Cultural Anthropology Website,* website, June 8, 2017, https://culanth.org/fieldsights/1133-is-there -a-progressive-politics-after-progress. More generally Wendy Brown underscored how continental philosophy and critical theory have "radically reconceived the operations, mechanics, circulation, logics, venues, and vehicles of power." Brown, *Edgework*, 66.

23. Frantz Fanon, *The Wretched of the Earth*, trans. Richard Philcox (New York: Grove, 1963), 22.

24. Fanon, 5.

25. Dipesh Chakrabarty, "Forward: The Names and Repetitions of Postcolonial History," in *The Ambiguous Allure of the West: Traces of the Postcolonial in Thailand*, ed. Rachel V. Harrison and Peter A. Jackson (Hong Kong: Hong Kong University Press, 2010), xiv.

26. Herbert Marcuse, *One Dimensional Man: Studies in the Ideology of Advanced Industrial Society* (Boston: Beacon, 1964), 256.

27. Marcuse, 256.

28. Hannah Arendt, *The Origins of Totalitarianism* (New York: Meridian, 1958), 482. Hereafter cited parenthetically in the text.

29. Edward Said, *The World, the Text, and the Critic* (Cambridge, MA: Harvard University Press, 1983), 242. Hereafter cited parenthetically in the text.

30. The processes of professionalization, routinization, and co-optation of critical theory Said emphasizes are independent from epistemological questions and the internal conceptual operations of a theory.

31. Melanie Newton, "Reflections on Edward Said: A Caribbean Perspective," *Comparative Studies of South Asia, Africa and the Middle East* 23, no. 1 (2003): 11.

32. Tsing, "Is There a Progressive Politics After Progress?"

33. Césaire, "Letter to Maurice Thorez," 150.

Bibliography

Abu-Lughod, Lila. "Dialects of Women's Empowerment: The International Circuitry of the *Arab Human Development Report 2005.*" *International Journal of Middle Eastern Studies* 41 (2009): 83–103.

Allen, Amy. "Adorno, Foucault and the End of Progress: Critical Theory in Postcolonial Times." In *Critical Theory in Critical Times: Transforming the Global and Political Economic Order,* edited by Penelope Deutscher and Christina Lafont, 183–206. New York: Columbia University Press, 2017.

Arendt, Hannah. *The Origins of Totalitarianism.* New York: Meridian, 1958.

Bardawil, Fadi. "Césaire with Adorno: Critical Theory and the Colonial Problem." *South Atlantic Quarterly* 117, no. 4 (2018): 773–89.

——. "Forsaking the Syrian Revolution: An Anti-Imperialist Handbook." *al-Jumhuriya,* December 22, 2016. www.aljumhuriya.net/en/content/forsaking-syrian-revolution-anti -imperialist-handbook.

Bayat, Asef. *Revolution Without Revolutionaries: Making Sense of the Arab Spring.* Stanford: Stanford University Press, 2017.

Brown, Wendy. *Edgework: Critical Essays on Knowledge and Politics.* Princeton: Princeton University Press, 2005.

Césaire, Aimé. "Letter to Maurice Thorez." *Social Text* 103, vol. 28, no. 2 (2010): 145–52.

Chakrabarty, Dipesh. "Forward: The Names and Repetitions of Postcolonial History." In *The Ambiguous Allure of the West: Traces of the Postcolonial in Thailand,* edited by Rachel V. Harrison and Peter A. Jackson. Hong Kong: Hong Kong University Press, 2010.

Fanon, Frantz. *The Wretched of the Earth.* Translated by Richard Philcox. New York: Grove, 1963.

Fassin, Didier. "The Endurance of Critique." *Anthropological Theory* 17, no. 1 (2017): 1–26.

al-Haj Saleh, Yassin. "A Critique of Solidarity." *al-Jumhuriya.* Translated by Alex Rowell. July 16, 2018. www.aljumhuriya.net/en/content/critique-solidarity.

——. *The Impossible Revolution: Making Sense of the Syrian Tragedy.* Translated by Ibtihal Mahmoud. London: C. Hurst, 2017.

Harding, Susan. *The Book of Jerry Falwell: Fundamentalist Politics and Language.* Princeton: Princeton University Press, 2000.

Jacoby, Russell. *Dialectic of Defeat: Contours of Western Marxism.* Cambridge: Cambridge University Press, 1981.

Latour, Bruno. "Why Has Critique Run out of Steam? From Matters of Fact to Matters of Concern." *Critical Inquiry* 30 (2004): 225–48.

Marcuse, Herbert. *One Dimensional Man: Studies in the Ideology of Advanced Industrial Society.* Boston: Beacon, 1964.

Morris, Rosalind C. "Introduction." In *Can the Subaltern Speak? Reflections on the History of an Idea,* edited by Rosalind C. Morris. New York: Columbia University Press, 2010.

Newton, Melanie. "Reflections on Edward Said: A Caribbean Perspective." *Comparative Studies of South Asia, Africa and the Middle East* 23, no. 1 (2003): 11.

Said, Edward. *Orientalism.* New York: Vintage Books, 1994.

——. *The World, the Text and the Critic.* Cambridge, MA: Harvard University Press, 1983.

Scott, David. *Conscripts of Modernity: The Tragedy of Colonial Enlightenment.* Durham: Duke University Press, 2004.

——. *Stuart Hall's Voice: Intimations of an Ethics of Receptive Generosity.* Durham: Duke University Press, 2017.

Traverso, Enzo. *Left-Wing Melancholia: Marxism, History, and Memory.* New York: Columbia University Press, 2017.

Tsing, Anna. "Is There a Progressive Politics After Progress?" Dialogues, *Cultural Anthropology* website, June 8, 2017. https://culanth.org/fieldsights/1133-is-there-a-progressive-politics-after-progress.

CHAPTER 10

PRAGMATIC CRITIQUE OF TORTURE IN SRI LANKA

NICK CHEESMAN

To ask not *what* is critique but *how* is it, as Didier Fassin does in his contribution to this volume, is not only to ask after the condition of critique in its specific historical and geographic circumstances.[1] It is also to invite us to think through how else *could* critique be: to open up its possibilities and variations, including through inquiries into different times and places. It is to be attentive to the possibility of critique in other contexts from those with which critique is ordinarily associated—among them, the possibility of critique in nonscholarly idioms and postcolonial settings.[2]

Here I attend to one such possibility, under the guise of a type of critique that I characterize as pragmatic. In its rudiments, pragmatic critique consists in exploring, through methods of relating to the world via observation and experience, the conditions for the existence of a particular instituted practice—an established activity, learned and repeated over time. Its pragmatic sensibility encourages doubt about conventional explanations for the practice, which motivates inquiry.[3] Its critical attitude imbues the search for alternative explanations with a political imperative for action to effect transformative change.[4]

In its analysis of conditions for the existence of an instituted practice, pragmatic critique couples what Seyla Benhabib has labeled an explanatory-diagnostic aspect with an anticipatory-utopian dimension.[5] The former conjoins its pragmatic sensibility with its critical attitude. The latter is concerned with the transformative potential that can follow, via critique, from epistemologically and methodologically pragmatic interventions to address experienced injustice in specific cases. In both its critical attitude and pragmatic sensibility it is characteristically hopeful of making improvements to human conditions.[6]

This type of critique is opposed to "vernacular" pragmatism, which equates the pragmatic with the practical, and critique with criticism.[7] The critic, so the vernacular pragmatic line goes, obstructs practical men of action from doing whatever needs to be done under specified circumstances to obtain a certain result. Critique is, by this interpretation, impractical, inert, and antithetical to the pragmatic.

Vernacular pragmatism is no new coin. But in today's neoliberal academy its value has increased, while that of critique—understood not in the vernacular sense but as an attitude that aims at emancipation and alteration of society—has diminished. Erstwhile critical scholars now urge their counterparts to abandon critique and go in for the kind of "socially useful professional activity" that Max Horkheimer associated with traditional theory, which is to say, ostensibly pragmatic, noncritical activity.[8]

Carroll Seron, for instance, used her presidential address in 2015 to the US-based Law and Society Association to urge its membership to "get back in the game of advocacy" by recognizing that the time had come to turn away from critique and instead, with the economist Thomas Piketty, "take the role of *pragmatic policy* seriously."[9] By this, she continued, she meant that law-and-society scholars—who typically study law as action in everyday life—should concentrate on research that might contribute to ameliorative rather than radical policies for change. Working in this way, she suggested, they might contribute better to efforts to relieve growing inequalities, and make scholarly work more influential by communicating to a wide audience.

I welcome calls like Seron's for scholarship to engage with worsening political and social problems, among which she lists employment, housing, and voting as three of general concern to her predominantly American audience. I agree that one of the basic responsibilities of the academy is to address general problems like these, and others that are more particular to time and place: from where I sit presently, in the office of an advocacy group in suburban Bangkok, the list might include military and police impunity for killings of civilians, the targeting of minority groups through physical and structural violence, and, to go to the topic of this chapter, the persistent use of torture by state security forces and their proxies across Southeast and South Asia.

But I do not accept Seron's inference that to advocate for social changes of the sort she identifies and to communicate to a wide audience are to be pragmatic and that to critique is not. I see no necessary relationship between these activities and the categories of practice to which she assigns them. Calls like hers to move beyond critique toward the pragmatic, which reverse Horkheimer's turn from traditional to critical theory but do not interrogate it, insofar as they remain within his dichotomy of critical-emancipatory versus traditional-pragmatic action, miss the point. Critique, understood as a research practice that opens up the possibilities for effecting transformative change through politically animated, historically situated inquiry into conditions of the present, is not an obstacle to pragmatic inquiry into instituted practices of violence and injustice. To the contrary, a pragmatic sensibility can enable precisely this kind of inquiry.

I aim to show how this might be the case through study of a campaign against torture practiced by police in the south of Sri Lanka during the 2000s. The background to this campaign, my reasons for studying it, and my narrative and interpretation of it comprise the next section and substance of this chapter. The closing section works from the campaign to elucidate further the type of critique with which the chapter is concerned, and consider how in general terms pragmatic critique might be possible.

A Pragmatic Critique of Police Torture

While not a diagnosis of conditions of the sort with which Fassin is concerned in his chapter, in agreement with him that critique is always at least partly a response to a certain state of the world developed through a configuration of power and knowledge in both the academic and the public domains, this section shares with his diagnostic mode a special concern for the specificity of critique in time and place. It does so by narrating how a model of torture prevention emerged from a campaign in the south and center of Sri Lanka during the early to mid-2000s.

The campaign in Sri Lanka is central to my elucidating the practice and promise of pragmatic critique in this chapter for two primary reasons. First, while those involved in the campaign expressly sought to end torture by police, theirs was not *just* a campaign against torture. Its larger goal was to motivate hopeful action for the possibility of social equality. They surmised that torture persisted in Sri Lanka because social conditions stifled communication of the sort necessary for substantive rather than merely formal equality. The campaign aimed to make communication of that sort possible, so as to change those social conditions. Modern historians today argue that international and regional human rights movements supplanted emancipatory social projects with minimalist apolitical agendas.[10] I point to the campaign as an example of how human rights advocacy might also sometimes aim to reinvigorate critique and invite political engagement toward larger social goals.

Second, I had a partisan affiliation with the campaign. For five years I was employed by an organization allied to those leading the work in Sri Lanka, namely, the Asian Legal Resource Centre, based in Hong Kong. I traveled to the country frequently from 2000 to 2006. The contents of this chapter are assembled from diaries, correspondence, and recollections of this period, as well as a number of books and reports that spelled out the campaign in detail.[11] Insofar as the chapter draws on the contents of these publications and personal records, its goals are interpretive rather than descriptive. It is concerned with elucidating the practice of pragmatic critique by recalling salient features of the campaign, rather than with an ethnographic description of it.

To be clear, my partisanship does not make me starry eyed about the campaign. As in all human endeavors, the campaign suffered from inadequacies and oversights, some of which became more glaring as time went on. As in all projects with a utopian dimension, it fell short of its goals. However, I do not dwell on these inadequacies, oversights, or shortcomings here. My purpose in writing on this topic is not to make the campaign itself the object of critique. It is to work with those records of the campaign so as to think through the practice of, and possibilities for, the type of critique that I characterize as pragmatic.

By the time of the campaign, Sri Lanka was in the latter years of protracted violent conflict. In the north and east of the South Asian island country, a separatist war that had begun in the 1970s came to a bloody end with the defeat of the Liberation Tigers of Tamil Eelam on the battlefield. The south had in the 1980s experienced a second bout of a relatively short-lived but extremely violent Marxist insurgency, during a period of government led by a party notorious for its use of paramilitary groups and death squads. Torture was a feature of both wars, in the north and south.[12]

Responding to the savagery of the conflict in the south especially, in the early 1990s a new government set up commissions of inquiry into the abduction and killing of tens of thousands of people. It ratified international human rights laws, including the UN Convention Against Torture, to signal an intention to draw a line on the events of the past. In 1994 it passed a law to criminalize torture. These changed conditions gave human rights defenders more opportunities and resources with which to do their work. The seeds for the campaign of the 2000s were planted in this period.

The early days of the campaign are spelled out in a study authored by the activist lawyer and writer Shyamali Puvimanasinghe, based on her interview, archival, and documentary research with members of groups in Sri Lanka and in Hong Kong.[13] Puvimanasinghe takes as a starting point for the antitorture advocacy a moment in the mid-1990s when Chitral Perera, a boisterous community organizer, was surprised to learn of a torture chamber in the headquarters of a high-ranking police officer.

Perera was not naïve. Like other people he was well aware of the stories about torture and atrocities in counterinsurgency operations. He too had witnessed periods of intense violence. But he had not entertained the notion that into the 1990s torture chambers were a feature of routine policing in urban areas removed from the main battlegrounds of the country's ongoing separatist war. He inquired into the story and met a former detainee who confirmed it.

Perera's experience might be expressed in the form of a statement of surprise followed by a plausible explanatory hypothesis, as follows: "The surprising fact, that a high-ranking police officer has a torture chamber inside his headquarters, is observed; but if torture were systemic in the police force, then the torture chamber would be a matter of course; hence, there is reason to suspect that torture is systemic."[14] He started gathering cases with which to test the hypothesis. By the late 1990s he had heard hundreds of stories that validated it.

Perera founded Janasansadaya (or People's Forum) at a house on the southernmost edge of the capital city, Colombo, from which to work on cases he had gathered. He linked up with a number of other groups based in periurban and rural areas across the south and center of the island that had been working haphazardly on cases of torture too. He also found a kindred spirit and like mind in the exiled activist lawyer Basil Fernando, director of the Asian Human Rights Commission.[15] The commission started publicizing cases through its urgent appeals program. In 2002, fifteen local groups formed an alliance called People Against Torture, led by a Catholic priest with a background in liberation theology and strong social justice credentials that transcended religious lines.

People Against Torture worked to document and act on as many cases with survivors of torture and families as possible.[16] Although its members worked on some cases more extensively than others, they did not invest heavily in cases with special symbolic value of the sort that might have attracted international human rights groups. The members of People Against Torture saw themselves as grappling with a ubiquitous problem that required copious recordkeeping and advocacy, no matter how insignificant each individual case might seem, or how unremarkable the survivors of torture were.

The cases documented, then, were emphatically not of charismatic political detainees or photogenic social activists suffering at the hands of oppressive dictators and their secret police. They were cases of a quotidian, uncelebrated type, happening in grubby circumstances onto which no particular evil face could be projected. A house cleaner in Colombo accused by her employer of stealing a watch told of how she was assaulted by three police officers armed with a rubber hose, a wooden club, and an object with wires wrapped around it. A dockworker described being hung from a beam, burned, and beaten with an iron bar to have him admit to murder, in what turned out to be a case of mistaken identity. Another man accused of a petty crime said that police officers assaulted him all over his body with broomsticks and poured illicit liquor down his nostrils until he lost consciousness. A woman in the center of the country recounted being beaten repeatedly and raped in police custody before being forced to sign a statement the contents of which were unknown to her.

A welder in the capital said that police beat him with sticks and leather belts, and strangulated him while threatening to kill him if he did not confess to a theft from the company where he worked.[17]

Doubt about the practice of torture by police motivated empirical inquiry, not skepticism. This motivation marks an important difference between the work of the campaign and that of state agencies, like courts and national human rights commissions—not only in Sri Lanka but also in other parts of Southeast and South Asia. Official agencies, or groups that mimic state techniques for documenting and producing knowledge about the violence of state agents, tend to approach stories of wrongdoing by state officers skeptically, treating them as matters that must be thoroughly investigated and proven before steps, if any, are taken to address the complainant's grievance. The campaigners, by contrast, did not suspend belief of alleged wrongdoing until the facts had been assembled. This is not to say that they did not seek to affirm and validate factual truths. The factual details of testimonies were precious resources for them. They put these details in affidavits so as to bring criminal cases and seek compensation from the Supreme Court for breaches of constitutional rights. They supplemented them with medico-legal reports taken at hospitals. But People Against Torture produced and obtained these kinds of records trusting that the basic facts of the stories that survivors of torture told were truthful. They did not obtain or produce these records so as to convince themselves of the facts.

Authoritative records, then, had important legal and administrative purposes for the campaign, rather than any special epistemological function. They enabled the campaigners to make knowledge claims in conversations with government officials and UN experts, but they did not settle all doubts about the character and prevalence of torture in Sri Lanka. Not only did doubt not need to be settled for epistemological reasons, but also, to insist upon settling doubts before taking action would have been unethical. A certain amount of evidence mattered to the campaigners. They could not work with nothing. But equally important, if not more so, was the timeliness of their interventions through public statements, interviews, news articles, and public gatherings. A sense of urgency demanded that action proceed with and animate inquiry. This concern with getting enough detail on which to intervene speedily so as to combat the onset of demoralization in the aftermath of acts of torture came to occupy a special place in the model for torture prevention.

Research and action for quick intervention required of the campaigners that they be in close contact with survivors. Close contact became a working principle for the campaign.[18] They had to get as close to the torture situations that they were documenting as possible, in both space and time. They had to be close by when torture happened, not only so that they could intervene quickly but also so that they could try to make sense of what had happened. They also had to be there for the long haul. In some cases close contact extended to years of counseling and housing afforded to people who had to relocate away from their hometowns and villages.

The principle that the campaigners had to have close contact with people who had suffered torture was in no small part informed by the backgrounds of key figures in the campaign. Perera had had a middle-class upbringing but was a no-nonsense type who had cut his teeth working as a schoolteacher upcountry and as a trade unionist. Fernando had been raised the child of a family from the washer persons' caste in a fishing village and had spent some years as a revolutionary communist party organizer. From a young age he had an acute sense of both class and caste prejudice. He intuited that large parts of the Sri Lankan population had, like people in his own village, been alienated from public life. He was intent upon working in what Eyal Weizman has called a condition of "critical proximity," so as to arrive at a critique of Sri Lankan society "through friction with the world."[19] Absent this friction, the campaign would have lacked both the intellectual energy and political momentum that gave it its distinctive character.

The campaign organizers' backgrounds also meant that they did not come at the problem of torture in Sri Lanka deductively, working from the contents of a treaty or protocol with a general definition of a right not to be tortured toward the particulars of each case. Theirs was an exercise in understanding the social conditions in which torture was imbricated. It was not an exercise in ticking off the elements of a crime under international law each time someone was tortured. Of course, the campaigners were attentive to those definitions, treaties, and protocols that might be useful for their interventions. But they came at them crab-like, sideways rather than head-on. They used whatever resources they could find to make gains in specific cases, working to get some survivors compensated, to get official recognition of wrongdoing, and, wherever possible, to prosecute perpetrators. They took matters to UN experts and committees mandated to prevent torture. For want of a state witness protection program they set up their own. With support from medical professionals in Sri Lanka and the Rehabilitation and Research Centre for Torture Victims, based in Denmark, they got funding and training for the counseling of survivors.

Although all of these activities were tremendously important they were not the ends of the campaign. The ultimate goal was not to bring cases of torture to the attention of some officeholders in Geneva, or to bring some fundamental rights cases to the country's apex court. Those were steps on a longer journey to encourage dialogue and action for social change.

Police torture in Sri Lanka was part of a continuum of violence directed against certain types of people.[20] Another kind of campaign might have crisscrossed the continuum, identifying a range of different types of violence in order to develop a critique of the sort that mattered to the antitorture advocates. That they did not address other types of violence on the continuum was not because they thought those other types of violence were unimportant. Rather, the antitorture orientation gave the work a sharper focus. It enabled the campaigners to draw on a range of resources that they might not have had at their disposal to address other categories of violence. At the same time it opened up possibilities for the all-important critique of attendant social conditions. That is to say, the campaign coupled its explanatory-diagnostic aspect, namely, the analysis of the conditions giving rise to the practice of torture, with an anticipatory-utopian dimension, concerned with the transformative potential of bringing people and issues ordinarily excluded from public debate into it, through pragmatic interventions to address experienced injustice in specific cases of torture.

Since the campaigners needed to understand and plausibly explain the conditions for the existence of torture, they concentrated initially on institutional inadequacies. They needed to identify these to press for changes that might make possible the kind of incremental gains that were built into their larger program for transformative action. These included systemic failures to inquire into cases of torture when they occurred, and to hold perpetrators accountable. They also included procedural obstacles that had the effect of granting police impunity, despite the law of 1994 and formal institutional changes to ostensibly address the incidence of torture.

But institutional criticism did not itself get the campaigners to the larger problem of social inequality that, as they saw it, made torture possible. That could only come via a critique informed by and emergent from people affected by torture. One day, Fernando met the grandfather of a young man whom police detained over two alleged thefts and strung up on a pole, crossing his legs and arms in a position called the *dharmachakra*, or wheel of natural law (a Buddhist idiom), so as to beat him on the feet to have him confess to theft. The grandfather said: "These things happen to us because we are poor."[21] His reading resonated with Fernando's and, to the latter's mind, validated the approach he had taken to the problem. By the mid-2000s the campaigners had developed a critique of torture in the south and center of Sri Lanka that went beyond institutional particularities to the historical and sociological conditions for the existence of the practice as a problem of political economy.

The nub of the political economic critique was that the distinguishing characteristic of "the torturable class" was, as the young man's father had put it, that its members were poor.[22] Who got tortured? The poor did. Who tortured them? Police officers did, not only in pursuit of their own goals but also to satisfy the interests or desires of the members of other classes. The house cleaner accused of stealing a watch was tortured at the behest of her employer, who sat around drinking with the officer in charge of the police station after they were done with her. The officers who beat the welder also accused of stealing from his employer dragged him to a window to show the company's managers that they were giving him a going over. The dockworker whose name happened to be the same as a murder suspect was an easy and unsuspecting target. When he had the audacity to try to appear as a witness against them in court, they sent a couple of men who calmly shot him dead as he rode a public bus. Others were tortured for the most trivial of reasons: a young man whose shoulders were dislocated after being hung from a ceiling and beaten had allegedly taken a bunch of bananas. A group of police sexually tortured two junior schoolboys over the disappearance of some food from their canteen. The torture situations documented revealed not just abuses of the body, but also the abuse of a social class, in matters both grave and banal.

The political economic critique had strategic implications. The campaigners needed partners from among or proximate to the class of people affected, people who would recognize that the work was also in their own interests, more than they did from among people for whom the antitorture campaign was a kind of compassionate or humanitarian enterprise for others less fortunate and more vulnerable than themselves. Although they gained allies among senior journalists, professors, retired judges, clergy, and even a high-ranking policeman, who publicly validated many of their observations, the campaigners did not seek out or anticipate the support of those persons. They did not need them to confirm what was going on. Nor did they think that the involvement of those people would bring solutions to their problems. In dialogue and acting together with people who were directly or closely affected by torture, they sought to cultivate hopeful possibilities for transformative social change, via a critique of the conditions in Sri Lanka that gave rise to persistent human rights abuses across the island.

The campaigners also had strategic reasons for the turn to the south and center, toward the practice of torture in ordinary criminal cases. Human rights groups working in conditions of intense civil war up north had for years documented torture, killings, disappearances, rapes, and other military atrocities. But although the scale of violence in those areas exceeded anything elsewhere, these accounts had been unsuccessful in effecting change. Groups working in those areas could not have sustained close contact with the people whose stories they recorded. And to the extent that they could get details of atrocities, the government would deny they had occurred at all, or insist that they had occurred at the hands of their opponents, or concede that they had occurred but that the circumstances were exceptional and the violence regrettable but necessary. Even the most rudimentary facts were the subject of vigorous dispute by a state determined to rebut allegations of wrongdoing in the civil war, and keen to justify its use of violence.

The routine use of torture by police in the country's south was not subject to the same kinds of politics. The denials and justifications offered for events in the north were inapplicable to it. Furthermore, analytically the pragmatic critique of torture at police stations in the south and center of the country not only stood on its own terms, but also cast doubt on the explanations offered for the persistence of torture in other parts of the country. The practice could no longer be passed off as a regrettable response to exigencies. Nor could it be described as a type of political violence peculiarly suffered by minorities.

The critique of police torture in the south, then, was a corrective to the tendency to attribute personal and structural violence in Sri Lanka to the persistence of war in the north and east. Without denying that the scale of violence and militarization of the police force had contributed to the incidence of torture, it cast doubt on prevailing explanations that hinged on the war and the exigencies of periods of emergency rule. These explanations were necessary, but not sufficient. Study of torture in the south revealed that torture had deeper historical and sociological causes than most analyses of conditions in Sri Lanka had suggested or were prepared to admit.

By turning toward the south and center, the campaigners also aimed for results in specific cases, so as to give people hope that would motivate action for more substantive change. They did this not just to give hope to the survivors of torture and their families. They themselves needed hope. Perera earlier had been responsible for a project to teach people in the countryside about law. He recalled that one day a villager who had had a few drinks stood up to lambast him and a lawyer with whom he was partnered for their useless suggestions about how Sri Lankans could protect their fundamental rights. "The lawyer was annoyed," he said. "But I noticed that the rest of the audience agreed with the man."[23] A sense that the human rights work with which he had become accustomed was "limited to expressions of frustration" was what had brought him to establish Janasansadaya, and into his alliance with other members of People Against Torture.[24]

Like the injunction to work in close contact with survivors, hopeful action to effect change was not just a felt need but also a working principle of the alliance. Fernando posited that the main obstacle to change in Sri Lanka was demoralization caused by social inequality—understood, after the Indian polymath, constitutionalist, and Dalit leader B. R. Ambedkar, to be an appreciation for a kind of living togetherness, beyond the formal political and juridical equality assigned by bills of rights.[25]

The campaign aimed to have people think and then communicate their way out of their demoralized state, to build solidarity through a shared commitment to the possibilities of change, rather than shared identification as people who were politically oppressed. It did not make torture of the poor, as Wendy Brown has put it in her critique of moralistic identity-based struggles, "a cultural or political fetish."[26] The shared class identity of torture survivors mattered only insofar as it could serve as a basis for hopeful change.

Against expressions of frustration, for expressions of hope: this is how I heard the antitorture campaigners in Sri Lanka characterize their work again and again. This attitude and practice of hope align with what Colin Koopman has celebrated as pragmatism's insistence upon hope as a guide for critique and inquiry.[27] Like the classical pragmatists, the Sri Lankan antitorture advocates adhered to the view that absent of hope one cannot make a go of improving anything. Earlier human rights campaigns in Sri Lanka, they thought, had not stirred people to act because they had failed to inspire hope. They had failed to do so because they had not been able to communicate and act in ways that were meaningful for people bearing the brunt of state violence, or to bring those people into active communication for the kind of critique that might contribute to lasting social change. If Sri Lanka at the time was a country in crisis, it was for want of hopeful interventions of the sort that the campaigners sought to make. They hoped these might bring about change to the debate on torture in particular, through which they might generate dialogue on the possibilities for social justice in Sri Lanka in general.

A Model for Pragmatic Critique, of Torture

Puvimanasinghe's study presents the campaign against torture in Sri Lanka as a "model" for torture prevention in Asia. At one level, it is a narrative of the thought and action that contributed to the campaign to prevent torture, which was from the beginning intended both to test conjectures that came from early inquiry and to acquire the necessary experience on which to act for change. At another, it is a grounded theory of how people might try to think their way out of social inequality, and recognize that any number of unactualized possible alternatives to our present-day conditions exist and might be realized: hence, its anticipatory-utopian character.

The model is not an instruction manual for how to prevent torture elsewhere. The campaign that is its subject of inquiry resisted the idea that a manual of that sort could ever be produced or, if it could, that it would be meaningful. The book contains no flow charts setting out a process to prevent torture that might be duplicated, summaries of key ideas for action, or short lists of recommendations to decision makers of the sort conventionally found in studies by groups that claim to have uncovered solutions to human rights problems like torture. Neither the campaign that is its subject matter nor the model itself had that goal. Instead it invites readers to consider how a contingent admixture of inquiry and intervention might inform and guide action against torture, whether by advocacy groups, academics, or others, with the larger goal that through those actions social inequality might no longer appear inevitable.

So what does the model offer the reader thinking about how the practice of pragmatic critique might contribute to hopeful intervention into instituted practices of torture, or other categories of state violence elsewhere?

If the business of thinking a way out of a practice like torture consists in exploring the conditions that give rise to that practice so as to act on it, but not on the terms assigned by existing arrangements, then the essential problem for the campaigners might, with parenthetical adjustment to Michel Foucault's characterization of the impetus for critique, be said to be one of "how not to be [treated] like that, by that, in the name of those principles, with such and such an objective in mind and by means of such procedures, not like that, not for that, not by them."[28]

The answer to the question of how not to be treated like that, the model suggests, begins in the observed and experienced world, with an irritation or irritations of doubt that motivate inquiry. Observations followed by plausible explanatory diagnoses of the conditions for the existence of a particular instituted practice give rise to the hope of effecting transformative change with the resources already at hand.

This is a radically different starting point from those campaigns that begin with a normative statement from a human rights treaty or general position or question to guide inquiry, even if these may be relevant to whatever actions follow. It is also fundamentally different from the traditional scientific method of drawing up a neatly delineated typology of practices that are the subject of inquiry, or the political regimes responsible for instituting them, to which to assign and select cases for further research.

That is not to say that universal norms, general questions, or typologies are uninteresting or unimportant. The campaigners in Sri Lanka opposed torture as a matter of principle. Their principled opposition to torture partly motivated their political action for social equality. And they tacitly or explicitly organized cases into certain types so as to enable their critique—including the analytical category of torture of the poor. But they did not start with a typology, or an ethical statement on the repugnance of torture, or the contents of a law prohibiting the practice. Instead their work dovetailed with those. Political goals drove them to study situations closely from which to make conjectures that challenged established views. From these conjectures came the search for plausible explanations, and the sketching of types, with which to get some purchase on the problem and encourage action to effect change. With encouragement of action came the possibility to do something about conditions that went beyond the particularities of the torture situation.

While the pragmatic critique of torture was concentrated on the practice itself, beyond the immediacy of intervention in each specific case the campaign remained attentive to the need to move *through* the particular situation to the conditions that gave rise to it, and from there to explore the possibilities for transformative change, so as both to prevent the recurrence of the practice and to motivate people to work for conditions of social equality.

That is why, if the specific question for the campaign was how to act to prevent torture, then the general one was, how is it possible to *think* a way out of conditions of social inequality? Since torture was a characteristic of deeply iniquitous social hierarchies, the possibility of addressing the one was, in the view of those involved in the campaign, contingent on the other. This larger goal gave the campaign certain distinctive contents, in defiance of the politics of demoralization that pervaded Sri Lanka in this period. The campaign was never simply about showing a commitment to help some vulnerable other. It was always about how to have people recognize that to act in the interests of others was to act in their own interests.

The possibility of acting for social equality is contingent on the thought that equality is possible. But the thought cannot arise absent some evidence of its possibility. The antitorture advocacy in Sri Lanka sought to create conditions that would allow for that thought, through a politics of the possible. As the idea of holding a police officer in Sri Lanka responsible for practically any type of serious wrongdoing was at the time beyond the imagination of most of the people with whom the groups were working, their task was in part to show that what might appear, seen from afar, as relatively trivial gains in specific cases nevertheless constituted evidence that progress was possible. And evidence of progress was cause for hope. In taking up "the task of articulating the demands of justice and human worthiness" inherent in the antitorture norm, they sought to portray what Benhabib has characterized as utopian "modes of friendship, solidarity, and human happiness," which could emerge out of shared struggle for improvement.[29]

In sum, in general terms pragmatic critique entails the study of particular instituted practices so as to get at the configuration of power and knowledge that enables certain conditions to exist. It is concerned with the possibilities for hopefully changing situations, through the resources available to those affected by them. It seeks to understand and plausibly explain those arrangements that allow for a practice to be instituted, and to identify the resources needed to change it. Its epistemology and methodologies are portable. Its idiom is historically and geographically contingent.

Pragmatic critique does not in its pragmatic sensibility stand for any particular program of action or results. Nevertheless, it is more than just a method of observation and inquiry. It also entails, in its critical attitude, an abiding concern for political and social change. A pragmatic critique of any particular instituted practice does not observe that practice as a matter of scholarly or intellectual interest alone. Instead it enters into inquiry so as to address the question of how the practice is part of larger arrangements to dominate people whose place in the body politic is tenuous, who are in the margins or on the frontiers of the political community, already humiliated in disproportion to other groups, either from the moment of birth or by virtue of something that they are accused of having done.

Torture of the poor is just one category through which to engage in a critique of this sort, one that was sensible and efficacious for the campaigners in Sri Lanka during the 2000s. Pragmatic inquiry into other conditions, informed by different critical sensibilities, will recommend other salient categories for inquiry, other starting points for action, not because pragmatic critique is infinitely malleable (it is not), but because attention to contingency is among its methodological imperatives. Against aspirations for a kind of precision and determinacy that are demanded by positivistic human rights work, and scholarship in a similar vein, in which violence is rendered legible through standardized templates to classify violations, which reorganize and homogenize the experiences of those involved, pragmatic critique insists on the possibility of illuminating the peculiarities of conditions that make practices possible.

Whether pragmatic critique succeeds in reaching its goals or not is, of course, another matter entirely. In its explanatory diagnostic mode, the campaign in Sri Lanka certainly made a persuasive case for rethinking the problem of torture in the country. And it put police torturers on notice that they would no longer be able to get away with the kinds of practices that they had in the past. In its anticipatory utopian aspect it succeeded in motivating people to speak, act, and be seen in ways, times, and places that they had not hitherto been heard and seen. It did not ultimately make a discernible difference to conditions of social inequality. But if it fell short of its utopian telos it did at least sustain hopes that Sri Lankans could reimagine and practice different kinds of social relations than those to which they had for centuries been accustomed. In doing so, it kept alive possibilities for further pragmatic critique, in still other times and contexts.

Notes

Thank you to Didier Fassin and Bernard Harcourt for convening the critique seminar at the Institute for Advanced Study, Princeton in 2016–17 that gave rise to this book, and for their work as editors. Thanks too to all other colleagues whose chapters appear in this volume for their thoughtful and attentive questions and comments on a draft of the chapter at an authors' gathering in November 2017, especially Max Tomba, who led the discussion on this chapter, and Lori Allen for generous comments on a preliminary outline of it. Special thanks to Danielle Celermajer, Chris Cusano, Marija Grujić, Kishali Pinto-Jayawardena, and Dvora Yanow for close reading and helpful advice on subsequent drafts, as well as to April Biccum and other colleagues at the Australian National University who heard and commented on a reading of the chapter at a seminar hosted by the Interpretation, Method, and Critique Network in September 2018.

1. Didier Fassin, "How Is Critique?," in this volume.
2. See Lori Allen, "Subaltern Critique and the History of Palestine," in this volume.
3. See Karen Locke, Karen Golden-Biddle, and Martha S. Feldman, "Making Doubt Generative: Rethinking the Role of Doubt in the Research Process," *Organization Science* 19, no. 6 (November-December 2008): 907–18; Charles S. Peirce, "The Fixation of Belief," *Popular Science Monthly* 12 (1977): 1–15.
4. See Nancy Fraser, "What's Critical About Critical Theory? The Case of Habermas and Gender," in *Unruly Practices: Power, Discourse and Gender in Contemporary Social Theory* (Cambridge: Polity, 1989).
5. Seyla Benhabib, *Critique, Norm, and Utopia: A Study of the Foundations of Critical Theory* (New York: Columbia University Press, 1986), 226.
6. See Colin Koopman, *Pragmatism as Transition: Historicity and Hope in James, Dewey, and Rorty* (New York: Columbia University Press, 2009).
7. Joshua U. Galperin, "Trust Me, I'm a Pragmatist: A Partially Pragmatic Critique of Pragmatic Activism," *Columbia Journal of Environmental Law* 42, no. 2 (2017): 425–95, 433.
8. Max Horkheimer, "Traditional and Critical Theory," in *Critical Theory: Selected Essays* (New York: Herder and Herder, 1972), 208.
9. Carroll Seron, "The Two Faces of Law and Inequality: From Critique to the Promise of Situated, Pragmatic Policy," *Law and Society Review* 50, no. 1 (2016): 9–33, 12, 13, italics added.
10. See in particular, Patrick William Kelly, *Sovereign Emergencies: Latin America and the Making of Global Human Rights Politics* (Cambridge: Cambridge University Press, 2018); Samuel Moyn, *The Last Utopia: Human Rights in History* (Cambridge, MA: Belknap Press of Harvard University Press, 2010).
11. Although the work continued after the mid-2000s as the key texts used for this chapter were published from around 2004 to 2006, and as my work with the Asian Legal Resource Centre ceased in 2008, I restrict the discussion in this chapter to this period.
12. See Dhana Hughes, *Violence, Torture and Memory in Sri Lanka: Life After Terror* (London: Routledge, 2013); Chandrasekaram Visakesa, "Do Tigers Confess? An Interdisciplinary Study of Confessionary Evidence in Counter-Terrorism Measures of Sri Lanka," PhD thesis, Australian National University, 2012.
13. Shyamali Puvimanasinghe, *A Model for Torture Prevention in Asia* (Hong Kong: Asian Human Rights Commission; Copenhagen: Rehabilitation and Research Centre for Torture Victims, 2005).
14. Adapted from Peirce's schematic representation of a method of pragmatic inference that he labeled "abductive," in K. T. Fann, *Peirce's Theory of Abduction* (The Hague: Martinus Nijhoff, 1970), 47.
15. The Asian Legal Resource Centre and the Asian Human Rights Commission in practice operated out of the same office and shared staff and resources, although for legal and administrative reasons they were separate entities.
16. From 1998 to 2011, the organizations claim to have documented some fifteen hundred cases of police torture, of which four hundred are compiled in Basil Fernando, *Narrative of Justice in Sri Lanka Told Through Stories of Torture Victims* (Hong Kong: Asian Legal Resource Centre, 2013).
17. Each of these cases is documented in Asian Legal Resource Centre, "Torture Committed by the Police in Sri Lanka," *Article 2* 1, no. 4 (2002): 1–72.
18. See Josefina Bergsten, Meryam Dabhoiwala, and Phillip Setunga, *Close Contact with Victims Makes Human Rights Work Meaningful and Effective* (Hong Kong: Asian Human Rights Commission, 2004).

19. Eyal Weizman and Zachary Manfredi, " 'From Figure to Ground': A Conversation with Eyal Weizman on the Politics of the Humanitarian Present," *Qui Parle: Critical Humanities and Social Sciences* 22, no. 1 (2013): 167–92, 172.

20. See Vidura Munasinghe and Danielle Celermajer, "Acute and Everyday Violence in Sri Lanka," *Journal of Contemporary Asia* 47, no. 4 (2017): 615–40.

21. Basil Fernando and Shyamali Puvimanasinghe, eds., *An X-Ray of the Sri Lankan Policing System and Torture of the Poor* (Hong Kong: Asian Human Rights Commission, 2005), 163.

22. Graham Greene, *Our Man in Havana* (London: Penguin, 2007), 159.

23. Patrick Lawrence, *Conversations in a Failing State* (Hong Kong: Asian Human Rights Commission, 2008), 127.

24. Puvimanasinghe, *A Model for Torture Prevention in Asia*, 47.

25. Basil Fernando, *Demoralization and Hope: Creating the Social Foundation for Sustaining Democracy* (Hong Kong: Asian Human Rights Commission, 2000), 5.

26. Wendy Brown, "Symptoms: Moralism as Anti-Politics," in *Politics out of History* (Princeton: Princeton University Press, 2001), 26.

27. Koopman, *Pragmatism as Transition*, 16.

28. Michel Foucault, "What Is Critique?," in *The Political*, ed. David Ingram (Malden, MA: Blackwell, 2002), 193. The parenthetical "treated" replaces "governed" in the English translation of the original.

29. Benhabib, *Critique, Norm, and Utopia*, 13.

Bibliography

Allen, Lori. "Subaltern Critique and the History of Palestine." In *A Time for Critique*, edited by Didier Fassin and Bernard E. Harcourt. New York: Columbia University Press, 2019.

Asian Legal Resource Centre. "Torture Committed by the Police in Sri Lanka." *Article 2* 1 no. 4 (2002): 1–72.

Benhabib, Seyla. *Critique, Norm, and Utopia: A Study of the Foundations of Critical Theory*. New York: Columbia University Press, 1986.

Bergsten, Josefina, Meryam Dabhoiwala, and Phillip Setunga. *Close Contact with Victims Makes Human Rights Work Meaningful and Effective*. Hong Kong: Asian Human Rights Commission, 2004.

Brown, Wendy. "Symptoms: Moralism as Anti-Politics." In *Politics Out of History*. Princeton: Princeton University Press, 2001.

Fann, K. T. *Peirce's Theory of Abduction*. The Hague: Martinus Nijhoff, 1970.

Fassin, Didier. "How Is Critique?" In *A Time for Critique*, edited by Didier Fassin and Bernard E. Harcourt. New York: Columbia University Press, 2019.

Fernando, Basil. *Demoralization and Hope: Creating the Social Foundation for Sustaining Democracy*. Hong Kong: Asian Human Rights Commission, 2000.

——. *Narrative of Justice in Sri Lanka Told Through Stories of Torture Victims*. Hong Kong: Asian Legal Resource Centre, 2013.

Fernando, Basil, and Shyamali Puvimanasinghe, eds. *An X-ray of the Sri Lankan Policing System and Torture of the Poor*. Hong Kong: Asian Human Rights Commission, 2005.

Foucault, Michel. "What Is Critique?" In *The Political*, edited by David Ingram. Malden, MA: Blackwell, 2002.

Fraser, Nancy. "What's Critical About Critical Theory? The Case of Habermas and Gender." In *Unruly Practices: Power, Discourse and Gender in Contemporary Social Theory*. Cambridge: Polity, 1989.

Galperin, Joshua U. "Trust Me, I'm a Pragmatist: A Partially Pragmatic Critique of Pragmatic Activism." *Columbia Journal of Environmental Law* 42, no. 2 (2017): 425–95.

Greene, Graham. *Our Man in Havana*. London: Penguin, 2007.

Horkheimer, Max. "Traditional and Critical Theory." In *Critical Theory: Selected Essays*. New York: Herder and Herder, 1972.

Hughes, Dhana. *Violence, Torture and Memory in Sri Lanka: Life After Terror*. London: Routledge, 2013.

Kelly, Patrick William. *Sovereign Emergencies: Latin America and the Making of Global Human Rights Politics*. Cambridge: Cambridge University Press, 2018.

Koopman, Colin. *Pragmatism as Transition: Historicity and Hope in James, Dewey, and Rorty*. New York: Columbia University Press, 2009.

Lawrence, Patrick. *Conversations in a Failing State*. Hong Kong: Asian Human Rights Commission, 2008.

Locke, Karen, Karen Golden-Biddle, and Martha S. Feldman. "Making Doubt Generative: Rethinking the Role of Doubt in the Research Process." *Organization Science* 19, no. 6 (November-December 2008): 907–18.

Moyn, Samuel. *The Last Utopia: Human Rights in History*. Cambridge, MA: Belknap Press of Harvard University Press, 2010.

Munasinghe, Vidura, and Danielle Celermajer. "Acute and Everyday Violence in Sri Lanka." *Journal of Contemporary Asia* 47, no. 4 (2017): 615–40.

Peirce, Charles S. "The Fixation of Belief." *Popular Science Monthly* 12 (1877): 1–15.

Puvimanasinghe, Shyamali. *A Model for Torture Prevention in Asia*. Hong Kong: Asian Human Rights Commission; Copenhagen: Rehabilitation and Research Centre for Torture Victims, 2005.

Seron, Carroll. "The Two Faces of Law and Inequality: From Critique to the Promise of Situated, Pragmatic Policy." *Law and Society Review* 50, no. 1 (2016): 9–33.

Visakesa, Chandrasekaram. "Do Tigers Confess? An Interdisciplinary Study of Confessionary Evidence in Counter-Terrorism Measures of Sri Lanka." PhD thesis, Australian National University, 2012.

Weizman, Eyal, and Zachary Manfredi. "'From Figure to Ground': A Conversation with Eyal Weizman on the Politics of the Humanitarian Present." *Qui Parle: Critical Humanities and Social Sciences* 22, no. 1 (2013): 167–92.

CHAPTER 11

DISPOSSESSION, REIMAGINED FROM THE 1690s

DAVID KAZANJIAN

Contemporary critiques of dispossession in the Americas at times presuppose that those who have been dispossessed previously owned what was taken from them. This presupposition, in turn, has led some anti-dispossessive politics either to seek the return of what was taken or to imagine a future characterized by "the commons" or "commoning," which is to say, a collective ownership that would repurpose an older form of collective possession understood to have existed before dispossession began. That presupposition and those politics are typically backed up by a historical narrative of "primitive" or "originary" accumulation that places the beginning of dispossession in a broad period from the fifteenth to the nineteenth centuries, in which capitalism is said to have established itself by enclosing commons; stealing the land, labor, and the very bodies principally of native and African-descended people; and enshrining property, waged-work, and racial forms in legal and extralegal norms.[1]

In this essay, I offer a somewhat different narrative of "primitive" or "originary" accumulation in North America in order to show how critiques of dispossession do not need to presuppose that the dispossessed previously owned what was stolen from them, and to suggest that other forms of anti-dispossessive politics might follow from such critiques.[2] I focus on one legal case from the 1690s involving an enslaved black man from Boston named Adam.[3] The late seventeenth century was a crucial period for dispossession in the British North American colonies, which intensified later than in Europe or Spanish America, for it represented a transition from indentured servitude to legally codified and racialized chattel slavery. Adam's case allows us a glimpse into this transition, in medias res. In particular, the case exposes the ways Adam's dispossessors *imputed to* him an ownership of himself *in order to* facilitate the dispossession of his body and its capacities. In response to such accumulation by (the imputation of) possession—rather than by the dispossession of something Adam originally owned—Adam could be said to have eschewed claims to prior possession and reparative recovery in favor of a robust critique of dispossession expressed as a fugitive politics "exorbitant" from, or outside the orbit of, possession as such. I take the term *exorbitant*—which originally meant to go out of a wheel-track, as a cart might stray from a road—from testimony Adam's master John Saffin gave against him in the case, bitterly criticizing the way Adam dared to move about Boston "at his pleasure, in open Defiance of me his Master . . . to the great scandall and evill example of all Negros both in Town and countrey whose eyes are upon this wretched Negro to see the Issue of these his exorbitant practices."[4] Imagining Saffin's criticism from the subaltern perspective of Adam, whose own words do not appear in the archive, raises the possibility that Adam did not so much assert his own possession of himself or demand the return of possessions that were stolen from him as he "issued" "exorbitant practices" that defied possession as such. In the archive of Adam's case, then, we can find traces of a challenge to what Karl Marx dubbed "so-called originary accumulation" that imagined a future outside what C. B. MacPherson has called "possessive individualism," or the Lockean tradition that understands self-ownership as the essence of proper subjectivity and private property as the normative relationship of subjects to the so-called natural world.[5] This challenge also troubles contemporary efforts to imagine such a future in terms of "commons" or "commoning."

Furthermore, Adam's exorbitance cannot be said to come from a subjective will or anything we could comfortably call his own desire to realize individual agency. No such ground can be imputed to Adam because he never represents himself in the archive; he is only ever represented by others. I thus suggest that we read "Adam" more as a name for a theory of anti-dispossession, or as a trajectory of thought and action, suggestively different from the trajectory that has gone under the name of John Locke. Indeed, the potency of Adam's case is ever more evident when we recall that Locke bases his seminal theory of possession, published in 1689–90 as *Two Treatises on Government*, on a critique of Robert Filmer's royalist interpretation of the biblical Adam. While Locke displaces Filmer's Adam to found a certain liberal trajectory that leads to the present, the case of Adam offers an alternative trajectory from the 1690s.

To the extent that contemporary analyses of, and political projects against, dispossession rely on a historical narrative that presumes individual or common possession prior to dispossession, my account of Adam's dispossession presents a challenge to, and demands a revision of, those analyses and political projects. I thus urge contemporary critiques of dispossession to take stock of the implicit or explicit historical narratives that ground their analytical and political projects, and to entertain alternative, speculative narratives of the past that lead to different political futures.

Dispossession

There is an account of dispossession that has become widely accepted in many academic and activist circles, and that on initial consideration seems hardly objectionable. Under capitalism, so this account goes, exploited people have what they own stolen from them: indigenous people and rural peasants have their land stolen from them, as well as their labor stolen from them; African-descended people have their freedom stolen from them, and thus their labor and their very bodies stolen from them. Some have argued that this theft was initially driven by overt violence such as colonization, chattel slavery, enclosure, and the criminalization of poverty and landlessness via what Marx called "bloody legislation against the expropriated." Then, the account goes, this overt violence gave way to, or was developed into, what Marx famously called the "silent compulsion of economic relations which 'sets the seal' on the domination of the capitalist over the worker."[6] In other words, workers learned to "work by themselves," as Louis Althusser put it, to get up and get to the factory at the proper time without being dragged out of bed by an overseer, boss, or cop, whose overt violence did not disappear but became an exceptional exercise rather than a quotidian one.[7]

This classic account of dispossession has long been critiqued as too developmentalist, giving way to an understanding of "accumulation by dispossession" as a structure or an ongoing and recursive element of capitalism. Scholars of indigenous and Native American studies and of white settler colonialism in particular have of late theorized dispossession in its contemporary urgency.[8] Yet despite this shift from a developmentalist to a structural account of dispossession, and the power of social movements that have both theorized and activated this account, a foundationalist presupposition still often animates the concept: namely that the dispossessed owned what was stolen from them. This foundationalist presupposition operates on two relatively distinct if often intertwined levels. First, it can be taken to mean that the dispossessed owned themselves, their bodies, or their labor before they were appropriated, and thus that a properly critical response entails returning selves, bodies, and labor to the subjects who originally owned them. Second, it can also be taken to mean that the dispossessed owned the land that was stolen from them, either privately or "in common" as codified commons or as collectively inhabited space, and thus that a properly critical response entails returning that land to its original owners or inhabitants. This foundationalist presupposition is to some extent entrenched in Marx's own formative accounts of dispossession. His preferred words for the concept were *Enteignung*, usually translated as "expropriation," and *Aneignung*, usually translated as "usurpation" or "appropriation." Yet throughout part 8 of *Capital*, vol. 1, and elsewhere, he allows those terms to mingle with terms like *Raub*, or "robbery," *Diebstahl*, or "theft," and especially the phrase "theft of land," as Robert Nichols shows.[9] Marx was also fond of describing so-called wage slavery as a situation in which the dispossessed were left with "nothing to sell but their *own* skins" (my italics).[10] Many contemporary accounts of dispossession continue to presume, if not necessarily arguing explicitly, that subjects always already owned themselves, until their selves were stolen from them.

Of this account we must ask: In what sense can it be said that the dispossessed owned land, themselves, or even their "skins" such that those possessions could be stolen from them? What do we mean when we impute such prior possession, such ownership, or such propriety to the dispossessed? And what are the implications of such imputations for our anti-dispossessive politics?

As it turns out, one of the most influential seventeenth-century arguments for dispossession, which still underwrites contemporary practices of dispossession, was also an argument that imputed prior possession to the dispossessed: John Locke's *Two Treatises on Government* (1690). The *First Treatise* critiques Robert Filmer's claim that kings inherit their paternal and regal authority by divine right passed down from the presumptively first man, father, and ruler: the biblical Adam.[11] The biblical Adam emerges from the *First Treatise* not as a universal foundation linked to kings, but rather as a particular representative of "the whole Species of Man, as the chief Inhabitant, who is the Image of his Maker." This whole species—rather than Adam himself—is given "the Dominion over the other Creatures."[12] This particularization of the biblical Adam does not necessarily question paternal power over women or the power of mastery over the enslaved; rather, it refuses to take those powers as analogous to political power. For Locke, any authority imputed to the biblical Adam ceased once the tendency of the state of nature ("men living together according to reason, without a common Superior on Earth, with Authority to judge between them") to slide into the state of war ("a declared design of force upon the Person of another, where there is no common Superior on Earth to appeal to for relief") led men to leave the state of nature and enter into properly political "Society."[13] At that point, political authority passed not to kings, but to "*men under Government* . . . a standing Rule to live by, common to every one of that Society."[14]

This depoliticization of the biblical Adam's foundational authority, in turn, leads Locke to formulate his famous theory of property. Although "God gave the World to *Adam* and his Posterity in common," it does not follow that only "one universal Monarch, should have any *Property*"; in other words, that Adam was first does not mean that an individual monarch can claim to be an inheritor of Adam's power or property. Nor does it follow that common ownership prevails over individual ownership: "the taking of this or that part, does not depend on the express consent of all the Commoners." Rather, "Though the Earth, and all inferior Creatures be common to all Men, yet every Man has a *Property* in his own *Person*. . . . Whatsoever then he removes out of the State that Nature hath provided, and left it in, he hath mixed his *Labour* with, and joyned to it something that is his own, and thereby makes it his *Property*." Foundationally and presumptively ("of necessity"), then, people own their labor, and when that labor is "mixed" with natural things, those things become the property of those who labored upon them: "The *labour* that was mine, removing them out of that common state they were in, hath *fixed* my *Property* in them."[15] Since the value of something of nature derives principally from the willful exercise of labor upon it, rather than from any value inherent in natural things themselves, willful subjectivity is the condition of possibility for the removal of nature from commonality and the transformation of it into property.

For Locke, this principle is consistent with both servitude and the expropriation of native lands by settlers, but not because the enslaved or the "Indian" are not "men" or do not potentially own themselves, their labor, or their land.[16] To the contrary, precisely because servants and native people are imputed to have the capacity for ownership over themselves, their labor, and their land, their ownership can appropriated by others as an outcome either of just war or of insufficient "industry." Of servitude, Locke argues in chapter 4 of the *Second Treatise* that "A Man" cannot offer himself up for enslavement, if enslavement is taken to be giving the power over one's own death to another, because "No body can give more Power than he has himself." But if by one's own "fault" one has "forfeited his own Life, by some Act that deserves Death," he may give the power to delay that death to another with whom he effectively enters into a compact to remain alive and serve. Servitude, here, is the preservation of a life that has actively forfeited its own right to remain alive.[17] The precise "fault" or "Act" that could justify entering into such a relationship of servitude is not specified in chapter 4 of the *Second Treatise*. Quite apart from the specificity of such a "fault" or "Act," however, it is crucial to recognize that the principle of servitude here is not the inhumanity or unreason of the enslaved, nor is it the inability of the enslaved to be an autonomous and willful master of their own desire. Rather, the enslaved are presumed to have a willful subjectivity that they surrender actively, through the willful exercise of that very subjectivity: "by his fault, forfeited his own Life, by some Act." The condition of possibility for Lockean just servitude is thus the imputation of willful subjectivity to the enslaved prior to their enslavement.

The principle of willful subjectivity, expressed through labor, is for Locke also not inconsistent with the expropriation of native lands by settlers. "Indians" are not inhuman in the *Second Treatise*; they are not lacking in willful subjectivity: "Thus this Law of reason makes the Deer that *Indian's* who hath killed it; 'tis allowed to be his goods who hath bestowed his labour upon it, though before, it was the common right of every one."[18] Their lands can be appropriated, rather, precisely because they do not properly utilize their presumptively willful subjectivity through sufficient or appropriate labor. Title to land, then, is determined by Locke's quite particular determination of the quality and quantity of labor "mixed" with the land. The more one "Tills, Plants, Improves, Cultivates, and can use the Product of," the greater the claim to title. It is not the inability to till, plant, improve, cultivate, and use the product of that labor that justifies appropriation of land; rather, it is the failure extensively and intensively to use the very ability that is imputed to all, "Indians" included.[19]

This is where Locke's famous passages on the "Waste" land that can be rightly appropriated by settlers come into play. America, in particular, is full of "Land . . . lyeing wast in common" because "the Inhabitants valued it not, nor claimed Property in any more than they made use of": "For I aske whether in the wild woods and uncultivated wast of America left to Nature, without any improvement, tillage or husbandry, a thousand acres will yield the needy and wretched inhabitants as many conveniencies of life as ten acres of equally fertile land doe in Devonshire where they are well cultivated?"[20] The comparison between the "waste of America" and the "fertile land . . . in Devonshire" is not a comparison between a place where inhuman or subhuman creatures called "Indians" live and a place where fully human Englishmen live; rather, it is a comparison between two groups of humans, both of whom are imputed to have a willful subjectivity expressed principally by labor, but one of whom fails to express that subjectivity adequately. Again and crucially, the condition of possibility for the devaluation of land as waste, as well as the subsequent justification for settler dispossession of that land from native peoples, is the imputation of self-ownership to the dispossessed.

Some contemporary scholarship has attended to this feature of dispossession. C. B. MacPherson shows how possessive individualism, or one's presumptive ownership of one's belongings and of oneself and as an autonomous and self-sufficient subject, was a feature of the rise of capitalism rather than a precapitalist precondition or even some ahistorical, ontological ground. Subsequently, scholars such as Cheryl I. Harris, Carole Pateman and Charles Mills, and Aileen Moreton-Robinson have shown how such possessive individualism has always been racialized.[21] But by revisiting Locke's *Two Treatises* here, I want to emphasize how racialized dispossession entails a quite specific, foundationalist presupposition and condition: the imputation of willful subjectivity to the dispossessed prior to their dispossession.

Since Locke constructs such a stark opposition between the commons and property, it might seem that casting possession prior to dispossession in terms of a more positively valued notion of collective possession—an anticapitalist commons or practice of "commoning," rather than Locke's negatively valued "waste"—would unsettle the foundationalist presupposition of Lockean dispossession.[22] Yet E. P. Thompson has taught us how being "in common" with one's lands or customs in England in the eighteenth century was a fluid practice constantly changing in response to unfolding conditions rather than a stable, idyllic state of collective possession. To the extent that they antagonized capitalism, the commons did so by repurposing themselves in the face of the quite specific techniques of capitalist expropriation, not by maintaining some precapitalist, nonpossessive purity rooted in time immemorial.[23] Indeed, any white settler commons in the Americas were themselves previously expropriated from indigenous peoples, and so should not function as the model for a prior state to which we ought to return or which we can simply revive. Additionally, although indigenous people had a diverse range of relationships to land, we know not only that many indigenous people did not conceive of land as property prior to the dispossession of their land, but also that sometimes indigenous people appropriated land from other indigenous people before it was stolen from them by white settlers.[24] If the opposition between so-called commons and possession is not as clear cut as either Locke or many critiques of dispossession presume, then we ought to be cautious about positing commons or commoning as a foundation upon which to generate a critique of possessive individualism and the dispossession it works to justify.

Some contemporary theories of the subject put an even sharper critical focus on dispossession's tendency to impute prior proprieties to subjectivity. Such theories have long considered what might be called the constitutive dispossessions that make subjectivity possible, a consideration many link to any radical challenge to liberal, capitalist regimes of power and knowledge. Writes Judith Butler: "Let's face it. We're undone by each other. And if we're not, we're missing something":

> Even when we have our rights, we are dependent on a mode of governance and a legal regime that confers and sustains those rights. And so we are already outside of ourselves before any possibility of being dispossessed of our rights, land, and modes of belonging. In other words, we are interdependent beings whose pleasure and suffering depend from the start on a sustained social world, a sustaining environment. . . . We can only be dispossessed because we are already dispossessed. Our interdependency establishes our vulnerability to social forms of deprivation.[25]

When contemporary theories of dispossession rely on foundationalist presuppositions about people owning themselves, by contrast, they become a politics of morality. Such theories certainly have the advantage of revealing that the criminals are not those relentlessly criminalized subjects of dispossession, but rather the dispossessors themselves—despite their control over juridical and police apparatuses. But they also run the risk of implicating themselves in the very dispossessive modes of power and knowledge that they seek to oppose. That is, when current theories of dispossession remain within the terms of good and evil, innocent and criminal, they position anti-dispossessive critics and activists as detectives and cops, judges and juries. As is no doubt clear by now, I am concerned with the effects and affects of such foundationalism: how it might imagine justice as the return to what once was, how it could insist on a renewed conformity to identities imagined to have been lost, how it implicates anti-dispossessive politics in that which it seeks to challenge, how it melancholically aspires to recognition, restoration, and reparation.

What if people who were dispossessed under conditions of "so-called originary accumulation" sometimes understood dispossession differently than all this? What if they offered vigorous opposition to the theft of land, labor, and bodies from the dispossessed without always presupposing prior historical or ontological possession? And how might we spot such opposition in the worn and fragmentary archives of "so-called primitive accumulation" in the Americas?

Adam

I offer my interpretation of Adam's case as an exercise in critical or speculative historiography about what has been called the black radical tradition, rather than as a historiographic recovery of black lives or an empirically verifiable interpretation of who Adam was or what he did.[26] While recovery as a historiographic aim in the narrowest sense has been critiqued from literary, philosophical, and historical perspectives, the tendency to interpret documents from the past as if they only provided answers to the questions of who did what, where, when, and why endures.[27] Elsewhere I have argued that, while such interpretations are valuable, their focus on the empirical evidence of subjective agency tends also to foreclose viewing such documents as scenes of speculative, subaltern theory.[28]

In the case of Adam, we also confront a problematic that theorists of subalternity have long thematized. Adam was not in a position to write and publish texts that could become powerful trajectories of thought like his more empowered contemporaries did, texts we still read and theorize with, such as Locke's *Two Treatises of Government*. He also seems not to have testified directly in his case, or at least the extant court records do not contain his own testimony. Consequently, what we know about Adam comes from what others said and wrote about him, and even those accounts exist as incomplete fragments, sometimes literally worn beyond legibility. Certainly, in the absence of his own words, we can neither retry his case nor make verifiable historical or juridical claims about him. Indeed, there is no subject in this archive whom we could confidently call Adam and to whom we could impute desire, will, intention, or agency. In the face of this, we could despair of the possibility of discerning Adam's perspective on his own dispossession, leaving his case in the control of those who sought to dispossess him.

I take a different approach. Those who sought to dispossess Adam were clearly unsettled by Adam's challenges to their efforts, to such an extent that they went to great lengths to oppose him both in and out of court, as their own testimony clearly shows. By reading what others say about Adam's efforts as highly mediated, archival traces of what he might have done or said or thought—as something like negative prints or distorted echoes—I speculate upon how the name "Adam" might figure a set of perspectives on and actions against dispossession.[29] This approach, in turn, asks us to rethink what theoretical practice itself might entail. It can generate a potent if unverifiable account of subaltern theoretical practices that do not conform to contemporary presumptions about theory or practice, in particular to quite Lockean presumptions about how proper theory and politics are grounded in a subject's willful pursuit of their own desire.[30] The referent of what I call "Adam," then, is not so much the historical subject of this case; that subject certainly did exist, but a verifiable account of his existence is not my aim. Rather, Adam's actions clearly made an impression upon these archives, and I am after that impression, distorted though it certainly is. In this way, we can give "Adam" the chance to prompt our rethinking of both the theory of dispossession and anti-dispossessive politics.

In the Massachusetts State Archive in Boston, one finds a set of bound volumes, created in the nineteenth century, containing the extant files of the Suffolk Court, some of the earliest judicial records of the Massachusetts Bay Colony. On about fifty pages of one such volume, one finds appended the records of a late-seventeenth-century conflict between John Saffin, a wealthy and well-connected Boston merchant and judge, and Adam, a black man enslaved to Saffin. These records are rich but fragmentary, due largely to the underdeveloped judicial system of the colony and the rather haphazard record keeping of British colonial authorities. We have a series of filings by Saffin, statements by witnesses, and determinations by court officials, but little that links one document to another beyond chronology. The documents cannot on their own be said to narrate much of a coherent story. We can, however, reconstruct something like a narrative of the conflict between Saffin and Adam by taking these Suffolk Court files together with a few other key texts.[31] We can do this as long as we remember that it is we who are synthesizing this version of the tale, with the help of a few contemporary historians who have also written briefly about the case.[32] Here is a version of that narrative.

It seems that in 1694, Saffin indentured his slave Adam, as well as a parcel of land and a few animals, to a tenant farmer of his called Thomas Shepherd, who lived in Bristol, Massachusetts. Adam was told that if he worked for Shepherd for seven years, he would be freed. When that term expired, Saffin refused to free Adam and indeed sought to make Adam work further for him, and then to indenture Adam to yet another man. Adam refused this second indenture and fled. In the face of legal action taken against him by Saffin, Adam turned to another prominent Boston merchant and judge named Samuel Sewell for help. Sewell, who was critical of slavery and also held the controversial distinction of being the only judge in the Salem witch trials subsequently to express regret for his involvement in that affair, became an advocate for Adam. The initial jury hearing the case ruled against Adam, who quickly appealed on the sensible grounds that his master Saffin had himself presided over the case, and thus had improperly influenced the jury. As the appeal moved slowly through the courts, Adam got smallpox and had to be cared for at Saffin's expense. Once Adam recovered, Saffin tried to indenture him again to a Captain Timothy Clarke, who got into a fight with Adam. At this point, Adam sued Saffin for harassment. Saffin then tried to sell Adam out of the colony, but was blocked by the courts, and eventually petitioned the governor and legislature for summary judgment on the matter, but was denied. Finally, in November 1703, the Superior Court of Judicature ruled in Adam's favor and freed him from Saffin.[33] To give some demographic context for this moment, Wendy Warren tells us that by the end of the seventeenth century there were about ninety thousand English colonizers in New England, perhaps fifteen hundred enslaved Africans, and another fifteen hundred enslaved or indentured Native Americans, all of whom lived alongside an undetermined number of as yet uncolonized Native Americans.[34]

What would it mean to say that Saffin sought to dispossess Adam, as it seems we ought to say? The court records repeatedly point to a document at the center of this conflict: the indenture agreement Saffin penned when he first hired Adam out to Shepherd on November 15, 1694. Here is how that document is recorded in the Suffolk Court Files:

Bee it known unto all men by these presents That I John Saffin of Bristol in the Province of the Massachusetts Bay in New England out of meer kindness to and for the Encouragement of my negro man Adam to go on chearfully in his Business & Imployment by me now putt into, the Custody Service and command of Thomas Shepherd my Tenant on boundfield Farm in Bristol aforesaid for and During the Terme of Seaven years from the Twenty fifth day of March last past 1694—fully to be compleat and Ended or as I may otherwise See cause to Imploy him. I say I doe by these presents of my own free & Voluntary Will & pleasure from and after the full end & Expiration of Seven years beginning on the Twenty fifth day of March last past and from thenceforth fully to be compleat and Ended, Enfranchise clear and make free my said negro man named Adam to be fully at his own Dispose and Liberty as other free men are or ought to be according to all true Intents & purposes whatsoever. Allways provided that the said Adam my servant do in the mean time go on chearfully quietly and Industriously in the Lawfull Business that either my Self or my Assigns shall from time to time reasonably Sett him about or imploy him in and doe behave and abear himself as an Honest true and failthful Servant ought to doe during the Tearm of Seven years as aforesaid. In Witness whereof I the said John Saffin have hereunto sett my hand and Seal this Twenty Sixth day of June 1694—In the Sixth year of their Magestys Reign.[35]

In turn, Saffin repeatedly explains to the court his decision not to follow through on the promise to free Adam after his service to Shepherd in these terms: "the said Negro hath in no wise performed the Conditions on which he was to be free But on the Contrary hath behaved him self Turbulently Neglegently Insolently and Outragiously both to your Petitioner and his Tenant Thomas Shepard and his wife and family, and Others."[36]

Crucially here, Saffin does not charge simply that Adam did not do the work that was required of him. Indeed, nowhere in the case records does Saffin claim Adam failed to work for Shepherd during his indenture, nor does Adam claim that he refused to work for Shepherd. Instead, Saffin charges that Adam did not work for Shepherd with the appropriate affect, with the proper mode of being, as it was described in the original indenture agreement of 1694. Rather than "chearfully quietly and Industriously . . . behave and abear himself as an Honest true and faithfull Servant ought to," Adam "on the contrary . . . behaved him self Turbulently Neglegently Insolently and Outragiously." This suggests that Saffin did not simply seek to *dispossess* Adam of something that was essentially his, such as his labor or his body. Rather, Saffin imputed to Adam a certain mode of being as a condition of possibility for the labor Adam was to perform. Rather than telling us that Saffin just sought to *dispossess* Adam of his own labor, these documents more strenuously emphasize that Saffin sought to *possess* Adam with, or *conjure* in him, the cheerful and quiet desire for, or love of, industry on behalf of his master.

In one of Saffin's other statements we can see even more clearly that what is at stake in the case is not so much Saffin's theft of Adam's possessions, which is to say, Saffin's dispossession of something Adam previously owned, as Saffin's effort to *possess* or *animate* Adam with a certain being, to *conjure* Adam as a cheerful laborer who desires his master's desire. As Saffin explains to the court in 1703:

The thing in brief is this. Your Petitioner hath a certaine Negro man named Adam that is withheld or taken from him your Petitioner under countenance of authority (not collour of law) which Negro hath sooner or later cost your Petitioner above Threescore pounds. . . . [I]n the mean time your Petitioner is made a meer Vassall to his slave . . . for all this the said vile Negro is at this Day set at large to goe at his pleasure, in open Defiance of me his Master in danger of my life, he having threatned to be Revenged of me and all them that have cross't his turbulent Humour, to the great scandall and evill example of all Negros both in Town and countery whose eyes are upon this wretched Negro to see the Issue of these his exorbitant practices.[37]

Saffin here complains not simply that Adam stopped working for him, or that Adam improperly reappropriated the labor that Saffin had expropriated; rather, Saffin complains that Adam's "pleasure" and "practices" are "exorbitant" to the cheerful, quiet industry he demanded of and imputed to Adam, in their original agreement. This *immaterial* demand could be said to supplement the material dispossession of Adam's labor, forming a constitutive part of Saffin's regime of accumulation.

This is a crucial point about which I want to be clear: Saffin's effort to possess Adam with "chearful, quiet industry" does not occur *after* Adam has been dispossessed of his labor; it is not merely a discursive *justification* of a prior, more concrete dispossession of something Adam properly owned. Rather, Saffin's attempted possession of Adam occurs alongside, and is intimately bound up with, his attempted dispossession of Adam's labor. We could even more precisely say that Saffin paradoxically tries to "give" Adam exactly what he then seeks to "take" from him, according to a logic we might call Lockean.

This case offers insight into the way racialized systems of accumulation proceed by dispossession and possession at once. It also suggests that a critique of such systems need not rely upon an understanding, either explicit or implicit, of what is possessed, essentially and prior to dispossession, by those who are dispossessed. That is, we do not need to make claims about who Adam essentially was or what he owned prior to his encounter with Saffin; we do not need to generate an account of the possessions of which Adam was dispossessed. To the contrary, a critique of Saffin's regime of accumulation must attend to the paradoxical ways Adam had imputed to him the very possession—in this case, cheerful, quiet, and industrious behavior—that Saffin sought to accumulate.

What would such a critical shift mean for how we understand the ways the dispossessed responded to dispossession? This is not to ask just what they did do, where, and when, but more crucially to ask how might they be said to have theorized dispossession, or how we might read their subaltern theories of dispossession in and from such an archive. Adam, as I have mentioned, did not have much access to the institutional discourses that would find their way into the archives of his case. He offers almost no direct testimony, no account of himself as it were. So we must read for his theoretical work in and through what is said about him by others, and in turn read what we learn about or from Adam as a trajectory of theorized practice rather than a story about an individual's agency.

The court records never suggest that Adam demanded the return of his labor capacity and the restoration of his ownership over his own body. In fact, the founding conditions of Adam's initial enslavement to Saffin never come up in the case. As we have already seen, however, the archive does tell us a good deal about how Adam acted while working for Shepherd and what he did once he completed his term of indenture and judged himself to be free. The last two passages I quoted earlier indicate that while working for Shepherd, Adam did not perform a love of his work. He rather seems to have expressed his disdain for the very work he nonetheless seems to have performed. Once free from Shepherd and Saffin, he seems to have moved around quite a bit "at his pleasure," "both in Town and countrey" in and around Boston, particularly among "all Negros." These movements—whatever they were precisely, and we can only imagine—did not simply embarrass Saffin, they made Saffin feel as if he were "a meer Vassall to his slave," with such a manner of "open Defiance" that Saffin feared for his very life.

So Adam's "crime"—which is to say, his challenge to Saffin's regime of accumulation—was for Saffin not so much Adam's failure to do material labor as it was his successful spectacle of freedom, in which he dis-possessed his master's putative possession of his own desire, for "all Negros both in Town and countrey whose eyes are upon" him to see. We might say that, rather than seeking the return of his labor so that he could work industriously as he so chose, or the return of his body so that he could possess himself as he supposedly once did, Adam spectacularly indulged in what Saffin quite precisely calls "exorbitant practices": practices that were outside the track of industry itself. Adam's turbulent, negligent, insolent, and outrageous actions—as they appear textually in this archive—thus transvalue the laboring being Saffin sought to conjure him as.

What is more, that this ex-orbitance was said by Saffin to play out "both in Town and countrey" suggests that Adam also transvalues the spaces in which he moved. This possibility puts some pressure on a key feature of contemporary critiques of dispossession: the use of "the commons" as a name for that which the dispossessed possessed prior to dispossession, and thus as a foundationalist figure for opposition to accumulation by dispossession. When we use "the commons" in that way, we have to tell a story about how the enclosure or expropriation of the commons was a protracted, bloody, and violent process that entailed the loss of a prior state of anticapitalist collective possession; in turn, we risk tethering ourselves to the desire for a return to or a restoration of the commons or something modeled on the commons.[38]

That desire actively forgets that any commons in the Americas were themselves "settled," which is to say, expropriated from native peoples and worked by the indentured and the enslaved. To acknowledge such expropriation is not to impute prior possession in the Lockean sense, but rather to emphasize the taking of that which was not previously subject to such a notion of possession. Think, for instance, of Adam's own city of Boston and its Common, one of the places where Adam may well have gone "at his pleasure" and perhaps even issued "exorbitant practices" like speaking ill of his master, as Saffin charges. Expropriated from the Wampanoag tribes (particularly the Massachusett) whom European settlers first encountered, the area of Boston Common is first recorded to have been owned by William Blackstone, who held it until it was purchased by the Massachusetts Bay Colony in 1634 to be a communal park. Boston Common was during Adam's lifetime a collective space for cattle grazing and cultivation, both of which were tactics of white settler colonization, as well as for public gathering. But it was also a gallows where thousands of people whom John Saffin might have called turbulent, negligent, insolent, outrageous, and exorbitant were hung, including suspected witches, petty thieves, pirates, dissenters, servants, and slaves.[39] Because a collectively settled space like Boston Common did not include black and indentured people like Adam in its commonality, it could not function for Adam as a foundational home or stable site: that is, we cannot say that Adam had his proper commons enclosed. In fact, Adam likely had no such home or site at all, no place we could say he originally owned and then had taken from him. Boston Common could, however, be one of many places Adam passed through or lingered temporarily within "at his pleasure." That passing-through or temporary lingering, in turn, could be understood as the modality of his "pleasure" and the scene of his "exorbitant practices," in opposition to Saffin's effort to assign him a settled place of possession like Thomas Shepherd's farm. That is, rather than having lost and sought to recover a settled place stolen from him by Saffin, we find Adam setting out and about, publicly humiliating Saffin "to the great scandall and evill example of all Negros both in Town and countrey whose eyes are upon" him, such that, as Saffin writes in another submission to the court, "he grew so intollerably insolent, quarrelsome and outragious, that the Earth could not bear his rudeness."[40]

Born upon no Earth, not even a commons like Boston Common, Adam cannot be said to have been taken from a site of prior possession or to have sought a return to such a site. But he can be said to have exuberantly enacted a certain social vagabondage in and among "all Negros," much to Saffin's vexation. Going about town at his pleasure, refusing to be possessed by Saffin's regime of accumulation, Adam's communalism was itinerant and performative, critical and riotous, pleasurable and exorbitant.

The condition of possibility for Locke's critique of absolute monarchy is an insistence, against Filmer, "that *Adam* had not either by natural Right of Fatherhood, or by positive Donation from God, any such Authority over his Children, or Dominion over the World as is pretended." With the biblical Adam's presumptively foundational, political authority removed, Locke is able to found a liberal, universal theory of possessive individualism that imputes ownership over one's self and one's belongings not only to those who would dispossess black and brown people around the globe, but also to those very dispossessed people as a condition of their dispossession. His theory effectively gives the dispossessed that which he then advocates dispossessing them of. To the extent that anti-dispossessive politics today reasserts and seeks to recover the possessions of the dispossessed on the ground that they previously owned—and thus have and will always by right own—themselves and their belongings, such politics risks further entrenching the very Lockean principle that made dispossession in the Anglo-American liberal tradition ongoingly possible.

While Locke was formulating *Treatises* that would become a constitutive part of our present, another Adam set out toward a different future. If those politics are not yet part of our present, it is not because they are of a too-distant or outdated past. Rather, the case of Adam deserves the most careful consideration as we reflect upon our dispossessed pasts and plot our fugitive futures. For perhaps we can glean from its extant fragments an alternative theory of dispossession, which is to say, perhaps Adam can teach us to read and to act not only with outrage for the loss of all that we think we had and knew, and not only with hope for efforts to restore or repair our stolen prior possessions. Rather, perhaps Adam can teach us how to live exorbitantly, to wander deviantly from possession as such.

Notes

I would like to thank a number of people whose comments on this essay have helped me immensely, even as I have as yet not adequately responded to all of their insights: Lori Allen, Lalaie Ameeriar, Fadi Bardawil, Margo Crawford, Andrew Dilts, David L. Eng, Didier Fassin, Bernard Harcourt, Suvir Kaul, Ania Loomba, Allegra McLeod, Ayşe Parla, Jennifer Ponce de León, Peter Redfield, Josie Saldaña, Joan Scott, Massimiliano Tomba, Dillon Vrana, Dagmawi Woubshet, Chi-ming Yang.

1. For work that either implicitly or explicitly presumes such prior possession, see Veronika Bennholdt-Thomsen and Maria Mies, *The Subsistence Perspective: Beyond the Globalised Economy* (London: Zed, 1999); David Bollier and Silke Helfrich, eds., *The Wealth of the Commons: A World Beyond Market and State* (Amherst: Levellers, 2012); Cesare Casarino and Antonio Negri, *In Praise of the Common: A Conversation on Philosophy and Politics* (Minneapolis: University of Minnesota Press, 2008); Silvia Federici, "Women, Land Struggles, and the Reconstruction of the Commons," *WorkingUSA: The Journal of Labor and Society* (WUSA) 14, no. 61 (March 2011); Federici "Witch-Hunting, Globalization and Feminist Solidarity in Africa Today," *Journal of International Women's Studies*, special issue, *Women's Gender Activism in Africa*, Joint Special Issue with *WAGADU*, 10, no. 1 (October 2008): 29–35; Federici, "Feminism and the Politics of the Commons," http://wealthofthecommons.org/essay/feminism-and-politics-commons; David Harvey, *The New Imperialism* (Oxford: Oxford University

Press, 2003); Peter Linebaugh, *Stop, Thief! The Commons, Enclosures, and Resistance* (Oakland, CA: PM Press, 2014) and Linebaugh, *Magna Carta Manifesto: Liberties and Commons for All* (Berkeley: University of California Press, 2008).

2. For work that has inspired my shift in perspective on dispossession, and is not cited elsewhere in this essay, see Swapna Banerjee-Guha, *Accumulation by Dispossession: Transformative Cities in the New Global Order* (New Delhi: SAGE, 2010); Marisa Belau-steguigoitia Ruis and María Josefina Saldaña-Portillo, *Des/posesión: Género, territorio y luchas por la autodeterminación* (México: PUEG-UNAM, 2014); Marisa J. Fuentes, *Dispossessed Lives: Enslaved Women, Violence, and the Archive* (Philadelphia: University of Pennsylvania Press, 2016); Jodi A. Byrd, Alyosha Goldstein, Jodi Melamed, and Chandan Reddy, eds., special issue on economies of dispossession, *Social Text* 135, 36, no. 2 (June 2018); Glen Sean Coulthard, *Red Skin, White Masks: Rejecting the Colonial Politics of Dispossession* (Minneapolis: University of Minnesota Press, 2014); Craig Fortier, *Unsettling the Commons: Social Movements Within, Against, and Beyond Settler Colonialism* (Winnipeg: ARP, 2017); Alyosha Goldstein and Alex Lubin, eds., "Settler Colonialism," special issue of the *South Atlantic Quarterly* 107, no. 4 (Fall 2008); Tania Murray Li, *Land's End: Capitalist Relations on an Indigenous Frontier* (Durham: Duke University Press, 2014); Fred Moten, *Black and Blur: Consent Not to Be A Single Being* (Durham: Duke University Press, 2017), 85; Moten, *Stolen Life: Consent Not to Be a Single Being* (Durham: Duke University Press, 2017); Daniel Nemser, "Primitive Spiritual Accumulation and the Colonial Extraction Economy," *Política Común* 5 (2014): 1–21; Karen R. Roybal, *Archives of Dispossession: Recovering the Testimonios of Mexican American Herederas* (Chapel Hill: University of North Carolina Press, 2017); Audra Simpson and Andrea Smith, eds., *Theorizing Native Studies* (Durham: Duke University Press, 2014); Audra Simpson, *Mohawk Interruptus: Political Life Across the Borders of Settler States* (Durham: Duke University Press, 2014); Gavin Walker, "Primitive Accumulation and the Formation of Difference: On Marx and Schmitt," *Rethinking Marxism* 23, no. 3 (2011): 384–404; Jackie Wang, *Carceral Capitalism* (South Pasadena, CA: Semiotext[e], 2018).

3. Although in the limited space of this essay I discuss only this one case, in the larger project on which I am at work I examine a range of such cases from New England and the Yucatán peninsula in the 1690s. For an example of the latter, see my forthcoming essay " 'I Am He': A History of Dispossession's Not-Yet-Present in Colonial Yucatán," in *Accumulation and Subjectivity*, ed. Karen Benezra (New York: State University of New York Press, forthcoming).

4. Massachusetts Archives, Suffolk Court Files (Author's image 0827); Abner C. Goodell, "John Saffin and His Slave Adam," *Publications of The Colonial Society of Massachusetts* (March 1893): 96. On *exorbitant*, see *Oxford English Dictionary* online.

5. Karl Marx, *Capital: A Critique of Political Economy*, vol. 1 (New York: Penguin, 1990), 873–940. Though typically translated as "so-called primitive accumulation," the phrase Marx used was *Die sogenannte ursprüngliche Akkumulation*, which is perhaps better translated as "so-called original accumulation." The phrase "accumulation by dispossession" is usually associated with Harvey, *The New Imperialism*; C. B. MacPherson, *The Political Theory of Possessive Individualism: Hobbes to Locke* (Oxford: Oxford University Press, 2011).

6. Marx, *Capital*, 1:899.

7. Louis Althusser, "Ideology and Ideological State Apparatuses (Notes Towards an Investigation)," in *Lenin and Philosophy*, trans. Ben Brewster (New York: Monthly Review Press, 1971), 181.

8. For earlier accounts of dispossession as ongoing rather than originary, see the work of Peter Kropotkin, Rosa Luxemburg, and W. E. B. Du Bois in the nineteenth and early twentieth centuries, and dependency theory, world-system theory, South Asian and Latin American subaltern studies, Eric Williams, Cedric Robinson, David Harvey, and Glen Coulthard, among many others, in the twentieth and twenty-first centuries. This is a point many think Marx himself made repeatedly if unsystematically in part 8 of *Capital*, vol. 1, as well as in the *Grundrisse*, the *Ethnographic Notebooks*, and his famous letter to Nikolay Mikhaylovsky from 1877. See Robert Nichols, "Indigeneity and the Settler Contract Today," *Philosophy and Social Criticism* 39, no. 2 (2013): 165–86; Nichols, "Disaggregating Primitive Accumulation," *Radical Philosophy* 194 (November-December 2015): 18–28.

9. Nichols, "Disaggregating Primitive Accumulation," 20. The "theft" framework was popularized by Pierre-Joseph Proudhon's slogan "property is theft," from his *What is Property?* (Cambridge: Cambridge University Press, 1994). Proudhon may himself have drawn on earlier, eighteenth-century iterations of that claim, such as Jacques Pierre Brissot de Warville's *Philosophical Inquiries on the Right of Property* (*Recherches philosophiques sur le droit de propriété*) (Paris: Editions d/Histoire Sociale, 1780; Milan: Galli Thierry, 1966) and Marquis de Sade's *Juliette*, trans. Austryn Wainhouse (New York: Grove, 1968). See Frederick A. de Luna, "The Dean Street Style of Revolution: J.-P. Brissot, Jeune Philosophe," *French Historical Studies* 17, no. 1 (Spring 1991): 159–90. Even as he at times reproduces the "property is theft" formulation, Marx also critiqued Proudhon's foundationalist presupposition: "The upshot is at best that the bourgeois legal conceptions of '*theft*' apply equally well to the '*honest*' gains of the bourgeois himself. On the other hand, since '*theft*' as a forcible violation of property *presupposes the existence of property*, Proudhon entangled himself in all sorts of fantasies, obscure even to himself, about *true bourgeois property*." Marx, "On Proudhon," Letter to J. B. Schweizer, *Der Social-Demokrat* 16 (February 1, 1865), in www .marxists.org/archive/marx/works/1865/letters/65_01_24.htm as well as Karl Marx, *The Poverty of Philosophy* (New York: Prometheus, 1995), 195–96.

10. Marx, *Capital*, 1:873.

11. John Locke, *Two Treatises of Government* (Cambridge: Cambridge University Press, 1988), 142, 149, 268.

12. Locke, 168.

13. Locke, 278–85.

14. Locke, 284.

15. Locke, 286–88.

16. It is important to note that Locke himself participated in enslavement and land dispossession as an investor in the Royal African Company, as well as a member of the Council of Trade and Plantations and also the Board of Trade, both of which oversaw the American colonies.

17. Locke, *Two Treatises*, 284.

18. Locke, 289.

19. Locke, 290–91.

20. Locke, 294–95.

21. MacPherson, *The Political Theory of Possessive Individualism*; Cheryl I. Harris, "Whiteness as Property," *Harvard Law Review* 106, no. 8 (June 1993): 1707–91; Aileen Moreton-Robinson, *The White Possessive: Property, Power, and Indigenous Sovereignty* (Minneapolis: University of Minnesota Press, 2015); Carole Pateman and Charles Mills, *Contract and Domination* (Cambridge: Polity, 2007).

22. For an extensive critique of this view, which unfortunately I encountered too late to incorporate adequately into this essay, see Allan Greer, *Property and Dispossession: Native Empires and Land in Early Modern North America* (Cambridge: Cambridge University Press, 2018).

23. E. P. Thompson, *Customs in Common: Studies in Traditional Popular Culture* (New York: New Press, 1993). Marx also consistently refused to idealize precapitalist collectives: "Let us now transport ourselves from Robinson's island, bathed in light [the classical political economists' idealized figure for so-called primitive accumulation], to medieval Europe, shrouded in darkness. Here, instead of the independent man, we find everyone dependent—serfs and lords, vassals and suzerains, laymen and clerics." Marx, *Capital*, 1:170.

24. See, for instance, Coulthard, *Red Skin, White Masks*; Brian DeLay, *War of a Thousand Deserts: Indian Raids and the U.S.-Mexican War* (New Haven: Yale University Press, 2009); Fortier, *Unsettling the Commons*; Greer, *Property and Dispossession*; Pekka Hämäläinen, *The Comanche Empire* (New Haven: Yale University Press, 2008); Simpson, *Mohawk Interruptus*.

25. Judith Butler, *Undoing Gender* (New York: Routledge, 2004), 19; Butler and Athena Athanasiou, *Dispossession: The Performative in the Political* (Cambridge: Polity, 2013), 4–5.

26. Cedric Robinson, *Black Marxism: The Making of the Black Radical Tradition* (London: Zed, 1983). See also Gaye Theresa Johnson and Alex Lubin, eds., *Futures of Black Radicalism* (New York: Verso, 2017); Fred Moten, "Knowledge of Freedom," *CR: The New Centennial Review* 4, no. 2 (2004): 269–310.

27. For critiques of recovery as a historiographic aim, see, for example, Giorgio Agamben, *Remnants of Auschwitz: The Witness and the Archive* (New York: Zone, 1999); Saidiya Hartman, *Scenes of Subjection: Terror, Slavery, and Self-Making in Nineteenth-Century America* (Oxford: Oxford University Press, 1997); Marc Nichanian, *The Historiographic Perversion*, trans. Gil Anidjar (New York: Columbia University Press, 2009); Laura Helton, Justin Leroy, Max A. Mishler, Samantha Seeley, and Shauna Sweeney, eds., "The Question of Recovery: Slavery, Freedom, and the Archive," special issue of *Social Text* 33, no. 4 (December 2015); Brian Connolly and Marisa Fuentes, eds., "From the Archives of Slavery to Liberated Futures?," special issue of *Journal of the History of the Present* 6, no. 2 (2016).

28. David Kazanjian, *The Brink of Freedom: Improvising Life in the Nineteenth-Century Atlantic World* (Durham: Duke University Press, 2016); Kazanjian, "Freedom's Surprise: Two Paths Through Slavery's Archives," *History of the Present: A Journal of Critical History* 6, no. 2 (Fall 2016): 133–45; Kazanjian, "Scenes of Speculation," *Social Text* 125 33, no. 4 (December 2015): 77–83.

29. While such speculative readings are not strictly speaking verifiable, they build on a long tradition in anthropology of attending to the specificities of so-called local knowledges. A foundational text in this tradition is Claude Lévi-Strauss, *The Savage Mind* (Chicago: University of Chicago Press, 1966).

30. I am inspired by the calls of Gayatri Chakravorty Spivak and Saidiya Hartman to allow the hermeneutics of the social sciences (principally history) and humanities (principally literary studies) to bring each other to crisis. Saidiya Hartman, "Venus in Two Acts," *Small Axe* 26, vol. 12, no. 2 (June 2008): 1–14; Gayatri Chakravorty Spivak, *Death of a Discipline* (New York: Columbia University Press, 2003); Spivak, "Our Asias—2001: How to Be a Continentalist," in *Other Asias* (Malden, MA: Blackwell, 2008). See also Walter Johnson, "On Agency," *Journal of Social History* 37, no. 1 (Fall 2003): 113–24;

Saba Mahmood, *The Politics of Piety: The Islamic Revival and the Feminist Subject* (Princeton: Princeton University Press, 2005).

31. During this conflict, Saffin and Sewell engaged in a now famous pamphlet war over whether the enslavement of Africans was just or unjust. While this pamphlet war between prominent white colonists has long been considered one of the first debates of its kind in the British North American colonies, few have attended to the case involving Adam that was its principal precipitating cause. See Samuel Sewell, *The Selling of Joseph: A Memorial* (Boston, 1700); and John Saffin, *A Brief and Candid Answer to a Late Printed Sheet, Entituled, The Selling of Joseph* (Boston, 1701); Sewall, *Diary of Samuel Sewall, 1674–1729*, vols. 1 and 2, ed. M. Halsey Thomas (New York: Farrar, Straus and Giroux, 1973). See also Lawrence W. Towner, "The Sewall-Saffin Dialogue on Slavery," *William and Mary Quarterly*, 3rd ser., 21, no. 1 (January 1964): 40–52.

32. Richard Francis, *Judge Sewall's Apology, a Biography: The Salem Witch Trials and the Forming of An American Conscience* (New York: Harper, 2005); Goodell, "John Saffin and His Slave Adam"; Wendy Warren, *New England Bound: Slavery and Colonization in Early America* (New York: Norton, 2016).

33. "Its therefore Considered by the Court That the s^d Adam & his heirs be at peace & quiet & free with all their Chattles from the s^d John Saffin Esqr & his heirs for Ever." Records of the Superior Court of Judicature, 1700–14; Goodell, "John Saffin and His Slave Adam," 100.

34. Warren, *New England Bound*.

35. Massachusetts Archives, Suffolk Court Files [image 0827]; Goodell, "John Saffin and His Slave Adam," 88.

36. Suffolk Court Files; Goodell, "John Saffin and His Slave Adam," 101.

37. Suffolk Court Files; Goodell, "John Saffin and His Slave Adam," 96.

38. For a comprehensive challenge to the idealization of the commons in the Americas, see Greer, *Property and Dispossession*, especially 241–70.

39. See *The Public Rights in Boston Common, Being the Report of a Committee of Citizens* (Boston: Press of Rockwell and Churchill, 1877); Lawrence W. Kennedy, *Planning the City Upon a Hill: Boston Since 1630* (Amherst: University of Massachusetts Press, 1994).

40. Suffolk Files; Goodell, "John Saffin and His Slave Adam," 104.

Bibliography

Butler, Judith. *Undoing Gender*. New York: Routledge, 2004.

Butler, Judith, and Athena Athanasiou. *Dispossession: The Performative in the Political*. Cambridge: Polity, 2013.

Byrd, Jodi A., Alyosha Goldstein, Jodi Melamed, and Chandan Reddy, eds. Special Issue on Economies of Dispossession, *Social Text* 135, vol. 36, no. 2 (June 2018).

Coulthard, Glen Sean. *Red Skin, White Masks: Rejecting the Colonial Politics of Dispossession*. Minneapolis: University of Minnesota Press, 2014.

DeLay, Brian. *War of a Thousand Deserts: Indian Raids and the U.S.-Mexican War*. New Haven: Yale University Press, 2009.

Francis, Richard. *Judge Sewall's Apology, a Biography: The Salem Witch Trials and the Forming of An American Conscience*. New York: Harper, 2005.

Fuentes, Marisa J. *Dispossessed Lives: Enslaved Women, Violence, and the Archive*. Philadelphia: University of Pennsylvania Press, 2016.

Goldstein, Alyosha, and Alex Lubin, eds. "Settler Colonialism." Special Issue of *The South Atlantic Quarterly* 107, no. 4 (Fall 2008).

Goodell, Abner C. "John Saffin and His Slave Adam." *Publications of The Colonial Society of Massachusetts* (March 1893).

Hämäläinen, Pekka. *The Comanche Empire*. New Haven: Yale University Press, 2008.

Harris, Cheryl I. "Whiteness as Property." *Harvard Law Review* 106, no. 8 (June 1993): 1707–91.

Harvey, David. *The New Imperialism*. Oxford: Oxford University Press, 2003.

Locke, John. *Two Treatises of Government*. Cambridge: Cambridge University Press, 1988.

MacPherson, C. B. *The Political Theory of Possessive Individualism: Hobbes to Locke*. Oxford: Oxford University Press, 2011.

Marx, Karl. *Capital: A Critique of Political Economy*. Vol. 1. New York: Penguin, 1990.

Moreton-Robinson, Aileen. *The White Possessive: Property, Power, and Indigenous Sovereignty*. Minneapolis: University of Minnesota Press, 2015.

Nichols, Robert. "Disaggregating Primitive Accumulation." *Radical Philosophy* 194 (November-December 2015): 18–28.

———. "Indigeneity and the Settler Contract Today." *Philosophy and Social Criticism* 39, no. 2 (2013): 165–86.

Pateman, Carole, and Charles Mills. *Contract and Domination*. Cambridge, Polity, 2007.

Roybal, Karen R. *Archives of Dispossession: Recovering the Testimonios of Mexican American Herederas*. Chapel Hill: University of North Carolina Press, 2017.

Simpson, Audra. *Mohawk Interruptus: Political Life Across the Borders of Settler States*. Durham: Duke University Press, 2014.

Simpson, Audra, and Andrea Smith, eds. *Theorizing Native Studies*. Durham: Duke University Press, 2014.

Thompson, E. P. *Customs in Common: Studies in Traditional Popular Culture*. New York: New Press, 1993.

Towner, Lawrence W. "The Sewall-Saffin Dialogue on Slavery." *William and Mary Quarterly*, 3rd series, 21, no. 1 (January 1964): 40–52.

Warren, Wendy. *New England Bound: Slavery and Colonization in Early America*. New York: Norton, 2016.

CHAPTER 12

CRISIS, CRITIQUE, AND ABOLITION

ANDREW DILTS

In a series of essays in the *Boston Review*, published over the course of the year following Donald Trump's election to the presidency of the United States, the historian Robin D. G. Kelley takes stock of the crisis posed by the electoral success of Trumpism.[1] The election of Trump, Kelley notes, was not to be taken lightly. "Donald J. Trump's election," Kelley writes, "was a national trauma, an epic catastrophe that has left millions in the United States and around the world in a state of utter shock, uncertainty, deep depression, and genuine fear." But, he continues, "the outcome should not have surprised us."[2]

As a historian of African American culture and politics, Kelley has always drawn attention to how the experience and thought of Black people in the United States demonstrates how white supremacy is, as the philosopher Charles Mills puts it, "the unnamed political system that has made the modern world what it is today."[3] Kelley's analysis does not deny that reinvigorated and growing fascist movements are seizing on electoral successes, consolidating and legitimating their power. But it would be wrong, Kelley insists, to see this as a profoundly "new" crisis. "We are not facing an aberration," he writes, "an unexpected crisis in a system that is otherwise a well-oiled democracy."[4] If the crisis of Trumpism appears "new," this is less because of a radical break with US traditions of domination and oppression, but more because we are seeing a *return* to an unapologetic and open form of white supremacy as a political system. Kelley reminds us that we ought to understand this crisis as the most recent in the long series of crises faced by putatively democratic nations founded on and maintained by mass exclusion, forced labor, colonialism, and genocide. Or as Kelley put it more succinctly during a plenary lecture in the summer of 2017: "Crisis for whom? My folks have been living in crisis for years before Trump."[5]

Across these essays, Kelley reflects on how the sense of crisis felt by many in the United States found its sharpest form not merely among those on the political left, but moreover as a crisis *within* in the left. When the election outcome was quickly framed in terms of "economic anxiety" (overlooking evidence that racial resentment was a far stronger predictor of support for Trump), many on the left turned their anger toward organizers of color and left critics of establishment Democratic politics. "The response on the part of high-profile liberals and leftists," Kelley wrote shortly after Trump's inauguration, "has been to blame 'identity politics' for undermining the potential for working-class solidarity."[6] According to such an account, "people of color, queer folks, feminist-minded women, and liberal Democrats alienated the white working class, driving it into the arms of Trump."[7] This argument, as Kelley notes, "is both inept and confused":

> The movements associated with "identity liberalism" have not been obsessed with narrow group identities but with forms of oppression, exclusion, and marginalization. And these movements are not exclusionary—not Black Lives Matter, not prison abolitionists, not movements for LGBTQ, immigrant, Muslim, and reproductive rights. They are serious efforts to interrogate the sources of persistent inequality, the barriers to equal opportunity, and the structures and policies that do harm to some groups at the expense of others.[8]

It has been with disturbing frequency that those who might otherwise insist that they are "allies" to movements for Black, queer, indigenous, or gender liberation seem to be among the first to reject demands for the end to the violence of police, for the end of incarceration (in all its forms, and not only its "mass" formation), for the end of borders, capitalism, patriarchy, and settler colonialism. Such demands, the argument goes, are not only taken to be impossible, but, in the light of rising fascism, irresponsible. Even well before the 2016 US presidential election, hyperbolic forms of concern appeared from within the left, insisting that *criticism* and *critique* would result in electoral losses for the left, and that critics themselves would be responsible for things like "left-wing voter suppression."[9]

Perhaps this is not surprising: when traditionally liberal and center-left political positions appear to be under direct attack, there is a tendency to shy away from more radical political positions, and retrench around a nostalgia for welfare-liberalism, in which the norms of multiculturalism and inclusion were subsumed under the neoliberal consensus between the center-left and reactionary conservatism. And as part of this latest iteration of left-wing melancholia, there is a powerful incentive to invest in electoral politics (rather than support radical confrontations with fascists), to be "realistic" (rather than demand the impossible), and to support the reform of police or prisons (rather than abolish them). But what if the *particular* danger of this crisis is that our responses to it remain deeply *attached* to settler-colonial-hetero-patriarchal-white-supremacist institutions and practices? What if, rather than break these attachments, we rearticulate these attachments as necessary given "what is currently possible" during a crisis?

If the current crisis is a *new* crisis—rather than also a continuation of the ongoing crisis marked by the intersecting exclusions of indigenous people, Black folks, and women—then it is very much a crisis of center-left liberalism. And it is one in which radical critique is most necessary. In this essay, I argue that a mode of radical critique that is particularly suited to this moment is already available. It is a tradition of historical and critical analysis that builds (in part) on the work W. E. B. Du Bois, extended theoretically by the philosopher Angela Davis (among others), and practiced widely by social movement organizers under the name of abolitionist politics. "Abolition Democracy" is the name given by Du Bois to the short-lived period of time in the years following the Civil War in which abolishing chattel slavery included both the "negative" emancipation of Black people from bondage and the "positive" building of institutions, practices, and resources necessary for Black freedom. As invoked by twentieth-century abolitionist thinkers and organizers, it serves as one basis for the broader abolitionist movement (typically focused on prison and police abolition but operating in concert with a variety of movements for self-determination and liberation). And, as I will argue here, abolition offers a robust model of critique, especially suited to our current moment, precisely because it is an open-ended project of world-building.[10]

I carry this brief for abolitionist critique in three parts, moving from higher levels of abstraction to the concrete. First, I give a general account of abolitionist *theory*, connecting Du Bois's historical account of the "Abolition Democracy" to a dialectical theory of critique and analysis. Second, I narrow my focus to consider contemporary abolitionist *practice*, showing how abolitionist critique is always connected to specific political and social action, but in which action is better understood as an ongoing practice or organizing strategy in which positive building and negative dismantling move together. Third, I demonstrate the interconnection between abolitionist theory and practice with the case of Critical Resistance, one of the best known and oldest prison abolition organizations in the United States. It is my claim that the work and thought of Critical Resistance mobilizes rather than demobilizes people through—and not in spite of—their commitment to a ruthless critique of reformism. As such, I close by considering what this ought to mean for those of us concerned not merely for the health of "critique" in the face of fascism and liberal retrenchment, but also for those concerned for the ongoing work of liberation from the settler-colonial, white supremacist, and heteropatriarchal systems in which we continue to find ourselves.

Abolition Democracy and Critique

For we have, built into all of us, old blueprints of expectation and response, old structures of oppression, and these must be altered at the same time as we alter the living conditions which are a result of those structures.

—Audre Lorde

The imperative of abolition, its political and theoretical force, is to dismantle, build, and transform from within existing systems of oppression. It is to acknowledge given conditions as real, material, and compelling. Yet in doing so, the abolitionist imperative recognizes *how* those conditions have been given their reality, their materiality, and their force. It is a refusal to let those conditions remain fixed or naturalized, even when the project of dismantling, building, and transforming appears to be impossible. It does not allow the *current* crisis to foreclose acknowledgment of the *ongoing* crisis. Abolition is itself the work of radical negation, of an immoderate and even fanatical saying "no." It is the "no" against the current order that opens the ground for other ways of living and acting that do not rely on that current order's logic or demands.

As a *political* and *theoretical* project, abolition identifies specific institutions (such as the police or the prison) and traces out their constitutive practices and ways of thinking, marking these practices and epistemes as the *objects* to be dismantled and transformed. It names these institutions as themselves *problems* to be confronted, even when they do not *appear* as problems. Far too often, "problems" are often already presented in digestible and understandable terms, as things with which we are already familiar and which trouble us because they disrupt the normal flow of practices and events. In such a framing, problems seem obvious. Yet this seeming obviousness of what is (and what is not) a problem is itself a way to direct our thinking about them and action in response to them. To take problems as stated, or as given, is to approach problems as the domain of "policy" expertise, which typically forecloses critical analysis.[11]

The question is to trace *how* such problems can present themselves "as such." As the philosopher Sarah Tyson describes it: critique is the practice of inhabiting something in a meaningful way such that one learns where and how that thing breaks down, and *then* pursuing *that breakdown* as an object of thought and action.[12] Critique occurs when one moves beyond the normative description or evaluation of something, some event, or some practice, to include those things taken for granted in the evaluation of that thing. It is a tracing of the breakdown, as a way of discovering how a problem has come to appear as one: a genealogy of becoming a problem. And it requires an immanence (an inhabiting, a staying close) with the object of critique that is necessarily uncomfortable, disturbing, and risky. It reframes "problems" and corresponding "solutions" as the outcomes of political projects, rather than as natural kinds.

Such analysis is always already historical, and this should be no surprise, given the connections that contemporary abolitionist theory draws with its historical antecedents. In the United States, this connection is invoked as the "unfinished" or "unfulfilled" project of abolishing chattel slavery. As the ethnic studies scholar and abolitionist Dylan Rodríguez explains:

> It's both a tremendous obligation and honor to undertake the unfulfilled work of the best of our abolitionist precursors—those who did not only want the abolition of white supremacist slavery and normalized anti-Black violence, but who also recognized that the greatest promise of abolitionism was a comprehensive transformation of a civilization in which the sanctity of white civil society was defined by its capacity to define "community" and "safety" through the effectiveness of its ability to wage racial genocides. The present day work of . . . abolition has to proceed with organic recognition of its historical roots in liberation struggles against slavery, colonization, and conquest.[13]

Such a historical approach draws directly from Du Bois's account of the Abolition Democracy. In addition to Rodríguez, theorists such as Angela Davis, Robin D. G. Kelley, George Lipsitz, and Joel Olson have all pointed to Du Bois's account of Abolition Democracy to describe an open-ended project of building a world in which black liberation would be positively assured beyond the negative freedom of nineteenth-century emancipation from chattel slavery.

Du Bois introduces the term *Abolition Democracy* in *Black Reconstruction*, his materialist history of the twenty-year period following the Civil War, spanning from 1860 to 1880. The political theorist Cedric Robinson—one of the most careful analysts of historical and conceptual connections between race and capitalism—notes that in *Black Reconstruction*, Du Bois describes US chattel slavery as "a particular historical development of capitalism organizing the exploitation of the surplus value of labor of African-American works. It was a *sub-system* of world capitalism."[14] Du Bois demonstrates how the abolition of slavery had both a "negative" form (the release from bondage) and a "positive" form (the building of institutions, practices, and resources necessary for Black freedom).[15] Yet the project of positive abolition was short lived. Had the ongoing positive emancipation of Black workers continued, there would have been a radical reorganization and transformation not only of political life (including, but not limited to, meaningful political enfranchisement) but also of economic and social life.

As Robinson notes, drawing heavily on Du Bois's analysis, modern capitalism was made possible by the integration of the Black *worker* into the industrial economy through slavery and *then* remade by "the dismantling and destruction of the 'dictatorship of labor' established in the southern U.S. during the Reconstruction."[16] The failure to maintain the Abolition Democracy and its program of institution building and economic transformation for the sake of Black liberation also produced a "new capitalism and a new enslavement of labor."[17] As Robin Kelley reminds us, Du Bois's account shows us how momentary spaces of positive Black liberation across the South were dismantled, through a *consensus* between liberal and conservative whites. As the political theorist Joel Olson describes this moment in his own reading of Du Bois, the "cross-class alliance" that was forged between would-be-white workers and the capitalist classes—who sought to continue to exploit labor (southern and northern) at the expense of Black workers, "white" workers, and cross-racial solidarity between all workers—would spell the end of "positive" emancipation.[18] By 1876, whatever gains had been achieved under the period of Abolition Democracy gave way instead to what Du Bois called the "splendid failure" of emancipation.[19]

Of those who have invoked Du Bois's term, it is primarily the philosopher and prison abolitionist Angela Davis who has popularized Abolition Democracy as a *framework* for analysis. In her *Abolition Democracy: Beyond Empire, Prisons and Torture*, Davis offers an account of the post-9/11 connections between the so-called war on terror as prosecuted by (and within) the United States and the far longer histories of incarceration, detention, and bodily torture practiced by (and within) the United States. Building on her earlier studies of the racialized nature of incarceration and "criminal" punishment in the United States, Davis links the end of chattel slavery in the nineteenth century directly to the use of prisons in the postbellum era. These historical and functional connections between slavery and the US criminal punishment system have become widely known in recent years in both academic and popular circles. Popular frameworks and terms such as the "prison-industrial-complex," "mass incarceration," or "the new Jim Crow" have purchase in a variety of political spaces (even if they are often poorly articulated and misunderstood). Yet each of these terms point to how "the prison" is a location of *ongoing* crisis, of *persistent* racial and gender subordination, and also an object of necessary "reform." The question, of course, is if the prison (or any object of critique) can be "reformed" without attending to the underlying practices that produced it.

The moment when calls for "reform" of a practice or institution appear as intelligible is where the work of problem definition has *ceased* rather than begun. And this is why it is so important that Davis invokes Du Bois's notion of "Abolition Democracy" as a *framework* for understanding "the prison" not merely as a place, but as a way of thinking about broader carceral practices of torture, confinement, and racialized and gendered subjugation. She repeats Du

Bois's fundamental insight of *Black Reconstruction*—that slavery was only negatively abolished by 1865 and that "comprehensive" abolition was never realized—and reads that argument forward into two subsequent abolitionist movements in the United States: death penalty abolition and prison abolition. As Davis writes, "In order to achieve the *comprehensive* abolition of slavery—after the institution was rendered illegal and black people were released from their chains—new institutions should have been created to incorporate black people into the social order."[20] Just as the negative dismantling of chattel slavery was incomplete without corresponding institutions and practices of freedom were a productive failure, the mere ends of execution and of caging, absent the creation of new social, economic, and political institutions designed to emancipate those persons criminalized by the state, will likewise be a continuing of this failure. Davis continues:

> In thinking specifically about the abolition of prisons *using the approach of abolition democracy*, we would propose the creation of an array of social institutions that would begin to solve the social problems that set people on the track to the prison, thereby helping to render the prison obsolete. There is a direct connection with slavery: when slavery was abolished [negatively], black people were set free, but they lacked access to the material resources that would enable them to fashion new, free lives. Prisons have thrived over the last century precisely because of the absence of those resources and the persistence of some of the deep structures of slavery.[21]

For Davis, Abolition Democracy is not merely a period in US history, but also an "approach" for critical analysis. As a framework, Abolition Democracy is a dialectical understanding of how the achievement of meaningful freedom requires building new institutions in and through the abolition of old ones. By acknowledging the negative and positive aspects of abolition as an ongoing movement toward a new horizon, Davis indicates that the "how" of abolition matters a great deal. For instance, as Davis notes, if you think about death penalty abolition in isolation from prison abolition, it becomes possible to endorse an expansion of the prison as a way to "abolish" the death penalty: using life without the possibility of parole (LWOP) in place of "death." But the trading of one "death" (execution) for "life" (LWOP) is not an abolition worthy of the name, but rather a splendid failure. Not only does such an "abolition" fail to end death (it trades one mode of death for another: execution for death in prison), it also reinforces the practice of punitive confinement and the logic of the "unredeemable offender." Nevertheless, life without parole sentencing is routinely offered as a part of "abolishing" or "ending" the death penalty and as politically "pragmatic" by many anti–death penalty activists in the United States. It is here that a more radical abolition, a more thoroughgoing critique, and a vision of the ongoing project of freedom are necessary to resist the lure of mere "reform."

Abolition Democracy offers a critical *framework* of analysis, in which the analysis of one problem (the death penalty) is traced through its relation to other concrete problems, historically, genealogically, and theoretically (from the death penalty to incarceration and from incarceration to racialized criminality). Thus, it also provides a different appraisal of the situation at hand (noting that death penalty abolition cannot be achieved without keeping the horizon of prison abolition in mind). This is to embrace what the criminologist Thomas Mathiesen calls "unfinished solutions" as part of the ongoing dialectical process of abolitionist politics. Unfinished solutions are those in which an "alternative" to current practices and conditions is *never* offered as complete or definitive. As the theorist and legal scholar Allegra McLeod explains, turning to partial and unfinished solutions to existing unjust social practices thought to be "necessary" opens a space of (im)possibility, "because it is not possible to generate an alternative that is truly and utterly distinct from the status quo as our imaginations are constrained by our existing social arrangements. The unfinished alternative emerges when we refuse 'to remain silent concerning that which we cannot talk about.'"[22] McLeod's reworking of Mathiesen shows that abolition offers ways of talking about living with others that acknowledge that work as a necessarily ongoing and open-ended project. The desire for closure and finality interrupts this project as part of the violence of the state.

Figured in this way—not merely as a historical period of comprehensive abolition, but also as a framework for critical analysis of interlocking problems—Abolition Democracy names an ongoing, dialectical, and fugitive project of mutual liberation. It escapes our grasp, yes, but it does so by pointing toward a democratically conceived horizon in which, as abolitionists frequently insist, no one is disposable. It is an inherently *critical* project, refusing to point to a fixed reference point, teleological end, or finished solution. As such, Abolition Democracy operates always in relation to both the world as it *has become* and the world that is *otherwise*. Even while deeply materialist, it is also a project to expand our political imagination. It theorizes what might become possible and takes particular interest, therefore, in those things that are thought to be impossible. Abolition Democracy reveals that those practices, configurations of political life, and lives themselves taken as impossible are in fact already present, vibrant sources for collective mobilization.[23] Such a reversal of terms demonstrates the simultaneously critical and pragmatic thrust of the abolitionist imperative, as Lorde puts it in this section's epigraph: we must alter the oppressive institutions at the same time as we find ways to survive within them. Such an approach is anything but purely theoretical or abstract, even as it pushes us to think expansively and in seemingly impossible terms. Abolitionist critique and the movement for Abolition Democracy take the negativity of abolition as a motivating force for positive political, social, and interpersonal action.

Abolitionist Action

> *Abolition means, fundamentally, the returning of resources, not their revoking. Taking away police and prisons is meaningless if they are not replaced with the resources that prevent violence—housing, healthcare, mental health services, public education, nutritious food, transportation, etc. When we say "abolition," we are talking about taking back the resources that have been extracted from our communities and funneled towards their militarization. We are talking about reclaiming them, and channeling them into the options and opportunities that make our communities healthier, happier and stronger. This is the safety we seek. Police and prisons have nothing to do with it.*
>
> —Benji Hart

The "prison" and the "police" are not simply given or natural. If they appear to be, this is because they have *become* naturalized in a particular form and with an identifiable material history and thus appear to be given. And as Benji Hart notes in the epigraph, police and prisons are supported by an extensive set of resources that could be used otherwise. Often, the specific skepticism (and sometimes hostility and outright dismissal) directed toward abolitionist projects focuses on the notion that abolition will require far more resources than are currently available: abolition is figured as impossible *because* it is impractical. Marginal reform of prison conditions and police practices, it is therefore argued, is all that is possible. And the ongoing crises of police and prison legitimacy or efficiency, the logic continues, open a political opportunity for such marginal reform, restoring these "natural" institutions to their equilibria. The question of a broader redistribution of resources and power that would be implied by shuttering the jails or disbanding the police is taken off the table.

But what almost always underlies the reformist position hostile to abolition are two unstated assumptions: first, that the current state of affairs is largely just and only in need of marginal adjustment to return to "normal"; and second, that the harms of the police and prison are exceptions to their normal operation. The granting of these assumptions is *how* the naturalization of the prison and the police take place. As a radical critique, however, abolition takes on these assumptions directly in the concrete terms of safety and community health and strength. First, the current state of affairs is far from just or near some kind of equilibrium. Maintenance of the current state of affairs in fact requires constantly expanding economic, political, and affective resources. Consider, for instance, the portion of the state and local budgets that goes toward policing and prisons, expanding persistently over the last forty years. These are resources, as Hart notes, that can go elsewhere. Second, abolitionist organizing does not take the harms of the "prison" or the police as exceptions to the normal operation of the state's use of violence, or as evidence of a merely dysfunctional system. Rather, this violence is exemplary and integral to the state's genocidal, colonial, and hetero-normative project of white supremacy (itself a political project of hierarchical rule). Abolitionist organizers ask: What if the prison isn't broken at all? What if it is working exactly like it is supposed to?

Abolitionist critique thus offers a far more realistic account of the enormous costs—in lives, talent, treasure, time, and energy—of keeping things the way they currently are. Reformers, on the other hand, steeped in economistic cost-benefit analysis, often measure welfare gains and losses within the term of marginal analysis. But this approach places the current state of affairs at an imagined "zero" point against which proposals either increase or decrease social welfare in relation to that point. The effect, however, is that the status quo becomes normalized as neutral, rather than what a more realistic accounting ought to tell us: we live within a deeply stratified and massively unequal world in which a huge number of people (if not most people) must *survive* within an oppressive, dominating, and unjust society. The *starting* point of an abolitionist perspective is that the current state of affairs is in fact *intolerable* and must be dismantled, rebuilt, and transformed in order to help communities survive and flourish. It is, in this sense, already in the tradition of nonideal theory, material rather than abstract, historical rather than counterfactual.

While "abolition" (as a theoretical framework and object of analysis) has found a marginal home in the academy, its primary location is practical, as a framework for social and political organizing. Abolition functions *as an approach to organizing* as much as a goal to be realized by abolitionists. Many abolitionist organizations in the United States organize around specific issues or public services besides the police and prisons and do so in an abolitionist manner. As the prison abolitionist Rose Braz puts it: "Abolition defines both the end goal we week and the way we do our work today. Abolition means a world where we do not use prisons, policing, and the larger system of the prison industrial complex as an 'answer' to what are social, political, and economics problems. Abolition is not just an end goal but a strategy today."[24]

This is what Allegra McLeod identifies as the "abolitionist ethic." As McLeod puts it, the abolitionist ethic is a "moral orientation . . . committed to ending the practice of confining people in cages and eliminating the control of human beings through imminently threatened police use of violent force."[25] This ethic can be deployed in nearly any political movement as a principle of agreement among members of how to pursue their aims.

Abolitionist organizing under such an ethic recognizes that "the prison" (as both an abstract form and a very real and material place of confinement and suffering) and "the police" have become deeply integrated into social and political projects that *ought* to be antithetical to them. This can be seen immediately in the rise of carceral "solutions" to problems such as drug abuse, sexual and gender-based violence, reproductive health, homelessness, or mental health. Movement organizations have thus rightly taken up an abolitionist ethic to reject the use of state violence as providing such solutions. For instance, organizations like the Black Youth Project 100 (BYP100), the Sylvia Rivera Law Project (SRLP), Survived and Punished, generationFIVE, and Southerners on a New Ground (SONG) all function as abolitionist movement organizations (in that they seek prison and police abolition as well as organizing in an abolitionist way, building coalitions without relying on the violence of the state), but at the same time, they do specific service work and mobilization that may not appear to be directly about prisons or the police.

For example, the BYP100, an outgrowth of the Black Youth Project at the University of Chicago (a long-term research project founded by Cathy Cohen) describes itself as a "member-based organization of Black youth activists creating justice and freedom for all Black people." Founded in 2013 in the immediate aftermath of the acquittal of George Zimmerman for the killing of Trayvon Martin, the BYP100 works across a broad set of policy items, organized (most recently) around a model of divestment/investment. They call for the mass (and immediate) divestment from institutions and practices that reduce the life chances of Black youth (and all Black people) and a corresponding reinvestment in "Black futures." Addressing the violence of policing (especially in Chicago, following the murder of Laquan McDonald by Officer Jason Van Dyke of the Chicago Police Department in 2014), the BYP100 organized a campaign to defund police departments across the nation and redirect those funds into housing, education, jobs, and healthcare for Black people. They expressly identify themselves as abolitionists, writing: "As an abolitionist organization that seeks to dismantle current systems of policing, incarceration, and punishment, BYP100 has always been committed to directly confronting police power."[26] What is telling—beyond the organization's incredible success in changing policy conversations, forcing politicians out of office (including both a district attorney and possibly the mayor of Chicago), and redirecting the goals of Black politics (especially in Chicago)—is the way in which the organization understands abolitionist politics as part and parcel with their wider project of building Black futures and collective liberation for all people.[27]

While one may have to search for the express language of "abolition" in the self-descriptions of organizations like those noted earlier, they are exemplary (rather than exceptional) abolitionist critics of the status quo in the work that they take up. This is because the *action* of abolitionist critique (as perhaps distinct but inseparable from abolitionist *ethics*) focuses on the institutions of the police and prisons, but never in insolation from other social and political spaces. Following the broader framework of Abolition Democracy, in which institutions and practices are always understood as produced by a material history of struggle, abolitionist critique focuses on questioning and confronting the conditions of possibility of the police and prisons. Contrary to reformist positions that presume that the crises of police violence or mass incarceration are the products of only the current conditions (and thus reformable), abolitionist critique reads the prison and police as both produced by *and reproducing* the historically determined conditions. Thus, positive building and negative dismantling always move together within abolitionist critique. And an abolitionist political agenda seeks to build the world in which prisons and police would be rendered *impossible* because the functions they serve would be made *obsolete* (as Angela Davis puts it). It seeks to build the world in which the state's use of violence is not granted the status of a "solution" to a problem but rather is understood as a problem itself.

Abolitionist movement organizations thus do not limit themselves to narrow understandings of the police or prisons as institutions in isolation from broadly social and political organization. Rather, they may *appear* to not be *primarily* focused on prison and police abolition and to not incorporate abolitionist principles into their practice. Yet, by virtue of being an essentially open-ended political project (directed toward horizons rather than static ends), these organizations practice abolition as *critical* in form and practice. Surveying what abolitionists *do*, Dan Berger, Mariame Kaba, and David Stein write: "Abolitionists have worked to end solitary confinement and the death penalty, stop the construction of new prisons, eradicate cash bail, organized to free people from prison, opposed the expansion of punishment through hate crime laws and surveillance, pushed for universal health care, and developed alternative modes of conflict resolution that do not rely on the criminal punishment system."[28]

That is to say, perhaps the most important way that an abolitionist critical framework connects the practical and theoretical is in its practices of mobilization.

Critical Resistance

No matter what your approach or political leanings, one thing should stand out: if we're imagining that a world without prisons is going to look like the world we live in now, we aren't really imagining abolition.

—The Critical Resistance Abolitionist Toolkit

Abolitionist critique is both a powerful mode of critical analysis and a mobilizer of political action. It is especially suited to this moment of punctuated crisis within an ongoing crisis. While some of the organizations discussed earlier articulate their abolitionist critique implicitly through a shared background commitment (to abolish the prison or the police) and through methods of organizing that refuse to enlist the help of the state, some important abolitionist organizations explicitly identify their *primary* goal as the abolition of the prison itself and organize expressly around that project. One of the best known of these organizations is Critical Resistance (CR).

Founded in 1997 as a nonhierarchical collective dedicated to the abolition of the Prison Industrial Complex (the PIC), Critical Resistance is one of the most important abolitionist organizations in the United States. Based out of their national office in Oakland (and with regional chapters in Los Angeles, New York, and Portland), Critical Resistance has an open membership structure, a professional organizing staff, and an advisory board that includes activists, organizers, and scholars. They work on a wide variety of specific projects, including open meetings focused on political education, letter-writing campaigns, publishing a newspaper with incarcerated members called the *Abolitionist*, producing books and videos for organizing use, supporting other abolitionist campaigns with direct material resources, and organizing national conferences. Ari Wohlfeiler (an early member of Critical Resistance) summarizes the breadth of this work and its central organizing point: "We've worked to meet the PIC at every point: anti-expansion work, reading groups, legal services, parties, radio shows, copwatching, lobbying, political education, publishing, grassroots fundraising, bodywork and healing projects, letter writing with prisoners, housing and environmental justice organizing."[29]

Critical Resistance's mission statement is instructive in both its form and its content. It is a straightforward declaration of their opposition to the prison industrial complex as well as the deeper underlying beliefs, practices, and mentalities that support prisons and all forms of "caging":

> Critical Resistance seeks to build an international movement to end the Prison Industrial Complex [PIC] by challenging the belief that caging and controlling people makes us safe. We believe that basic necessities such as food, shelter, and freedom are what really make our communities secure. As such, our work is part of global struggles against inequality and powerlessness. The success of the movement requires that it reflect communities most affected by the PIC. Because we seek to abolish the PIC, we cannot support any work that extends its life or scope.

First, CR identifies itself as focused on building a movement, to which policy change is subordinate. The work is immediately practical organizing work, directed toward its stated goal: to end the Prison Industrial Complex. And this goal—abolishing the PIC—is defined in specifically critical terms: challenging widespread ideological beliefs that a set of particular practices (caging and controlling people) produces a desired outcome (safety). CR thus offers an alternative definition of how safety is produced (through the provision of food, shelter, and freedom, all defined as *basic* necessities). The unstated implication of this redefinition rests on the material claim that many communities lack these basic necessities, specifically those whose inequality and powerlessness are produced by the functioning of the PIC. At each level of this statement, then, CR engages in a kind of ideology critique, operating not merely on the level of policy or legal change, but also at the level of beliefs and ideological attachments that support those policies and laws. Most importantly, the mission lays out two guiding organizing principles: (1) that "success" will be measured from the point of view of the most affected communities (i.e., that the criteria for what counts as a win will not be offered by those who benefit from the PIC), and (2) that any policy, project, or proposal that CR will support will be empirically tested against supporting the "life or scope" of the PIC.

Even in this brief statement, the hallmarks of critique (beginning in material rather than abstract considerations, as normatively situated reflection, and based in the needs of those most effected by a concrete political problem) are apparent. The relatively abstract terms of analysis are grounded in an awareness of the material (and global) conditions of inequality and powerlessness, in the lack of basic necessities (which include *freedom* as a fundamental human need), and in the straightforward redefinition of the dominant terms of analysis (safety) and a stated understanding that the PIC reflects a broader set of concerns that are global in nature (and, we can infer, that are historical as well, in that they see the PIC as a particular manifestation of a much longer history and larger set of political crises of domination and subjugation). Moreover, it follows Tyson's definition of critique offered earlier: CR looks to the apparent breakdown of the PIC, marked as a dysfunctional or "failed" institution: it is taken as a starting point, but then takes up that breakdown itself as a question, asking not how the institution has "failed" but rather how its constitutive terms (safety, harm, freedom, and the like) underlie how we define failure.

Critical Resistance is perhaps best known for a joint statement in 2001 published with INCITE! Women of Color Against Violence.[30] INCITE!, a national organization which has a similar organizing model as CR, works to end violence against women of color through grassroots direct action. Their joint statement, *Gender Violence and the Prison-Industrial Complex*, has become canonical in critical carceral studies, gender studies, and critical race theory, and is a widely cited document that is both an artifact of the two organizations' practice and an ongoing organizing tool. It is important to emphasize here that a clean distinction between "texts" and "action" is difficult to sustain. CR and

INCITE! both engage in a wide variety of organizing practices, just one of which is the production of reflective texts. I turn to such texts here because they track—both in their production as collaboratively produced statements and in their rhetorical form—the blurring between theory and practice that I take to be essential to abolitionist critique (and critique more generally).

Written collectively by (primarily) women of color members of both organizations in 2001, the joint statement is a mutual "holding to account" of the two movements for their shared organizing failings. On the one hand the anti-prison movement had largely failed to take seriously the question of gender-based violence against women as central to its mission, and on the other hand, the movement to end sexual and gender-based violence against women had far too often relied on the violence of the state in ways that diminished rather than promoted the safety of marginalized people, women of color in particular. As the statement puts it: "We call social justice movements to develop strategies and analysis that address both state *and* interpersonal violence against women. Currently, activists/movements that address state violence (such as anti-prison, anti-police brutality groups) often work in isolation from activists/movements that address domestic and sexual violence" (21). Structured through a series of shared points of analysis, the joint statement thus operates both as a critical diagnosis of the contradictions between two radical movements and as itself a performance of solidarity between the two movements, collectively affirming their shared mission of creating meaningful safety for all people.

The statement itself moves through three sections. First, it takes on the anti-violence movement, noting five specific ways that movement's reliance on the state's use of violence (i.e., a reliance on law enforcement, criminalization, prisons, state-funding, and the criminal justice system) has diminished the safety of women (especially women of color) rather than supported it. In its second section, the statement takes on the mainstream antiprison movement, again noting five specific ways that movement has failed to account for the lives and experiences of those most vulnerable to sexual and gender-based violence in its work (i.e., by rendering women invisible in their analyses, by not addressing everyday forms of harassment and sexual violence faced by women, by failing to attend to LGBTTI exposure to violence, by sidelining concerns about serial murder and rape, and by relying on "romanticized" notions of community in response to real concerns about safety held by survivors of sexual and domestic violence). These pointed and direct criticisms are then followed in the final section with eleven concrete steps for movement actors to take to address these contradictions between the two movements. The authors close with a statement of their goal: "We seek to build movements that not only end violence, but that create a society based on radical freedom, mutual accountability, and passionate reciprocity. In this society, safety and security will not be premised on violence or the threat of violence; it will be based on a collective commitment to guaranteeing the survival and care of all peoples" (25). The structure of the statement itself models a self-reflective and critical appraisal of organizing work, using opposing perspectives between the two movements' failings as a new ground for listening and responding to each other. From this confrontation, a new coalition emerges for future organizing.

Reprinted in 2008 as part of CR's *Abolition Now: Ten Years of Strategy and Struggle Against the Prison Industrial Complex*, the statement is introduced with a genealogical account of its production, a brief statement of its reception and follow-up, and a series of open-ended questions through which to frame (re)readings in years to come. As the editors of the volume note, the original statement's concrete steps and its open-ended call for action made it a powerful organizing tool. They write that these steps could allow "each movement . . . to transform the contradictory position between movements into a position of a *critically integrated politic*" (16). Rather than merely countering the shortcomings and failings of each movement, the work of the joint statement would be to *overcome* those contradictions in a way that produces a *new* political body. While circulated in advance of the conference in 2008, the inclusion of a series of concrete questions to guide discussion continues to serve this dialectical purpose even in the reprinting.

The use of such discussion questions is a hallmark of Critical Resistance's (and INCITE!'s) approach to prison abolition, gender justice, and organizing for mutual liberation. Questions motivate both theoretical analysis and collective action. What might appear as merely a rhetorical presentational choice is itself part of the ongoing work of digging deeper, asking further critical questions, and engaging in an openly dialectical approach as part of the organizing work. As they self-reflectively note, "Radical social movements that we are building together are being challenged and pushed to incorporate critical and potentially movement-altering agendas and practices. Perhaps at the next tenyear anniversary, we will celebrate the ways in which these rich and transformative cross-movement collaborations have created unique and productive pathways towards liberation for us all" (21). Rather than bemoan the difficulty of strong critique from within its membership, the CR/INCITE! statement (in its multiple iterations) *celebrates* these challenges. This is because they believe that the organizing work of liberation emerges from within critical responses to their own shortcomings and contradictions between movements.

In addition to the questions that frame the reprinted CR/INCITE! statement, the *Critical Resistance Abolitionist Toolkit*—a freely available online PDF running over a hundred pages in length, designed expressly to facilitate understanding of the concept of prison abolition in order to organize individuals to take concrete action against the PIC—offers theoretical analyses in concert with questions intended to prompt conversations either between real people attending an abolitionist meeting or with oneself as an isolated reader. The questions are pedagogical (helping to clarify concepts and definitions), substantive (forcing readers to confront their own assumptions, attachments, and beliefs), and practical (demanding concrete proposals for action, such as what one can do instead of calling the police during emergencies). Such questions, interspersed throughout accessible theoretical discussions, show how critical thinking takes place in dialog with others. And in that dialog, accountability and solidarity between people are directly built.

It is thus a hallmark of Critical Resistance's approach that it brings together both ruthless critique and mobilization. This pattern is discernable throughout their work. First, through deep connections to incarcerated people near local chapters or through their nationally circulated newspaper, the *Abolitionist*, CR organizes actions in direct support of incarcerated people. Theoretical and empirical analysis follows, framed and articulated through questioning specific policy proposals and strategies. The guiding principles of the mission direct their work—no strategies or proposals which extend the life or scope of the PIC are acceptable, and priority is given to the self-determination of those most affected by the PIC, namely, incarcerated people and their loved ones. The most important question—does this policy or project extend the life or scope of the PIC?—is asked persistently. As one CR organizer explained to me, this question is often phrased. "What happens if we win? Will we be fighting against what we asked for ten years from now?" And lastly, a confrontation with the extended reach of the PIC is organized and the process begins again. Because CR understands abolition both as a goal to be achieved (a world without prisons and police) and as a way of organizing, it produces the world that it seeks to build.

* * *

Which isn't to say liberals can't eventually come around to radical concepts like abolition. I was a liberal once. But it is to say that radicalism is an exorcism of liberalism, not an evolution of it.

—Hari Ziyad

I've tried to show throughout this essay—moving from the question of the crisis, to the framework of Abolition Democracy in general, to the case of prison and police abolition in particular, grounded and reflected in a particular set of texts by an abolitionist organization—that we already possess resources necessary to counter the critique of critique and the current crisis of left-liberalism. It may be a practice of organizing that is unfamiliar to those of us who have not taken part in collaborative work, have not thought beyond legislative policy or the ballot box, and whose imaginations of mass mobilization still reflect nostalgic memories of what direct action looked like before the rise of mass incarceration. And at this moment in particular, when we might rightly feel the need to abandon a ruthless critique of everything existing and when demands are issued to unify the "left" around liberal principles that leave systems of domination and oppression intact, we ought to resist that feeling and that demand. Now is the time to (re)commit to a radical stance and to an immoderate negation of those unjust institutions whose presence feels so natural that to oppose them seems impossible. And moreover, abolitionist politics as critique offers a powerful resource in this moment: it is a way of organizing and mobilizing people. It is a framework *and* practice of critical thinking and engagement with the world, analyzing, appraising, and confronting concrete political problems faced by marginalized and oppressed people. And it has been well known for generations. Far from leading us into a dead end of political paralysis, abolition as it has been theorized by its practitioners brings together critique and mobilization by democratizing both.

It is worth returning to the *democratic* force of the historic Abolition Democracy. Even limited as it was (especially by gender and disability), the period of Abolition Democracy documented by Du Bois was radical because it moved the polity toward a truer, deeper, and more meaningful democratic practice. More than mere inclusion of formerly enslaved people into the polity on given terms, it was necessarily a reconfiguration of those terms itself. It was a period in which the emancipation of black workers entailed political and economic enfranchisement and a rejection of domination in all its forms. It was a period of self-rule, the sort of which has rarely been seen in the history the enlightenment. This is because the promise and force of Abolition Democracy were in the work of building it, not in spite of its being *impossible, impractical*, and *excessively critical*, but *because* it was.

Abolitionist critique teaches us that the work of prison and political abolition, while surely directed toward the horizon of a world without prisons or police, *is in the building* of communities of safety, mutual accountability, and shared liberation. It is in the democratic building of democracy. Even as there is a goal in mind, the pursuit of that goal on abolitionist terms is also disruptive of the very terms of political success. It is, in this sense, an insurgency from within. Because abolitionist critique is a form of concrete political action, organizing people to confront concrete political problems as the work of politics, it is the work of negative and positive transformation.

Abolitionist critique offers us an alternative to the seduction of retrenched liberalism and reformism, especially when the temptation of retrenchment is heightened by the crises of the particular moment. But precisely in such moments, immoderate and insurgent political action is more necessary than ever. And while we may worry that radical critique asks too much or risks demoralizing political agents, the tradition of abolitionist political action and theory shows us that such worries can be addressed, and that another way has already been possible. Because abolitionist critique demands that we directly confront and challenge white supremacy, hetero-patriarchy, and contemporary fascism, it both acknowledges the ongoing crisis and is a bulwark against the crisis at hand. It is the transformation of the current world through the building of a new world.

Notes

1. Kelley, "Trump Says Go Back, We Say Fight Back," *Boston Review*, November 15, 2016, https://bostonreview.net/forum/after-trump/robin-d-g-kelley-trump-says-go-back-we-say-fight-back; Kelley, "Births of a Nation," *Boston Review*, March 6, 2017, https://bostonreview.net/race-politics/robin-d-g-kelley-births-nation; Kelley, "One Year Later," *Boston Review*, November 8, 2017, https://bostonreview.net/race-politics/robin-d-g-kelley-one-year-later.
2. Kelley, "Trump Says Go Back, We Say Fight Back."
3. Charles W. Mills, *The Racial Contract* (Ithaca: Cornell University Press, 1997), 1.
4. Kelley, "One Year Later."
5. Kelley, "Trumpism and the Crisis of the Left."
6. Kelley, "Births of a Nation."
7. Kelley.
8. Kelley.
9. This particular accusation comes from a widely circulated article by Rebecca Solnit from 2012, in which she argues that criticism within the left itself is a source of political demobilization. Rebecca Solnit, "Rain on Our Parade: A Letter to the Dismal Left," *Common Dreams*, September 27, 2012, www.commondreams.org/views/2012/09/27/rain-our-parade-letter-dismal-left.
10. I am hardly the first person to make direct connections between abolitionist politics and the traditions of critical theory and critique. For just a set of sources that make this connection explicit see Che Gossett, "Abolitionist Imaginings: A Conversation with Bo Brown, Reina Gossett, and Dylan Rodríguez," in *Captive Genders: Trans Embodiment and the Prison Industrial Complex*, ed. Eric A. Stanley and Nat Smith, 323–42 (Oakland, CA: AK, 2011); Liat Ben-Moshe, Che Gossett, Nick Mitchell, and Eric A. Stanley, "Critical Theory, Queer Resistance, and the Ends of Capture," in *Death and Other Penalties: Philosophy in a Time of Mass Incarceration*, ed. Geoffrey Adelsberg, Lisa Guenther, and Scott Zeman, 266–95 (New York: Fordham University Press, 2015).
11. See F. Moten and S. Harney, "Policy and Planning," *Social Text* 27, no. 3 (September 1, 2009): 182–87, 183.
12. Personal correspondence, June 1, 2018.
13. Liz Samuels and David Stein, eds., "Perspectives on Critical Resistance," in *Abolition Now!: Ten Years of Strategy and Struggle Against the Prison Industrial Complex*, 1–14 (Oakland, CA: AK, 2008), 8.
14. Cedric Robinson, "A Critique of W. E. B. Du Bois' Black Reconstruction," *Black Scholar* 8, no. 7 (May 1977): 44–50, 45, https://doi.org/10.1080/00064246.1977.11413913.

15. On Du Bois's distinction between "positive" and "negative" abolitionists in the nineteenth century, see Jasmine Noelle Yarish, "#IfIDieInPoliceCustody: Neo-Abolitionism, New Social Media, and Queering the Politics of Respectability," *National Political Science Review* 19, no. 2 (2018).

16. Robinson, "A Critique of W.E.B. Du Bois' Black Reconstruction," 46.

17. W. E. B. Du Bois, *Black Reconstruction in America: Toward a History of the Part of Which Black Folk Played in the Attempt to Reconstruct Democracy in America, 1860–1880* (New Brunswick, NJ: Transaction, 2012), 566; Robinson, "A Critique of W. E. B. Du Bois' Black Reconstruction," 46.

18. Joel Olson, *The Abolition of White Democracy* (Minneapolis: University of Minnesota Press, 2004).

19. Du Bois, *Black Reconstruction in America*, 633.

20. Angela Davis, *Abolition Democracy: Beyond Empire, Prisons, and Torture* (New York: Seven Stories, 2005), 95.

21. Davis, 96–97, emphasis added.

22. Allegra M. McLeod, "Confronting Criminal Law's Violence: The Possibilities of Unfinished Alternatives," *Harvard Unbound* 8 (2013): 109–32, 121, citing Mathesien.

23. For instance, consider the rhetoric and action of queer and trans prison abolitionists, such as Reina Gossett and Dean Spade, who have recently argued for an embrace of the impossible and building a movement of nobodies (rather than accept the neoliberal framing that everybody is somebody). Reina Gossett, "Commencement Address at Hampshire College," *Reina Gossett* (blog), May 17, 2016, www.reinagossett.com/commencement-address-hampshire-college/; Sarah Lazare, "Now Is the Time for 'Nobodies': Dean Spade on Mutual Aid and Resistance in the Trump Era," *AlterNet*, January 9, 2017, www.alternet.org/activism/now-time-nobodies-dean-spade-mutual-aid-and-resistance-trump-era.

24. Samuels and Stein, "Perspectives on Critical Resistance," 11.

25. McLeod, "Prison Abolition and Grounded Justice," *UCLA Law Review* 62 (2015): 1156–239, 1161–62.

26. BYP100, "Our Impact," BYP100, https://byp100.org/our-impact-2/.

27. For an excellent account of the formation of the BYP100 and its abolitionist grounding, see Barbara Ransby, *Making All Black Lives Matter: Reimagining Freedom in the Twenty-First Century* (Oakland: University of California Press, 2018).

28. Dan Berger, Mariame Kaba, and David Stein, "What Abolitionists Do," *Jacobin*, August 24, 2017, http://jacobinmag.com/2017/08/prison-abolition-reform-mass-incarceration.

29. Samuels and Stein, "Perspectives on Critical Resistance," 5.

30. INCITE! Women of Color Against Violence and Critical Resistance, "The Critical Resistance INCITE! Statement on Gender Violence and the Prison Industrial Complex," in *Abolition Now!: Ten Years of Strategy and Struggle Against the Prison Industrial Complex*, by the CR10 Publications Collective, 15–29. Oakland, CA: AK, 2008. Hereafter cited parenthetically in the text.

Bibliography

Ben-Moshe, Liat, Che Gossett, Nick Mitchell, and Eric A. Stanley. "Critical Theory, Queer Resistance, and the Ends of Capture." In *Death and Other Penalties: Philosophy in a Time of Mass Incarceration*, edited by Geoffrey Adelsberg, Lisa Guenther, and Scott Zeman, 266–95. New York: Fordham University Press, 2015.

Berger, Dan, Mariame Kaba, and David Stein. "What Abolitionists Do." *Jacobin*, August 24, 2017, http://jacobinmag.com/2017/08/prison-abolition-reform-mass-incarceration.

BYP100. "Our Impact." BYP100, https://byp100.org/our-impact-2/.

Davis, Angela. *Abolition Democracy: Beyond Empire, Prisons, and Torture*. New York: Seven Stories, 2005.

Du Bois, W. E. B. *Black Reconstruction in America: Toward a History of the Part of Which Black Folk Played in the Attempt to Reconstruct Democracy in America, 1860–1880*. New Brunswick, NJ: Transaction, 2012.

Gossett, Che. "Abolitionist Imaginings: A Conversation with Bo Brown, Reina Gossett, and Dylan Rodríguez." In *Captive Genders: Trans Embodiment and the Prison Industrial Complex*, edited by Eric A. Stanley and Nat Smith, 323–42. Oakland, CA: AK, 2011.

Gossett, Reina. "Commencement Address at Hampshire College." *Reina Gossett* (blog), May 17, 2016, www.reinagossett.com/commencement-address-hampshire-college/.

Hart, Benji. "To Fight for Black Lives Is to Be Anti-Police." *Radical Faggot* (blog), July 21, 2016, https://radfag.com/2016/07/21/to-fight-for-black-lives-is-to-be-anti-police/.

INCITE! Women of Color Against Violence and Critical Resistance. "The Critical Resistance INCITE! Statement on Gender Violence and the Prison Industrial Complex." In *Abolition Now! Ten Years of Strategy and Struggle Against the Prison Industrial Complex*, by the CR10 Publications Collective, 15–29. Oakland, CA: AK, 2008.

Kelley, Robin D. G. "Births of a Nation," *Boston Review*, March 6, 2017, https://bostonreview.net/race-politics/robin-d-g-kelley-births-nation.

——. "One Year Later," *Boston Review*, November 8, 2017, https://bostonreview.net/race-politics/robin-d-g-kelley-one-year-later.

——. "Trumpism and the Crisis of the Left." Plenary presented at the American Political Science Association Annual Meeting, San Francisco, CA, September 1, 2017.

——. "Trump Says Go Back, We Say Fight Back." *Boston Review*, November 15, 2016, https://bostonreview.net/forum/after-trump/robin-d-g-kelley-trump-says-go-back-we-say-fight-back.

Lazare, Sarah. "Now Is the Time for 'Nobodies': Dean Spade on Mutual Aid and Resistance in the Trump Era." *AlterNet*, January 9, 2017, www.alternet.org/activism/now-time-nobodies-dean-spade-mutual-aid-and-resistance-trump-era.

Lorde, Audre. "Age, Race, Class, and Sex: Women Redefining Difference." In *Zami; Sister Outsider; Undersong*, 114–23. New York: Quality Paperback Book Club, 1993.

McLeod, Allegra M. "Confronting Criminal Law's Violence: The Possibilities of Unfinished Alternatives." *Harvard Unbound* 8 (2013): 109–32.

——. "Prison Abolition and Grounded Justice." *UCLA Law Review* 62 (2015): 1156–239.

Mills, Charles W. *The Racial Contract*. Ithaca: Cornell University Press, 1997.

Moten, F., and S. Harney. "Policy and Planning." *Social Text* 27, no. 3 (September 1, 2009): 182–87.

Olson, Joel. *The Abolition of White Democracy*. Minneapolis: University of Minnesota Press, 2004.

Ransby, Barbara. *Making All Black Lives Matter: Reimagining Freedom in the Twenty-First Century*. Oakland, CA: University of California Press, 2018.

Robinson, Cedric. "A Critique of W. E. B. Du Bois' Black Reconstruction." *Black Scholar* 8, no. 7 (May 1977): 44–50, https://doi.org/10.1080/00064246.1977.11413913.

Samuels, Liz, and David Stein, eds. "Perspectives on Critical Resistance." In *Abolition Now! Ten Years of Strategy and Struggle Against the Prison Industrial Complex*, 1–14. Oakland, CA: AK, 2008.

Solnit, Rebecca. "Rain on Our Parade: A Letter to the Dismal Left." *Common Dreams*, September 27, 2012, www.commondreams.org/views/2012/09/27/rain-our-parade-letter-dismal-left.

Yarish, Jasmine Noelle. "#IfIDieInPoliceCustody: Neo-Abolitionism, New Social Media, and Queering the Politics of Respectability." *National Political Science Review* 19, no. 2 (2018).

Ziyad, Hari. "What I Was Trying to Get at Is That All of The . . ." Facebook, October 12, 2017, www.facebook.com/hziyad/posts/10155848345136934.

CHAPTER 13

LAW, CRITIQUE, AND
THE UNDERCOMMONS

ALLEGRA M. MCLEOD

*If the designing of the future and the proclamation of ready-made solu-
tions for all time is not our affair, then we realize all the more clearly what
we have to accomplish in the present—I am speaking of a ruthless criticism of everything existing, ruthless in two senses: The criticism must not
be afraid of its own conclusions, nor of conflict with the powers that be.*

—Karl Marx

T he law calls out for critique—for a ruthless criticism of law's complicity in racialized inequality, poverty, environmental devastation, and violence. But critique—"unafraid of its own conclusions" or of "conflict with the powers that be"—occupies at most a marginal
place in the American legal academy.[1] Legal scholarly critique remains largely
bound by the formal dictates of law, focused narrowly on legalistic conceptions
of the problems at hand, reluctant to undertake critical analysis without positing an immediately practicable policy solution, and reticent to engage in a bold
reimagination of what justice would actually require. As the legal scholar Pierre
Schlag writes of contemporary critical legal scholarship, with only slight over-
statement, it is "dead—totally dead. . . . more dead, vastly and exponentially
more dead, than critical legal studies was ever dead during its most dead

period."[2] The scarcity of ruthlessly critical thought in US law schools, with rare exception, not only is due to the fact that, as Schlag argues, much legal scholarship amounts to "highly elaborated, carefully crafted mediocrity," but is also a product of the homogeneity of law faculties and the more general neoliberalization and hyperprofessionalization of American universities and particularly US law schools.[3] Although the law daily constitutes and rationalizes the dispossession and caging of millions of human beings, a thorough unmasking and dissection of these practices and especially the creative imagination of alternative futures are largely absent from the scene.[4]

Yet, by focusing elsewhere, by shifting where we look for critique, new subjects and objects of critique come into view. Inside US prisons and in the movements protesting the violence of American policing, powerful critiques of law have emerged, constituting in the process new intellectual and political formations.[5] These critical movements manifest an extension of what Fred Moten and Stefano Harney have described as the "undercommons"—a "down-low, low-down maroon community" that aims for a form of critique or an "emancipatory enlightenment" at odds with the professionalization of intellectual life.[6] This essay will examine the contributions to a critique of law set in motion by these critical movements and the ways in which their creative coalitional politics enables new understandings and possibilities.

The Undercommons

In "The University and the Undercommons," Fred Moten and Stefano Harney explore how the contemporary university is at odds with emancipatory critical thought; at the same time, Moten and Harney exhort a commitment to critique and to intellectual life that exceeds the confines of the university's professionalizing demands—a form of critical collective study they associate with the "undercommons." In Moten and Harney's account, a commitment to an emancipatory project of critical study is kept alive in the undercommons by "the subversive intellectual," who "came under false pretenses, with bad documents, out of love." For Moten and Harney, it is a love for "thinking through the skin of teaching toward a collective orientation to the knowledge object as future project" that drives the subversive intellectual to the university in the first instance, in search of its refuge:

> It is teaching that brings us in. Before there are grants, research conferences, books, and journals there is the experience of being taught and of teaching. Before the research post with no teaching, before the graduate students to mark exams, before the string of sabbaticals, before the permanent reduction in

teaching load, the appointment to run the Center, the consignment of pedagogy to a discipline called education, before the course designed to be a new
book, teaching happened.[7]

Through some early experience of collective questioning, overcome, grasping
together toward provisional understanding—an experience of genuine excite-
ment for learning and being taught—the subversive intellectual turns to critique wanting more.

But all too quickly, the university disappoints, through its demands for professionalization, its individualism, its alignment with capitalist interests, its
refusal of unanswered questions. In fact, US universities, and especially American law schools, are constituted by "skyrocketing tuition prices, soaring
student debt, the hyperexploitation of precarious service workers, the proliferation of highly paid senior administrative positions, and the increased
commercialization and corporatization of higher education."[8] Law schools are
particularly beholden to the corporate sector as the schools depend on law
firm salaries and corporate largesse to fund institutional projects and service
student debts. Most law school faculty have been trained and shaped by time
spent in the nation's three or four most elite law schools and at elite corporate
law firms—institutions wedded to the status quo. Moreover, according to the
Undercommoning Collective—a "network" of critical "organizers within and
beyond the university" who draw inspiration from Moten and Harney's writings on the undercommons—US universities are at odds with emancipatory
critical thought in virtue of their complicity in "the marginalization and con-
tainment of nontraditional inquiry," "training corporate kleptocrats," "from the
white supremacist and Eurocentric knowledge ... exalt[ed] ... to ... dark collaborations with the military-industrial complex."[9]

So, Moten and Harney explain, the "critical academic questions the university, questions the state, questions art, politics, culture."[10] Moten and Harney
argue, however, that "to distance oneself professionally through critique" is ultimately a "consent to privatize the social individual." In other words, the turn to
critique as a professional project in the face of the university's professionalization and privatization is an act of "negligence"—a failure to confront the critical
academic's own implication in these dynamics. As a consequence, those who
remain committed to a project of collective, emancipatory study that exceeds
or even rejects professionalization—the denizens of the undercommons—are
"wary of critique, weary of it, and at the same time dedicated to the collectivity
of its future."[11]

What might it mean to be "dedicated to the collectivity" of the future of critique? Moten and Harney describe the slogan, popular on the left, "universities, not jails," as consisting of a certain misconception or delusion, because
rather than a simple opposition between the university and the prison, we must

understand both as "involved in their [own] way with the reduction and command of the social individual"—consequently, Moten and Harney conclude, "perhaps it is necessary finally to see that the university produces incarceration as the product of its negligence."[12] More specifically, the work of the university system in legitimating the myth of meritocracy, implicitly rationalizing the upward distribution of wealth, and professionalizing, individualizing, and privatizing the pursuit of knowledge serves to reinforce the zones of despair and precarity and the scenes of violence that fill American prisons. Therefore, Moten and Harney explain, it is this relation between the university and the prison that "the undercommons reserves as the object . . . of another abolitionism."[13] Moten and Harney end with this exhortation: that the "object of abolition" is "not so much the abolition of prisons but the abolition of a society that could have prisons, that could have slavery . . . and therefore not abolition as the elimination of anything but abolition as the founding of a new society."[14] The future of critique, then, lies in the quest for a new collectivity formed in part through critical study in the undercommons—what Moten and Harney call "Black study," drawing on a black radical tradition of critical collective inquiry.

We might understand critique in these terms as a project of focused skeptical and creative collective study of a text or context, with the goal of calling the object of critique fundamentally into question, and even beginning to transcend it. Whereas for Michel Foucault, as other contributors to this volume describe, critique entailed a certain "art of not being governed *like this*" and a project of creative self-governance, in the undercommons it is in part through critique—through a project of critical collective study—that new social forms, new forms of truly democratic collective governance, and a new society may take shape.[15]

Marx wrote of ruthless criticism in that same letter excerpted as an epigraph to this essay that "everyone will have to admit to himself that he has no exact idea of what the future ought to be." Instead, through critique "we do not dogmatically anticipate the world, but . . . want to find the new world through criticism of the old one."[16] Critique of this sort holds the potential to be a means of working toward that preliminary transcendence or transformation of the status quo by unmasking, deconstructing, laying bare, describing the world carefully in all its awful and mundane violence, and then refusing together the existing understandings of the world as it is and thereby beginning to make it anew.

According to Moten and Harney, the university serves in this project as a "place of refuge"—a place to escape or refuse other forms of complicity and alienated labor—but not itself as a place of "enlightenment." The subversive intellectual "can only sneak into the university and steal what one can." On Moten and Harney's account: "To abuse its hospitality, to spite its mission, to join its refugee colony, its gypsy encampment, to be in but not of—this is the path of the subversive intellectual in the modern university."[17]

Likewise, the work of the critical intellectual working in the legal academy today should include a certain redistribution of resources from the university toward other people, places, and movements, a shift in attention and opportunities to other sites of critical collective study. While Moten and Harney identify the denizens of the undercommons as those convening in the interstices of the university committed to collectivity and critique, a vital critique of law is being taken up, and perhaps should be understood as more clearly located outside the university in the critical work transpiring in prisons and in the resistance movements confronting the violence of American policing.

The Short Corridor Collective and Prisoner Hunger Strike Solidarity Movements

In one of the most dreaded and isolated prisons—the California Pelican Bay State Prison Security Housing Unit, composed of long-term solitary confinement cells—a group of men subjected to isolation over decades formed a reading group they termed the "Short Corridor Collective."[18] Along with other members of the Collective, Todd Ashker, Sitawa Jamaa, Arturo Castellanos, and Antonio Guillen—each deemed by the State of California to be affiliated with a different racially identified prison gang—began to read together and to critically engage the legal and political conditions of their confinement.[19] The Short Corridor Collective engaged scholarship on the Irish Prison Hunger Strikes, the work of Michel Foucault, and the legacies of Cesar Chavez and the Black Panthers.[20] Although the men could not meet face to face or even see one another from their solitary cells, they were able to organize to read the same texts and to pass notes and talk to one another about those texts and about their circumstances through the small openings in their cells created by vents and drains. Through their writings and discussions, the Collective came to articulate an analysis of the illegitimacy and injustice of their legally rationalized confinement, and ultimately its connections to a regime of racially organized brutality that unfolds not only throughout California's prisons and jails, but across the country's segregated and gentrified landscapes, composing the conditions of inequality and desperation that fuel the carceral state.[21]

Todd Ashker, in his fifties, had been incarcerated in the Pelican Bay Solitary Housing Unit (SHU) since 1984, for roughly thirty years, because prison officials identified him as a member of the Aryan Brotherhood gang. He described his conditions of confinement in these terms, reported ultimately in a petition to the United Nations filed by the Center for Human Rights and Constitutional Law:

Mr Ashker's outdoors time is in a small, concrete enclosed dog-like yard 1 ½ hours a day with no exercise equipment other than a hand-ball. . . . [H]is yard time is always cancelled due to "staff training," and from the years 1989–2011 he received zero time outside, other than when he was allowed to go . . . into a small enclosed concrete yard. He spent 24 hours a day 7 days a week in a small concrete cell. . . . Mr. Ashker's meals are under-portioned, watered down, under-cooked, food is spoiled, cold, no nutrition, salad is rotten, trays are always dirty and covered with dirty dish water.

Addressing himself in the third person in his petition but offering a description in his own words of the first-person perspective of someone subject to this treatment, Ashker's critical writings present a challenge to existing discourses on criminal punishment by positioning the incarcerated person as author and offering a vantage point "from inside," sharpened through the process of developing a collective understanding of these shared experiences. This critique of the law and practice of solitary confinement does away with formal legal distinctions characteristic of much legal analysis—Ashker focuses our attention not on what is legally cognizable but on the dog-like yard where he is brought in shackles for barely one hour each day, on the concrete that composes his world, and on his rotting food and filthy water. Ashker and other writers in the Collective illuminate the lived, felt experience of degradation entailed by such confinement in their own voices, in words deployed not primarily or exclusively to win legal redress but to challenge fundamentally and collectively the continued legitimacy and possibility of their confinement—a critical descriptive practice that Lisa Guenther refers to as a phenomenology of solitary confinement.[22] This critique renders vivid law's violence from the perspective of those brutalized by it, who are typically excluded from active participation in legal discourse altogether. The Collective confronts the law with its own viciousness by exposing its mundane and horrific details, in voices that would otherwise be absent and in terms arrived at together. The collective character of these critical practices is especially significant because it is precisely the sociality of the men in the SHU that the state has sought to vanquish by their confinement in isolation. The mere existence of the Collective's collaborative, critical writing is itself a confrontation with the powers that be. It is also significant that the Collective's writings eschew or move beyond legal categories and legalist language in collective terms, introducing new vocabularies and understandings.

As the Short Corridor Collective developed a critique of their conditions, their critical analyses also began to extend beyond the physical dimensions of their ordeals. The Collective sought to identify the legal rationalizations of their prolonged solitary confinement. They discovered that many hundreds, even thousands of men, like Ashker, were held in indefinite solitary confinement primarily or even solely because of alleged affiliations with gangs. Some of those so confined denied any such continuing affiliations, but more than that, the Collective decried the injustice of being subject to the torture of prolonged solitary on the basis of, for example, the possession of drawings believed to indicate gang affiliation or other indicia of gang membership absent any harmful conduct.

Kijana Tashiri Askari, also known as Marcus Harrison, had been locked in solitary confinement since 1994 on the grounds that he was a member of the Black Guerilla Family gang. Askari reported through later published writings how the California Department of Corrections officials' policies on gangs or "security threat groups" ultimately lacked any definitive criteria that could be subject to contestation. Thus, these many hundreds, even thousands of imprisoned human beings were subjected to indefinite solitary confinement because of alleged gang activity without any, in Askari's terms, "behavioral basis." Askari conveyed that "any and everything can and will still be considered . . . gang activity, in spite of how innocuous the activity may be."[23]

Through its critical investigation of these practices, the Collective began to reinterpret the conduct of prison administrators so that their punishments came to appear as criminal—a violation of basic human decency. In turn, the purported crimes used to justify indefinite solitary confinement—possession of drawings believed to indicate gang affiliation absent other harmful conduct—came to be understood as innocuous, even as forms of expression worthy of protection and reflective of strategies for survival under conditions of state-perpetrated criminal torture. Unafraid of these conclusions, the Collective recast the fundamental terms of the social arrangements its members inhabited, offering a critical account in which the law itself came to be revealed as criminal and in which those subject to the state's worse possible punishments were rendered relatively innocent—survivors and authors of an alternative ethics and politics. This work of reconceptualizing the contours of criminality, moral wrong, deservingness, and survivorship, and ultimately the contours of what justice requires, is a core part of what a meaningful critique of law should entail.

A book by Denis O'Hearn, *Nothing but an Unfinished Song: The Life and Times of Bobby Sands*, which addresses the Irish Republican Army hunger strike in the Maze Prison, became a particular source of inspiration for the Collective, and the group decided to organize a series of statewide hunger strikes to demand change to these policies and practices in California's prisons. The Collective issued a call to initiate the hunger strike that functioned as a critique of the illegitimacy of their continued confinement and an effort to forge new solidarities between previously polarized groups of incarcerated citizens. The call—authored by Mutope Duguma, who is also known as James Crawford, what he calls his "slave name"—read as follows:

> This is a call for all prisoners in Security Housing Units (SHUs), Administrative Segregation (Ad-Seg), and General Populations (GP), as well as the free oppressed and non-oppressed people to support the indefinite July 1st 2011

peaceful Hunger Strike in protest of the violation of our civil/human rights, here at Pelican Bay State Prison Security Housing Unit (PBSP-SHU). . . . It should be clear to everyone that none of the hunger strike participants want to die, but due to our circumstances, whereas that state of California has sentenced all of us on Indeterminate SHU program to a "civil death." . . . The purpose of the Hunger Strike is to combat both the Ad-Seg/SHU psychological and physical torture, as well as the justifications used to support treatment of the type that lends to prisoners being subjected to a civil death. Those subjected to indeterminate SHU programs are neglected and deprived of the basic human necessities while withering away in a very isolated and hostile environment. . . . This protracted attack on SHU prisoners cuts across every aspect of the prison's function: Food, mail, visiting, medical, yard, hot/cold temperatures, privileges (canteen, packages, property, etc.), isolation, cell searches, family/friends, and socio-culture, economic, and political deprivation. . . . day in and day out, without a break or rest. . . . It is these ongoing attacks that have led . . . prisoners to organize . . . around an indefinite Hunger Strike in an effort to combat the dehumanizing treatment we prisoners of all races are subjected to.[24]

This call spread to those incarcerated elsewhere in the state, who then joined the strike and shared their experiences and analyses of long-term confinement. Over time, organizing through channels inside and outside California prisons, some thirty thousand prisoners joined the hunger strikes, with a network of individuals and organizations outside of prisons across the state announcing their solidarity with the protestors and producing together a trove of critical writings on California's carceral landscape.

Michael "Zaharibu" Dorrough, a fifty-nine-year-old man incarcerated in the Corcoran State Prison SHU since 1988 for being a member of the Black Guerilla Family gang and subsequently for writing black nationalist newspapers, shared his writings, which then circulated through the Prison Hunger Strike Solidarity forum. Dorrough describes witnessing in SHU "other people snap," "human beings cutting themselves," "eating their own waste[]," "smearing themselves in it," "throwing it," "human beings not just talking outloud to themselves—but screaming at and cursing themselves." J. Heshima Denham, also incarcerated in the Corcoran State Prison SHU for over a decade, wrote of the effects of isolation on his mind and body, of the "psychological and physical devastation of the torture unit," and of being punished for possessing a drawing of a dragon, which was alleged to be a symbol of the Black Guerilla Family gang.[25]

The writings of the hunger strikers gave fuller meaning to the conceptions of "civil death" offered by scholars to describe the effects of incarceration—giving voice to the particular forms of embodied and legally rationalized suffering produced through law. It was significant that again the authors of this critique of law, connected to the Prison Hunger Strike Solidarity network, were also those subject most intimately and intensely to the horrors perpetrated by and through law and whose voices the state sought to erase from public through imprisonment. The authors of this critique make plain that a meaningful critique of law must not just learn from but place at its center those most vulnerable to law's violence, who are typically excluded entirely from legal discourse.

The actions of the Collective also included the issuance of an agreement to end racial hostilities between the state's prison gangs. The Collective issued a call to solidarity among those racially classified groups of prisoners that prison authorities rely on to maintain a certain discipline and division. In an "Agreement to End Hostilities," the Short Corridor Collective proposed: "now is the time for us to collectively seize this moment ... and put an end to more than 20–30 years of hostilities between our racial groups." The Agreement continued: "collectively, we are an empowered, mighty force, that can positively change this entire corrupt system." Later, the Youth Justice Coalition, which represents incarcerated youth in California jails, prisons, and juvenile detention centers issued a parallel call:

> For all of us, there must be a cut off point—a time at which we stop participating in our own destruction. As young people who have experienced bloodshed on the streets of Los Angeles, and the violence and humiliation within juvenile halls, Probation camps and Division of Juvenile Justice Youth Prisons, we are also calling for an end to the war between the youth. We are challenging all youth in the streets, schools and lock-ups throughout California, to ... Declare a temporary cease fire and work toward building lasting truces. Take the same mentality and skills we have used to hustle drugs, bang our hoods and promote our crews to unite in a powerful movement to demand dignity, respect and equality for all our people.... We must also demand an end to police and sheriff violence, an end to the mass incarceration of youth—especially Black and Brown youth, an end to ICE detention and deportation, living wage jobs, and a quality education that prepares all youth for college and a career.[26]

Through these critical interventions, the prison hunger strike movement forged a collective voice inside and outside prison walls, in jails, in immigration detention, and elsewhere—critical of their conditions of confinement but also oriented at the same time to transcending their circumstances through their critical writings and beginning to make their worlds anew. Through this new collective power and solidarity, the prison hunger strikes in California fundamentally challenged the state's processes of confinement. In conjunction with litigation initially filed pro se by members of the Short Corridor Collective, the hunger strikes brought about substantial if partial changes to California's practices of solitary confinement. The litigation settlement requires the state to use a behavior-based allegation rather than vague and unsubstantiated allegations of gang affiliation in order to impose solitary confinement and the state may only do so for a more limited period of time. As a result, hundreds of people have been released from decades of long-term solitary confinement and the Collective has encouraged all people incarcerated in California to continue to report on and protest prison conditions. In response, state officials in California have sought cynically to meet the requirements of the agreement by transferring imprisoned people to other prison facilities or to jails, but the collective outcry has persisted. Hunger strikes continue regularly across the state and prison officials have begun to negotiate more routinely to meet the strikers' demands.[27]

These hunger strikes have produced solidarities and proliferating protests from Washington State to Palestine. The hunger strike solidarity network publicized and galvanized support for imprisoned Palestinians in Israeli prisons who engaged in a hunger strike and who, despite encountering intense repression, managed to negotiate concessions meaningful to the strikers including more lengthy family visits, access to improved communication media, and other basic necessities. The network has also raised up the voices and demands of hunger strikers in immigration detention in the United States.[28] Through these connections, the critical project of the Short Corridor Collective has extended across space, with those most vulnerable to the abuses of confinement changing the extent to which they are able to be controlled and have their grievances considered.[29]

Ultimately, the work of the hunger strikers has also extended beyond challenging the legitimacy of long-term solitary confinement, by identifying connections between these practices and other forms of injustice. Their critique rejects the legalistic silos that constrain much critical analysis of law emanating from the legal academy, which addresses, for example, pretrial jail detention, policing, juvenile detention, immigration detention and enforcement, and postconviction incarceration in prisons as separate and distinct problems— mirroring the law's treatment of these practices as separate and distinct. Instead, the hunger strikers recognize the interconnections and similarities between these institutions, rather than approaching them as discrete concerns.

The emergent movement to challenge the violence of solitary confinement has come to refer to itself as the New Abolition movement. In protests from Washington, DC, to San Jose, California, in 2017, the New Abolitionists condemned the complicity of US constitutional jurisprudence in the brutality of incarceration, and called for an end to the extortion of prisoners and their families for needed goods and services, an end to the militarization of police, to voter disenfranchisement of up to six million people, to indefinite detention of entire families by Immigration and Customs Enforcement, and to a bail bond system that unjustly penalizes the poor and dispossessed—underscoring consistently the connections between these practices of degradation and dispossession.[30] Through ongoing protests, the critical work of the Collective has given rise in the span of several years to an increasingly global movement, myriad new collectivities engaged in critique and committed to revealing and ending the ravages of caging human beings.[31] In contrast to the university's privatizing and individualizing dynamics, these critical efforts emphasize collectivity and through the process of critique have formed new collectivities and new configurations of power and politics.

The Movement for Black Lives, BYP100, Alternative Visions of Justice and Accountability

During this same period, the Movement for Black Lives, a coalition of more than fifty organizations associated with Black Lives Matter and representing thousands of Black people across the United States, sought to confront the racialized violence of policing and criminal law enforcement in the United States. In 2016, the Movement authored a "Platform" and "Vision for Black Lives" to develop a critical analysis of racialized brutality in policing and to envision far-reaching transformative change, but to do so while holding in mind more specific, immediate goals. Like the critique of the hunger strikers, the Platform identifies the connections between the violence associated with criminal law enforcement and other forms of social, economic, and racial injustice, moving beyond the formal strictures that typify legal academic criticism. For example, the Movement's Vision considers problems related to policing and incarceration—focusing on the extensive federal, state-level, and local investments in policing and caging—as tied to other repressive state policies and practices that distribute wealth upward and lead to immiseration for vast numbers of people of color. The Platform and Vision likewise advance an account of what would make communities safer, freer, and more secure. In this regard, the Platform states: "there's no evidence that the massive spending on incarceration reduces crime rates or keeps communities safer. Studies do show that jobs. . . . [and i]nvestments in community based drug and mental health treatment, education, universal pre-K, and other social institutions can make communities safer while improving life outcomes for all." Those studies are then explored in detail and the Vision identifies particular state and local initiatives that may provide achievable means to these ends as well as more aspirational, radical accounts of necessary change, including fundamental socioeconomic transformation.[32]

In conjunction with its critical writings, the Movement has also organized virtual seminars on these topics, exploring themes from local democratic control of policing and other public resources to reparations. These seminars or webinars convene scholar-activists, organizers, and others associated with the Movement before a national audience to think together about how to effectuate change not just to the status quo in policing but to the broader dynamics of racial, economic, and social injustice the Movement has called into question. Some of this work includes careful study of emergent forms of how communities have organized to ensure their safety without prisons and police or how communities have organized to begin the process of redistributing social and economic resources. Through these critical discussions, affiliated organizations engage at one and the same time in new experiments in collective self-governance—seeking to critically confront police violence and carceral responses while beginning to realize a world in which other forms of security and peaceful coexistence are possible.

For instance, Rachel Herzing, a cofounder of the national grassroots abolitionist organization Critical Resistance, and codirector of the Center for Political Education, a resource center for progressive political organizations serving working-class people of color in the Bay area, has worked to reduce the demand for police emergency responses in Oakland, California, and around the country, by increasing residents' capacity to resolve conflict without having to call the police. Following an extensive community survey in which Oakland residents identified problems for which they most needed support, Herzing and other organizers have worked locally to convene alternative first responders not tied to law enforcement—health workers, community volunteers, social workers, and antiviolence advocates—who are available to respond to community members with family in mental health crisis or who face other emergencies. Herzing, who is committed to an abolitionist project, conceives of abolition in this regard as, in her words, a "set of political responsibilities" to organize collective responses to ensure security in other terms.[33]

Movement participants have also engaged in critical experiments in collective self-governance in response to harm perpetrated by certain members of the movement against others. The Black Youth Project 100 (BYP100)—a national member-based organization of eighteen- to thirty-five-year-old activists and organizers associated with the Movement for Black Lives—has authored critiques of policing and criminal prosecution as means of realizing justice, and when one of BYP100's leaders was accused of sexual assault, the organization and the survivor, who is also a Movement member, convened a transformative justice process to come to terms with the harm done.[34] The survivor, Kyra, made BYP100 aware of the assault in a letter when the perpetrator, Malcolm, became the focus of widespread attention on social media and elsewhere after his arrest at a protest in Chicago of the police killing of Laquan McDonald. Kyra wrote:

> The assault happened three years ago on this exact day. I had met him a few days prior and he asked me if I wanted to go see a movie. . . . After the movie, he asked to come up to my apartment for coffee and I obliged because I thought

he needed it to stay awake during his drive home. But when I offered it to him he said he didn't actually want any, and just wanted an excuse to come upstairs. He made a few sexual advances, and each time I asked him to stop. I was clear that I did not consent, and I thought he got the picture that he'd made me uncomfortable. But because it was late, at some point I dosed off and I woke up with Malcolm's fingers in my vagina. . . . I immediately asked him to leave and once he was gone I told him what he did was an act of sexual violence. He was apologetic, but did not understand why what he did to me was assault.[35]

At the same time that Kyra made her experience of assault public, she also underscored that she did not believe the criminal process could deliver justice or provide meaningful redress. She wrote:

We can't trust the justice system to protect us or to hold perpetrators accountable—that much is clear. So, we need to work towards a way to do that ourselves. By sharing my experience, my short term goal is to come up with a system by which we can hold people in the organizing community accountable when they hurt people, and to educate folks both before and after harm is done. And maybe that system can turn into inspiration for ways we can protect the community at large without police. I'm not exactly sure what that looks like yet, but I am looking forward to working with you to figure out a plan.[36]

BYP100 responded by meeting with Kyra, and all concerned parties decided to participate in a transformative justice process as Kyra, Malcolm, and BYP100's leadership were all critical of criminal prosecution as a response to sexual harm.[37] Kyra, Malcolm, and the transformative justice facilitators then published accounts of their experience. Rather than a prescription of how to respond to wrongdoing across the board in all circumstances, all participants understood their work together and associated writings as offering a framework for an alternative response, one that was consistent with their critiques of criminal legal practices and with their commitment to realize justice in other terms.[38] Through this process and the writings associated with it, Movement members have followed their critiques of criminal law enforcement to their own conclusions, unafraid of the risks that may entail. Harsha Walia has described such efforts to realize critical commitments at a local scale as a politics of prefiguration in which participants seek through their own choices and relationships to prefigure the sort of world in which they wish to live.[39]

Beyond these projects of critical engagement and transcendence of conventional forms of criminal law enforcement, Movement participants have also critically engaged state and local budgeting processes, aiming to challenge the allocation and distribution of public funds to policing and punishment rather than to social, restorative, or other projects. Zachary Norris, the executive director of the Ella Baker Center for Human Rights in Oakland, California, has launched a Truth in Reinvestment campaign tracing how public funds allocated for reinvestment outside the criminal process are actually spent. Norris, the Ella Baker Center, and organized community members have called their campaign "healthcare and housing not handcuffs" and much of their work has involved local advocacy around budgeting decisions, for example, working to redistribute dollars from sheriff and probation offices to community-based worker resource centers for people returning to communities after incarceration. Anthony Newby, working with Neighborhoods Organizing for Change (NOC), a black-led community organization based in Minneapolis, pressured the city and state to reinvest state funds after the killing of Jamar Clark by police in 2015. Newby and other organizers widely publicized their critique of policing and promised justice reinvestment through writings, interviews, and direct actions, shutting down airports, bridges, and the Mall of America. Ultimately, Newby and his collaborators managed to secure thirty million dollars for reinvestment. Newby has described the next stage for his organization and the movement as to think about how to most meaningfully invest that money so it does not simply go to providers who are committed to preserving the status quo.[40]

In Washington, DC, in 2015 and 2016, local Black Lives Matter activists successfully opposed the mayor's proposed anticrime legislation, which would have expanded funding for policing and increased the size of the police force as well as raising penalties for a range of offenses.[41] Organizers successfully pushed instead for a separate initiative that would offer jobs and stipends to at-risk youth.[42] These activists have also pressed the city to increase investment in community land trusts, a form of collective property ownership that maintains the affordability of homes in gentrifying neighborhoods over time, and they have recently concluded a successful initiative to work toward implementing a living wage.[43]

As the Movement has undertaken these projects, the Vision and accompanying webinars also explore litigation and legislative advocacy strategies as well as model domestic and foreign legislation—compiling hyperlinked resources. The idea is that other communities may turn to these resources and writings to devise their own related projects. Through these and other efforts, local organizers have built through their critical analyses of policing and criminal punishment a national movement that serves to denaturalize common assumptions about crime and punishment, connecting criminal law reform to mobilizations for a living wage, affordable housing, cooperative ownership, and a redistribution of public resources.

Keeyanga-Yamhatta Taylor has underscored how the Movement for Black Lives has reshaped public discourse on crime, policing, and race.[44] But the Movement has also revitalized local democratic politics, reshaping local and state budgeting efforts, in large part by organizing communities to actively redirect their own state and local governments.[45] The Platform and Vision represent a large-scale collective effort to critically confront order-maintenance policing and also at one and the same time to conceptualize democracy, security, freedom, and justice in other terms. Then, in localities around the United States, the Movement is engaging in the critical and collective institution-building political work essential to realize what W. E. B. Du Bois called Abolition Democracy—that form of transcendent collective egalitarian democratic governance that ought to have emerged after the end of slavery and the Civil War in the United States, but that was never realized then or in the years to follow. Abolition Democracy recognizes as crucial to abolition the *negative* abolition of the objects of critique but also the *positive* project of reconstituting democratic self-governance and human flourishing in truly egalitarian terms.[46]

The Possible Futures of Critique

In the end, it is not clear what the future of these critical projects will hold and how far these efforts to imagine and manifest new forms of abolitionist democratic coexistence may reach. But they should at least radically expand the canon of critique such that we understand the work of ruthless criticism, and of a critique of law, to consist in the writings, actions, and imaginings of those most intimately affected by imprisonment, the violence of policing, and legally rationalized dispossession. Moreover, through the work of these critical movements, it is worth recognizing that we bear witness to critical practices that are engaged at once in a formidable unmasking and critical analysis, simultaneously constituting new collectivities and forms of self-governance that challenge existing structures of power and control, and ultimately create the beginnings of new forms of democratic coexistence.

Perhaps too these critical projects might teach those of us located elsewhere—at a greater distance from the immediate violence of imprisonment and policing—to summon the courage and imagination to produce our own ruthless criticism less afraid of its own conclusion and of conflict with the powers that be. This critical work, perhaps emanating in part from those very sites of complicity, from within universities and other institutions of formalized critical study, should be motivated, though, not by a sympathetic solidarity. Instead such critical work must emanate from the recognition, as Jack Halberstam writes of the undercommons, that "the structures . . . oppose[d] are not only bad for some of us, they are bad for all of us." As Halberstam puts it, critical coalitional work within the undercommons, as it may seek ultimately "to make things better" must take up this work not just "for the Other"; rather, "you must also be doing it for yourself."[47]

Halberstam continues: "no one will really be able to embrace the mission of tearing 'this shit down' until they realize that. . . . gender hierarchies are bad for men as well as women and they are really bad for the rest of us. Racial hierarchies are not rational and ordered, they are chaotic and nonsensical and must be opposed by precisely all those who benefit in any way from them."[48]

Or, as Moten puts it: "the coalition emerges out of your recognition that it's fucked up for you, in the same way that we've already recognized that it's fucked up for us. I don't need your help. I just need you to recognize that this shit is killing you, too, however much more softly, you stupid motherfucker, you know?"[49]

Along these lines, those in the hunger strike solidarity network and those engaged in contemporary struggles for racial justice through the Movement for Black Lives do not simply aim to serve as a source of support to people incarcerated in solitary confinement, or those subject to police violence, lifting up their voices, but work instead toward a more thoroughgoing cooperation, as Lisa Guenther has proposed, in the role of "accomplices rather than allies."[50] These efforts suggest a model for how, despite great obstacles and sometimes seemingly insurmountable challenges, across large distances and differences, emancipatory critical collaboration might take shape. This is a call for a critical practice, self-aware, impassioned, even enraged, motivated by an irresistible impulse to justice. It is a call that remains to be answered.

Notes

1. Karl Marx, "Letter to Arnold Ruge," *Deutsch-Franzosische Jahrbucher*, 1844.
2. Pierre Schlag, "Spam Jurisprudence, Air Law, and the Rank Anxiety of Nothing Happening (A Report on the State of the Art)," *Georgetown Law Journal* 97 (2009).
3. Wendy Brown, *Undoing the Demos: Neoliberalism's Stealth Revolution* (Cambridge, MA: MIT Press, 2015), 180–200.
4. For an instance of an exceptional departure from this trend, see, for example, Amna Akbar, "Toward a Radical Imagination of Law," *New York University Law Review* 93 (2018): 405–79.
5. Prison Hunger Strike Solidarity, Collected Writings, https://prisonerhungerstrikesolidarity.wordpress.com; Movement for Black Lives, *A Vision for Black Lives: Policy Demands for Black Power, Freedom, and Justice*, August 2016, https://policy.m4bl.org.
6. Fred Moten and Stefano Harney, *The Undercommons: Fugitive Planning and Black Study* (London: Minor Compositions, 2013).
7. Moten and Harney, 27.
8. Undercommoning, "Undercommoning Within, Against and Beyond the University-as-Such," *ROAR Magazine*, June 4, 2016.
9. Undercommoning.
10. Moten and Harney, *The Undercommons*, 38.
11. Moten and Harney, 38.
12. Moten and Harney, 41, 42.

13. Moten and Harney, 41.
14. Moten and Harney, 41.
15. Michel Foucault, "What Is Critique?," in *The Politics of Truth*, ed. Sylvère Lotringer, 41–81 (Los Angeles: Semiotext[e], 1997).
16. Marx, "Letter to Arnold Ruge."
17. Moten and Harney, *The Undercommons*.
18. Keramet Reiter, *23/7: Pelican Bay Prison and the Rise of Long-Term Solitary Confinement* (New Haven: Yale University Press, 2016).
19. Alessandro Camon, "The Short Corridor: How the Most Isolated Prisoners in America Took on the System, and Won," *Los Angeles Review of Books*, May 15, 2016.
20. Lisa Guenther, "Political Action at the End of the World: Hannah Arendt and the California Prison Hunger Strikes," *Canadian Journal of Human Rights* 4, no. 1 (2015); Antonio Guillen, "Why I Joined the Multi-Racial, Multi-Regional Human Rights Movement to Challenge Torture in the Pelican Bay SHU," *San Francisco Bay View National Black Newspaper*, August 29, 2013.
21. Camon, "The Short Corridor."
22. Lisa Guenther, *Solitary Confinement: Social Death and Its Afterlives* (Minneapolis: University of Minnesota Press, 2013).
23. Prisoner Hunger Strike Solidarity, https://prisonerhungerstrikesolidarity.wordpress.com.
24. Prisoner Hunger Strike Solidarity.
25. Prisoner Hunger Strike Solidarity.
26. Prisoner Hunger Strike Solidarity.
27. Lucas Guilkey, Nearly One Third of Glenn Dyer Prisoners Wrap Up Hunger Strike, October 27, 2017.
28. Prisoner Hunger Strike Solidarity, https://prisonerhungerstrikesolidarity.wordpress.com.
29. Prisoner Hunger Strike Solidarity.
30. Prisoner Hunger Strike Solidarity.
31. Prisoner Hunger Strike Solidarity.
32. Movement for Black Lives, "A Vision for Black Lives: Policy Demands for Black Power, Freedom, and Justice," August 2016, https://policy.m4bl.org.
33. Vision for Black Lives Webinar Series: Invest/Divest, April 12, 2017.
34. Black Youth Project (BYP 100) Community Accountability Process (Chicago 2015–16), posted by Sarah Daoud on behalf of Kyra, November 27, 2015 (on file with author).
35. Black Youth Project.
36. Black Youth Project.
37. Transforming Harm, Summary Statement Re: Community Accountability Process, March 8, 2017 (on file with author).
38. Transforming Harm.
39. Harsha Walia, *Undoing Border Imperialism* (Chico, CA: AK Press, 2013).
40. Vision for Black Lives Webinar Series: Invest/Divest, April 12, 2017.
41. Abigail Hauslohner and Aaron C. Davis, "Black Lives Matter Activists Disrupt Bowser Speech on How to Stop Killings," *Washington Post*, August 27, 2015; Brent J. Cohen, "Implementing the NEAR Act to Reduce Violence in D.C.," DC Policy Center, May 25, 2017.
42. Cohen, "Implementing the NEAR Act to Reduce Violence in D.C.," DC Policy Center, May 25, 2017.
43. Allegra McLeod, "Envisioning Abolition Democracy," *Harvard Law Review* (2019).

44. Keeyanga-Yamhatta Taylor, *From #BlackLivesMatter to Black Liberation* (Chicago: Haymarket, 2016).
45. McLeod, "Envisioning Abolition Democracy."
46. Angela Davis, *Abolition Democracy: Beyond Empire, Prisons, and Torture* (New York: Seven Stories, 2005), citing W. E. B. Du Bois, *Black Reconstruction in America* (1935).
47. Jack Halberstam, "The Wild Beyond: With and for the Undercommons," in *The Undercommons: Fugitive Planning and Black Study* (London: Minor Compositions, 2013), 10.
48. Halberstam, 10.
49. Moten and Harney, *The Undercommons*.
50. Lisa Guenther, "Beyond Guilt and Innocence: The Creaturely Politics of Prisoner Resistance Movements," citing Indigenous Action Media, "Accomplices Not Allies: Abolishing the Ally Industrial Complex," May 4, 2014, www.indigenousaction.org/accomplisces-not-allies-abolishing-the-ally-industrial-complex/, in *Active Intolerance: Michel Foucault, the Prisons Information Group, and the Future of Abolition*, ed. Perry Zurn and Andrew Dilts, 225–40 (New York: Palgrave, 2016).

Bibliography

Akbar, Amna. "Toward a Radical Imagination of Law." *New York University Law Review* 93 (2018): 405–79.

Black Youth Project (BYP100). Community Accountability Process (Chicago 2015–16). Posted by Sarah Daoud on behalf of Kyra, November 27, 2015 (on file with author).

Brown, Wendy. *Undoing the Demos: Neoliberalism's Stealth Revolution.* Cambridge, MA: MIT Press, 2015.

Camon, Alessandro. "The Short Corridor: How the Most Isolated Prisoners in America Took on the System, and Won." *Los Angeles Review of Books*, May 15, 2016.

Cohen, Brent J. "Implementing the NEAR Act to Reduce Violence in D.C." DC Policy Center, May 25, 2017.

Davis, Angela. *Abolition Democracy: Beyond Empire, Prisons, and Torture.* New York: Seven Stories, 2005.

Du Bois, W. E. B. *Black Reconstruction in America.* New York: Harcourt Brace, 1935.

Foucault, Michel. "What Is Critique?" In *The Politics of Truth*, edited by Sylvère Lotringer, 41–81. Los Angeles: Semiotext(e), 1997.

Guenther, Lisa. "Beyond Guilt and Innocence: The Creaturely Politics of Prisoner Resistance Movements," citing Indigenous Action Media, "Accomplices Not Allies: Abolishing the Ally Industrial Complex," May 4, 2014, www.indigenousaction.org/accomplisces-not-allics-abolishing-the-ally-industrial complex/. In *Active Intolerance: Michel Foucault, the Prisons Information Group, and the Future of Abolition*, edited by Perry Zurn and Andrew Dilts, 225–40. New York: Palgrave, 2016.

——. "Political Action at the End of the World: Hannah Arendt and the California Prison Hunger Strikes." *Canadian Journal of Human Rights* 4, no. 1 (2015): 33–56.

——. *Solitary Confinement: Social Death and Its Afterlives.* Minneapolis: University of Minnesota Press, 2013.

Guilkey, Lucas. "Nearly One Third of Glenn Dyer Prisoners Wrap Up Hunger Strike." *Oakland North*, October 27, 2017, https://oaklandnorth.net/2017/10/27/nearly-one-third-of-glenn-dyer-prisoners-wrap-up-hunger-strike/.

Guillen, Antonio. "Why I Joined the Multi-Racial, Multi-Regional Human Rights Movement to Challenge Torture in the Pelican Bay SHU." *San Francisco Bay View National Black Newspaper*, August 29, 2013.

Halberstam, Jack. "The Wild Beyond: With and for the Undercommons." In *The Undercommons: Fugitive Planning and Black Study*, edited by Stefano Harney and Fred Moten. London: Minor Compositions, 2013.

Hauslohner, Abigail, and Aaron C. Davis. "Black Lives Matter Activists Disrupt Bowser Speech on How to Stop Killings." *Washington Post*, August 27, 2015.

Marx, Karl. "Letter to Arnold Ruge." *Deutsch-Franzosische Jahrbucher* (1844).

McLeod, Allegra. "Envisioning Abolition Democracy." *Harvard Law Review* (2019).

Moten, Fred, and Stefano Harney. *The Undercommons: Fugitive Planning and Black Study*. London: Minor Compositions, 2013.

Movement for Black Lives. *A Vision for Black Lives: Policy Demands for Black Power, Freedom, and Justice*. August 2016. https://policy.m4bl.org.

Prison Hunger Strike Solidarity, Collected Writings. https://prisonerhungerstrikesolidarity.wordpress.com.

Reiter, Keramet. *23/7: Pelican Bay Prison and the Rise of Long-Term Solitary Confinement*. New Haven: Yale University Press, 2016.

Schlag, Pierre. "Spam Jurisprudence, Air Law, and the Rank Anxiety of Nothing Happening (A Report on the State of the Art)." *Georgetown Law Journal* 97 (2009).

Taylor, Keeyanga-Yamhatta. *From #BlackLivesMatter to Black Liberation*. Chicago: Haymarket, 2016.

Transforming Harm. Summary Statement Re: Community Accountability Process, March 8, 2017 (on file with author).

Undercommoning. "Undercommoning Within, Against and Beyond the University-as-Such." *ROAR Magazine*, June 4, 2016.

Vision for Black Lives Webinar Series: Invest/Divest, April 12, 2017.

Walia, Harsha. *Undoing Border Imperialism*. Chico, CA: AK, 2013.

CHAPTER 14

CRITICAL PRAXIS FOR THE TWENTY-FIRST CENTURY

BERNARD E. HARCOURT

W̲e face today an unprecedented constellation of global crises. With the rise of extreme-right populist movements, the international impact of neoliberal policies, increased xenophobic sentiment and attacks on minorities, and the fallout of a global war on terror, we are in the midst of a rare historical epoch of worldwide political turbulence. These times urgently call for critical analyses of our contemporary crises and for reflection on the future of critical praxis.

Earlier similar epochs were foundational moments for critical theory and praxis. The 1920s, especially in the Weimar Republic, gave rise to a whole generation of critical theorists—many of whom would emigrate in exile around the world and spawn a critical diaspora.[1] The 1960s, with its global student uprisings and government repression, stimulated another wave of critical theory and praxis, giving way to a formidable decade of critical thought during the 1970s.

Our critical times today demand an equal response from contemporary critical theorists, and we are fortunate to have inherited an abundant and diverse range of critical theories to help us analyze the present global crises. With regard to critical theory—as the contributions to this collected volume attest—we are in a promising condition. But with regard to critical praxis, we are in a slightly different situation. The trajectory of critical praxis, although influenced by similar forces as that of critical theory, landed us in a different place today. This raises a quandary, but it also presents an opportunity: we now need to rejuvenate critical praxis for the twenty-first century.

The contrast is revealing. On the one hand, in the domain of critical theory, the trajectory arched upward since its origins in the Frankfurt School, especially during the subsequent crises of the 1960s and 1970s. In the aftermath of May '68 and the repression of the student uprisings and anti–Vietnam War movements, a second generation of critical theorists refashioned conceptual tools to better diagnose the ongoing crises and grasp how power circulates through society—offering a remarkable range of competing critical perspectives. A series of antifoundational challenges within critical theory produced a deep fissure within the field that, although at first destabilizing, proved productive in generating new and promising critical theoretical approaches.[2]

The decade of the 1970s was particularly fruitful for critical theory. Some critics returned to foundations and enriched the earlier generation of critical theory. Louis Althusser, for instance, supplemented his scientific interpretation of Marx with concepts of ideology and ideological state apparatuses, in his "Ideology and Ideological State Apparatuses (Notes Towards an Investigation)," published in 1970. Hannah Arendt returned to notions of civil disobedience, violence, and revolution, to reconsider the active political life in her collection of essays *Crises of the Republic*, published in 1972. Jürgen Habermas reworked legitimation theory to offer a new diagnosis of crisis tendencies specific to advanced capitalism in *Legitimation Crisis*, published in 1973. Other critics challenged foundations and charted new directions for critique. Gilles Deleuze and Félix Guattari upended notions of desire and reconceived the will to power, turning the Oedipal myth into a bourgeois conspiracy in their *Anti-Oedipus*, published in 1973. Michel Foucault reconceptualized relations of power on the matrix of civil war in his lectures *Penal Theories and Institutions* in 1972 and *The Punitive Society* in 1973, and then in his book *Discipline and Punish*, published in 1975. A series of other innovative critical interventions erupted at the same time, including Frederic Jameson's *Marxism and Form* (1971), Jean Baudrillard's *The Mirror of Production* (1973), Hayden White's *Metahistory* (1973), Silvia Federici's *Wages Against Housework* (1975), Cornelius Castoriadis's *The Imaginary Institution of Society* (1975), Perry Anderson's *Considerations on Western Marxism* (1976), Luce Irigaray's *This Sex Which Is Not One* (1977), Mario Tronti's *On the Autonomy of the Political* (1977), Stuart Hall's *Policing the Crisis* (1978), Nicos Poulantzas's *The State, Power, Socialism* (1978), and Edward Said's *Orientalism* (1978), among others. The critical production from the 1970s was remarkable— stimulated as well by a historical epoch of global political upheaval.

In the decades that followed, a third generation of critical theorists augmented and, at times, rebelled against these critical frameworks. In the process, they developed new critical tools and concepts to address their own troubled times. They invented the concept of the Anthropocene, with important contributions by Dipesh Chakrabarty, and continued to develop the critical paradigm of neoliberalism, with key works by David Harvey, Wendy Brown, and Loïc Wacquant. They crafted new ideas of populism, in the writings of Chantal Mouffe and Ernesto Laclau, and new concepts of precarity, biopower, necropolitics, racialized assemblages, intersectionality, critical anthropology, and other theoretical frameworks, with significant contributions by Giorgio Agamben, Judith Butler, Kimberlé Crenshaw, Didier Fassin, Achille Mbembe, Alexander Weheliye, and others. These new and retooled critical concepts reinvigorated critical thought—challenging the cohesion of the field, but ultimately providing a rich array of critiques. And despite the fact that the historical, contextual, and disciplinary constellations have constrained the space of critique today, as Didier Fassin convincingly argues,[3] critical theory now offers promising avenues, building on a rich conversation over generations of critical thinkers.

On the other hand, the trajectory of critical praxis landed critical theorists, today, on less firm ground. The point of departure was cohesive and grounded. The first generation of critical thinkers was rooted in a Marxist orientation toward praxis. This was due, in large part, to its genetic makeup: Marxist scholars trying to rethink Marxism and its failures, the first Frankfurt School thinkers remained wedded to the framework of class struggle, dialectical materialism, and proletarian revolution. As a result, critical praxis was at first relatively straightforward and well defined: the task, essentially, was to demonstrate the truth of dialectical materialism.[4]

The second generation, during the 1960s and 1970s, would fragment the Marxist consensus. Many critics would liberate themselves from the strictures of Marxist praxis. New modes of uprising, insurrection, disobedience, and insubordination arose, and these would then inspire new experiments and forms of revolt by the next generation during the early twenty-first century. The Indignados uprising, the global Occupy movement, the Arab Spring would present new modalities of praxis. These would then lead to fruitful theorizing of the performativity of assembly, for instance, in Judith Butler's work, of the political potential of the multitude in Michael Hardt and Antonio Negri's writings, or of renewed concepts of civil and political disobedience in the works of W. J. T. Mitchell and Mick Taussig, Sandra Laugier and Albert Ogien, and Frédéric Gros. In the United States, the #BlackLivesMatter and #MeToo movements would prompt stimulating reflections on questions of leadership and representation in the writings of Cathy Cohen, Barbara Ransby, Deva Woodly, and others.

But often, those very practices—of general assemblies, of leaderless and ideologically agnostic occupations, of spiritually tinged uprisings, of hashtag social movements—clashed with classical conceptions of critical praxis and triggered uneasy reactions among many critical theorists. There was often a sense of frustration at the newer modalities of uprising. Leaderlessness was particularly fraught, and substantial disagreement emerged about the practices at Occupy Wall Street.

At other times, the political crises gave way to low-grade paralysis among critical thinkers, an unexpected quiescence at least by contrast to the more vocal interventions of liberal dissent, such as the ACLU, Human Rights Watch, or the Center for Constitutional Rights in New York. The critical responses appeared somewhat muted. The critical left, as opposed to the liberal left, appeared disarmed. To be sure, there were important interventions analyzing new forms of critical praxis, and several essays in this collection do precisely that with regard to the critical practices of new organizations like the Short Corridor Collective, prisoner hunger strike solidarity movements, and Black Youth Project 100 (BYP100), among others; but the ground of critical action seemed less firm than that of critical theory. It often felt that critical praxis was missing in action—as opposed, that is, to liberal forms of protest.

These troubled times offer a critical opportunity for renewed attention to praxis. They provide a unique opening for critique to map out and reorient the possible directions in which praxis might productively evolve over the twenty-first century. Any such effort must rest, naturally, on a better understanding of the historical trajectory of critical praxis, a history that has rarely been told—which itself may be an indicator of a problem. This essay is a first stride in this direction, and it will proceed in three steps. In part 1, the essay will trace the structural transformation in critical praxis over the twentieth century. In part 2, it will describe the major polarities of critical practice at the turn of the century. Then, in part 3, it will map out the possible directions for critical praxis in the twenty-first century. The essay will not advocate for any one direction, but rather underscore the need for openness and experimentation in these postfoundational times. In a short conclusion, I will confess my own orientation to the future. The point of the essay, though, is not to resolve the future of critical praxis, but to highlight the need for contemporary critical theorists to now return, in a far more sustained way, to the most critical question today in these times of global political turbulence: What is to be done?

The Structural Transformation of Critical Praxis Over the Twentieth Century

The field of critical praxis underwent fundamental change over the twentieth century—to the point where the term *praxis* has lost some of its meaning today and may even be jarring to some readers.[5] The reasons for this trace in large part to a disenchantment with the Marxist philosophy of history and an exhaustion with the notion of a proletarian revolution, which were at the heart of nineteenth-century notions of critical praxis, as well as to the decline of syndicalism and of the more radical factions of the international labor movement in the 1920s, and the gradual transformation of labor movements over the course of the twentieth century. Even as late as the 1970s, dialectical materialism remained more central to critical theory, either as an animating force or as a foil and point of resistance, reconceptualization, or augmentation. But the geopolitical changes at the turn of the twenty-first century, the dissipation of segments of the working class, and the exhaustion of metahistories dramatically eroded the hold of ambitious philosophies of history.

The reasons also trace, in part, to the transformation of the concept of revolution that was embedded in the more traditional idea of critical praxis. Reinhart Koselleck and Hannah Arendt famously traced the emergence of the "modern" concept of revolution to the seventeenth, eighteenth, and nineteenth centuries. By contrast to ancient conceptions of revolution tied to the etymology of revolving cycles—of the cyclical returning to a point of origin, of the astronomical cycle of the stars, or of the ancient philosophical progression of constitutions (from monarchy to its dark twin tyranny, to aristocracy and then oligarchy, and finally to democracy and ultimately ochlocracy, or mob rule)— the modern concept of revolution signified a watershed transformation or a binary break, a singular moment represented by the collective concept of "Revolution," with a capital "R" and in the singular. What characterized this conception of revolution was the passage from the idea of a merely political to a broadly social revolution: the idea that modern revolution was about social change, about "the social emancipation of all men, [about] transforming the social structure," in the words of Koselleck.[6]

Toward the latter half of the twentieth century, this modern concept of revolution seemed to collapse under the weight of its own exigency. It was eclipsed by a set of late-modern concepts of uprising, insurgency, insurrection, disobedience, and insubordination.[7] The transformation was brought about, in part, by the anticipated failure of modern revolution, which itself nourished a certain expectation or fear of miscarriage—what Étienne Balibar refers to as an "accumulation of factors which make the failure of revolutions their only possible outcome, therefore depriving them of their historical meaning and their political effectivity."[8] The transformation was due, in part also, to the recurring idea that revolutions lead only to terror—or, in Simona Forti's words, that revolution "hosts in its genetic code the mark of terror and totalitarianism,"[9] a thesis notoriously made famous by François Furet and other late-twentieth-century historians. It was partly due, as well, to the omnipresent fear that the prospect of revolution brought about a more powerful preemptive counterrevolution.

These historical transformations pushed critical praxis from its origins in Marxist class struggle, through the disruption of Maoist-inspired forms of insurrection, to more contemporary models of assemblies, occupations, strikes, and hashtag social movements that have a completely different texture than classical critical praxis. They were driven by factors that will have a lasting impact on critical praxis in our present times. Two in particular.

The first was the loosening grip of the philosophy of history. This was a gradual process, originally in Mao's thought, but more so in the later receptions of his writings in Western Europe starting in the 1960s and 1970s. Mao's early writings were heavily influenced by a Marxist philosophy of history. His *Report on an Investigation of the Peasant Movement in Hunan* (March 1927) firmly embraced dialectical materialism, trumpeting the coming revolution in resolute terms.[10] Similarly, Mao's more philosophical writings from the period, for instance, his essay *On Contradiction* (1937), represented a vigorous appropriation of Marxist dialectical materialism by contrast to what he called the metaphysical or vulgar evolutionist worldview—what we might refer to today as the liberal progressive view of history. But by the time of the Cultural Revolution, the urgency of the laws of history had dissipated: class struggle remained important, but the call to churn society was presented more as a productive, pragmatic idea than as historical necessity. The historical determinism was now muted, replaced by a practical sense of politics. This became even more accentuated with the Western reception of Maoist ideas in the 1960s and 1970s. With the Mao-Dadaism of the 1970s in Italy,[11] for instance, or Jean-Luc Godard's portrayal in *La Chinoise* (1967), the siren call of determinist history had all but vanished. By the time we got to the twenty-first century, even the more radical insurrectional writings had lost their Marxist history. Rather than a determinist future, history was described more as a doomsday scenario. Theories of contradiction were replaced by the powder keg: things were about to explode. Instead of history, we faced a ticking time bomb.[12]

The second factor was more conjunctural. The movement away from traditional Marxism and the reception of Maoist thought in the West and South in the 1960s was influenced by the historical conjuncture, on the one hand, of European communist parties that were captured by the Soviet Union and still suffered from a Stalinist hangover and, on the other hand, of the absence of an attractive socialist alternative. Young militants projected onto Maoism their hope for a substitute to Soviet communism. This was true across the political left—from the more hardcore Leninist or Jacobin or Bolshevik politics of someone like Alain Badiou and his *Union des communistes de France (marxiste-léniniste)* at one end, to the more aesthetic, libidinal, and subjective politics of the *Vive la revolution!* group in France at the other.[13]

These two factors brought about a transformation of the underlying map of critical praxis. At first, for Marx and still for the first generation of the Frankfurt School, the driving force of history was class struggle, imagined as a struggle between the bourgeoisie and the proletariat. The influence of Maoism on European militants during the late 1960s and 1970s represented a rejection of a more classical, unified, or coherent Marxist vision of proletarian revolution led by an organized, industrialized working class, guided by an intellectual vanguard, and determined by history. The shift was not simply the replacement of the working class by agricultural workers or colonial subjects, though that was of course an important, even foundational dimension. The more important shift was from a unitary notion of Revolution (with a capital R and in the singular, as Koselleck emphasized) to the idea of microinsurrections by minority insurgents that would culminate in a massive movement of the people. This entailed a struggle involving not two, but three parties: the active insurgents, the active counterinsurgents, and the masses. Insurgency theory directed the small minority of active insurgents to gain the allegiance of the masses in order to seize power from the counterrevolutionary minority. It involved far more microlevel insurrectional tactics and game-theoretic strategizing—which would inspire the *groupuscules* and anarchist cells of the 1960s, 1970s, and 1980s. In the following decades, the map of the political struggle was similar—in the sense that there was a tripartite demarcation between the small minority of activists, the police state, and the general population; however, it often felt that the more radical activists viewed themselves as an embattled minority with little interest in and even some disdain for the masses. The discourse of uprising became that of a pitched battle against the counterrevolutionary forces of the state, but at a distance from the majority of the population—masses that did not seem movable or winnable. The general population had become the consumerist, neoliberal bulk of individuals, more objects of disdain than a popular force to be won over.

The result was a fragmentation of different models of uprising during the later twentieth century. There was, first, a traditional *insurgency model of uprising* that could be traced directly to Mao's military strategies before 1949. This model rested on a tripartite division of society, and it promoted the growth of small, separatist cells or wider national liberation movements. This was the model of the FLN in Algeria and of other liberation movements throughout the global South—which eventually gave rise to counterinsurgency practices in Indochina, Algeria, and Vietnam. There was, second, a model of the *constant upending of revolutionary accomplishments*, modeled on the Cultural Revolution. This model rested on the idea of the inevitable return of self-dealing and self-interest, of elitism and complacency; it reflected the idea that the Communist Party would inevitably become the bourgeoisie. This model gave rise to the call for "permanent revolution" that would echo in Latin America. There was, third, a model of *creative insubordination*, especially in some of the inventive receptions of Maoism in the West in the 1960s and 1970s as an alternative to Soviet communism. Militants in France, Italy, and elsewhere developed alternative ways of thinking and challenging relations of power, some through new forms of popular justice, others through leaderless inquiries. A good illustration here is the debate between two young Maoists, Benny Lévy and André Glucksmann, and Michel Foucault that took place in June 1971, "On Popular Justice: A Debate with Maoists." And then, finally, there emerged a model of *separatist insurrection* that had elements of early insurgency theory, but was far more isolationist from the general population. This model was reflected in the more extreme violent movements of the 1970s and 1980s in Western Europe and the United States, such as the Baader-Meinhof Group, the Red Brigades in Italy, or the Weather Underground Organization. The model differed sharply from the modern concept of revolution. It had a sharply different episteme: a small-bore, tactical episteme of the guerilla fighter, associated with rebellion and insurrection, as opposed to the mass revolution. In this way, critical praxis moved away from the modern concept of revolution to more situated, localized events of insurrection, revolt, disobedience, insurrection, insubordination—the various modalities of uprising.

Critical Practices at the Turn of the Twenty-First Century

The structural transformation of critical practice over the twentieth century greatly influenced practices of critical resistance at the turn of century. There was, naturally, a range of critical praxis, but two modal paradigms: at one end, a set of more radical insurrectional movements in continuity with the historical transformations just discussed; and at the other end, a set of more open prefigurative social movements that evolved in part in opposition to the previous models. The latter prefigured the type of democratic egalitarian politics that they aspired to. Each of these poles was fruitfully theorized by contemporary collectives and critical thinkers.

The first style of separatist insurrectional movements manifested around the world, from El Salvador and Peru in the 1980s to Nepal and Kashmir in the 1990s. These insurrectional practices took different forms and inspired separatist cells in Europe and elsewhere. The Invisible Committee, an anonymous group of anarchist activists in France, gave theoretical expression to this approach in a series of books, beginning with their first, *The Coming Insurrection*, published in 2007. The Invisible Committee views the world through the prism of civil war between different visions of society—between "irreducible and irreconcilable ideas of happiness and their worlds."[14] It is useless, the Committee suggests, to get indignant, to get involved in citizens' groups, or to wait for change or the revolution. Rather, the Committee advocates a form of separatism, secession, or isolation: to withdraw to communes, to remove oneself from the people. Even anarchist milieus must be forsaken because what they do is "blunt the directness of direct action" (101). The masses are to be viewed with caution and suspicion, the Committee adds, not the least of which because "we expect a surge in police work being done by the population itself" (118). The Committee sets forth strategies for insurrection: demonstrations need to be wild and unexpected, not disclosed in advance to the police; they must lead the police, rather than be herded by them; they must take the initiative, harass and distract the police, in order to attack elsewhere; they must take up arms and maintain an armed presence, even if this does not mean an armed struggle, using arms sparingly and infrequently (131–36). The central call is for an uprising that represents "a vital impulse of youth as much as a popular wisdom" (14).

At the other extreme, there was a set of assemblies and nonviolent social movements with a different ethic. Reacting in part against the patriarchal, "great man," top-down character of conventional critical praxis, at least historically, these movements tended to aspire to be leaderless (or, inversely, what some of them called leaderful), peaceful and more egalitarian, democratic, and ideologically open. They attempted to prefigure the political processes that they aspired to, rather than view their militancy as an inevitable means to achieve a future society they wanted to live in. Naturally, these movements took different forms. Some of the organizations were more attentive to membership. BYP100, for instance, restricted membership to persons who were between eighteen and thirty-five, and it was by definition black and young; it nominated and elected leaders; and, to become a member of BYP100, a person had to attend an orientation meeting, had to participate in two chapter meetings, and had to attend a public event.[15] But many of the other organizations aspired to be leaderless, such as Occupy Wall Street, Nuit Debout, or other organizations within the Movement for Black Lives. Many were ideologically open, in the sense that there was no policing of views, censorship of political ideologies, or established party line. To the contrary, many of these movements took an ethical and political stance of equality and respect that went against the very idea of hierarchical power.

Critical theorists gave theoretical expression to these movements and assemblies as well. Barbara Ransby explored their "group-centered leadership practices" by means of which the movements often turned over the decision making to those people on the ground who had the best understanding of the problems they faced and who were in the best position to carry out their own solutions. "The Movement for Black Lives is distinctive," Ransby explained, "because it defers to the local wisdom of its members and affiliates, rather than trying to dictate from above." This was, in Ransby's words, a "better model for social movements," and it represented "a choice, not a deficiency."[16] In *Notes Toward A Performative Theory of Assembly* (2015), Judith Butler explored the performative dimensions of these assembly-based movements. Butler's central point was that the materiality of assembly, the corporeal presence of people assembled in the square, had a force of its own, independent of what was said, and served as the precondition for what got said. Peaceful assembly, in and of itself, mattered. The enactment of a "we" by means of physical assembly represented, for Butler, the medium within which claims for inclusion are expressed. It was the way to initiate claims to be "we the people" or, even more, "we are *still* the people."[17] This was, for Butler, the power and importance of these non-violent assemblies and movements.

Future Directions for Critical Practice

The historical context, though, has changed once again. In the last decade or more, the liberal veil has been lifted off the true face of the right across the globe. With the rise of extreme-right parties in Europe, the Tea Party and Trump presidency in the United States, and authoritarian leaders in Turkey, the Philippines, India, and elsewhere, the gloves have come off, and we now face far more vociferous and open attacks on minorities, immigrants, and leftist values. Even the more traditional conservative parties have begun to reveal their darkest underbellies. The lines of political demarcation, today, have become more polarized, violent, and confrontational.

This presents a real challenge for critical theory and praxis today. The truth is, critique was always sharper when it confronted liberal ideology. The reason is simple: critique operates most often and powerfully as an immanent form of criticism, using the aspirations and ideals of its object of critique to motivate a reassessment. Critique was always more cutting when it could show up liberal ideals—for instance, the promise of equality in the face of an unequal world, or the potential of freedom in an unjust society. It was always stronger when it could leverage the rhetoric of its interlocutor. But when the opposition is openly racist, sexist, homophobic, nationalistic, and supremacist, there is little to be gained from immanent critique. In the struggle over values, there is hardly any need for sophisticated critical theory.

It should not come as a surprise that the leading critical theorists in wartime so often joined the ranks of the state apparatuses that they previously or ordinarily would have critiqued. Where was critical theory in wartime? At the OSS, the US Office of Strategic Services, which was the forerunner to the CIA. Franz Neumann, who had just published his book on Nazi Germany, *Behemoth: The Structure and Practice of National Socialism* in 1942, as well as Herbert Marcuse and Otto Kirchheimer, author of *Punishment and Social Structure* with Georg Rusche in 1939, all worked for the OSS under its head, the Republican Wall Street lawyer William Donovan. Neumann in fact took charge of the Research and Analysis Branch of the OSS for Donovan. As John Herz, who worked in Neumann's unit, quipped, "It was as though the left-Hegelian World Spirit had briefly descended on the Central European Department of the OSS."[18] Max Horkheimer was also reportedly part of the OSS. Meanwhile, Theodor Adorno, Herta Herzog, and Paul Lazarsfeld became involved in the Princeton Radio Project, which later became Columbia University's Bureau of Applied Research, and which served intelligence functions.[19] And of course, what else would one do faced with a regime like Nazi Germany—especially as a Jew in exile in the United States?

Similarly, today, we face a new constellation that has shifted the landscape of critical practice. In response, a lot of critical thinkers today fold back onto the ACLU, the NAACP Legal Defense Fund, Human Rights Watch, or even the FBI and special counsel. They fall back on the liberal bastions—as critical theory did at mid-century. And it may well be that one effective strategy today is to lock arms with left-leaning liberals, tone down the critique, and work together until better times. But few critical theorists openly take that position. So instead, it is time to map out the possible directions for critical praxis for the twenty-first century. There are at least seven broad categories, plus a polyvalent approach that draws on them all.

Return to Vanguard Practices

Some critical theorists urge a return to vanguard revolutionary practices. In the context of the Arab Uprisings of 2011, for instance, thinkers such as Tariq Ali and Perry Anderson advocated a more concerted anti-imperialist strategy. The only way for the Arab uprisings "to become a revolution," Anderson wrote in 2011, was for the region as a whole to undo the Camp David Accords of 1979: "The litmus test of the recovery of a democratic Arab dignity lies there."[20] Tariq Ali, for his part, pointed us back to Lenin as the proper guide to rethink critical praxis.

In his book *The Dilemmas of Lenin: Terrorism, War, Empire, Love, Revolution* (2017), Ali draws our attention to Lenin's *April Theses*, originally pronounced at meetings of soviets in Saint Petersburg in early April 1917—in between the first revolution of February 1917 and the Bolshevik Revolution of October 1917. The *April Theses* were, as Ali reminds us, a clarion call to vanguard action at a time when the revolutionary leadership was adrift—a provocative, "explosive" (in Ali's words), and extremely controversial call for a second, truly socialist revolution to overcome the first, bourgeois political revolution.[21] Lenin called on his party members to unleash that second revolution in terms that would have had special resonance in Egypt in 2011: "The specific feature of the present situation in Russia is that the country is *passing* from the first stage of the revolution—which, owing to the insufficient class-consciousness and organisation of the proletariat, placed power in the hands of the bourgeoisie—to its *second stage*, which must place power in the hands of the proletariat and the poorest sections of the peasants."[22]

These words, Ali notes, "paved the way for the revolution in October 1917" (10). They laid the groundwork for a leaderful vanguard revolution—precisely the type of practice that was consciously avoided by many in Tahrir Square, and latter in Zuccotti Park and at the Place de la République. Ali's message is clear: what is needed at our assemblies today is a second uprising, a truly vanguard revolution. That alone will produce lasting change, according to Ali.

Revolutionary class struggle has and can always serve as a model for critical praxis. But if Lenin's theses are invoked, it is also important to remember certain dark sides of vanguard communism: how Leninism led to Stalinism, to the Terror-Famine in Ukraine in 1932–33, to the Molotov–Ribbentrop Pact of non-aggression in 1939, and the Soviet Gulag; or how Maoism led to the Great Chinese Famine of 1959–61 and to unconscionable violence during the Cultural Revolution. In armed warfare, naturally, there have been successful models of insurgency based on the military strategies of Mao, Che, and others; but those were armed insurrections led by armed insurgents attempting to gain independence or violently overthrow a government. That might still be a model for critical praxis today, but it is important to emphasize that it would likely be violently repressed and lead to wide-scale incarceration and death.

Continue with Insurrectional Practices

Other critical thinkers strenuously advocate for a continuation of microinsurrectional practices. Critical theorists such as Giorgio Agamben and Jacques Rancière, for instance, often have been associated with the anonymous collective the Invisible Committee, discussed earlier, which explicitly militates for insurrection in its books, including its more recent books *To Our Friends* (2014), and *Now* (2017). Some commentators have suggested that the writings of the Invisible Committee, in certain passages, bear striking resemblance to those of Agamben and Rancière.

"Abolish general assemblies": the Invisible Committee signals, in no uncertain terms, that it is writing against the recent tradition of occupations and general assemblies, and advocating a far more radical posture.[23] The Committee goes so far as to propose a weaponized insurgency, although it is careful to emphasize that it does not fetishize armed resistance. It embraces weapons in order not to use them. The idea is that an a priori refusal to arm oneself or to handle weapons is equivalent to powerlessness. Power is achieved by having weapons but not using them. The idea is to get to the point where it is no longer necessary to use arms through all the other strategies of unseating local authorities. "When power is in the gutter," the Committee writes, "it's enough to walk over it" (134).

Many of the tactics that have been deployed recently in antifascist and antigovernment protests draw on these insurrectional writings. In protests in 2018 in Berkeley, Oakland, or Paris, for instance, "black bloc" tactics are inscribed within an insurrectional frame. These tactics generally involve breaking windows, burning garbage, tires, or cars, and throwing projectiles at the police, and are generally carried out by black-clad protesters equipped with helmets, goggles, and face coverings. The tactics trace back to the squatter and other autonomist movements in Europe in the 1980s and to the Seattle WTO protests in 1999. In certain locations, such as in Western Europe, they have become routine at protest marches.

In France, for instance, protests were traditionally headed, in what was called the "cortège," by union representatives and were strictly policed by union security forces. In more recent times, the protest marches are now usually preceded by what is called the "tête de cortège," namely, individual protesters, including black bloc protesters, who defy the march permits and take on the law enforcement agents (national police, CRS, military gendarmes) that are policing the march. Individual protesters now also regroup in smaller clusters outside the perimeter of the permitted protest route in order to expand the space of protest and inject the protest more into the public space. These tactics violate the protest permit and are often severely repressed by the police, resulting in large-scale confrontations and arrests. These insurrectional practices are fraught with potential danger. At the 2018 May Day protests in Paris, for instance, a tête de cortège with hundreds of black bloc protesters violently encountered a police force, resulting in over two hundred arrests and a handful of injuries. Like vanguard revolutionary practices, these insurrectional strategies involve practices that may expose individuals to incarceration and physical injury.

Autonomous Zones

There have also emerged nonviolent, noninsurrectional separatist movements that seek to create communities, often through a squatting model that does not involve violence, but instead community, new forms of property, and various forms of collaboration. The ambition of these temporary spaces is generally to avoid formal state structures of control. They are often referred to as Temporary Autonomous Zones (TAZs), in part in homage to the poetic anarchist writings of Hakim Bey by that name. They can also aspire to be permanent autonomous zones, or as Bey suggested "Permanent TAZs" in an article from 1994 of that title.

A well-known example of a TAZ, which has attempted to become a permanent autonomous zone, is the autonomous zone of Notre-Dame-des-Landes outside of Nantes, France. This zone and others in France—in Rouen, Lyon, and elsewhere—are referred to as "Zones à defender," or "ZADs," and have generally involved peaceful occupations of lands often with a significant environmental aspect. In the case of the Notre-Dame-des-Landes, the zone began as a protest movement against the building of a large new airport outside Nantes to service all of Western France. The physical presence of the protesters, through a form of squatting of agricultural lands where the airport was going to be built, started a long-term alliance between leftist activists, anarchists, environmentalists, and local farmers. The ZAD eventually brought down the airport construction project after ten years of occupation and protest. In the process, the activists invented new forms of nonproperty, which the French state has tried to violently repress and demolish.

Civil and Political Disobedience

Civil and political disobedience have also recently received increased attention in critical circles. These practices build on the traditional notions of civil disobedience made famous in David Thoreau's *On the Duty of Civil Disobedience*, Mahatma Gandhi's writings on *Satyagraha*, or nonviolent resistance, Martin Luther King's *Letter from Birmingham Jail*, and Hannah Arendt's writings on civil disobedience as a form of lobbying in the *Crises of the Republic*. It is conventionally defined as the act of disobeying a positive law in order to suffer legal punishment and thereby convince others of the injustice of the law.

A number of contemporary critical theorists advocate a renewed attention to civil disobedience in democracies as a powerful tool to achieve social reform. Sandra Laugier and Albert Ogien in their work *Pourquoi désobéir en démocratie?* address head-on the countermajoritarian difficulties typically associated with civil disobedience and resolve in its favor. Frédéric Gros, in a book titled *Désobéir* (2017), explores and maps out the various forms of disobedience that mirror the different types of expected obedience to authority in political theory.

By contrast to civil disobedience, political disobedience can be defined as a form of insubordination that contests not only unjust positive law, but also the very political system that gives rise to those laws. It challenges the docility of civil disobedience, refusing to respect the punishment associated with breaking the law. It involves flouting rules, not just to challenge their legality, but because they are simply intolerable. W. J. T. Mitchell, Mick Taussig, and I theorized these new forms of political disobedience in the Occupy context in *Occupy: Three Inquiries in Disobedience* (2013). This type of practice has become increasingly common along state borders, where local farmers are giving aid and assistance to undocumented immigrants in defiance of the law, as well as in sanctuary cities that openly resist the legal enforcement of immigration laws. The ambition here is not to suffer punishment, as a way to reveal the immorality of the law, but to defy laws that are considered immoral. It takes a different ethical position toward praxis. It is much closer to what Foucault described in his lecture "What Is Critique?" (1978), where he suggested that critique is not being governed *"like this."* Not, as he had originally formulated, in being governed less or not at all, but in not being governed in this way.[24]

Gather in Assemblies, Occupations, and Movements

A number of critical theorists, including Judith Butler, Michael Hardt, Antonio Negri, and Deva Woodly, among others, rally around new practices of assembly, occupation, and nonviolent social movements. These practices build on the many occupations and assemblies that proliferated in the early twentieth century—such as Occupy, Standing Rock, Nuit Debout—as well as on many ongoing social movements, such as #BlackLivesMatter, or more broadly the Movement for Black Lives, and #MeToo. These assemblies and movements harken new political formations.

Deva Woodly emphasizes how the organizations within the Movement for Black Lives repoliticize the public sphere and demonstrate the potential of democratic experimentation. These movements revive the public sphere by countering a growing "politics of despair."[25] The different manifestations of #BlackLivesMatter protest, Woodly writes, are not just "pre-political" or prefigurative; they are inherently political practices that allow democracy to correct itself.

Judith Butler explicitly embraces these political forms. In reaction to black bloc protesters, who destroyed property at an antifascist demonstration in Berkeley in 2017, Butler condemns the violence and turns instead to an ethic of love. "The turn to violence," Butler writes, "further destroys hope and augments the violence of the world, undoing the livable world."[26] Instead of insurrection, Butler embraces these models of the general assembly and occupations. A frequent speaker at the global Occupy movement, Butler sees promise in such nonviolent strategies of assembly.

Michael Hardt and Antonio Negri in their book *Assembly* (2017) provide a handbook intended not just to analyze, as does Butler, but to stimulate, encourage, and foster assembly-style social movements.[27] Hardt and Negri offer guidance on how to organize, how to assemble, how to revolt, how to seize power, and how to transform society—not always agreeing with the practices on the ground. At the most concrete level and faced with leaderless social movements like Occupy Wall Street or the Arab Uprisings, Hardt and Negri offer a list of concrete organizational advice, almost commands, for leftist revolt: Do not give up on leadership. Do not go leaderless. Instead, "transform the role of leadership by inverting strategy and tactics": let the multitude decide on strategy, but the leaders decide on tactics (290). Do not give up on institutions and organizations, but instead build new institutions—specifically nonsovereign institutions (289). Most importantly, Hardt and Negri argue, seize power. Many of the current social movements focus all their attention on the movement itself, its general assemblies, and the insulated world of the resistance movement, rather than on taking power from the state. Many now create a hermetically sealed space of protest separate and independent from ordinary politics and political power. Hardt and Negri push in a very different direction, but within the rubric of assemblies: leftist movements must take power. They must seize the conventional instruments, institutions, and pathways of politics. "We have little sympathy with those who want to maintain their purity and keep their hands clean by refusing power," they proclaim. "In order to change the world we need to take power" (69).

Jam the System

Another strategy is to disrupt, to cause chaos, to jam the system—perhaps in a less constructive way than assemblies or social movements. This approach is traditionally associated with marginalized and disempowered populations. It has been theorized by James C. Scott under the rubric of infrapolitics and ordinary acts of resistance.

Infrapolitics is, according to Scott, the space of struggle of the nonelites and involves "surreptitious resistance."[28] It involves, for instance, "poaching and squatting on a large scale" that restructures the control of property, or "peasant tax evasion," or "massive desertion by serfs or peasant-conscripts" bringing down a regime (192). These are down-to-earth, low-profile stratagems designed to minimize appropriation. "In the case of slaves, for example, these stratagems have typically included theft, pilfering, feigned ignorance, shirking or careless labor, footdragging, secret trade and production for sale, sabotage of crops, livestock, and machinery, arson, flight, and so on" (198). These are the practices of the mob and the riot, the moral economy of the English crowd, in E. P. Thompson's terms. Scott argues that these stratagems of infrapolitics are a foundational form of politics. They are the building block for "more elaborate institutionalized political action that could not exist without it" (201). They rest on the model of being cornered, dominated, powerless in the face of an all-powerful state with all the tools—and lashing back in whatever way you can.

Political Organizing

Another direction for critical praxis is to organize politically in a more conventional fashion in order to pursue critical-theoretic goals. Along these lines, political organizing operates through traditional political parties and trade unions, and it resembles the basic strategies of leftist political parties. This approach has become increasingly visible in the United States in the wake of the campaign of Bernie Sanders for the Democratic presidential nomination in 2016 and 2020. The surprise victory of Alexandria Ocasio-Cortez in the Democratic primary for the Fourteenth Congressional District in the Bronx, New York, for the 2018 midterms, gave momentum to the Democratic Socialists of America party. In France, Jean-Luc Mélenchon rallied leftists behind a new populist and social democratic party he founded in 2016, La France insoumise, which advocates a constitutional convention and the creation of a new republic that would transform the private ownership of capital. In Spain, Pablo Iglesias founded in 2014 a leftist populist party, Podemos, which has challenged European austerity measures and has become one of the country's largest political parties.

Some critical theorists rally behind even more centrist leftist parties, such as the Social Democratic Party of Germany, the Democratic Party in the United States, or the French Socialist Party. In effect, the idea here is that the political ambitions are set by critical theory, but that the practical implementation follows more conventional political strategies of electoral politics. This approach may feel conventional, even noncritical, but if it is deployed in furtherance of critical objectives, there is no reason that it could not be considered an instrumental critical practice. (This would not be the case for adherence to right-wing parties, such as the Republican Party in the United States or the one in France, which embrace a conservative vision that not only eschews ideals of equality, but has abandoned basic notions of sufficiency, such as universal healthcare, subsistence benefits, refuge, or other basic welfare safeguards.)

A Polyvalent Approach

Critical theory may not necessitate theoretical purity, and may not preclude outright polyvalent forms of resistance—finding allies, embracing different strategies, triangulating praxis. Talal Asad argues for more polyvalent forms of political engagement that contest authority at different levels or, in his words, that "address numerous overlapping bodies and territories."[29] For Assad, this means aiming resistance at different targets—at times focusing on matters of national citizenship, at others of religious faith, and still at others of local governance. Asad reminds us of the remark Foucault made in the context of the Iranian Revolution: "Concerning the expression 'Islamic government,' why cast immediate suspicion on the adjective 'Islamic'? The word 'government' suffices, in itself, to awaken vigilance" (206). It is vigilance across the board that would be called for—without any specific privilege to tradition, to the national, or to the local: multiple different strategies of resistance at various different levels

(212). This represents, in effect, a polyvalent approach that draws and combines various praxis alternatives.

The many innovations and challenges to critical theory in the 1960s and 1970s are what proved so productive in the domain of theory, and are so promising today. Just as the antifoundational challenges to critical theory opened up a space for a diversity of critical approaches that will surely help us better analyze the crises we face today, a polyvalent approach could build on the promise of these new forms of critical praxis. We may need to harness the diversity in the domain of praxis, and, in a similar way, allow the field to breathe again. Insofar as we may be, at this point, beyond determinist philosophies of history, there may be more opportunities to open up, rethink, invent, and experiment in the field of critical praxis.

✳ ✳ ✳

The next challenge is to tranche the debate between these different modalities of critical praxis. Critical theory must now carefully attend to the dimension of praxis. That is, in my opinion, the most pressing and compelling task for contemporary critical theorists in the next decade.

In what follows, I speak only for myself. Rather than a determinist vision of history, I would embrace today the long laborious view of history. In this, paradoxically, I would bend some conservative thinking—and longtime opponents—toward a critical future. Their practices, after all, have proven effective in many regards. The long-term foundations built by conservative organizations, such as the Federalist Society and the Heritage Foundation, are demonstrably bearing fruit in these crises times. They have contributed importantly, for instance, to the capsizing of the federal judiciary in the United States. Conservative thinkers, such as Edward Banfield and James Q. Wilson in the United States, but Edmund Burke before them, praised the long-term and especially future-orientedness as a moral virtue and superiority.[30] The Annales School of historiography and their concept of *la longue durée*, which focused on the deeper structures that influence, but do not determine, history, could also serve here.[31] Rather than reject these ideas as reactionary, they may contribute importantly to critical praxis.

Much of the attention among contemporary critical thinkers is focused on the here and now. The assemblies are prefigurative models of democracy that we instantiate immediately—rather than wait any longer. Tariq Ali's call for a second revolution at Tahrir Square, similarly, was temporally immediate. The very title of the Invisible Committee's latest intervention, their book *Maintenant (Now)*, published in 2017, captures well this immediate temporal dimension. And similarly, most of the left-liberal interventions in the wake of the collapse of the Soviet Union, in the former Eastern European countries, for instance, involved immediate implementation of new Western-style constitutions without deeper labor.

What may have been lacking was sufficient attention to the future: to the deeper structures and forces that shape us, our desires, our ambitions—such that, in the former East, those new constitutions would easily become the weapons of ambitious new authoritarians, as has been the case in Hungary and Poland. The new constitutions become the new battleground for political struggle. The effort of the Polish government to retire older oppositional judges—placing a sixty-five-year-old age limit on judges, though granting exceptions—is precisely the kind of manipulation that presentism enables. A longer-term, more laborious effort may have been better.

To till the fields, laboriously, for rewards that we might reap in the future. To instill the values of the critical left in the next generations. To create social networks among critical theorists that reinforce leftist values and build lasting alliances. That may be the critical praxis necessary for the twenty-first century. There is, after all, no reason to believe that explicitly calling for revolution or insurrection advances the cause of social change when the soil is not prepared. The slow, time-consuming labor of shaping ideas and desires may be far more important. It is precisely how conservative organizations were built over decades and have now come to dominate. Popular dissatisfaction and the desire "not to be governed in this way" are what bring about social change, perhaps; but those desires and disaffections are shaped by decades-long struggles.

It may be that other paths to critical praxis prove more compelling than long-term laborious practices. They are hard, ungrateful work, not satisfying in the short term, thankless. They involve a time horizon that is hard to bear. They may rest on privilege: being able to wait when in fact present conditions are utterly intolerable, right now, even lethal. But these are the key questions we now need to address.

In the midst of the last major crises—after the events of May '68, the repressions, and the rethinking of power that took place—Foucault reminded us of the stakes of the political struggle. In his lecture *The Punitive Society*, delivered in 1973, where he began to map social relations on the matrix of civil war, Foucault emphasized the intelligence of the opposition. Foucault criticized intellectuals on the left who spoke of the stupidity of their opponents—who described them as narrow-minded, or mulish, or blind. He underscored instead the "lucidity and intelligence of this class, which has conquered and kept power under conditions" that should have led to its fall.[32] And he emphasized how serious the political struggle was.

I cannot stress that enough now. The political situation today is critical. And now, more than ever, we critical theorists need to reorient critical praxis for the twenty-first century. We now need renewed and sustained attention to the pressing question: What is to be done?

Notes

1. Seyla Benhabib traces the intertwined lives and thoughts of many of these exiled critical theorists and other intellectuals, including Theodor Adorno, Hannah Arendt, Walter Benjamin, Isaiah Berlin, Albert Hirschman, Gershom Scholem, and Judith Shklar, in Seyla Benhabib, *Exile, Statelessness, and Migration: Playing Chess with History from Hannah Arendt to Isaiah Berlin* (Princeton: Princeton University Press, 2018).

2. In "Counter-Critical Theory" (2018), I sketch out one such possible approach by showing how we might overcome the apparently irreconcilable conflict between the more positivist tradition and the antifoundational challenges. I propose there a pure theory of illusions that calls for the constant and unending analysis of our systems of belief and material conditions. Bernard E. Harcourt, "Counter-Critical Theory: An Intervention in Contemporary Critical Thought and Practice," *Critical Times* 1, no. 1 (2018).

3. Didier Fassin demonstrates this well in his opening essay "How Is Critique?" in this volume.

4. This is reflected, for instance, in the correspondence between Walter Benjamin and Bertolt Brecht regarding their plan for a critical journal in 1930–31. See generally Erdmut Wizisla, *Walter Benjamin and Bertolt Brecht—the Story of a Friendship*, trans. Christine Shuttleworth (New Haven: Yale University Press, 2009); Harcourt, "Counter-Critical Theory," 7–10.

5. Richard Bernstein analyzed the concept of praxis in a formative monograph in 1971 titled *Praxis and Action: Contemporary Philosophies of Human Activity* (Philadelphia: University of Pennsylvania Press, 1971). Bernstein there referenced another book, by Nicholas Lobkowicz, *Theory and Practice: History of a Concept from Aristotle to Marx* (Notre Dame: University of Notre Dame Press, 1967), that provides an exhaustive treatment of the concept of praxis from antiquity to Marx.

6. Reinhart Koselleck, "Historical Criteria of the Modern Concept of Revolution" (1968), in *Futures Past: On the Semantics of Historical Time* (New York: Columbia University Press, 2004), 52; see also Hannah Arendt, *On Revolution* (1963; New York: Penguin, 2006).

7. As Koselleck demonstrates, these concepts had precursors in earlier Middle Age uses of terms "from uprising and revolt to riot, insurrection, and rebellion, and on to *Zweiung*, internal and civil war." Koselleck, "Historical Criteria of the Modern Concept of Revolution," 47. The latter were connected, Koselleck argued, to a different form of struggle than the concept of modern revolution, one that was marked by religious confrontations and inquisitorial struggles. "Civil war, *guerre civile, Bürgerkrieg*—these were the central concepts by which the suffering and experience of fanatical confessional struggles were precipitated, by means of which, moreover, they were legally formulated" (47).

8. Etienne Balibar, "The Idea of Revolution: Yesterday, Today and Tomorrow," Keynote Lecture, International Society for Intellectual History Conference: "Rethinking Europe in Intellectual History," University of Crete, Rethymnon, May 3, 2016; revised with some changes and a new conclusion on May 6, 2016, for "Birkbeck in Athens Lectures in Critical and Cultural Theory" (draft on file with author), 6.

9. Simona Forti, "The Modern Concept of Revolution," September 11, 2017 (draft on file with author).

10. Mao Zedong, "Report on an Investigation of the Peasant Movement in Hunan," in *Selected Works of Mao Tse-tung* (Peking: Foreign Languages, 1967), 23–24.

11. Claire Fontaine, *1977: The Year That Is Never Commemorated*, 2017 (draft on file with author).

12. This is evident, for instance, in the books of the Invisible Committee, discussed later, whose first of now three books, *The Coming Insurrection*, was published in 2007. "The lid on the social kettle is shut triple-tight, and the pressure inside continues to build," they write. "There will be no *social* solution to the present situation." Invisible Committee, *The Coming Insurrection* (Cambridge, MA: Semiotext[e], 2009). See pages 10, 16, and 18 of the online version.

13. Richard Wolin describes this well in the book *The Wind from the East: French Intellectuals, the Cultural Revolution, and the Legacy of the 1960s* (Princeton: Princeton University Press, 2010). From lengthy conversations I had with Daniel Defert and François Ewald, who were both Maoists in the late 1960s and early 1970s—Defert belonged to the *Gauche prolétarienne* and Ewald was a Maoist militant in Lens during the crises there and at Bruay-en-Artois—it is clear that they turned to Maoism primarily as an alternative, as a way to avoid both the Stalinism of the French Communist Party and the dogmatism and top-down hierarchies of the French Socialist Party. Maoism was perceived by these young militants as offering an opening to a new leftist politics and new forms of insurrection—in essence, a new critical praxis. The subsequent political evolutions of these intellectuals are telling and relate to the variegated trajectories of critical theory and praxis. Defert would go on to found and run the first organization in France dedicated to fighting the HIV virus, named Aides. See Daniel Defert, *Une Vie politique: Entretiens avec Philippe Artières et Eric Favereau, avec la collaboration de Joséphine Gross* (Paris: Le Seuil, 2014). In addition to serving as general editor of Foucault's writings, Ewald would become a professor of insurance at the Conservatoire National des Arts et Métiers, and would found and direct the École nationale d'assurances in Paris.

14. Invisible Committee, *The Coming Insurrection*, 8. Hereafter citation given parenthetically in the text.

15. Darryl Holliday, "The New Black Power: They're Young. They're Radical. They're Organized. And They're a Thorn in Rahm's Side," *Chicago Magazine*, February 22, 2016, www.chicagomag.com/Chicago-Magazine/March-2016/black-leaders/.

16. Barbara Ransby, "Black Lives Matter Is Democracy in Action," *New York Times*, October 21, 2017.

17. Judith Butler, *Notes Toward a Performative Theory of Assembly* (Cambridge, MA: Harvard University Press, 2015), 181.

18. See, generally, Franz Neumann, Herbert Marcuse, and Otto Kirchheimer, *Secret Reports on Nazi Germany: The Frankfurt School Contribution to the War Effort*, ed. Raffaele Laudani (Princeton: Princeton University Press, 2013); as well as the book review by William Scheuerman in *Foreign Affairs*, July/August 2013.

19. Susan Cavin, "OSS and the Frankfurt School: Recycling the 'Damaged Lives of Cultural Outsiders,'" paper presented at the 2004 meeting of the American Sociological Association, https://alldocs.net/oss-the-frankfurt-school-recycling-the-damaged-lives -of-cultural-outsiders-office-of-strategic-services-theodor-w-adorno.

20. Perry Anderson, "On the Concatenation in the Arab World," *New Left Review* 68 (March-April 2011): 5.

21. Tariq Ali, *The Dilemmas of Lenin: Terrorism, War, Empire, Love, Revolution* (New York: Verso, 2017), 151, 164.

22. Vladimir Ilyich Lenin, "The Tasks of the Proletariat in the Present Revolution," aka "The April Theses," *Pravda* 26 (1917): 2.

23. Invisible Committee, *The Coming Insurrection*, 125 on online version.
24. Michel Foucault, *Qu'est-ce que la critique?*, ed. Henri-Paul Fruchaud and Daniele Lorenzini (Paris: Vrin, 2015), 37–38.
25. Deva Woodly, "#BlackLivesMatter and the Democratic Necessity of Social Movements," 2017 (on file with author).
26. Judith Butler, "Protest, Violent and Nonviolent," *Big Picture, Public Books*, October 13, 2017, www.publicbooks.org/the-big-picture-protest-violent-and-nonviolent/.
27. Michael Hardt and Antonio Negri, *Assembly* (New York: Oxford University Press, 2017). Hereafter citations given parenthetically in the text.
28. James C. Scott, "The Infrapolitics of Subordinate Groups," in *Domination and the Arts of Resistance*, 183–201 (New Haven: Yale University Press, 1990), 200.
29. Talal Asad, "Thinking About Tradition, Religion, and Politics in Egypt Today," *Critical Inquiry* 42 (Autumn 2015): 212.
30. I do not mean, in any way, to endorse the substantive views of Banfield or Wilson—but rather to bend their perspective on temporality. As I have argued at length elsewhere, their political views were reactionary and dangerous. See Harcourt, *Illusion of Order* (Cambridge, MA: Harvard University Press, 2001), 27–37, 127–159. Edward Banfield, for instance, published a book about Southern Italian society under the title *The Moral Basis of a Backward Society*, in which he argued—on the basis of his wife's interviews and discussions with some of the residents of the small town of Chiaromonte, in the region of Basilicata, in 1955 (she spoke some Italian, he did not)—that the short-sightedness of the Southern Italian people, who acted only on short-term immediate interests of their families, was the source of their "moral backwardness" and plight. But his and Wilson's conception of temporality, stripped of its moralism, can be productively deployed for critical praxis.
31. The term *la longue durée*, the long view of history, was coined by Marc Bloch and Lucien Febvre, two historians who founded the journal *Annales d'histoire économique et sociale* in 1929, which continues today under the name *Annales: Histoire, Sciences Sociales*. Their historiography avoided what they called "surface disturbances" in order to observe the medium- and long-term evolutions of economy and society, all the while attentive to the contingencies that disrupt historical trajectories. See Georges Duby, "Avant-propos," in *Le dimanche de Bouvines* (Paris: Gallimard, 1973), foreword.
32. Foucault, *La société punitive: Cours au Collège de France, 1972–1973*, ed. Bernard E. Harcourt (Paris: Gallimard/Seuil, 2013), 168.

Bibliography

Ali, Tariq. *The Dilemmas of Lenin: Terrorism, War, Empire, Love, Revolution*. New York: Verso, 2017.
Anderson, Perry. "On the Concatenation in the Arab World." *New Left Review* 68 (March-April 2011).
Arendt, Hannah. *On Revolution*. 1963; New York: Penguin, 2006.
Asad, Talal. "Thinking About Tradition, Religion, and Politics in Egypt Today." *Critical Inquiry* 42 (Autumn 2015).
Balibar, Etienne. "The Idea of Revolution: Yesterday, Today and Tomorrow." Keynote Lecture, International Society for Intellectual History Conference: "Rethinking Europe in Intellectual History," University of Crete, Rethymnon, May 3, 2016; revised with some

changes and a new conclusion on May 6, 2016, for "Birkbeck in Athens Lectures in Critical and Cultural Theory" (draft on file with author).

Benhabib, Seyla. *Exile, Statelessness, and Migration: Playing Chess with History from Hannah Arendt to Isaiah Berlin*. Princeton: Princeton University Press, 2018.

Butler, Judith. *Notes Toward a Performative Theory of Assembly*. Cambridge, MA: Harvard University Press, 2015.

——. "Protest, Violent and Nonviolent." *The Big Picture, Public Books*, October 13, 2017, www.publicbooks.org/the-big-picture-protest-violent-and-nonviolent/.

Defert, Daniel. *Une Vie politique: Entretiens avec Philippe Artières et Eric Favereau, avec la collaboration de Joséphine Gross*. Paris: Seuil, 2014.

Duby, Georges. "Avant-propos." In *Le dimanche de Bouvines*. Paris: Gallimard, 1973.

Fassin, Didier. "The Endurance of Critique." *Anthropological Theory* 17, no. 1 (2017): 4–29.

Fontaine, Claire. *1977: The Year That Is Never Commemorated*. 2017 (draft on file with author).

Forti, Simona. "The Modern Concept of Revolution." September 11, 2017 (draft on file with author).

Foucault, Michel. *Qu'est-ce que la critique?* Edited by Henri-Paul Fruchaud and Daniele Lorenzini. Paris: Vrin, 2015.

——. *La Société punitive: Cours au Collège de France, 1972–1973*, edited by Bernard E. Harcourt. Paris: Gallimard/Seuil, 2013.

Gros, Frédéric. *Désobéir*. Paris: Albin Michel, 2017.

Harcourt, Bernard E. "Counter-Critical Theory: An Intervention in Contemporary Critical Thought and Practice." *Critical Times* 1, no. 1 (2018).

Hardt, Michael, and Antonio Negri. *Assembly*. New York: Oxford University Press, 2017.

Invisible Committee. *The Coming Insurrection*. Cambridge, MA: Semiotext(e), 2009.

Koselleck, Reinhart. "Historical Criteria of the Modern Concept of Revolution" (1968), in *Futures Past: On the Semantics of Historical Time*. New York: Columbia University Press, 2004.

Laugier, Sandra, and Albert Ogien. *Pourquoi désobéir en démocratie?* Paris: La Découverte, 2011.

Lenin, Vladimir Ilyich. "The Tasks of the Proletariat in the Present Revolution," aka "The April Theses," *Pravda* 26 (1917).

Mitchell, W. J. T., Bernard E. Harcourt, and Michael Taussig. *Occupy: Three Inquiries in Disobedience*. Chicago: University of Chicago Press, 2013.

Ransby, Barbara. "Black Lives Matter Is Democracy in Action." *New York Times*, October 21, 2017.

Scott, James C. "The Infrapolitics of Subordinate Groups." In *Domination and the Arts of Resistance*, 183–201. New Haven: Yale University Press, 1990.

Wizisla, Erdmut. *Walter Benjamin and Bertolt Brecht—the Story of a Friendship*. Translated by Christine Shuttleworth. New Haven: Yale University Press, 2009.

Woodly, Deva. "#BlackLivesMatter and the Democratic Necessity of Social Movements." 2017 (on file with author).

Zedong, Mao. *Selected Works of Mao Tse-tung*. Peking: Foreign Languages, 1967.

CONTRIBUTORS

Lori Allen is a Senior Lecturer in Anthropology at SOAS, University of London. She is the author of *The Rise and Fall of Human Rights: Cynicism and Politics in Occupied Palestine* (Stanford University Press, 2013).

Fadi A. Bardawil is Assistant Professor of Contemporary Arab Cultures in the Department of Asian and Middle Eastern Studies at Duke University. He is the author of *Emancipation Binds: Arab Revolutionary Marxism, Disenchantment, Critique* (Duke University Press, forthcoming).

Nick Cheesman is a Fellow in the department of Political and Social Change at Australian National University. He is the author of *Opposing the Rule of Law: How Myanmar's Courts Make Law and Order* (Cambridge University Press, 2016).

Andrew Dilts is Associate Professor of Political Theory at Loyola Marymount University. He is the author of *Punishment and Inclusion: Race, Membership, and the Limits of American Liberalism* (Fordham University Press, 2014).

Karen Engle is Minerva House Drysdale Regents Chair in Law at the University of Texas, Austin. She is the author of *The Grip of Sexual Violence in Conflict: Feminist Interventions in International Law* (Stanford University Press, forthcoming).

Didier Fassin is the James D. Wolfensohn Professor in Social Science at the Institute for Advanced Study and Director of Studies at the École des Hautes Études en Sciences Sociales. He recently authored *Life: A Critical User's Manual* (Polity, 2018).

Vanja Hamzić is a Senior Lecturer in Legal History and Legal Anthropology at SOAS, University of London. He is the author of *Sexual and Gender Diversity in the Muslim World: History, Law and Vernacular Knowledge* (I. B. Tauris, 2015).

Bernard E. Harcourt is the Isidor and Seville Sulzbacher Professor of Law and
Professor of Political Science at Columbia University as well as Director of
Studies at the École des Hautes Études en Sciences Sociales. He recently authored
*The Counterrevolution: How Our Government Went to War Against Its Own
Citizens* (Basic Books, 2018).

David Kazanjian is Professor of English and Comparative Literature at the University
of Pennsylvania. He is the author of *The Brink of Freedom: Improvising Life in the
Nineteenth-Century Atlantic World* (Duke University Press, 2016).

Allegra M. McLeod is Professor of Law at Georgetown University Law Center. She is
the author of "Prison Abolition and Grounded Justice" (*UCLA Law Review*, 2015).

Ayşe Parla is Assistant Professor of Anthropology at Boston University. She is the
author of *Precarious Hope: Migration and the Limits of Belonging in Turkey*
(Stanford University Press, 2019).

Peter Redfield is Professor of Anthropology at the University of North Carolina,
Chapel Hill. He is the author of *Life in Crisis: The Ethical Journey of Doctors
Without Borders* (University of California Press, 2013).

Massimiliano Tomba is Professor of History of Consciousness at the University of
California, Santa Cruz. He is the author of *Marx's Temporalities* (Haymarket,
2013).

Linda M. G. Zerilli is the Charles E. Merriam Distinguished Service Professor of
Political Science and the College at the University of Chicago. She is the author
of *A Democratic Theory of Judgment* (University of Chicago Press, 2016).

INDEX

Abolition, 255, 263; contemporary abolitionist theory, 234; crisis, critique and, 230–49; Critical Resistance and, 241–46; of death penalty, 236–37; imperative of, 233; negative, 249n15; New Abolition movement, 10, 261; positive, 234, 249n15; of prison, 236; unfulfilled work of, 234

Abolition Democracy, 9, 232, 266; abolitionist action and, 241; critical analysis and, 236–37; critique and, 233–38; Davis on, 235–36; Du Bois on, 234–35; prison and, 235–36; radicalism and, 247

Abolitionist action: Abolition Democracy and, 241; Black Youth Project 100, 240; police and, 238–40

Abregú, Martin, 107

Absolute monarchy, 223–24

Academic world: corporate model of higher education, 22; critical thinking in, 30; critique in, 20–23; neoliberalism and, 21–22; positivism and, 22

Accountability, alternative visions of, 262–66

Adam (enslaved black man), 210–11, 217–24; Saffin and, 219–21

Adam, biblical, 213–14, 223–24

Adams, Vincanne, 75

Adorno, Theodor, 17, 280

Afro-pessimism, 5, 64–65; Blackness and, 65; politics of hope and, 65

Agamben, Giorgio, 141, 273, 282

Agger, Ben, 26, 32n19

Algerian revolution, 183

Ali, Tariq, 281, 288

Allen, Lori, 7

Alston, Philip, 107–8

Althusser, Louis, 212; "Ideology and Ideological State Apparatuses (Notes Towards an Investigation)," 225n7, 272

Ambedkar, B. R., 202

Anderson, Perry, 272, 281

Anthropocene, 272

Anthropology, 33n28, 86; activist research, 103; critical practice and, 153–54; global health and, 77–78; medical, 74; social, 7, 132–33; unknowable in, 134–35; utility of, 71. See also Ontological turn, in anthropology

Anticolonial movements, 181

Anticonstructivism, 104

Anti-dispossessive politics, 210

NEW DIRECTIONS IN CRITICAL THEORY

Amy Allen, General Editor

New Directions in Critical Theory presents outstanding classic and contemporary texts in the tradition of critical social theory, broadly construed. The series aims to renew and advance the program of critical social theory, with a particular focus on theorizing contemporary struggles around gender, race, sexuality, class, and globalization and their complex interconnections.